STREET ATLAS
Bedfordshire

Contents

III	Key to map symbols
IV-V	Key to map pages
VI-VII	Route planning
VIII	Administrative and postcode boundaries
1	Street maps
133	Index of hospitals, industrial estates, railway stations, schools, shopping centres, street names and universities

PHILIP'S

First published 2000 by

George Philip Ltd, a division of
Octopus Publishing Group Ltd
2-4 Heron Quays, London E14 4JP

First edition 2000
Second impression 2001

ISBN 0-540-07801-8 (hardback)
ISBN 0-540-07802-6 (spiral)

Printed and bound in Spain by Cayfosa-Quebecor

Digital Data

The exceptionally high-quality
mapping found in this book is
available as digital data in TIFF
format, which is easily convertible to
other bit-mapped (raster) image
formats. The data can be provided
as pages or, in some regions, as
larger extracts of up to 200 sq km.
The larger extracts can also be
supplied on paper.

The index is also available in digital
form as a standard database table.
It contains all the details found in the
printed index together with the
National Grid reference for the map
square in which each entry is named.

For further information and to
discuss your requirements, please
contact Philip's on 020 7531 8440 or
george.philip@philips-maps.co.uk

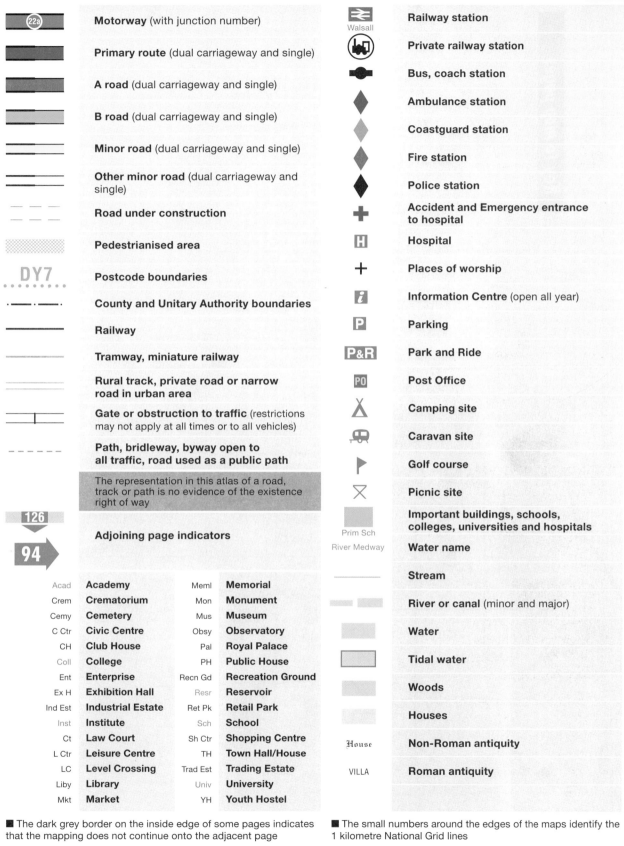

Motorway (with junction number)	
Primary route (dual carriageway and single)	
A road (dual carriageway and single)	
B road (dual carriageway and single)	
Minor road (dual carriageway and single)	
Other minor road (dual carriageway and single)	
Road under construction	
Pedestrianised area	
DY7 **Postcode boundaries**	
County and Unitary Authority boundaries	
Railway	
Tramway, miniature railway	
Rural track, private road or narrow road in urban area	
Gate or obstruction to traffic (restrictions may not apply at all times or to all vehicles)	
Path, bridleway, byway open to all traffic, road used as a public path	
The representation in this atlas of a road, track or path is no evidence of the existence right of way	
126	
94 **Adjoining page indicators**	

Railway station — Walsall

Private railway station

Bus, coach station

Ambulance station

Coastguard station

Fire station

Police station

Accident and Emergency entrance to hospital

H **Hospital**

Places of worship

i **Information Centre** (open all year)

P **Parking**

P&R **Park and Ride**

PO **Post Office**

Camping site

Caravan site

Golf course

Picnic site

Important buildings, schools, colleges, universities and hospitals — Prim Sch

Water name — River Medway

Stream

River or canal (minor and major)

Water

Tidal water

Woods

Houses

House **Non-Roman antiquity**

VILLA **Roman antiquity**

Acad	**Academy**	Meml	**Memorial**
Crem	**Crematorium**	Mon	**Monument**
Cemy	**Cemetery**	Mus	**Museum**
C Ctr	**Civic Centre**	Obsy	**Observatory**
CH	**Club House**	Pal	**Royal Palace**
Coll	**College**	PH	**Public House**
Ent	**Enterprise**	Recn Gd	**Recreation Ground**
Ex H	**Exhibition Hall**	Resr	**Reservoir**
Ind Est	**Industrial Estate**	Ret Pk	**Retail Park**
Inst	**Institute**	Sch	**School**
Ct	**Law Court**	Sh Ctr	**Shopping Centre**
L Ctr	**Leisure Centre**	TH	**Town Hall/House**
LC	**Level Crossing**	Trad Est	**Trading Estate**
Liby	**Library**	Univ	**University**
Mkt	**Market**	YH	**Youth Hostel**

■ The dark grey border on the inside edge of some pages indicates that the mapping does not continue onto the adjacent page

■ The small numbers around the edges of the maps identify the 1 kilometre National Grid lines

The scale of the maps is 5.52 cm to 1 km
3½ inches to 1 mile 1: 18103

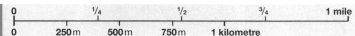

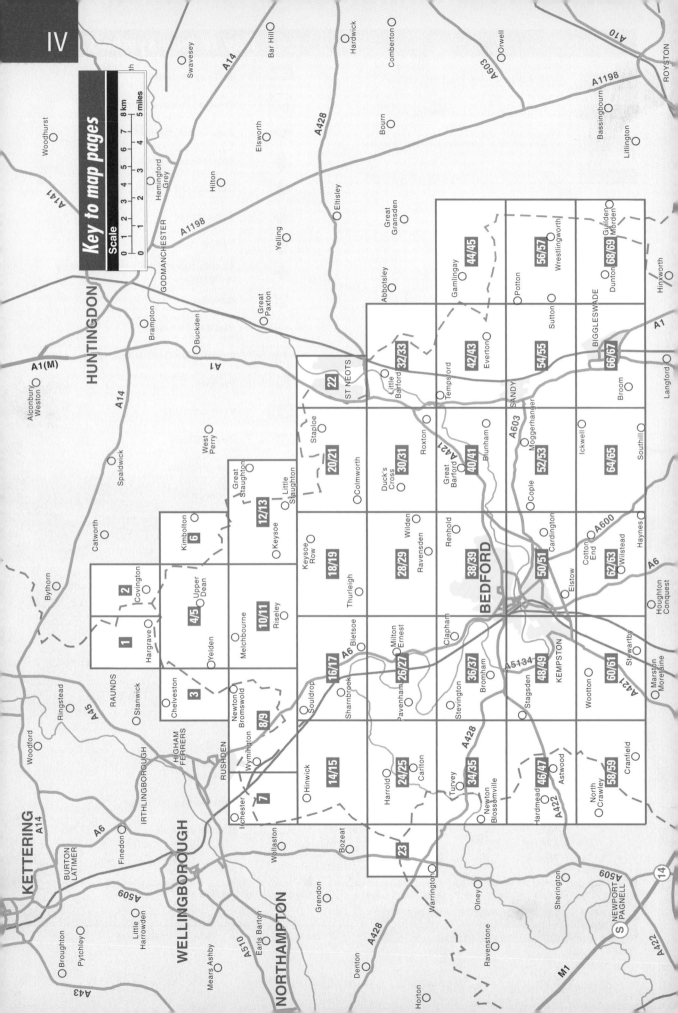

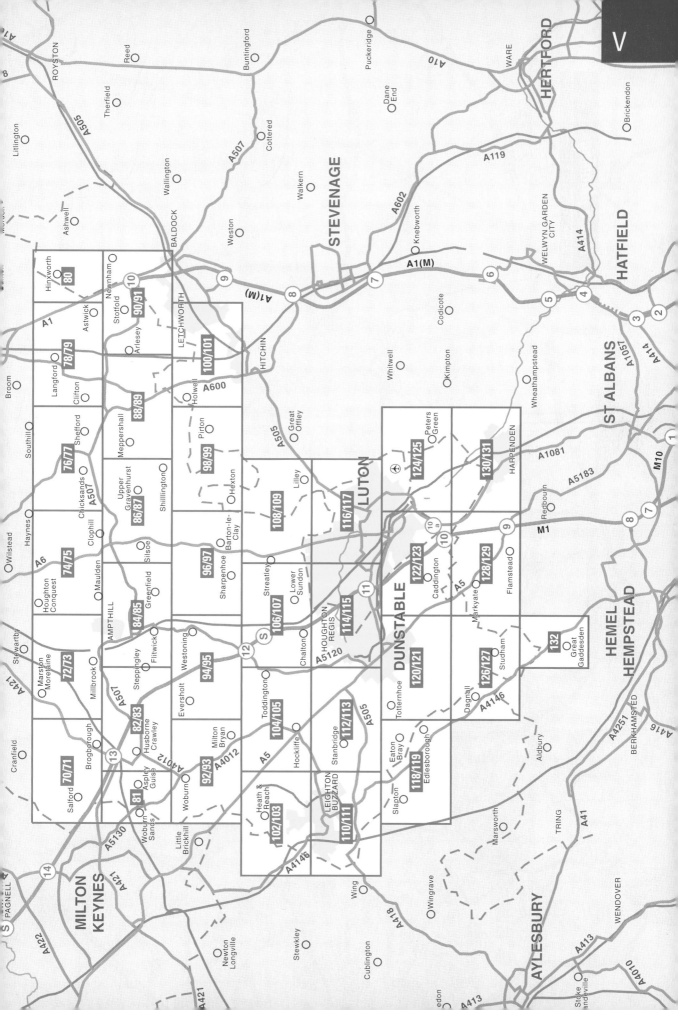

Route planning

Scale

```
0   1   2   3   4   5   6   7   8 km
0       1       2       3     4   5 miles
```

Pidley · Old Hurst · Woodhurst · Holywell · Fen Drayton · Swavesey · Needingworth
Broughton · Kings Ripton · Abbots Ripton · Little Stukeley · Great Stukeley
Alconbury Weston · Alconbury · Barham · Woolley · Easton · Spaldwick · Ellington · Brampton
Conington · Boxworth · Elsworth · Knapwell · Bar Hill · Boxworth · Fen Drayton
Caldecote · Toft · Highfields · Bourn · Kingston · Great Eversden · Little Eversden · Wimpole · Orwell
Croydon · Wendy · Shingay · Arrington · Abington Pigotts · Bassingbourn · Kneesworth · Litlington · Meldreth · Whaddon · Royston
GODMANCHESTER · Hemingford Grey · Hilton · Papworth Everard · Eltisley · Caxton · Great Gransden · Little Gransden · Longstowe · Hatley St George · East Hatley · Tadlow · Steeple Morden · Guilden Morden · Hinxworth · Edworth · Dunton
Offord Cluny · Offord D'Arcy · Papworth St Agnes · Graveley · Yelling · Croxton · Waresley · Gamlingay · Potton · Sutton · Wrestlingworth · Eyeworth · BIGGLESWADE · Langford
Buckden · Graham · Diddington · Southoe · Great Paxton · Little Paxton · ST NEOTS · Eynesbury · Little Barford · Tempsford · Blunham · SANDY · Beeston · Broom
East Perry · West Perry · Staughton Highway · Hail Weston · Duloe · Eaton Socon · Wyboston · Chawston · Roxton · Great Barford · Willington · Moggerhanger · Cople · Cardington · Northill · Ickwell · Old Warden · Southill · Stanford
Graham Water · Stow Longa · Stonely · Great Staughton · Little Staughton · Colmworth · Colesden · Reynold · Hatch · Cardington · Shortstown · Cotton End · Haynes · Haynes Church End
Kimbolton · Pertenhall · Keysoe · Keysoe Row · Bolnhurst · Wilden · Ravensden · Salph End · Clapham · BEDFORD · Harrowden · Elstow · Wilstead · Houghton Conquest
Catworth · Covington · Tilbrook · Lower Dean · Upper Dean · Swineshead · Riseley · Thurleigh · Milton Ernest · Bromham · Biddenham · KEMPSTON · Kempston Hardwick · Stewartby · Millbrook
Bythorn · Molesworth · Brington · Old Weston · Keyston · Shelton · Yelden · Knotting · Newton Bromswold · Bletsoe · Felmersham · Pavenham · Oakley · Stagsden · Wootton · Lower Shelton · Upper Shelton · Marston Moretaine · Cranfield
THRAPSTON · Denford · Ringstead · Hargrave · Caldecott · RAUNDS · Chelveston · Stanwick · Sharnbrook · Chellington · Carlton · West End · Stevington · Astwood · Bourne End
Woodford · Keyston · HIGHAM FERRERS · RUSHDEN · Wymington · Podington · Souldrop · Harrold · Turvey · Newton Blossomville · Hardmead · North Crawley
Twywell · IRTHLINGBOROUGH · Chelveston · Irchester · Farndish · Hinwick · Odell · Abbey · Clifton Reynes · Emberton · Sherington · Chicheley · Moulsoe
Cranford St Andrew · Cranford St John · BURTON LATIMER · Finedon · Great Addington · Little Addington · Strixton · Grendon · Easton Maudit · Yardley Hastings · Cold Brayfield · Lavendon · Filgrave · NEWPORT PAGNELL
Barton Seagrave · Isham · Great Harrowden · Little Harrowden · Hardwick · Mears Ashby · Wilby · Whiston · Castle Ashby · Denton · Brafield on-the-Green · Horton · Weston Underwood · Ravenstone · Stoke Goldington · Gayhurst · Tyringham · Lathbury
Broughton · Pytchley · Orlingbury · WELLINGBOROUGH · Ecton · Sywell · Overstone · Sywell Resr · Little Houghton · Hackleton · Hanslope
Great Cransley · Thorpe Malsor · Walgrave · Holcot · Moulton · Billing · Cogenhoe · Yardley Chase · Olney · Warrington · NEWPORT PAGNELL

Roads: A14, A141, A1(M), A1, A14, A428, A1198, A605, A10, A505, A603, A421, A6, A600, A43, A45, A509, A422, A510, A557, A4500, M1, B660, B661, B645, B663, B564, B5388, B565, B526, B530, B1040, B1042, B1046

R Great Ouse · R Cam or Rhee · R Kym · River Til

Major administrative and Postcode boundaries

— County and unitary authority boundaries
— District boundaries
····· Postcode boundaries
▓ Area covered by this atlas

SP TL

NN9
Hargrave Covington

PE18
Upper Dean Tilbrook

Yelden

Rushden
NN10
Farndish
NN29
Hinwick Souldrop
Northamptonshire

Riseley Little Staughton Great Staughton
Cambridgeshire

St Neots

MK44

Sharnbrook Thurleigh
PE19
Odell Milton Ernest Chawston
GU5
Harrold Bedford
MK46
Cold Brayfield Stevington Green End Tempsford Gamlingay
Turvey Clapham Ravensden
MK41 Renhold
Box End Bedford
MK40
MK16 Kempston Cardington Sandy SG19
Hardmead MK43 MK42 Shortstown
Wootton Biggleswade Eyeworth
SG8
Cranfield Dunton
SG18

Milton Keynes

Bedfordshire

Salford Ampthill Clophill Shefford Henlow SG7 Caldecote
MK45 SG17 SG15 SG5
Mid Bedfordshire SG16 Arlesey Stotfold
Flitwick SG6
Woburn Holwell Letchworth
Eversholt Barton-le-Clay SG5
MK17 SG4
Toddington SG4

Streatley
LU5
Tebworth Chalton Lilley
LU7 Houghton LU3 Stopsley
Leighton Buzzard Regis Hertfordshire
Tilsworth LU4 Luton SG4
South Bedfordshire LU2 Peter's Green
Dunstable Luton SG4
Buckinghamshire LU6 LU1
Slapton Whipsnade
HP4 AL3 AL5
Dagnall Markyate Harpenden AL4
HP2
HP1
Nettleden

SP TL

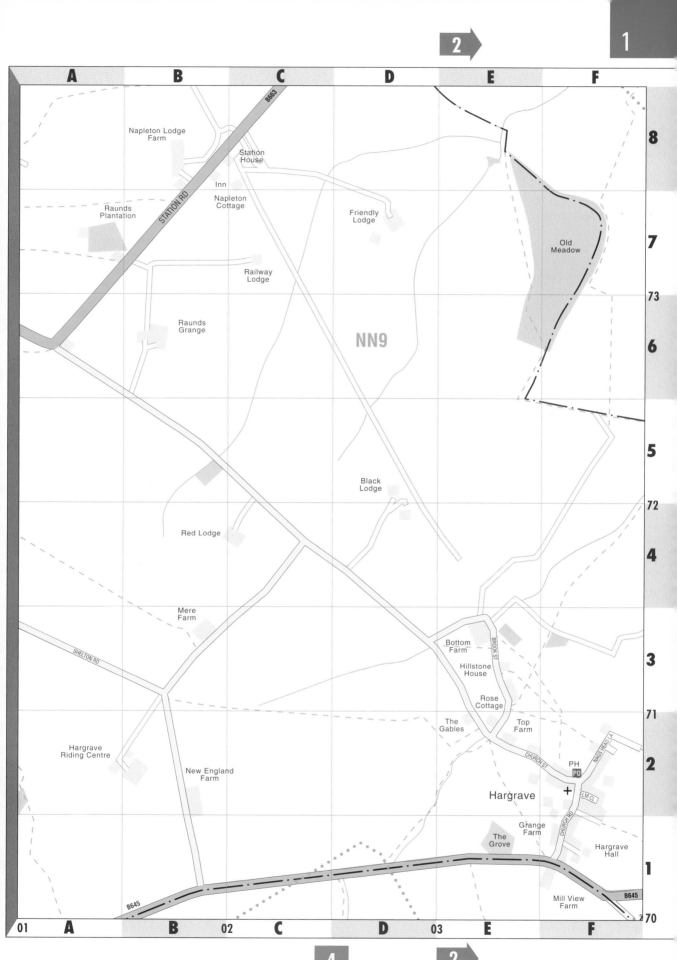

A B C D E F

8
7
73
6
5
72
4
3
71
2
1
70

Napleton Lodge Farm

Station House

B663

STATION RD

Inn

Napleton Cottage

Raunds Plantation

Friendly Lodge

Old Meadow

Railway Lodge

Raunds Grange

NN9

Black Lodge

Red Lodge

Mere Farm

SHELTON RD

Bottom Farm

Hillstone House

BROOK ST

Rose Cottage

The Gables

Top Farm

Hargrave Riding Centre

New England Farm

CHURCH ST

PH
PO

NAGS HEAD LA

Hargrave

ELM CL

The Grove

Grange Farm

CHURCH RD

Hargrave Hall

B645

Mill View Farm

B645

01 A B 02 C D 03 E F 70

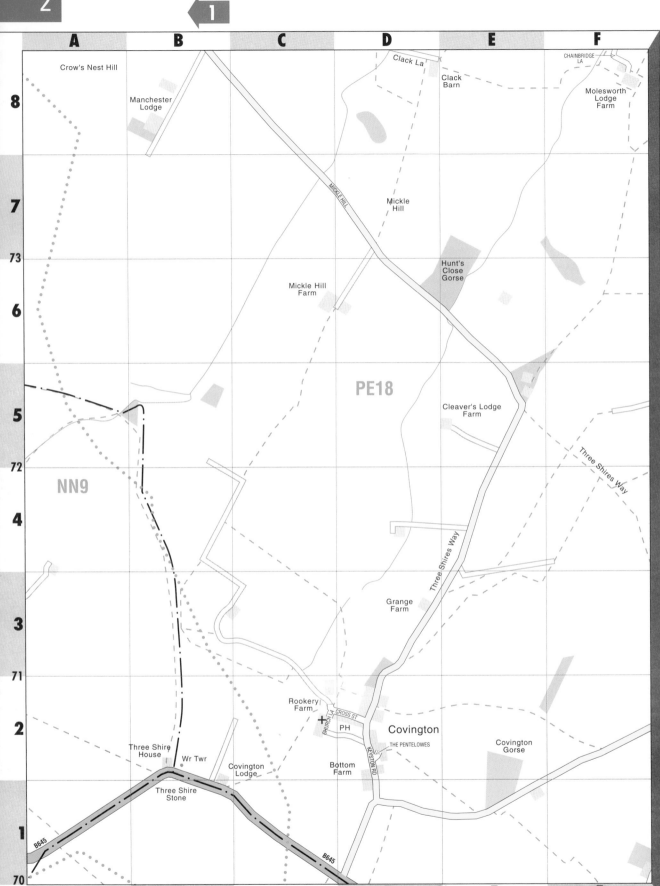

Crow's Nest Hill

Clack La

Clack Barn

CHAINBRIDGE LA

Molesworth Lodge Farm

Manchester Lodge

8

MICKLE HILL

Mickle Hill

7

73

Hunt's Close Gorse

Mickle Hill Farm

6

PE18

Cleaver's Lodge Farm

5

Three Shires Way

NN9

72

Three Shires Way

4

71

Grange Farm

3

Rookery Farm

CROSS ST

71

2

CHURCH LA

PH

Covington

THE PENTELOWES

Covington Gorse

Three Shire House

Wr Twr

Covington Lodge

KEYSTON RD

Bottom Farm

Three Shire Stone

1

B645

B645

70

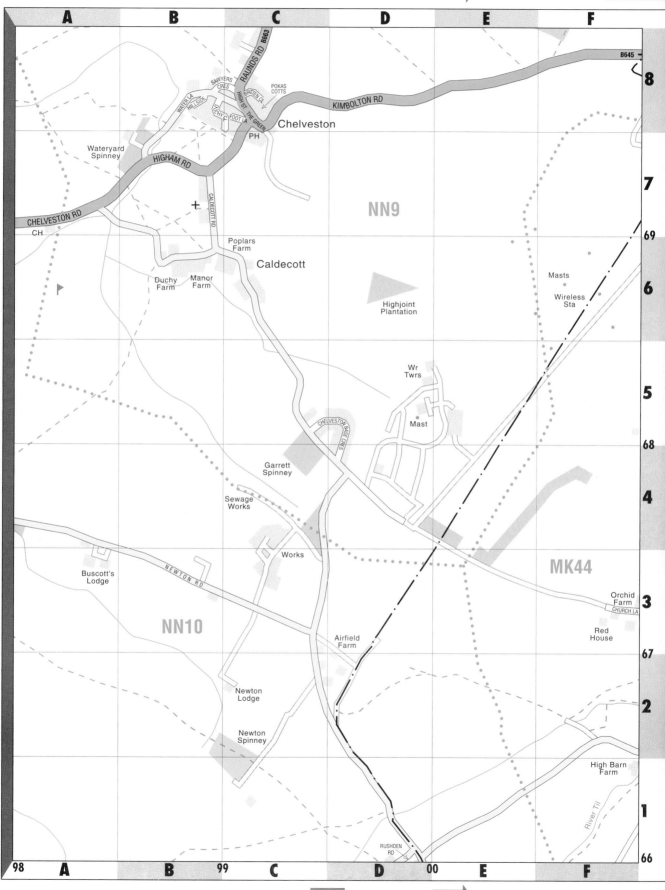

A   B   C   D   E   F

NN9   NN9

8

7

Mast

69

Mast

6

Shelton Gorse

Shelton

Shelton Grange Farm

Elmsleigh

Manor Farm

Shelton Spinney

Shelton Hall

PE18

Mill Farm

5

68

River Till

Three Shires Way

Middle Lodge

4

Dean Lodge

The Manor

Bottom Farm

Dean Lodge Spinney

3

STANBROOK WAY   FORGE   GDNS   CHURCH LA

TRAILLY CL

SPRING LA

Castle Hill

MK44

Yelden

67

HIGH ST

PH

Grange Farm

2

HIGH TOP BARNS

Top Farm

Yelden Spinney

1

PH

Crowfield Farm

66

01   A   B   02   C   D   03   E   F

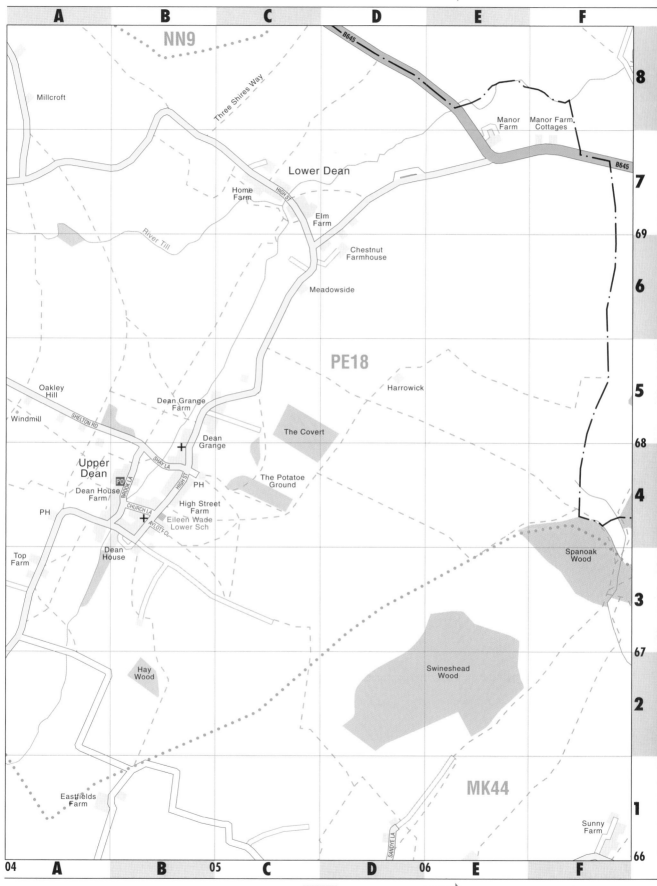

NN9

Millcroft

Three Shires Way

B645

Lower Dean

Manor Farm

Manor Farm Cottages

Home Farm

HIGH ST

Elm Farm

B645

River Till

Chestnut Farmhouse

Meadowside

PE18

Harrowick

Oakley Hill

Dean Grange Farm

SHELTON RD

The Covert

Windmill

Dean Grange

Upper Dean

PO

BROOK LA

SHAY LA

The Potatoe Ground

HIGH ST

PH

Dean House Farm

CHURCH LA

High Street Farm

PH

AYLOTT CL

Eileen Wade Lower Sch

Spanoak Wood

Top Farm

Dean House

Hay Wood

Swineshead Wood

MK44

Eastfields Farm

SANDYE LA

Sunny Farm

A　B　C　D　E　F

8

Hillson
Cottage

Cart-Land

B660 BUSTARD HILL

Manor
House

Tilbrook

STATION RD

Tilbrook
Mill

Brook
Farm

Wornditch
Hall

Vicarage
Farm

A645

7

CHURCH LA

69

HIGH ST

Bunyan
Lodge

Span Oak
Lodge

B645

River Kym

Wrights
Farm

Wornditch

6

SANDY LA

PE18

TILBROOK RD

Wornditch
Farm

Brittens
Farm

MAURICE CL

Kimbolton

VALENTINE GDNS 1
THE CHESTNUTS 2

ARGON PL
MONTAGU GDNS
NEWTOWN LA
NEWTOWN
STOW RD
PH
1
TUDOR CT
HUNTERS
Sch

Hardwicks

Blackquarter
Spinney

The Butts

ASH
DUKES ROW
LEYS
SONS
EAST

5

Kimbolton
Sch

B660

THRAPSTON RD

HIGH ST

FINBAR ST
PO

68

Tilbrook Bushes
Farm

Keys
Corner

Recn
Gd

TOLLFIELD

POUND LA

CASTLE GDNS

GRASS YD

St ANDREWS LA

B645

4

Honeyhill
Wood

Young
Quarters

Kimbolton Park

Kimbolton
Sch

Tilbrook
Bushes

Castle
Hill

B660

3

Old Park
Spinney

Old
Quarters

Park
Lodge

67

Bell's
Barn

Young
Spinney

Mountwood
Spinney

Park
Farm

2

Hungry
Hill

Wych Elm
Spinney

PARK LA

Grange
Farm

1

MK44

Horne
Farm

Wood End

Wood End
House

B660

66

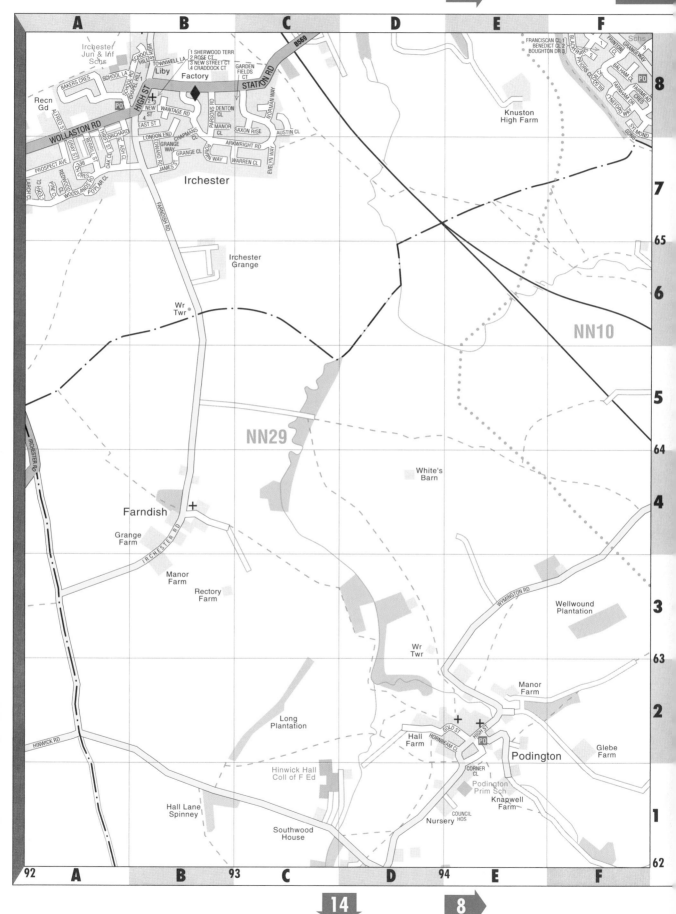

A B C D E F

8
7
65
6
5
64
4
63
3
2
1
62

Irchester Jun & Inf Schs

Recn Gd

BAKERS CRES

SCHOOL RD

SCHOOL LA

CHAPEL HILL

HILL ST

SCHOOL RD

HIGH ST

TOWNWELL LA

Liby

Factory

1 SHERWOOD TERR
2 ROSE CT
3 NEW STREET CT
4 CRADDOCK CT

STATION RD

B569

GARDEN FIELDS CT

FRANCISCAN CL 1
BENEDICT CL 2
BOUGHTON DR 3

FRINTON CL

GRANGEWAY

Schs

BLACKTHORN

FILLYERS CLOSE

BALHAM CL

FARNHAM DR

CHEFORD CL

FAIRMEAD CRES

ST MOND

GDNS

PO

Knuston High Farm

ALFRED'S RISE

PO

WOLLASTON RD

PROSPECT AVE

GRAY ST

THRIFT ST

ORCHARD PL

ASH CL

BERRILL ST

OAK CL

LARCH CL

PINE CL

REDWOOD CL

WOODLANDS RD

POPLAR CL

NEW ST

WANTAGE RD

EAST ST

LONDON END

EDWARD RD

JAMES ST

GRANGE WAY

GRANGE CL

DENTON CL

PARSONS RD

MANOR CL

SAXON RISE

ARKWRIGHT RD

NORMAN WAY

EVELYN WAY

AUSTIN CL

WARREN CL

Irchester

FARNDISH RD

Irchester Grange

Wr Twr

NN29

NN10

White's Barn

Farndish

Grange Farm

IRCHESTER RD

Manor Farm

Rectory Farm

IRCHESTER Rd

HINWICK RD

Long Plantation

Hinwick Hall Coll of F Ed

Hall Lane Spinney

Southwood House

Wr Twr

Wellwound Plantation

WYMINGTON RD

Manor Farm

Hall Farm

GOLD ST

HORNBEAM CL

HIGH ST

PO

Podington

Glebe Farm

CORNER CL

Podington Prim Sch

Nursery

COUNCIL HOS

Knapwell Farm

92 A B 93 C D 94 E F

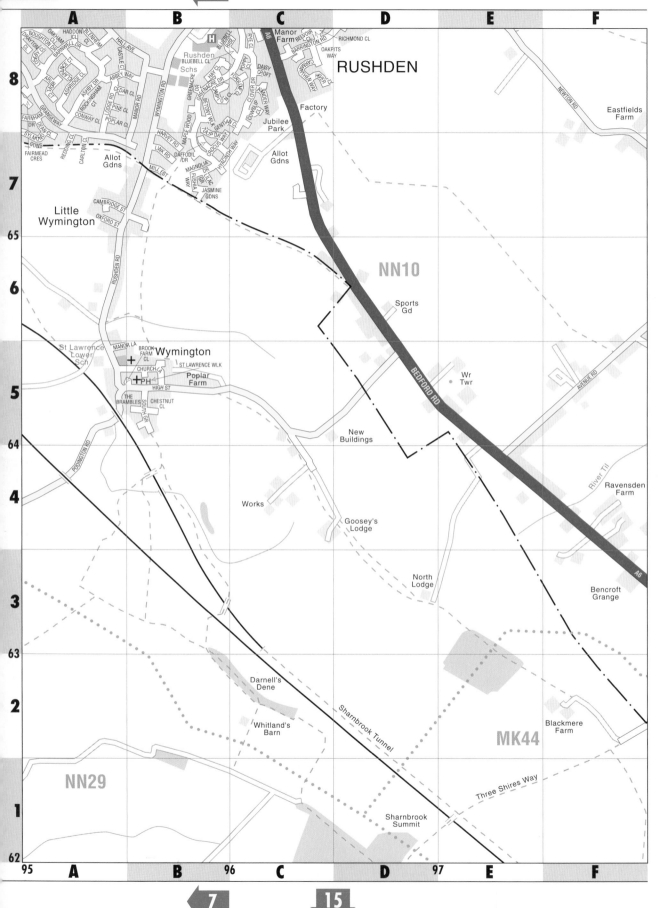

RUSHDEN

NN10

Manor Farm

Richmond Cl

Rushden Bluebell Cl Schs

H

Factory

Jubilee Park

Allot Gdns

Allot Gdns

Eastfields Farm

Little Wymington

Cambridge St

Oxford St

St Lawrence Lower Sch

Wymington

Manor La

Brook Farm Cl

St Lawrence Wlk

+ CHURCH

+ PH

High St

Poplar Farm

THE BRAMBLES

Chestnut Cl

Sports Gd

Wr Twr

Avenue Rd

New Buildings

River Til

Ravensden Farm

Works

Goosey's Lodge

North Lodge

Bencroft Grange

BEDFORD RD

A6

Darnell's Dene

Whitland's Barn

Sharnbrook Tunnel

MK44

Blackmere Farm

NN29

Three Shires Way

Sharnbrook Summit

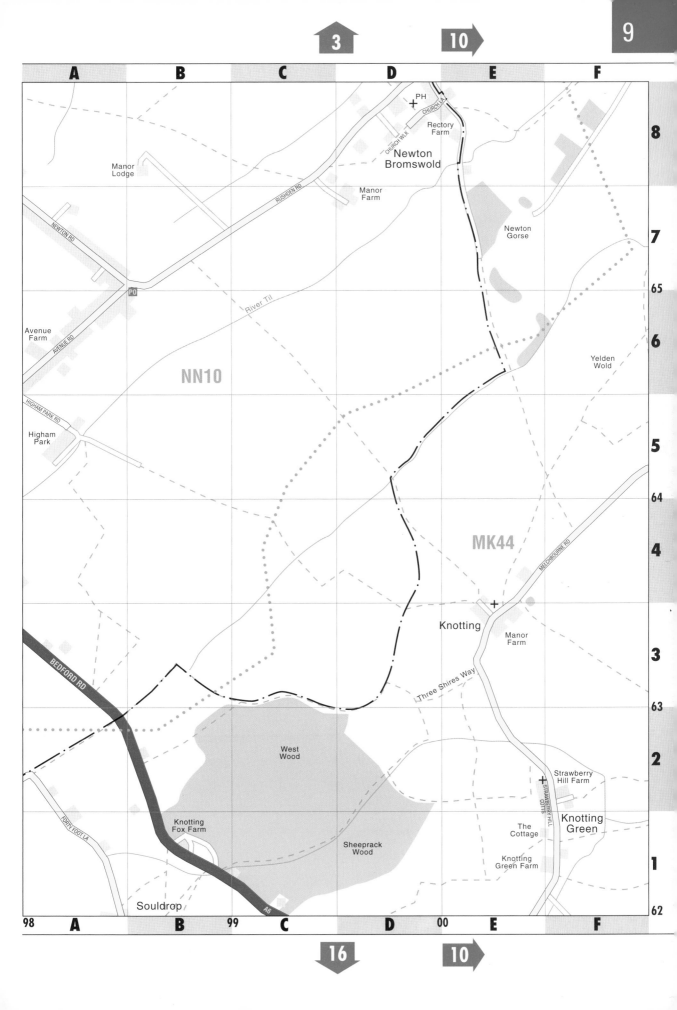

A B C D E F

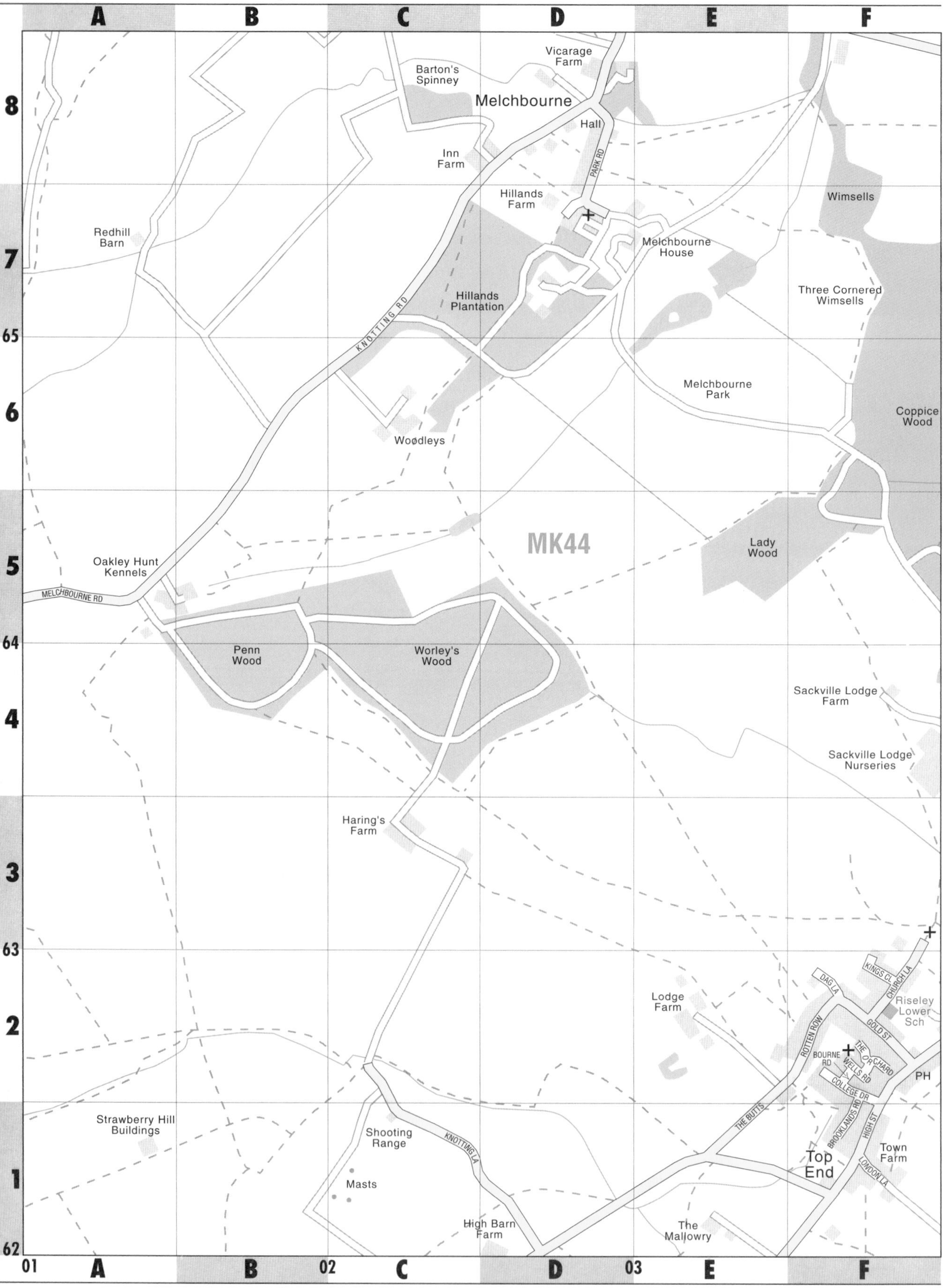

8 Barton's Spinney
Vicarage Farm
Melchbourne
Hall
Inn Farm
Hillands Farm
Redhill Barn
7 Melchbourne House
Wimsells
Hillands Plantation
Three Cornered Wimsells
65
Melchbourne Park
6 Coppice Wood
KNOTTING RD
Woodleys
MK44
5 Lady Wood
Oakley Hunt Kennels
MELCHBOURNE RD
64
Penn Wood
Worley's Wood
Sackville Lodge Farm
4 Sackville Lodge Nurseries
Haring's Farm
3
63
Lodge Farm
Kings Cl
Riseley Lower Sch
2 Dag La Church La
Gold St
Rotten Row
Bourne Rd
The Orchard
PH
Wells Rd
College Dr
Strawberry Hill Buildings
The Butts
Brooklands Way
High St
London La
Town Farm
1 Shooting Range
KNOTTING LA
Top End
Masts
High Barn Farm
The Mallowry
62
01 A B 02 C D 03 E F

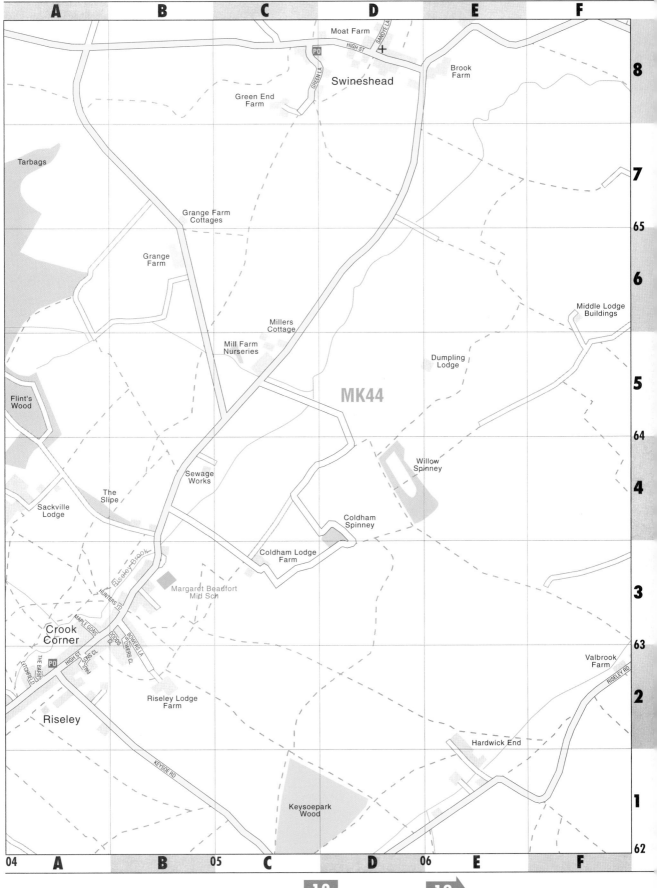

A   B   C   D   E   F

Moat Farm

High St

Swineshead

Green End
Farm

Brook
Farm

Tarbags

Grange Farm
Cottages

Grange
Farm

Middle Lodge
Buildings

Millers
Cottage

Mill Farm
Nurseries

Dumpling
Lodge

MK44

Flint's
Wood

Willow
Spinney

Sewage
Works

The
Slipe

Sackville
Lodge

Coldham
Spinney

Coldham Lodge
Farm

Riseley Brook

Margaret Beaufort
Mid Sch

Hunters Rd

Crook
Corner

Maple Gdns

Dodds
Sons Cl

Bonfers La

Valbrook
Farm

High St

Paul La

The Barns

Litchfield

Riseley Lodge
Farm

Riseley

Hardwick End

Riseley Rd

Keysoe Rd

Keysoepark
Wood

8

7

65

6

5

64

4

3

63

2

1

62

04 A   B 05 C   D 06 E   F

11
6

A B C D E F

8

7

65

6

5

64

4

3

63

2

1

62

07 A B 08 C D 09 E F

B660

The Old Vicarage

Pertenhall

Chadwell Farm

Chadwell End

KIMBOLTON RD

Hall Farm

Rosemary Cottage

Hoo Farm

Manor Farm

Green End

College Cottages

Gunnersbury Cottage

Pertenhall Brook

Galley Oak Spinney

STAUGHTON RD

Sowmead's Spinney

The Kangaroo

Home Close

The Grange

Rectory Farm

MK44

PERTENHALL RD

Lodge Farm

PH

Walnut Tree Farm

Brook Farm

Brook End

GREEN END

RISELEY RD

Brook End Farm

Circus Farm

MILL HILL

Keysoe

Vicarage

MILL LA

WYBRIDGE CL

Temple Farm

The Old Vicarage

CHURCH RD

WYBRIDGE

The Bungalow

Vicarage Farm

B660

London End Farm

London End

11
19

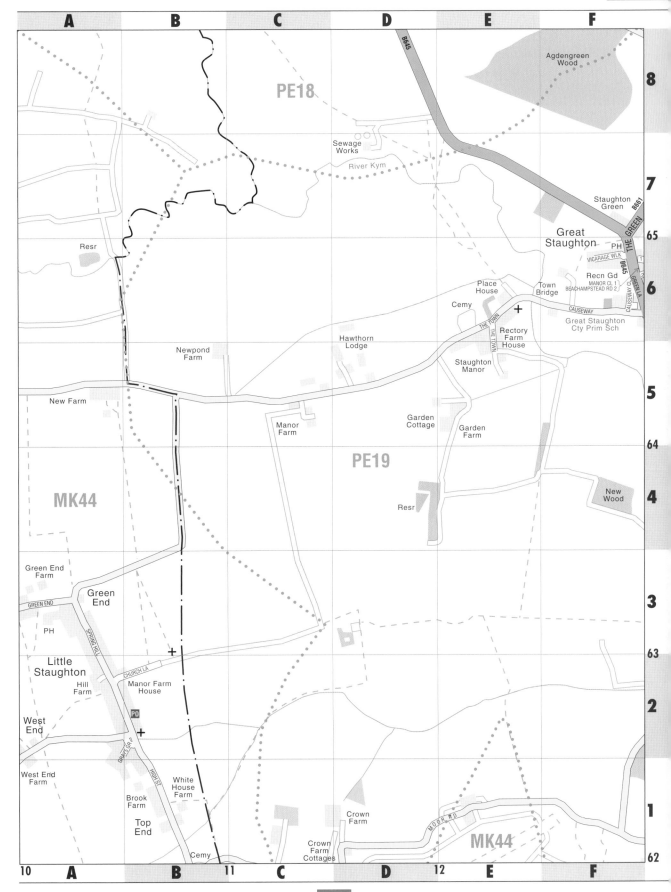

A B C D E F

PE18

Agdengreen
Wood

Sewage
Works

River Kym

B645

Staughton
Green

Great
Staughton

Resr

PH

VICARAGE WLK

Recn Gd

MANOR CL 1
BEACHAMPSTEAD RD 2

Place
House

Town
Bridge

CAUSEWAY

Cemy

Great Staughton
Cty Prim Sch

THE TOWN

Rectory
Farm
House

Newpond
Farm

Hawthorn
Lodge

Staughton
Manor

New Farm

Manor
Farm

Garden
Cottage

Garden
Farm

PE19

New
Wood

Resr

MK44

Green End
Farm

Green
End

GREEN END

SPRING HILL

PH

Little
Staughton

Hill
Farm

CHURCH LA

Manor Farm
House

West
End

PO

GRAYS GR

HIGH ST

West End
Farm

White
House
Farm

Brook
Farm

Crown
Farm

MOOR RD

MK44

Top
End

Cemy

Crown
Farm
Cottages

8

7

65

6

5

64

4

3

63

2

1

62

10 A B 11 C D 12 E F

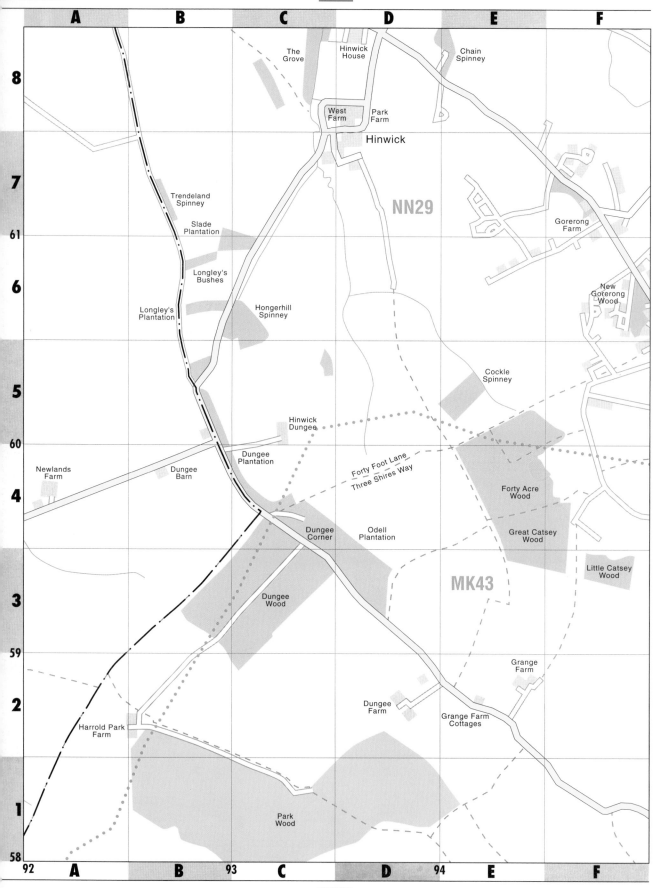

A B C D E F

8

7

61

6

5

60

4

3

59

2

1

58

92 A B 93 C D 94 E F

The Grove

Hinwick House

Chain Spinney

West Farm

Park Farm

Hinwick

NN29

Trendeland Spinney

Slade Plantation

Longley's Bushes

Longley's Plantation

Hongerhill Spinney

Gorerong Farm

New Gorerong Wood

Cockle Spinney

Hinwick Dungee

Dungee Plantation

Newlands Farm

Dungee Barn

Forty Foot Lane

Three Shires Way

Forty Acre Wood

Dungee Corner

Odell Plantation

Great Catsey Wood

Little Catsey Wood

MK43

Dungee Wood

Grange Farm

Dungee Farm

Grange Farm Cottages

Harrold Park Farm

Park Wood

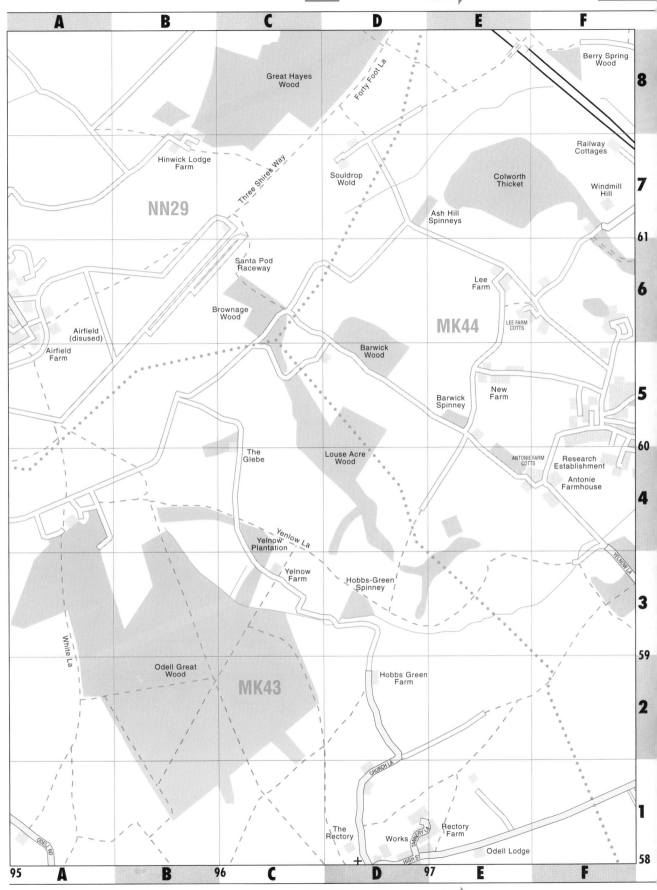

A B C D E F

8

Berry Spring Wood

Great Hayes Wood

Forty Foot La

Railway Cottages

7

Souldrop Wold

Colworth Thicket

Windmill Hill

Hinwick Lodge Farm

Three Shires Way

Ash Hill Spinneys

61

NN29

Lee Farm

6

Santa Pod Raceway

MK44

LEE FARM COTTS

Brownage Wood

Airfield (disused)

Barwick Wood

Airfield Farm

Barwick Spinney

New Farm

5

Louse Acre Wood

60

The Glebe

ANTONIE FARM COTTS

Research Establishment

Antonie Farmhouse

4

Yenlow La

Yelnow Plantation

Yelnow Farm

Hobbs-Green Spinney

YELNOW LA

3

White La

59

Odell Great Wood

Hobbs Green Farm

MK43

2

CHURCH LA

1

The Rectory

Works

Rectory Farm

TWINERY LA

Odell Lodge

ODELL RD

HIGH ST

58

95 A B 96 C D 97 E F

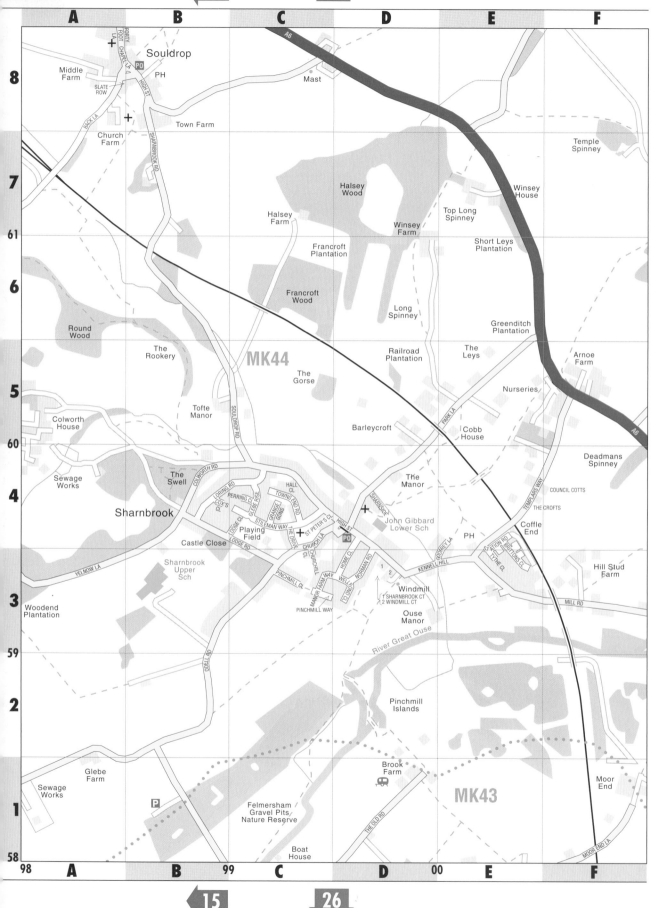

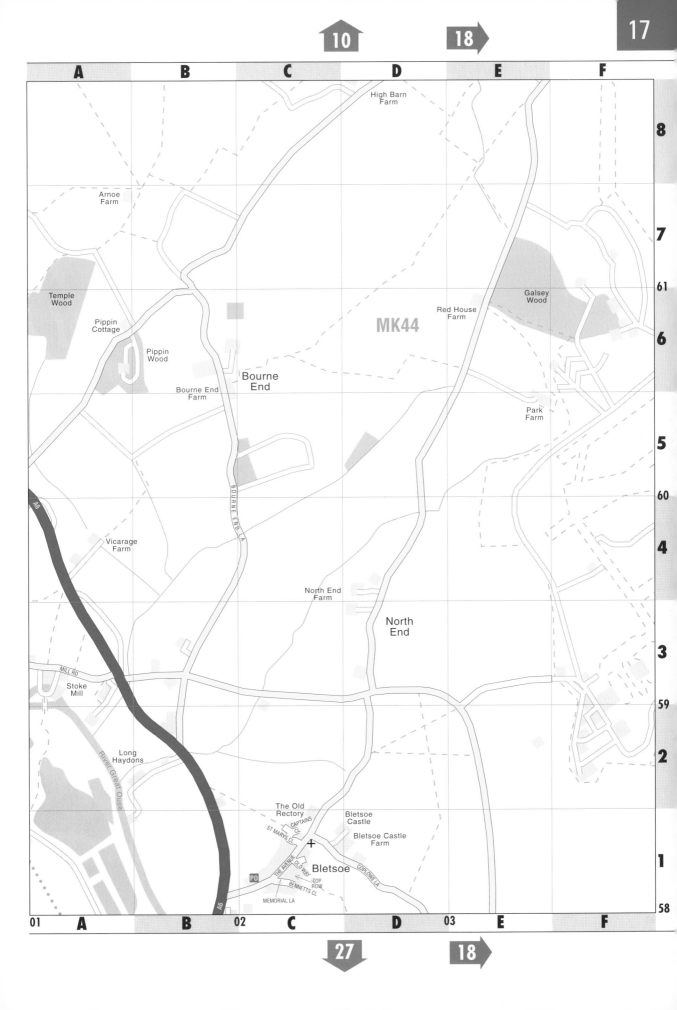

9

A B C D E F

8

7

61

6

Temple Wood

Arnoe Farm

High Barn Farm

Galsey Wood

Red House Farm

MK44

Pippin Cottage

Pippin Wood

Bourne End Farm

Bourne End

Park Farm

5

60

4

BOURNE END LA

Vicarage Farm

North End Farm

North End

A6

3

59

Mill Rd

Stoke Mill

Long Haydons

River Great Ouse

2

The Old Rectory

St Marys Cl

Captains Cl

Bletsoe Castle

Bletsoe Castle Farm

Coplowe La

1

PO

The Avenue

Old Way

Bletsoe

Top Row

Bennetts Cl

Memorial La

A6

58

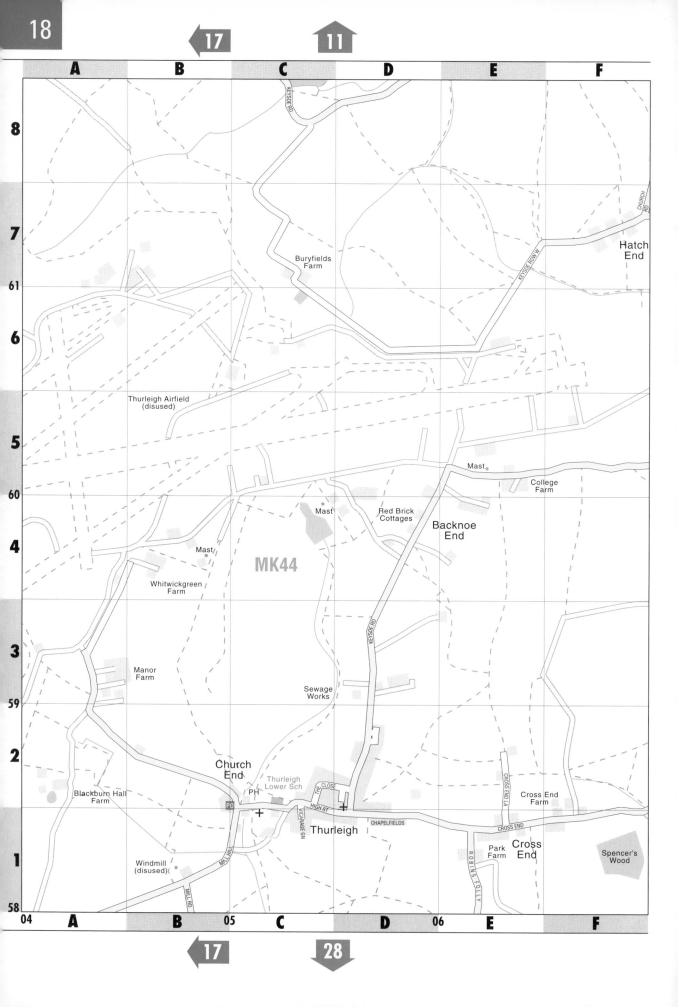

A   B   C   D   E   F

8

7

61

6

5

60

4

3

59

2

1

58

04   A   B   05   C   D   06   E   F

KEYSOE RD

CHURCH RD

Hatch
End

KEYSOE ROW W

Buryfields
Farm

Mast

College
Farm

Thurleigh Airfield
(disused)

Mast

Red Brick
Cottages

Backnoe
End

Mast

MK44

Mast

Whitwickgreen
Farm

KEYSOE RD

Manor
Farm

Sewage
Works

Church
End

Thurleigh
Lower Sch

THE CLOSE

CROSS END LA

Cross End
Farm

Blackburn Hall
Farm

PH

PO

HIGH ST

VICARAGE GN

CHAPELFIELDS

CROSS END

Thurleigh

Park
Farm

Cross
End

ROBINS FOLLY

Spencer's
Wood

Windmill
(disused)

MILL DALE

MILL RD

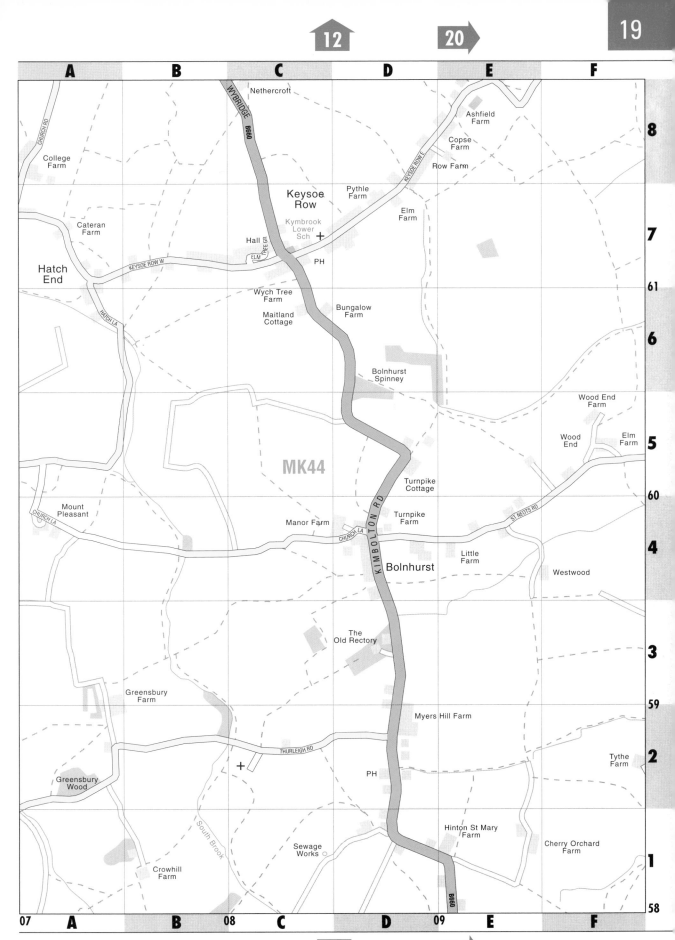

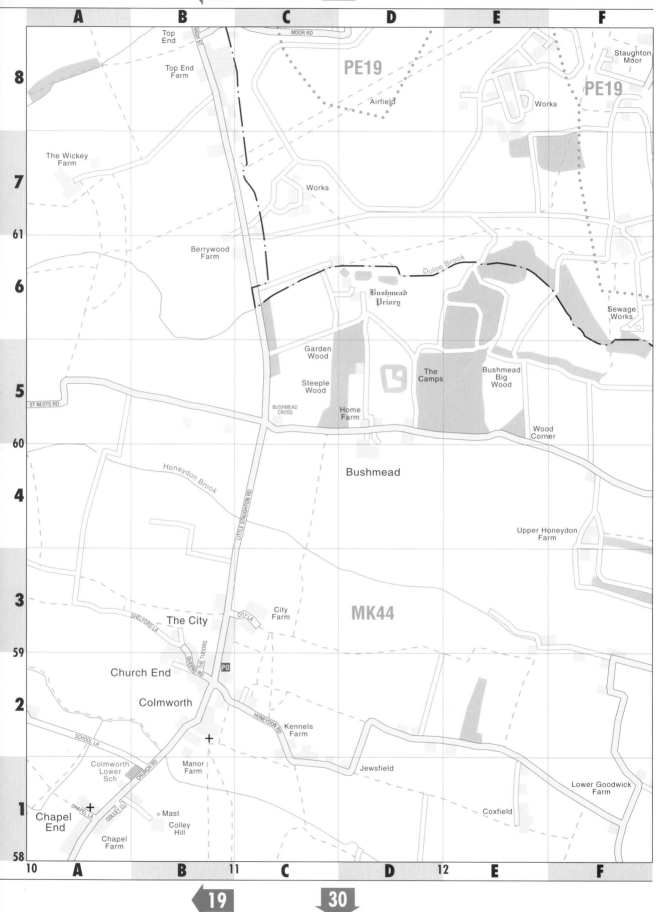

A B C D E F

8

7

61

6

5

60

4

3

59

2

1

58

10 A B 11 C D 12 E F

PE19
Staughton Moor
PE19
Airfield
Works
Top End
Top End Farm
MOOR RD
HIGH ST
The Wickey Farm
Works
Berrywood Farm
Duloe Brook
Bushmead Priory
Sewage Works
Garden Wood
Steeple Wood
The Camps
Bushmead Big Wood
ST NEOTS RD
BUSHMEAD CROSS
Home Farm
Wood Corner
Honeydon Brook
Bushmead
Upper Honeydon Farm
LITTLE STAUGHTON RD
The City
City Farm
CITY LA
MK44
SHELFORD LA
Church End
QUEENS RD
THE TUDORS
PO
Colmworth
HONEYDON RD
Kennels Farm
SCHOOL LA
Jewsfield
Lower Goodwick Farm
Colmworth Lower Sch
Manor Farm
CHURCH RD
CHAPEL LA
COLLEY CL
Mast
Colley Hill
Coxfield
Chapel End
Chapel Farm

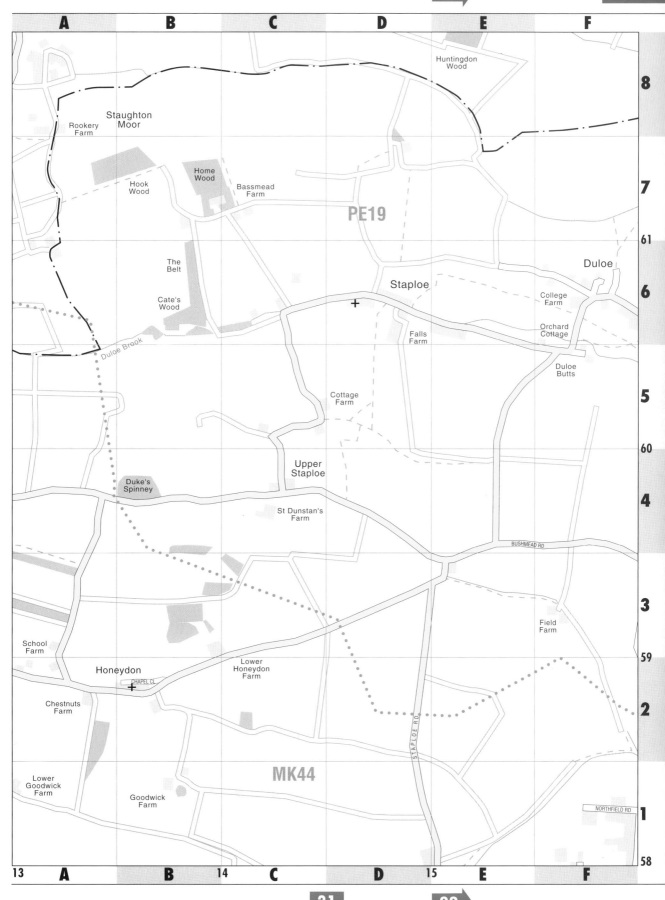

Huntingdon
Wood

8

Staughton
Moor

Rookery
Farm

7

Home
Wood

Hook
Wood

Bassmead
Farm

61

PE19

Duloe

The
Belt

6

Staploe

College
Farm

Cate's
Wood

Orchard
Cottage

Falls
Farm

Duloe Brook

Duloe
Butts

Cottage
Farm

5

Upper
Staploe

60

Duke's
Spinney

4

St Dunstan's
Farm

BUSHMEAD RD

3

Field
Farm

School
Farm

59

Honeydon

CHAPEL CL

Lower
Honeydon
Farm

2

Chestnuts
Farm

STAPLOE RD

MK44

Lower
Goodwick
Farm

1

Goodwick
Farm

NORTHFIELD RD

58

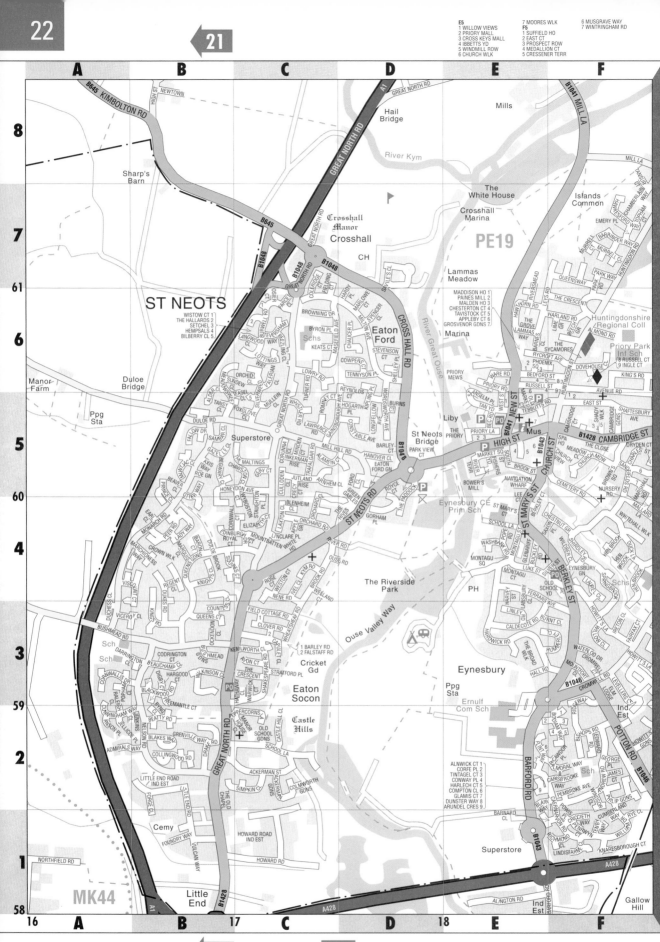

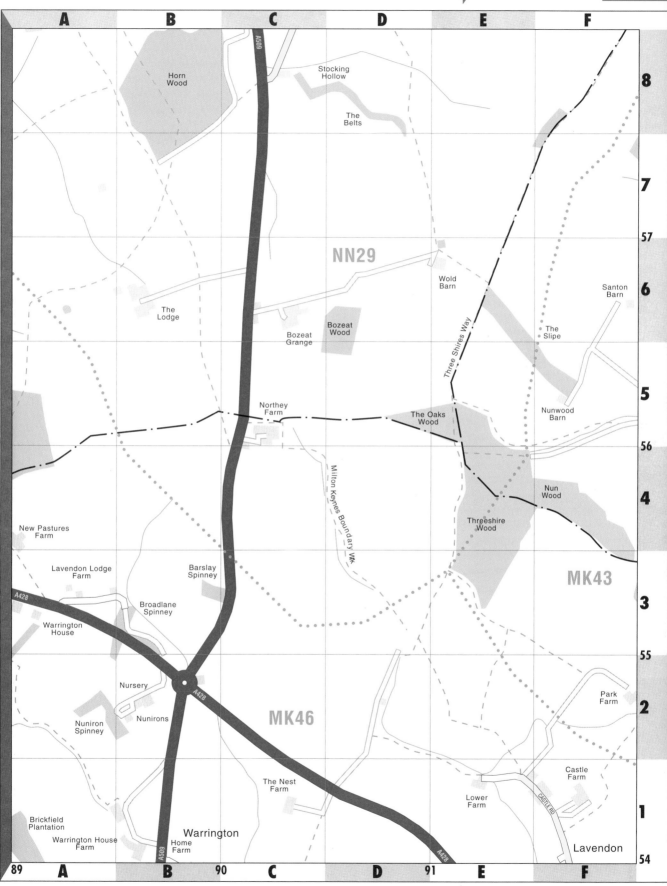

A B C D E F

8
7
57
6
5
56
4
55
2
54

Horn Wood

Stocking Hollow

The Belts

NN29

Wold Barn

Santon Barn

The Lodge

The Slipe

Bozeat Grange

Bozeat Wood

Three Shires Way

Nunwood Barn

Northey Farm

The Oaks Wood

Nun Wood

Milton Keynes Boundary Wk.

Threeshire Wood

MK43

New Pastures Farm

Lavendon Lodge Farm

Barslay Spinney

Broadlane Spinney

A428

Warrington House

Park Farm

Nursery

A428

MK46

Nuniron Spinney

Nunirons

Castle Farm

CASTLE RD

The Nest Farm

Lower Farm

Brickfield Plantation

Warrington

Warrington House Farm

A509

Home Farm

A428

Lavendon

A   B   C   D   E   F

← NN29

8

7

Templegrove
Spinney

Austin's
Spinney

New
Buildings

Allot
Gdns

WOOD RD

ORCHARD LA

Allot
Gdns

BROOK LA

57

Manor
Farm

The
Mansion

DICKENS CL

MANSION LA

HIGH ST

Harrold

BRAMLEY
CT

6

NEW RD

Harrold
Lower Sch

MOWHILLS

Priory
Farm

Harrold Priory
Mid Sch

Coldharbour
Hill

Cracknell Hill
House

Cracknell
Hill

5

Middle
Farm

MK43

56

4

River Great Ouse

Millholme
Island

3

Lavendon
Wood

Harrold Lodge
Farm

Marsh
Farm

Milton Keynes Bdy Wlk

55

Church
Farm

Spring Close
Farm

2

TURVEY RD

Tollgate
House

Carltonhall
Wood

Valley View
Farm

Snelson
Cotts

Carlton Hall
Farm

MK46

Snelson

1

HARROLD RD

Snelson
Cobs

CARLTON RD

54

92   A   B   93   C   D   94   E   F

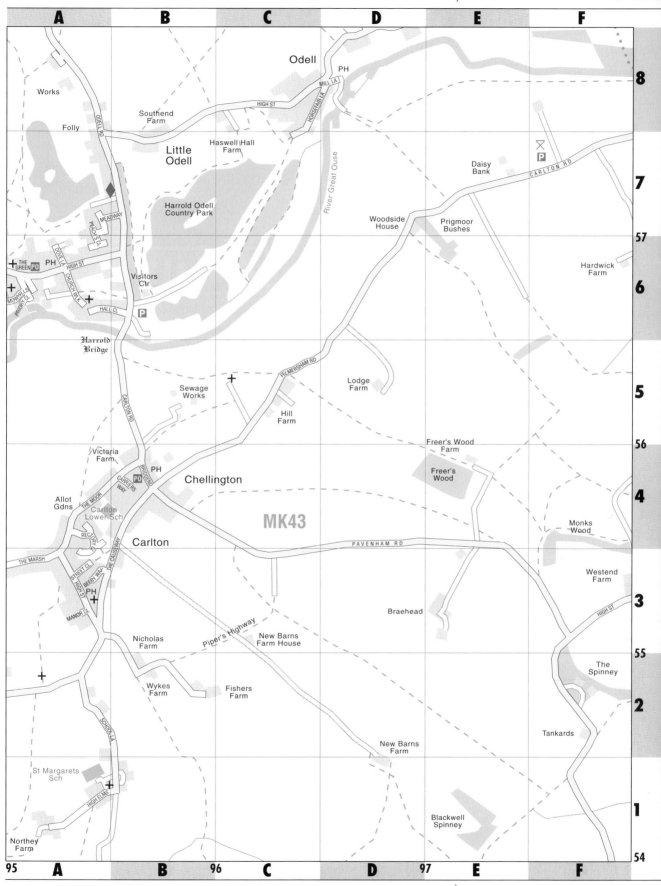

A   B   C   D   E   F

8

Odell

PH

MILL LA

HIGH ST

HORSEFAIR LA

Works

Folly

ODELL RD

Southend
Farm

Haswell Hall
Farm

Little
Odell

Daisy
Bank

CARLTON RD

7

River Great Ouse

Woodside
House

Prigmoor
Bushes

57

Harrold Odell
Country Park

MEADWAY

PEACH'S CL.

Hardwick
Farm

THE GREEN   PO   PH

HIGH ST

LOVE LA

CHURCH WLK

Visitors
Ctr

6

MONKWELLS
PRIORY CL

HALL CL.

P

Harrold
Bridge

Sewage
Works

Hill
Farm

Lodge
Farm

5

CARLTON RD

FELMERSHAM RD

Freer's Wood
Farm

56

Victoria
Farm

PH

Freer's
Wood

BROOMEND

CARRIERS WAY

PO

Chellington

MK43

4

Allot
Gdns

THE MOOR

Carlton
Lower Sch

Monks
Wood

REC.

THE CAUSEWAY

Carlton

PAVENHAM RD

Westend
Farm

THE MARSH

STREET CL.

BEDBY WAY

HIGH ST

PH

Braehead

HIGH ST

3

MANOR CL.

Piper's Highway

Nicholas
Farm

New Barns
Farm House

55

The
Spinney

SCHOOL LA

Wykes
Farm

Fishers
Farm

2

Tankards

St Margarets
Sch

New Barns
Farm

HIGH ELMS

1

Northey
Farm

Blackwell
Spinney

54

95   A   B   96   C   D   97   E   F

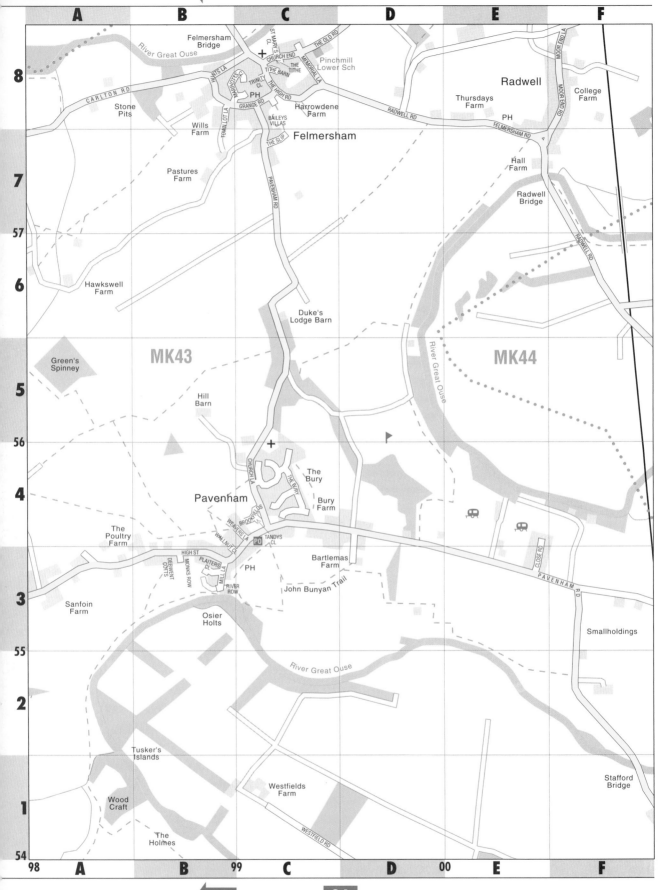

Felmersham
Bridge

River Great Ouse

Felmersham

Radwell

College
Farm

Thursdays
Farm

PH

Pinchmill
Lower Sch

Harrowdene
Farm

CARLTON RD

Stone
Pits

Wills
Farm

BAILEYS
VILLAS

Pastures
Farm

THE SLIP

PAVENHAM RD

RADWELL RD

FELMERSHAM RD

Hall
Farm

Radwell
Bridge

RADWELL RD

Hawkswell
Farm

MK43

MK44

River Great Ouse

Duke's
Lodge Barn

Green's
Spinney

Hill
Barn

The
Bury

Pavenham

CHURCH LA

THE BURY

Bury
Farm

The
Poultry
Farm

WEAVERS LA

BROOKFIELDS

WALNUT CL

PO

TANDYS
CL

Bartlemas
Farm

CLOSE RD

PAVENHAM RD

HIGH ST

DERWENT
COTTS

MONKS ROW

PLAITERS
CL

MILL LA

RIVER
ROW

PH

John Bunyan Trail

Smallholdings

Sanfoin
Farm

Osier
Holts

River Great Ouse

Tusker's
Islands

Westfields
Farm

Stafford
Bridge

Wood
Craft

The
Holmes

WESTFIELD RD

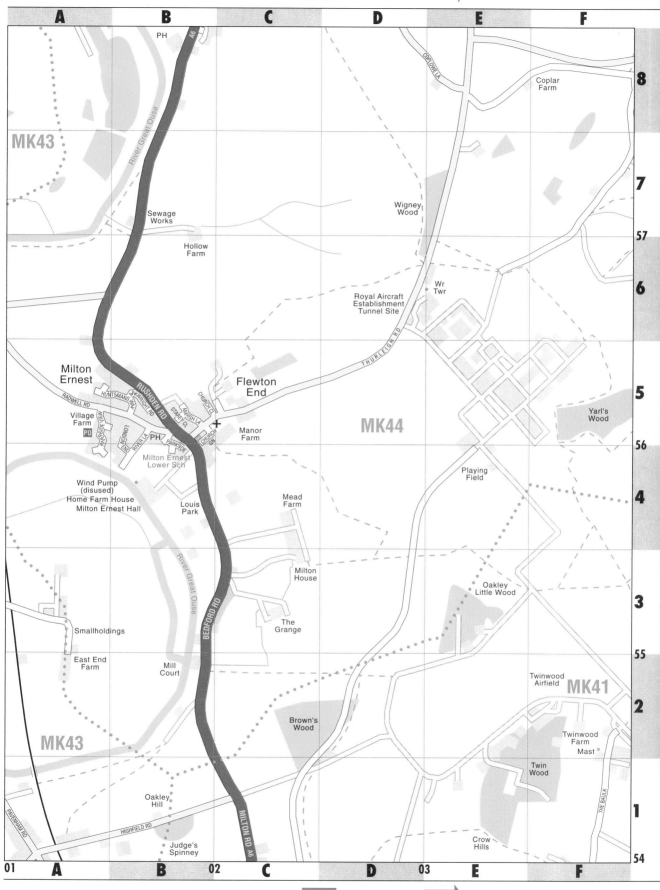

27
18

| | A | B | C | D | E | F |

8

Scald End Farm

Scald End

Robins Folly Farm

Romp Hall

Park End Farm

7

MILL RD

ROBINS FOLLY

Short Wood

Waterfall Farm

57

Rutter's Farm

6

Tilwick Wood

Red Gate Farm

MK44

Brook Farm

5

56

4

Little Wood

Traylesfield Farm

Great Wood

Manor Farm

Brook Farm

Outfields Farm

3

Wood End

Ravensden House

55

GRAZE HILL

Gray's Hill Farm

Ravensden Brook

THURLEIGH RD

SUNDERLAND HILL

B660

2

Highfield Farm

Graze Hill House

Willow Farm

SUNDERLAND CL

Fairfield Farm

PH

BUTLER ST

PO

MK41

Highfield House

BEDFORD RD

NEW CL

OLDWAYS RD

1

54

27
38

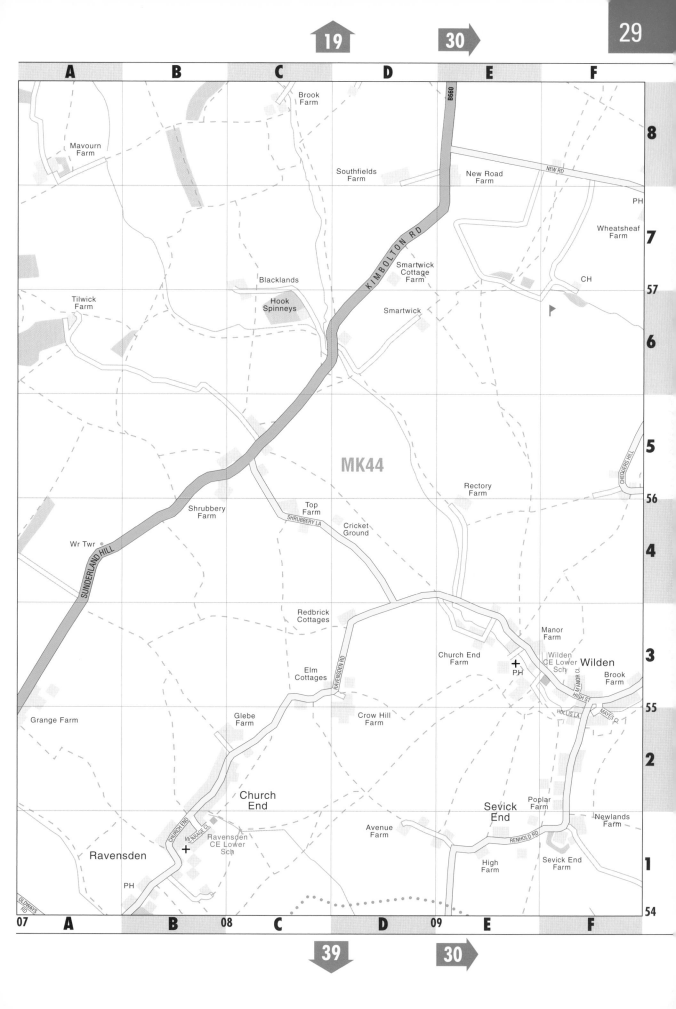

A B C D E F

8

7

57

6

5

56

4

3

55

2

1

54

Mavourn Farm

Brook Farm

Southfields Farm

New Road Farm

NEW RD

PH

B660

Wheatsheaf Farm

KIMBOLTON RD

CH

Blacklands

Hook Spinneys

Smartwick Cottage Farm

Smartwick

Tilwick Farm

MK44

Rectory Farm

CHEQUERS HILL

Shrubbery Farm

Top Farm

SHRUBBERY LA

Cricket Ground

Wr Twr

SUNDERLAND HILL

Redbrick Cottages

Manor Farm

Church End Farm

Wilden CE Lower Sch

Wilden

Brook Farm

MANOR CL

HIGH ST

Elm Cottages

RAVENSDEN RD

PH

HOLLIS LA

MAYES CL

Grange Farm

Glebe Farm

Crow Hill Farm

Poplar Farm

Sevick End

Newlands Farm

Church End

CHURCH END

VICARAGE CT

Ravensden CE Lower Sch

Avenue Farm

RENHOLD RD

Sevick End Farm

Ravensden

PH

OLDWAYS RD

High Farm

| | A | B | C | D | E | F |

8

CHURCH RD

NEW RD

Rootham's
Green

MILL RD

Mill End

7

Top
Farm

WILDEN RD

Begwary Brook

57

Channel's
End
Farm

CHANNELS END RD

6

Hillview
Farm

Finsbury Park
Farm

Channel's End
Farm

Channel's
End

Channel's End
Farm

Colesden
Wood

5

Dacca
Farm

Duck's
Cross

Colesden
Grange
Farm

56

Bryher
Farm

COLESDEN RD

MK44

Colesden

4

CHEQUERS HILL

Bell
Farm

Ley
Farm

3

East End
Farm

Sewage
Works

EAST END LA

HIGH ST

East End

Lady Wood

55

Hill
Farm

BARFORD RD

2

WOODEND LA

Hill Farm

Palaceyard
Wood

1

54

| 10 | A | B | 11 | C | D | 12 | E | F |

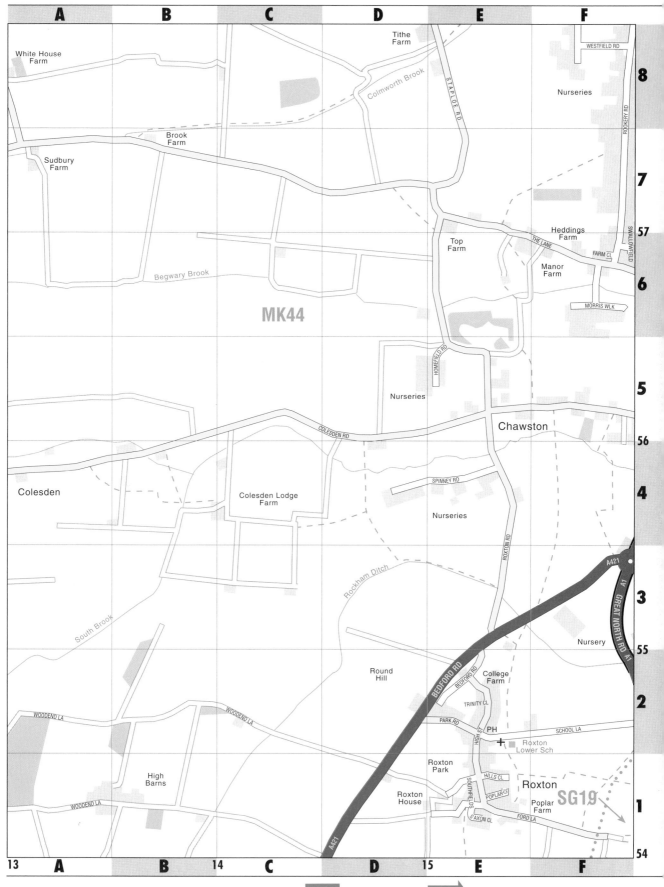

A   B   C   D   E   F

Tithe Farm

White House Farm

Colmworth Brook

STAPLOE RD

WESTFIELD RD

8

Nurseries

ROOKERY RD

Brook Farm

Sudbury Farm

7

57

SWALLOWFIELD

Heddings Farm

Top Farm

THE LANE

FARM CL

Begwary Brook

Manor Farm

6

MORRIS WLK

MK44

HOMEFIELD RD

Nurseries

5

Chawston

56

COLESDEN RD

Colesden

Colesden Lodge Farm

SPINNEY RD

4

Nurseries

ROXTON RD

Rockham Ditch

A421

GREAT NORTH RD A1

A1

3

South Brook

Nursery

55

Round Hill

BEDFORD RD

College Farm

BEDFORD RD

TRINITY CL

WOODEND LA

WOODEND LA

PARK RD

HIGH ST

PH

SCHOOL LA

2

Roxton Lower Sch

High Barns

Roxton Park

WLLS CL

SOUTHFIELDS

POPLAR CL

Roxton

SG19

Roxton House

Poplar Farm

WOODEND LA

SAXON CL

FORD LA

1

54

13 A 14 B C 15 D E F

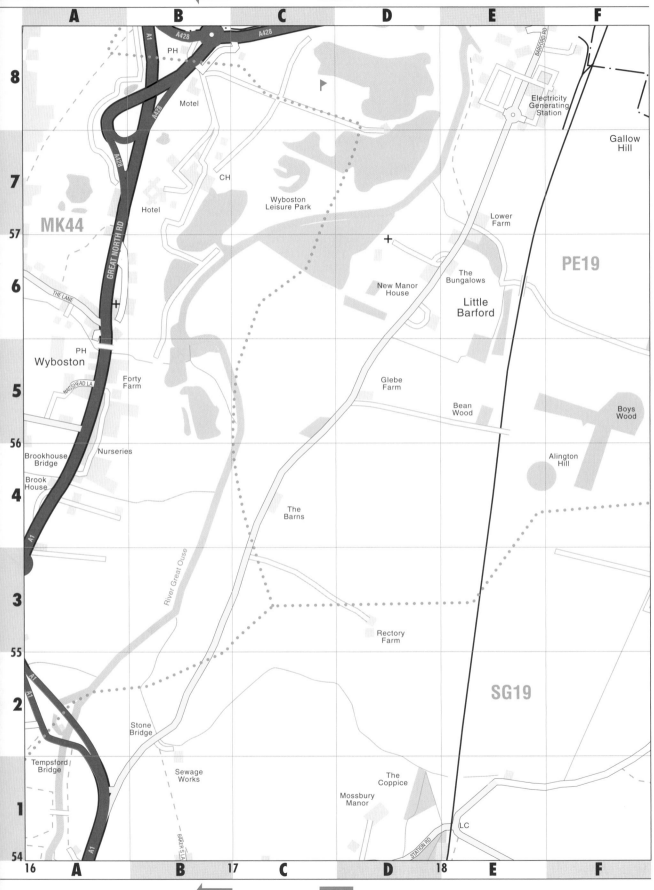

Rectory Farm

Parker's Farm

B1046

Lansbury Farm

Round Spinney

Hail Lane Plantation

ST NEOTS RD

B1046

CH

St Neots L Ctr

Hardwick Spinney

Long Plantation

CH

Hotel

Top Farm

Pear Tree Spinney

Abbotsley Downs

PE19

Gipsy Corner

Highbarns

Highfield Spinney

Downs Plantation

DREWELS LA

Highfield Kennels

Southwood Farm

PITSDEAN RD

Sir John's Wood

Highfield Farm

Bushy Common Plantation

Crane Hill

Highfield Cottages

Crab Tree Spinney

Hill's Farm

The Decoy

Stone Hill Farm

Ash Plantation

New Farm

SG19

Cold Arbour

Kims Spinney

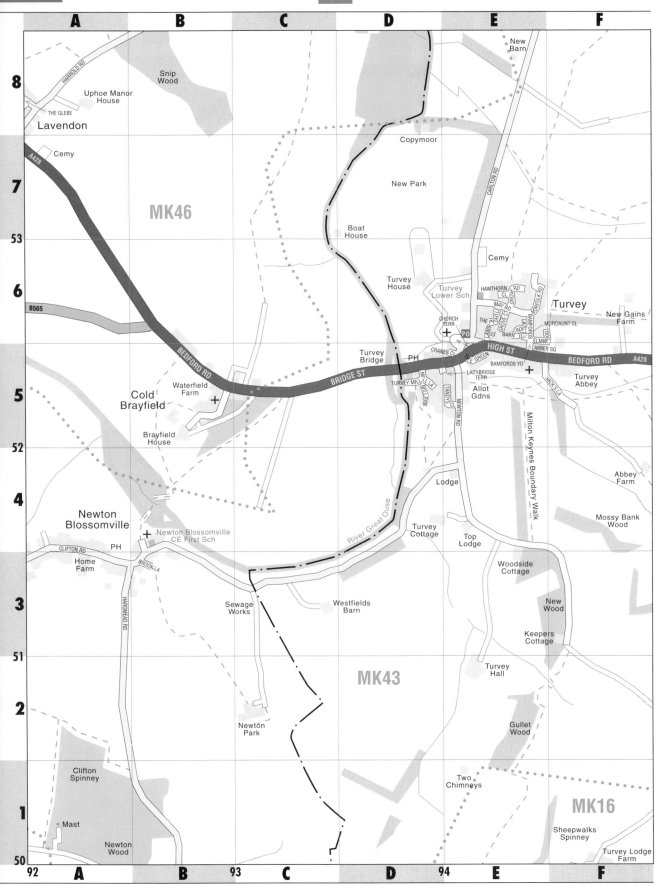

A   B   C   D   E   F

8

Snip Wood

New Barn

Uphoe Manor House

THE GLEBE

Lavendon

Copymoor

Cemy

A428

MK46

CARLTON RD

New Park

7

Boat House

53

Cemy

6

Turvey House

Turvey Lower Sch

HAWTHORN CL

RD

Turvey

B565

MAY RD

New Gains Farm

GROVE CT

CASTLE CT

CHURCH TERR

LEWIS CL

THE

BARN

BAMFORDS

LA

MORDAUNT CL

LOFT

BARFOLK RD

PO

ELM W

BEDFORD RD

Turvey Bridge

PH

CRANES CL

HIGH ST

ABBEY SQ

BEDFORD RD

A428

BRIDGE ST

THE GREEN

BAMFORDS YD

Waterfield Farm

TURVEY MILL

LADYBRIDGE TERR

Turvey Abbey

JACK S LA

5

Cold Brayfield

MILL LA

MILL RISE

TANDYS CL

Allot Gdns

NEWTON RD

Brayfield House

Milton Keynes Boundary Walk

Abbey Farm

52

Lodge

4

Newton Blossomville

River Great Ouse

Turvey Cottage

Top Lodge

Mossy Bank Wood

CLIFTON RD

PH

Newton Blossomville CE First Sch

BROOK LA

Woodside Cottage

New Wood

Home Farm

3

HARDMEAD RD

Sewage Works

Westfields Barn

Keepers Cottage

51

MK43

Turvey Hall

2

Newton Park

Gullet Wood

Clifton Spinney

Two Chimneys

MK16

1

Mast

Sheepwalks Spinney

Newton Wood

Turvey Lodge Farm

50

92   A   B   93   C   D   94   E   F

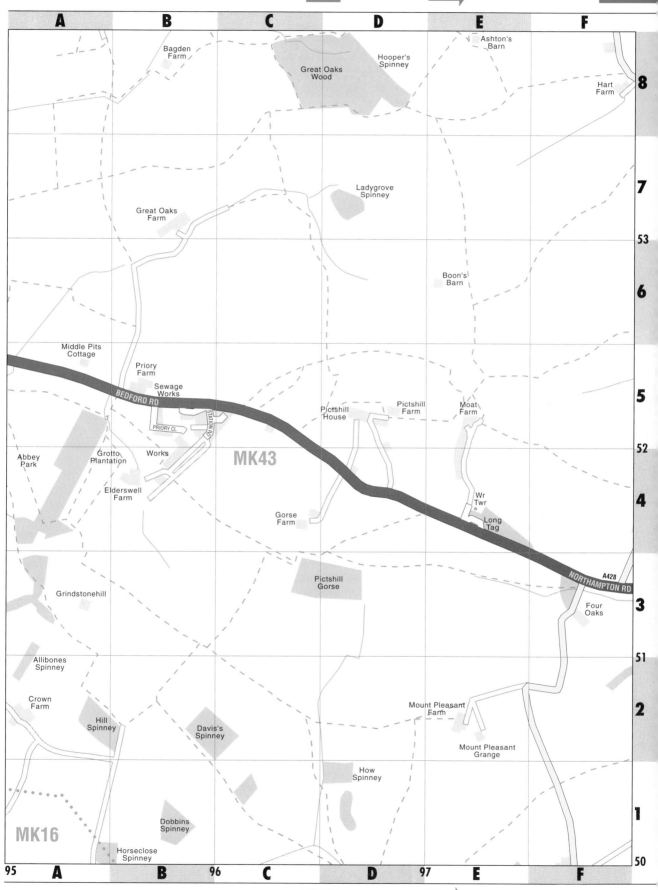

Bagden Farm

Great Oaks Wood

Hooper's Spinney

Ashton's Barn

Hart Farm

8

Ladygrove Spinney

7

Great Oaks Farm

53

Boon's Barn

6

Middle Pits Cottage

Priory Farm

Sewage Works

BEDFORD RD

STATION RD

PRIORY CL

Pictshill House

Pictshill Farm

Moat Farm

5

52

Abbey Park

Grotto Plantation

Works

MK43

Elderswell Farm

Gorse Farm

Wr Twr

Long Tag

4

Pictshill Gorse

Grindstonehill

NORTHAMPTON RD

A428

Four Oaks

3

51

Allibones Spinney

Crown Farm

Mount Pleasant Farm

2

Hill Spinney

Davis's Spinney

Mount Pleasant Grange

How Spinney

1

MK16

Dobbins Spinney

Horseclose Spinney

50

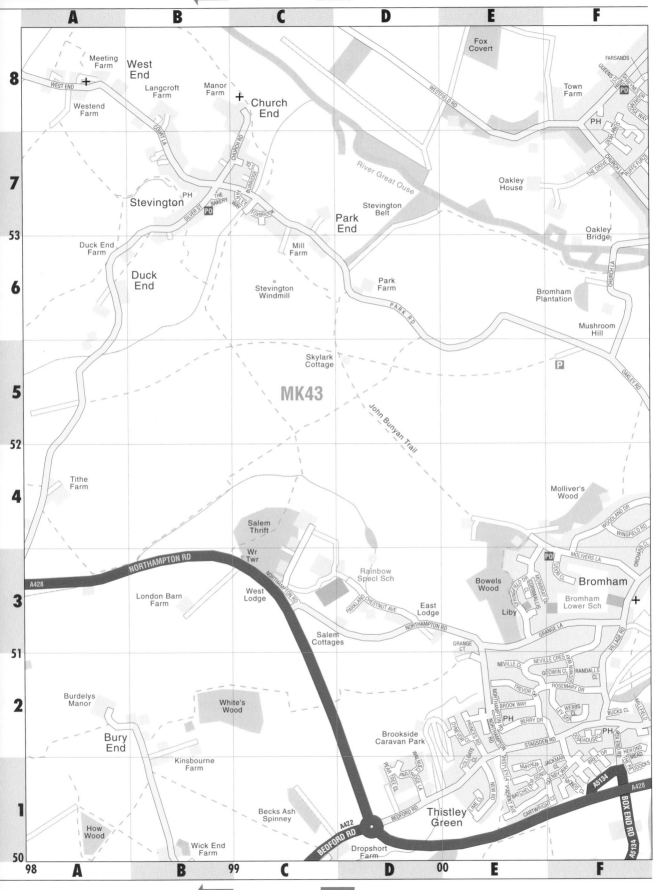

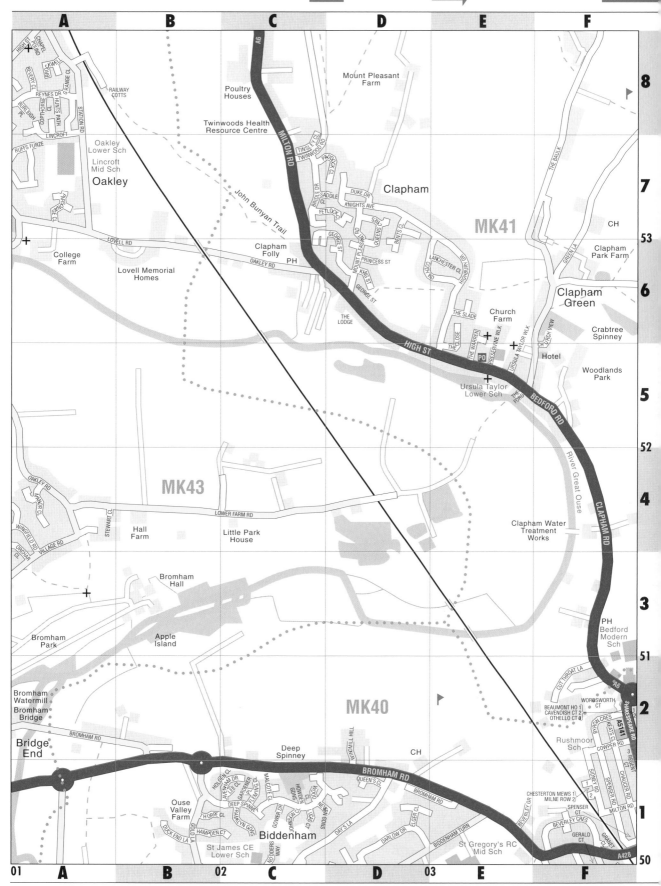

A B C D E F

8 7 53 6 5 52 4 3 51 2 1 50

MK44

MK41

MK40

College Farm
GREEN LA
Clapham Park Wood
Clapham Park
Little Park Farm
HAWK DR
John Bunyan Trail
Laboratory
Ind Est
MURDOCK RD
Mast
THE MANTON CTR
Mast
Bedford Modern Sch
Edith Cavell Lower Sch
Livingstone Lower Sch

Cleat Hill
CLEAT HILL
BEDFORD RD B660
CH
Mowsbury Hill
Putnoe Wood
Mowsbury Park
GLENROSE AVE
WAGSTAFFE CL
PARKSTONE CL

St Thomas More RC Upper Sch
KENNET RISE
WANSBECK RD
Beauchamp Mid Sch
Scott Lower Sch

Brickhill
Brickhill Lower Sch

BREAMISH WLK 1
PETTERIL WLK 2
THE GELT 3
SWALE PATH 4

AELFRIC CT 1
MERSEY WAY 2
WESTBURY CT 3
LEIGHTON CT 4
HIGHFIELD 5
EVESHAM CT 6
UPTON CT 7
FRAMPTON CT 8

1 IRVINE CT
2 MEDWAY CT
3 OULTON CT
4 WELLAND CT

1 SUNNINGDALE WLK
2 TURNBERRY WLK
3 LOWTHER RD
4 PERSHORE CL

Liby
1 LIBRARY WLK
2 LITTLE HEADLANDS
3 GREYSTOKE WLK

Putnoe
Newnham Mid Sch
Goldington Mid Sch
De Montfort Univ

KIMBOLTON RD
GOLDINGTON RD
B660
A428
A5140
NEWNHAM AVE

Bedford Park
RODEAN CT 1
ST MICHAEL'S CTS 2
KIMBOLTON CT 3

1 BANGWYN GDNS
2 ROMNEY WLK

Crem
Cemy

SHAKESPEARE RD
CLAPHAM RD
A6
A5141
BROMHAM RD
UNION ST
TAVISTOCK ST
ST PETER'S ST
A428
THE BROADWAY
HM Prison
DAME ALICE ST
MK40

1 LINDEN CT
2 CULVER HO
3 WARWICK RD
4 STRATFORD CT

Bedford Sch
Bedford (North Wing)
Castle Lower Sch
H

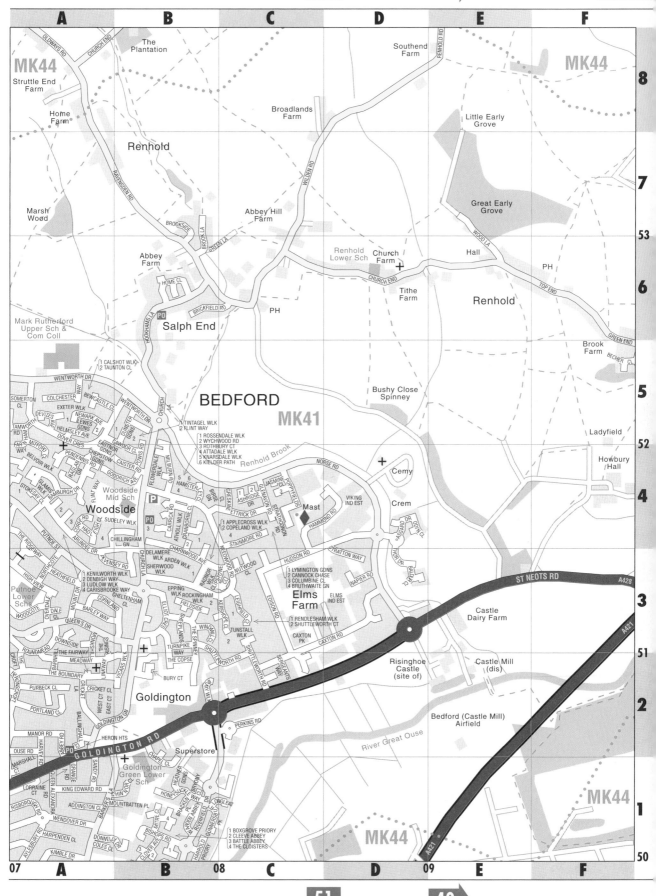

MK44

Struttle End Farm

Home Farm

Renhold

Marsh Wood

Abbey Farm

OLDWAYS RD
CHURCH END

The Plantation

Broadlands Farm

Southend Farm

RENHOLD RD

MK44

Little Early Grove

Great Early Grove

WOOD LA

Abbey Hill Farm

RAVENSDEN RD

BROOKSIDE

BROOK LA

GREEN LA

Renhold Lower Sch

Church Farm

Hall

PH

TOP END

Renhold

GREEN END

BECHER CL

Brook Farm

Mark Rutherford Upper Sch & Com Coll

HOOKHAMS LA

HOME CL

BRICKFIELD RD

Salph End

PO

CHURCH END

PH

Tithe Farm

CHURCH

BEDFORD

MK41

Bushy Close Spinney

Ladyfield

Howbury Hall

Renhold Brook

NORSE RD

Cemy

Woodside Mid Sch

Woodside

Crem

VIKING IND EST

Mast

ELMS IND EST

Putnoe Lower Schs

Elms Farm

ST NEOTS RD   A428

Castle Dairy Farm

A421

Goldington

GOLDINGTON RD

Castle Mill (dis)

Risinghoe Castle (site of)

Bedford (Castle Mill) Airfield

River Great Ouse

A421

MK44

Superstore

Goldington Green Lower Sch

PERKINS RD

CHAPEL CL

MK44

8
7
53
6
5
52
4
3
51
2
1
50

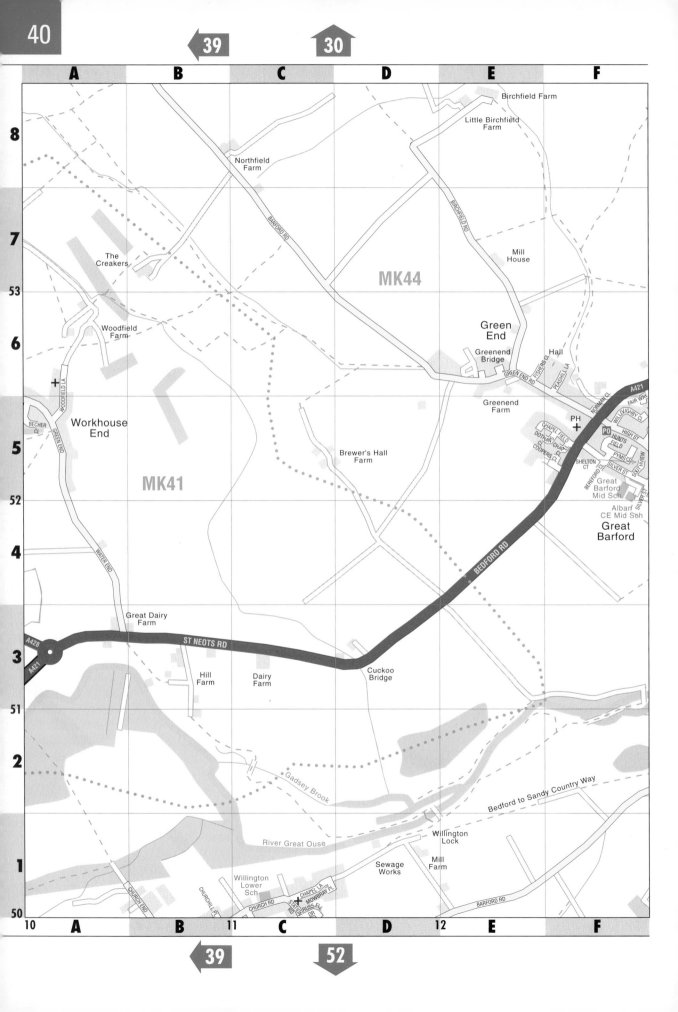

A B C D E F

8

Birchfield Farm

Little Birchfield Farm

Northfield Farm

BARFORD RD

BIRCHFIELD RD

7

The Creakers

53

MK44

Mill House

6

Woodfield Farm

Green End

Greenend Bridge

Hall

GREEN END RD

FISHERS CL

PEASHILL LA

WOODFIELD LA

A421

BECHER CL

GREEN END

Workhouse End

Greenend Farm

NORMAN CL

FAIR WAY

WILLOUGHBY CL

PH

CHAPEL FIELD

DOTHAN CL

CHARLTON CL

COOPERS CL

PO

HIGH ST

HUNTS FIELD

SILVER ST

SOUTH VIEW

PYMS CL

5

MK41

Brewer's Hall Farm

SHELTON CT

BEREFORD CT

Great Barford Mid Sch

52

Alban CE Mid Sch

Great Barford

4

WATER END

BEDFORD RD

Great Dairy Farm

A428

ST NEOTS RD

3

A421

Hill Farm

Dairy Farm

Cuckoo Bridge

51

2

Gadsey Brook

Bedford to Sandy Country Way

Willington Lock

River Great Ouse

1

Willington Lower Sch

Sewage Works

Mill Farm

BARFORD RD

CHURCH END

CHURCHILL PL

CHURCH RD

STATION RD

RUSSEL DR

MOWBRAY PL

CHAPEL LA

50

10 A B 11 C D 12 E F

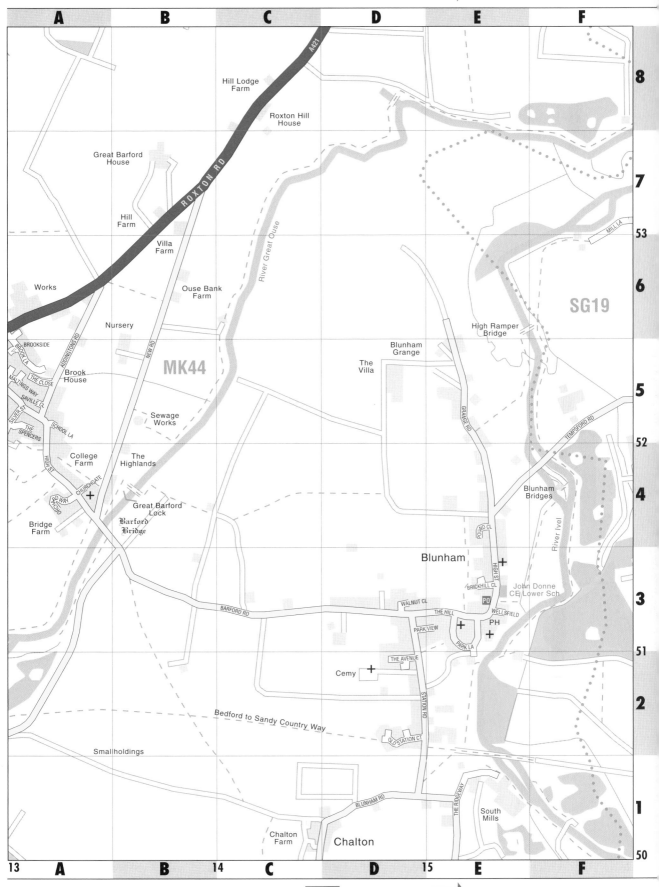

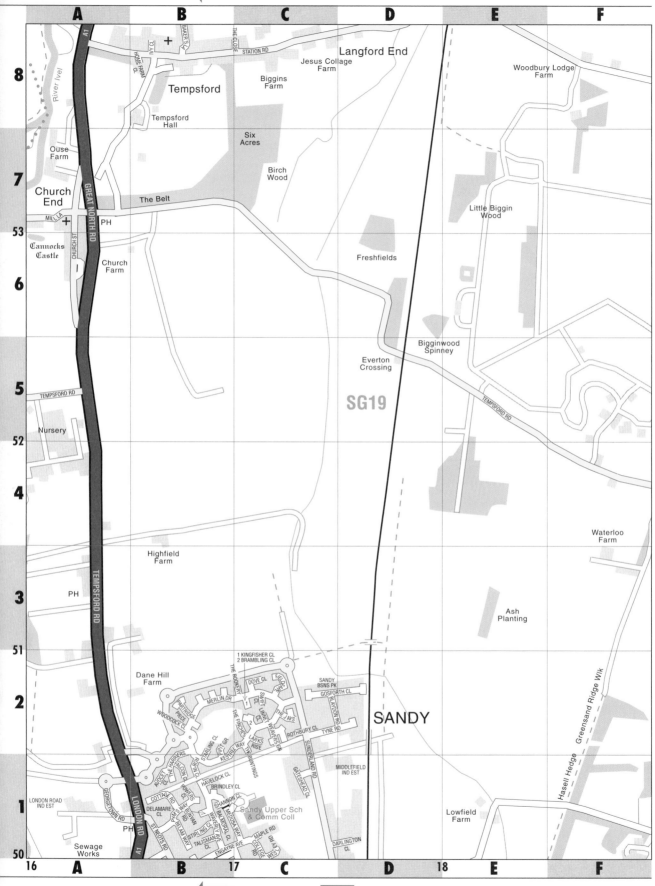

A   B   C   D   E   F

8

River Ivel

Tempsford

Langford End

Jesus Collage Farm

Biggins Farm

Woodbury Lodge Farm

Tempsford Hall

Six Acres

7

Ouse Farm

Birch Wood

Church End

The Belt

Little Biggin Wood

MILL LA

PH

53

Cannocks Castle

Church Farm

Freshfields

6

Bigginwood Spinney

Everton Crossing

5

TEMPSFORD RD

SG19

TEMPSFORD RD

Nursery

52

4

Waterloo Farm

Highfield Farm

Ash Planting

3

PH

51

1 KINGFISHER CL
2 BRAMBLING CL

Dane Hill Farm

SANDY BSNS PK

GOSFORTH CL

SANDY

2

Greensand Ridge Wlk

Hasell Hedge

MIDDLEFIELD IND EST

1

LONDON ROAD IND EST

Lowfield Farm

PH

50

Sewage Works

Sandy Upper Sch & Comm Coll

GREAT NORTH RD

LONDON RD

TEMPSFORD RD

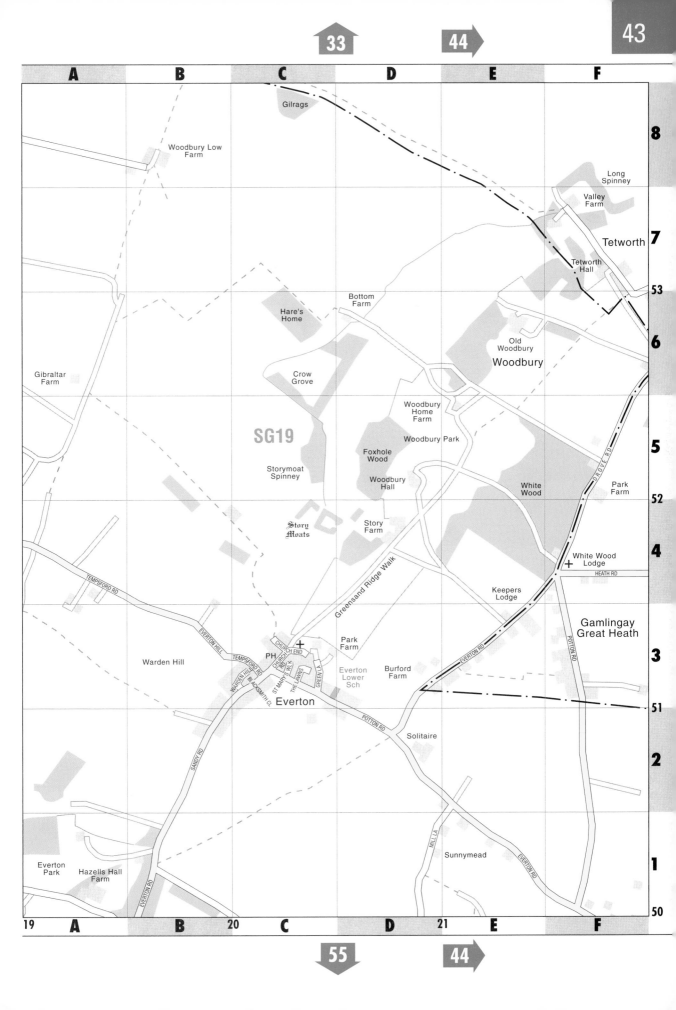

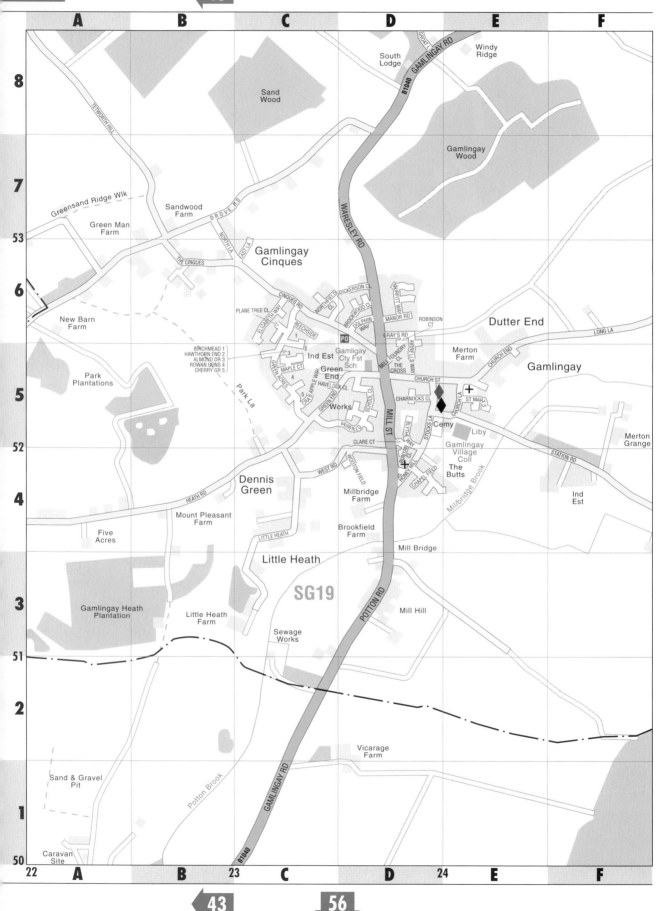

A B C D E F

8

Sand Wood

South Lodge

Windy Ridge

Gamlingay Wood

7

Greensand Ridge Wlk

Green Man Farm

Sandwood Farm

DROVE RD

TETWORTH HILL

NORTH LA

EAST LA

THE CINQUES

53

Gamlingay Cinques

CINQUES RD

PLANE TREE CL

MORTHFIELD CL

DICKERSON CL

BROOKWOOD CL

DOLPHIN WAY

LAURITT WAY

MANOR RD

ROBINSON CT

GRAY'S RD

Dutter End

LONG LA

6

New Barn Farm

ELIZABETH WAY

BEECHSIDE

1

2

3

GREEN ACRES

MAPLE CT

5

CRAB APPLE WAY

HAVELOCK CL

GREEN END

FAIRFIELD

BIRCHMEAD 1
HAWTHORN END 2
ALMOND DR 3
ROWAN GDNS 4
CHERRY GR 5

PO

Ind Est

Gamligay Cty Fst Sch

Green End

Works

BELL FOUNDRY CL

THE CROSS

ARDWELLS WAY

Merton Farm

CHURCH END

Gamlingay

Merton Grange

CHURCH ST

ST MARY

CHARNOCKS CL

Cemy

Liby

Gamlingay Village Coll

The Butts

STOCKS LA

BLYTHE WAY

SCHOOL LA

CHURCH LA

STATION RD

Ind Est

5

Park Plantations

Park La

52

CLARE CT

WEST RD

WOOTON FIELD

MILL ST

CHAPEL FIELD

HONEY HILL

Millbridge Brook

4

Dennis Green

HEATH RD

Mount Pleasant Farm

Five Acres

LITTLE HEATH

Millbridge Farm

Brookfield Farm

Mill Bridge

Little Heath

3

Gamlingay Heath Plantation

Little Heath Farm

SG19

Sewage Works

POTTON RD

Mill Hill

Mill Hill

51

WARESLEY RD

GAMLINGAY RD

GROAT RD

B1040

2

Vicarage Farm

1

Sand & Gravel Pit

Potton Brook

GAMLINGAY RD

B1040

50

Caravan Site

A B C D E F

8 Model Farm
Airfield
B1046
B1046

7 Fuller's Hill Farm
Ash Tree Cottage
53

6 Crooked Billet Farm
LONG LA

SG19

5 Millbridge Brook
52

4
HATLEY RD
Newlands Buildings
Newlands Cottages

Castle Farm
West Lodge
North Lodge
Church Farm
BAULK LA

3 Stud Bungalow
Hatley Park
Hatley St George
MAIN ST

Stud Cottage
Dower House
BAR LA

51

2 Wood Farm
Cockayne Hatley Wood
Hatley Park

1 Potton Wood

Pincote Barn
BUFF LA
50

25 A B 26 C D 27 E F

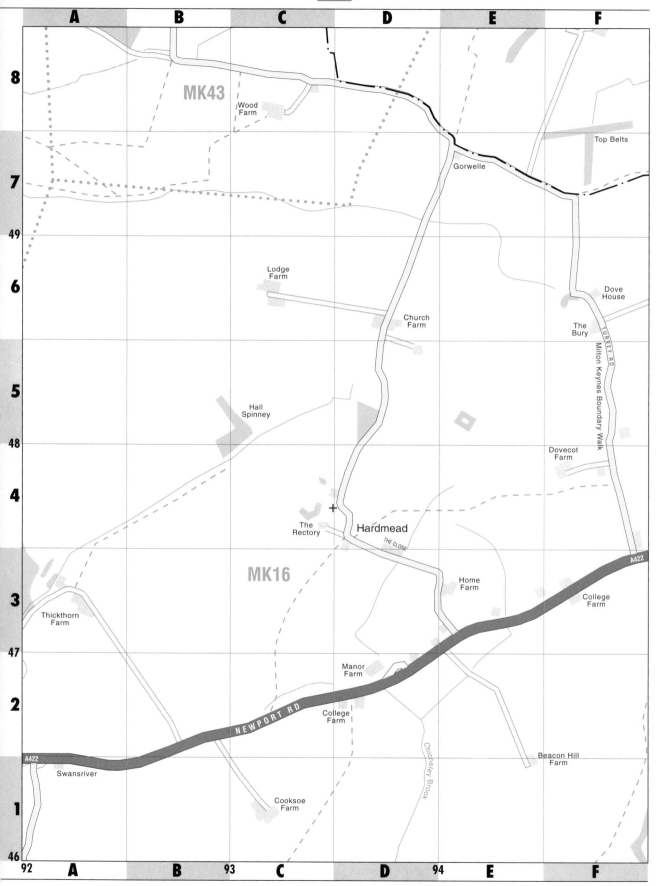

A B C D E F

8

7

49

6

5

48

4

3

47

2

1

46

MK43

Wood
Farm

Gorwelle

Top Belts

Dove
House

The
Bury

Lodge
Farm

Church
Farm

TURVEY RD

Milton Keynes Boundary Walk

Hall
Spinney

Dovecot
Farm

The
Rectory

Hardmead

THE CLOSE

Home
Farm

College
Farm

A422

MK16

Thickthorn
Farm

Manor
Farm

College
Farm

Beacon Hill
Farm

Chicheley Brook

NEWPORT RD

A422

Swansriver

Cooksoe
Farm

92 A 93 B C 94 D E F

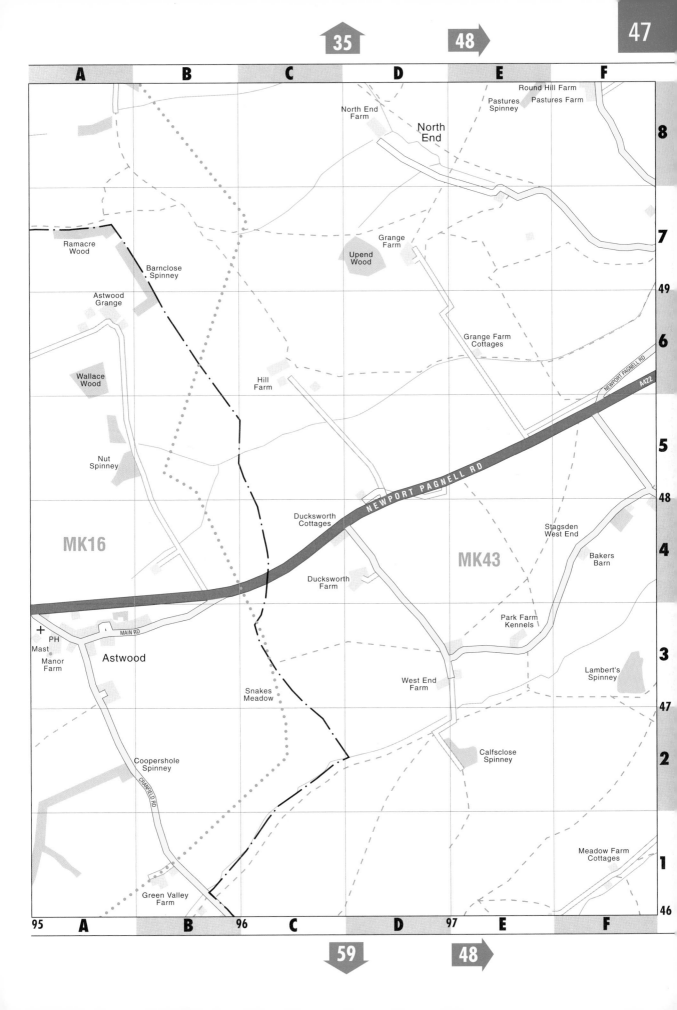

35
48

A B C D E F

8

Round Hill Farm
Pastures Spinney
Pastures Farm
North End Farm
North End

7

Ramacre Wood
Barnclose Spinney
Grange Farm
Upend Wood

49

Astwood Grange

Grange Farm Cottages

6

Wallace Wood
Hill Farm

NEWPORT PAGNELL RD
A422

5

Nut Spinney

48

Ducksworth Cottages

MK16

MK43

Stagsden West End

4

Ducksworth Farm

Bakers Barn

Park Farm Kennels

3

+
PH
Mast
MAIN RD
Manor Farm
Astwood

West End Farm

Lambert's Spinney

47

Snakes Meadow

Calfsclose Spinney

2

Coopershole Spinney

CRANFIELD RD

Meadow Farm Cottages

1

Green Valley Farm

46

95 A B 96 C D 97 E F

59
48

A B C D E F

8

7

49

6

5

48

4

47

3

2

1

46

Wick End

Stagsden

CHURCH LA

HIGH ST

OAKCROFT

PH

BEDFORD RD

Wickend Bridge

SPRING LA

B560

A422

A422

Sewage Works

Oxleys

Hanger Wood

John Bunyan Trail

Moorland

Box Farm

Box End

PH

BOX END RD

A5134

A5134

West End RD

Top Farm

Rushey Ford Farm

Astey Wood

SPRING LA

West End Farm

WEST END RD

MK43

Firs Farm

Kempston West End

WEST END RD

Glenbrook Farm

TITHE RD

Kempston House

GREEN END RD

HOME RD

Old Farm

Kempston Wood

Tythe Farm

John Bunyan Trail

Ransom's Wood

Wood Farm

Wood End

PH

WOOD END LA

Gibraltar Brook Farm

Wood End Farm

Gadfly Farm

Whitworth's Farm

Wootton Bourne End

WOOD END RD

TINKER'S CNR

HALL END

KEELEY LA

PH

Keeley Green

BEDFORD RD

KEELEY FARM CT

Mortal Man Farm

BOURNE END RD

98 A B 99 C D 00 E F

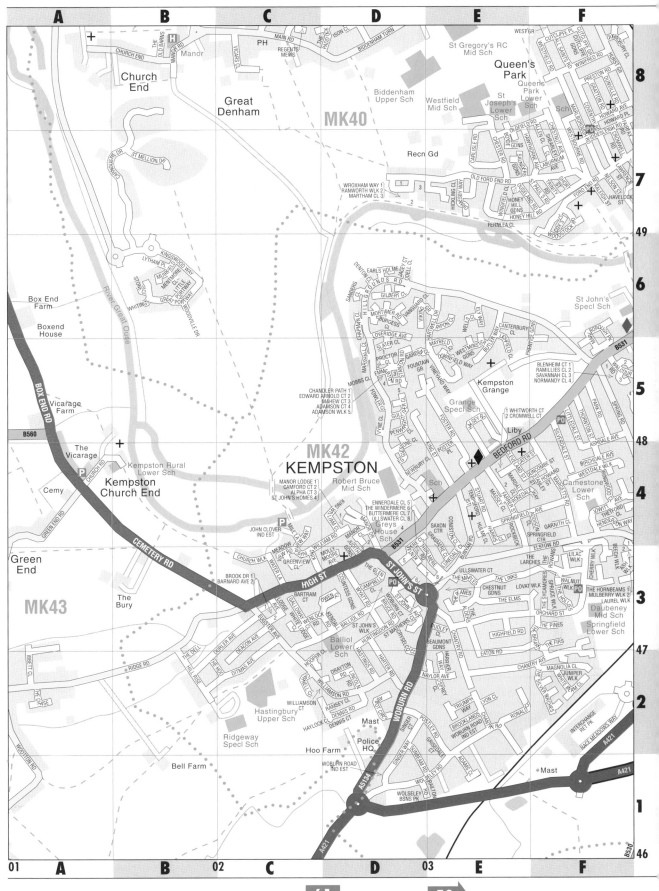

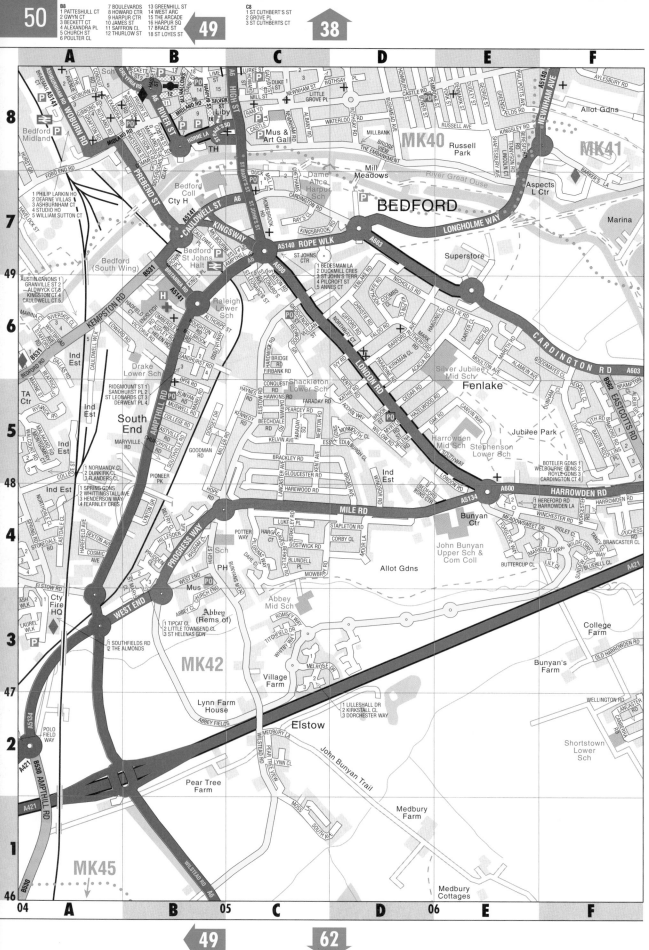

50

B8
1 PATTESHULL CT
2 GWYN CT
3 BECKETT CT
4 ALEXANDRA PL
5 CHURCH ST
6 POULTER CL

7 BOULEVARDS
8 HOWARD CTR
9 HARPUR CTR
10 JAMES ST
11 SAFFRON CL
12 THURLOW ST

13 GREENHILL ST
14 WEST ARC
15 THE ARCADE
16 HARPUR SQ
17 BRACE ST
18 ST LOYES ST

C8
1 ST CUTHBERT'S ST
2 GROVE PL
3 ST CUTHBERTS CT

49

38

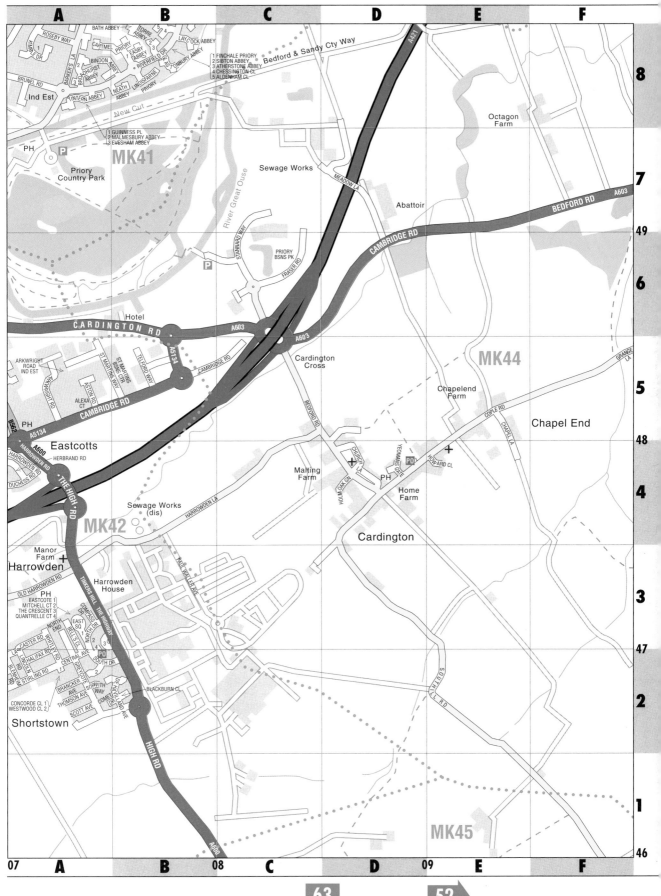

A B C D E F

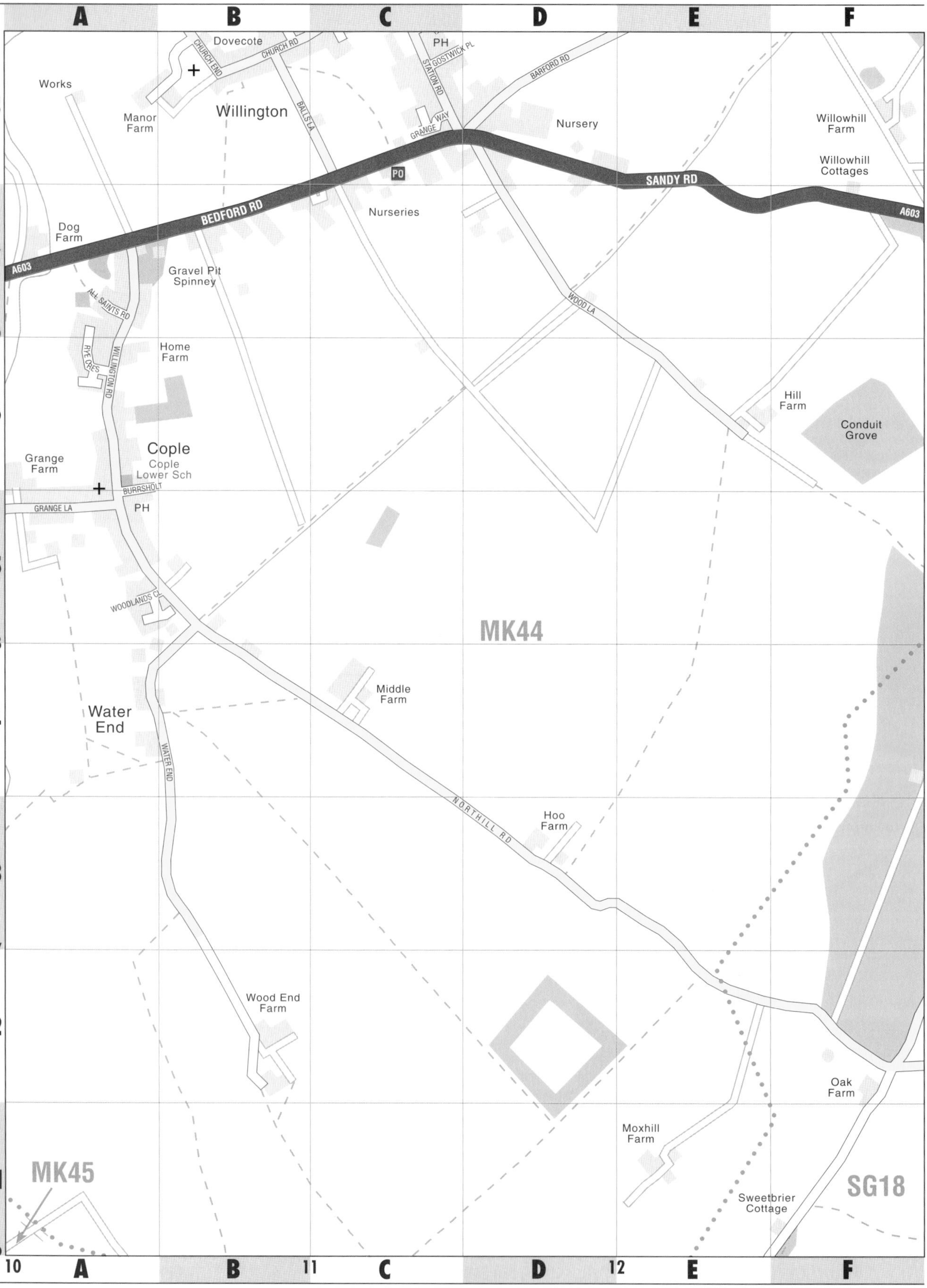

8
Works
Dovecote
Church Rd
Manor Farm
Willington
Balls La
Grange Way
PH
Gostwick Pl
Station Rd
Barford Rd
Nursery
Willowhill Farm
Willowhill Cottages

PO
Nurseries
SANDY RD
A603

7
A603
Dog Farm
BEDFORD RD
Gravel Pit Spinney
Wood La
A603

49
All Saints Rd
Willington Rd
Rye Cres
Home Farm
Hill Farm
Conduit Grove

6
Grange Farm
Cople
Cople Lower Sch
Burrsholt
PH
Grange La

5
Woodlands Cl
MK44

48
Middle Farm

4
Water End
Water End
Northill Rd
Hoo Farm

3

47

2
Wood End Farm
Oak Farm
Moxhill Farm

1
MK45
Sweetbrier Cottage
SG18

46
10 A B 11 C D 12 E F

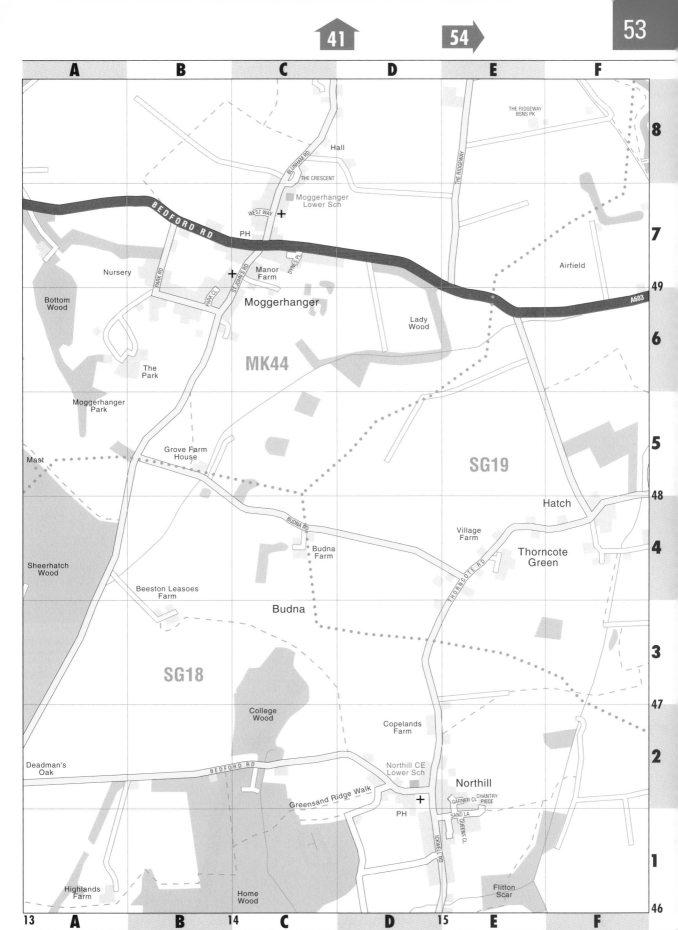

A B C D E F

8
7
49
6
5
48
4
3
47
2
1
46

THE RIDGEWAY
BSNS PK

Hall

BLUNHAM RD

THE CRESCENT

WEST WAY

Moggerhanger
Lower Sch

THE RIDGEWAY

BEDFORD RD

PH

DYKES PL

Nursery

PARK RD

ST JOHN'S RD

Manor
Farm

Airfield

A603

Bottom
Wood

PARK CL

Moggerhanger

Lady
Wood

MK44

The
Park

Moggerhanger
Park

SG19

Mast

Grove Farm
House

Hatch

Village
Farm

Thorncote
Green

Sheerhatch
Wood

BUDNA RD

Budna
Farm

THORNCOTE RD

Beeston Leasoes
Farm

Budna

SG18

College
Wood

Copelands
Farm

Deadman's
Oak

BEDFORD RD

Northill CE
Lower Sch

Northill

CHANTRY
PIECE

GARNER CL

Greensand Ridge Walk

PH

SAND LA

ICWELL RD

QUEENS CL

Highlands
Farm

Home
Wood

Flitton
Scar

13 A B 14 C D 15 E F

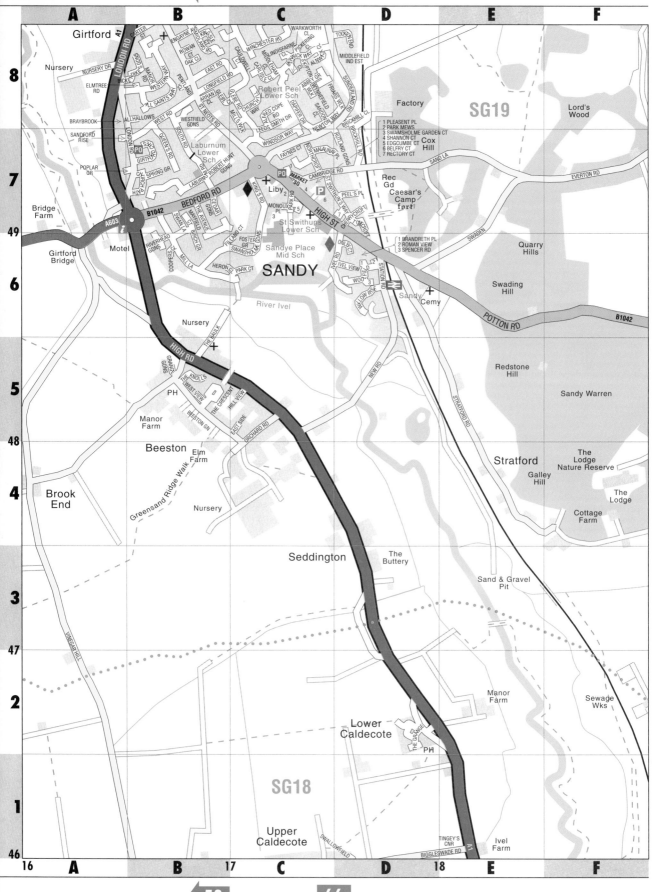

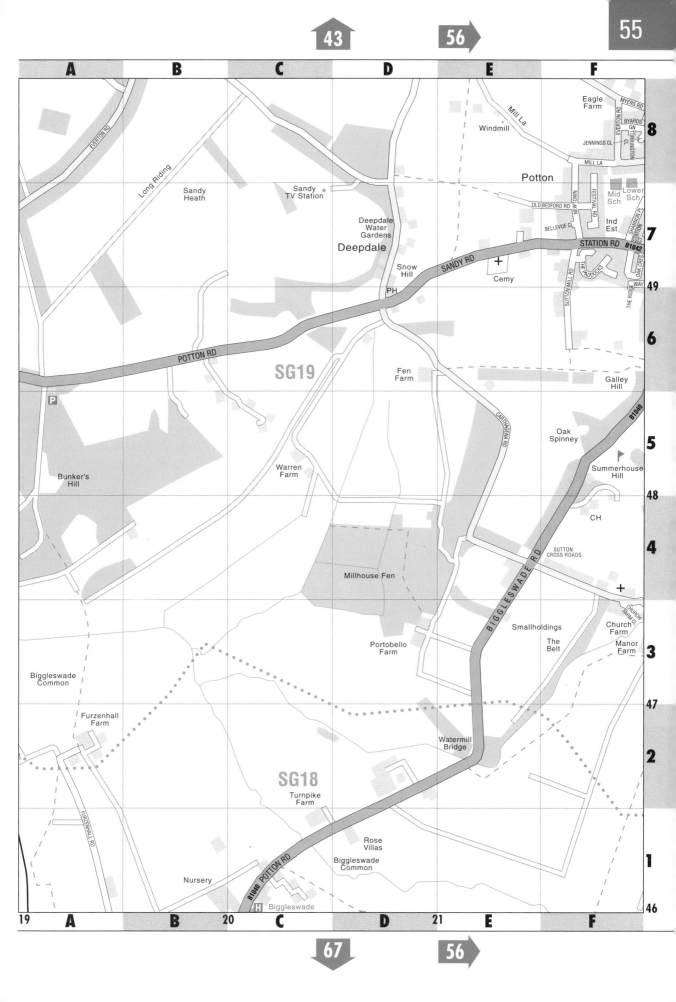

A   B   C   D   E   F

EVERTON RD

Long Riding

Sandy Heath

Sandy TV Station

Deepdale Water Gardens

Deepdale

Snow Hill

PH

SANDY RD

Cemy

8

Mill La

Windmill

Eagle Farm

MYERS RD

BYARDS

GN

EVERTON RD

TORRINGTON

JENNINGS CL

MILL LA

Potton

OLD BEDFORD RD

NW LA W'N

FESTIVAL RD

Mid Sch

Lower Sch

Ind Est

BELLEVUE CL

SHANNON PL

STATION

7

STATION RD   B1042

THE PADDOCKS

OAK CRES

WAY

THE RIDGE

49

POTTON RD

SG19

Fen Farm

CARTHAGENA RD

6

Galley Hill

B1040

Oak Spinney

5

Summerhouse Hill

P

Bunker's Hill

Warren Farm

48

CH

4

SUTTON CROSS ROADS

Millhouse Fen

BIGGLESWADE RD

Smallholdings

The Belt

CHURCH FARM CL

Church Farm

Manor Farm

3

Biggleswade Common

Portobello Farm

Furzenhall Farm

47

Watermill Bridge

2

SG18

FURZENHALL RD

Turnpike Farm

Rose Villas

Biggleswade Common

1

Nursery

B1040 POTTON RD

H   Biggleswade

46

19   A   B   20   C   D   21   E   F

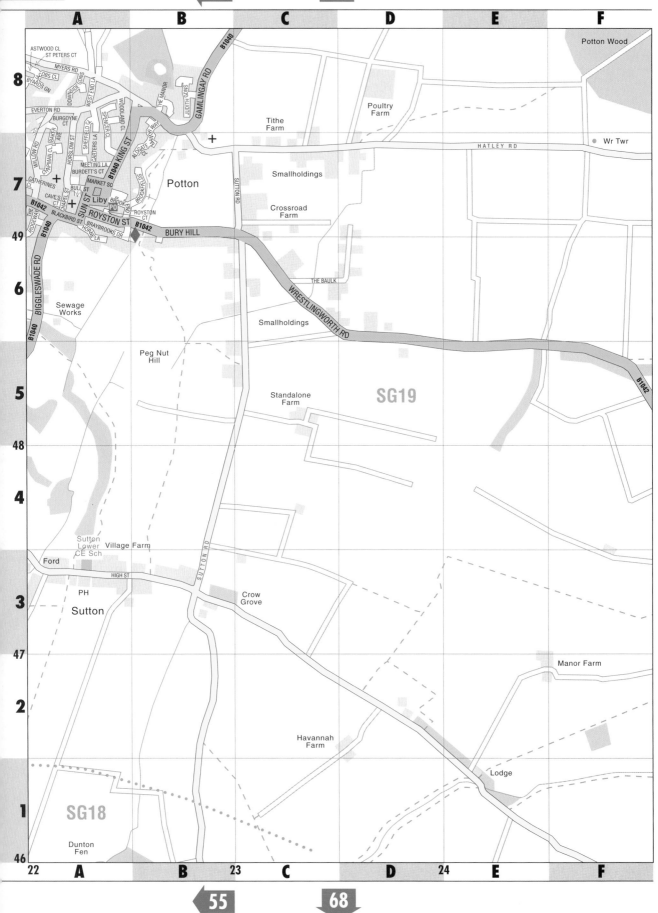

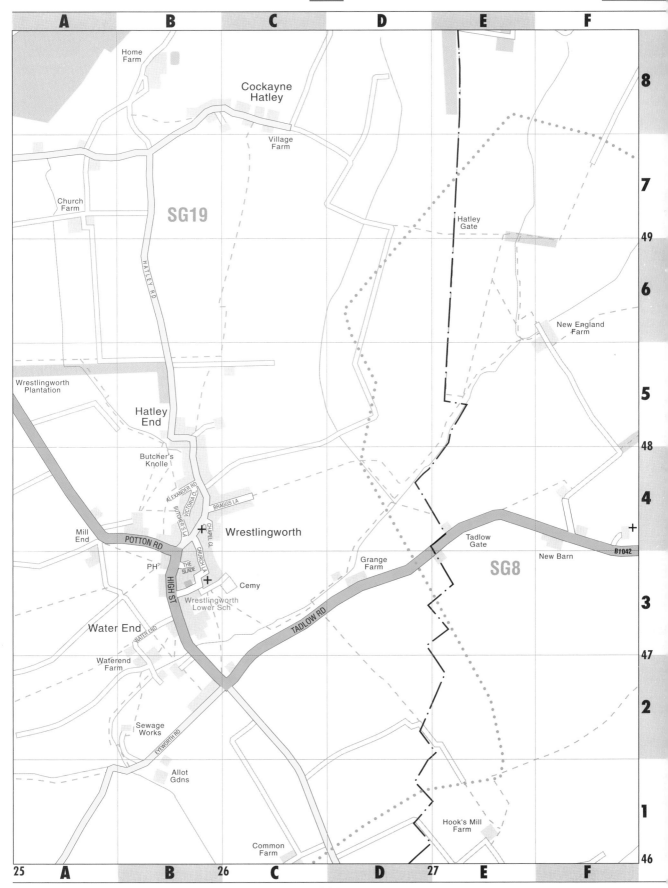

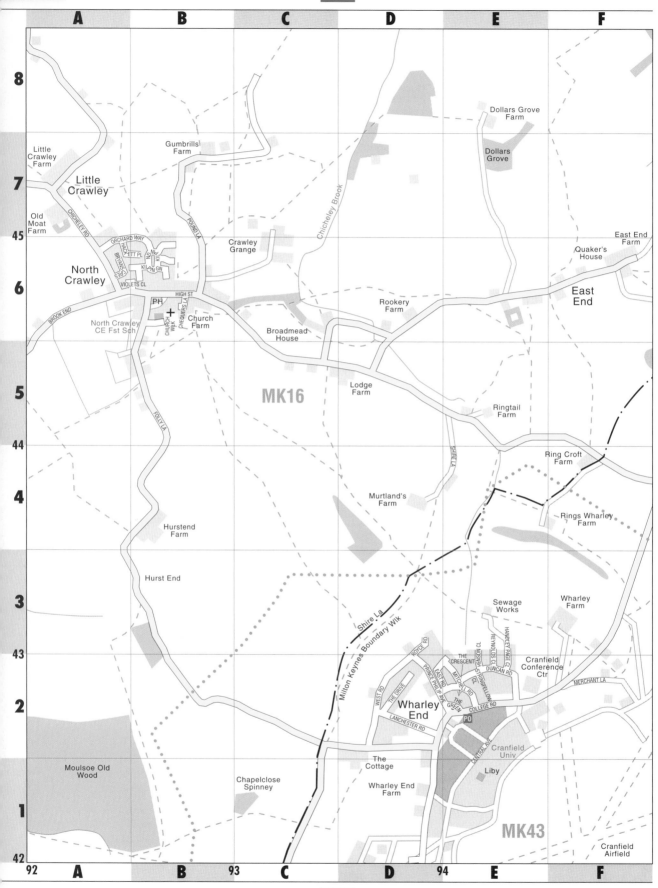

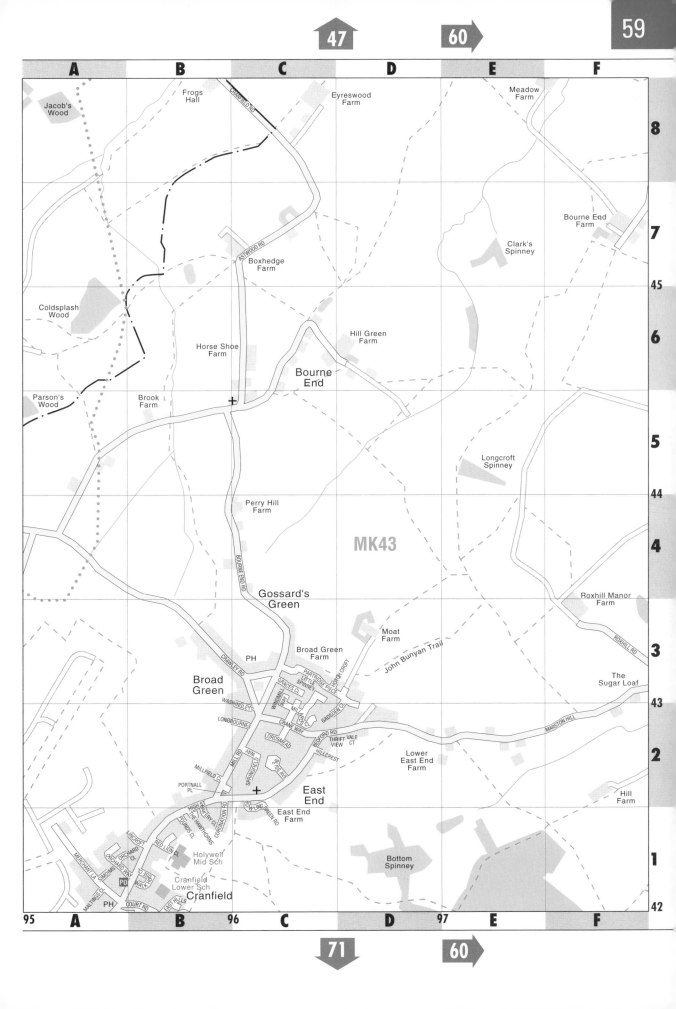

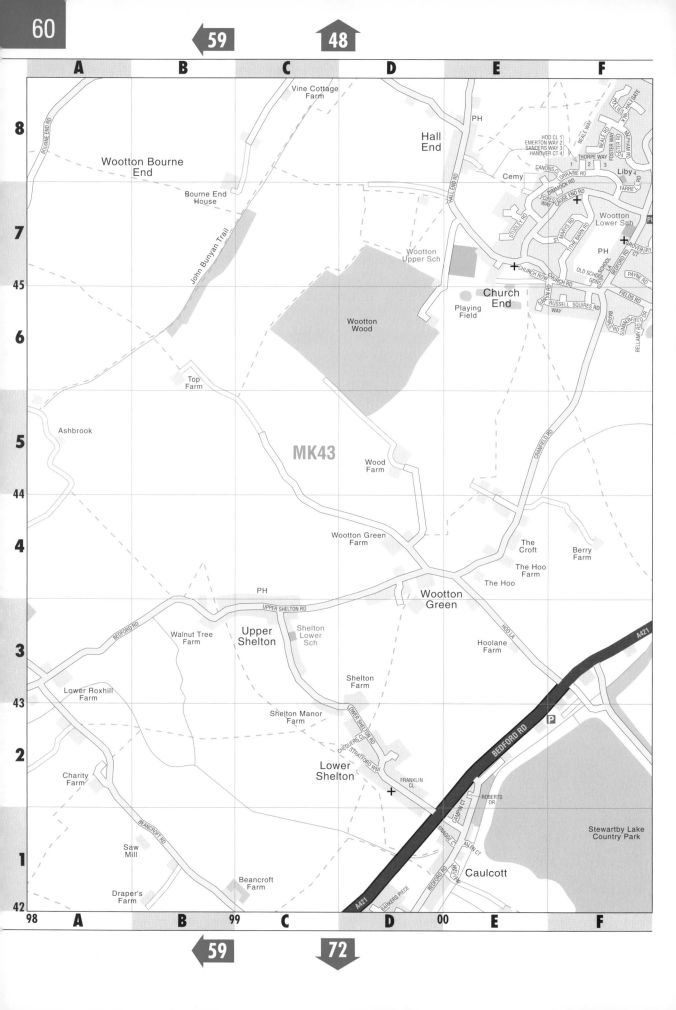

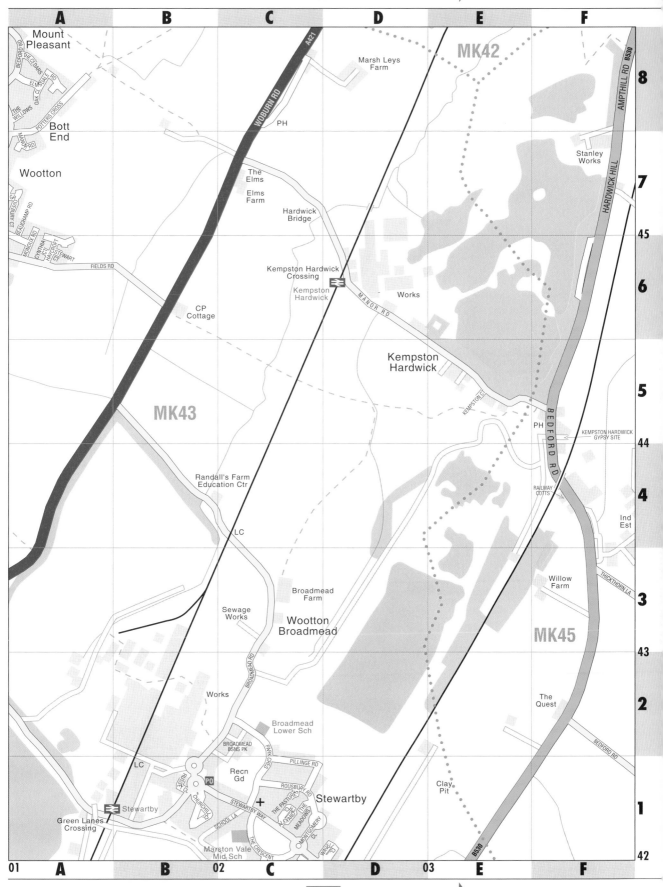

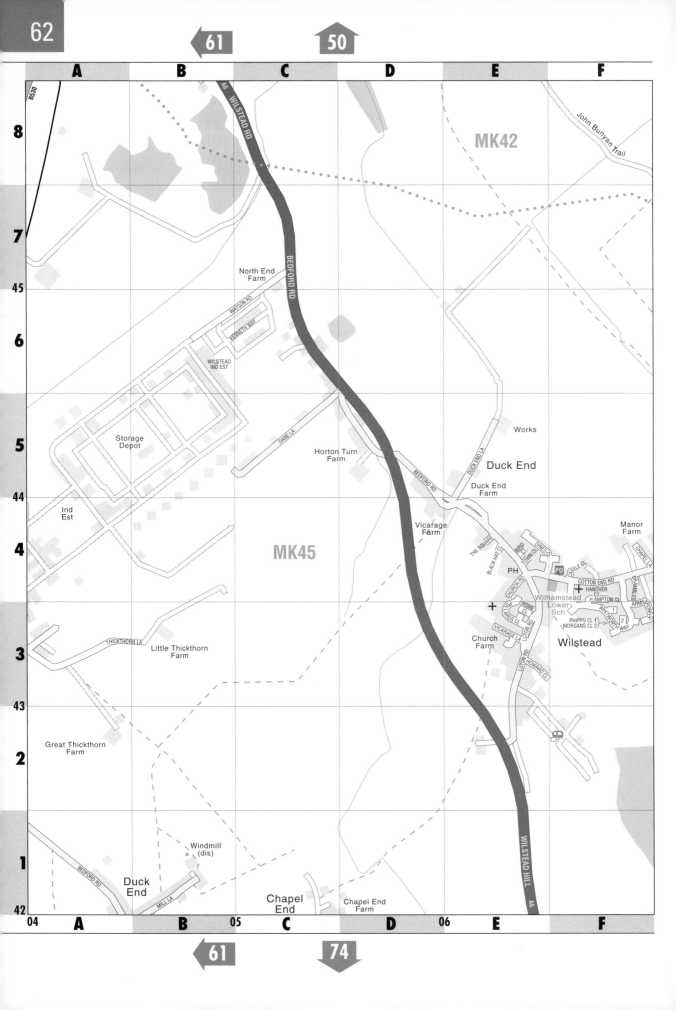

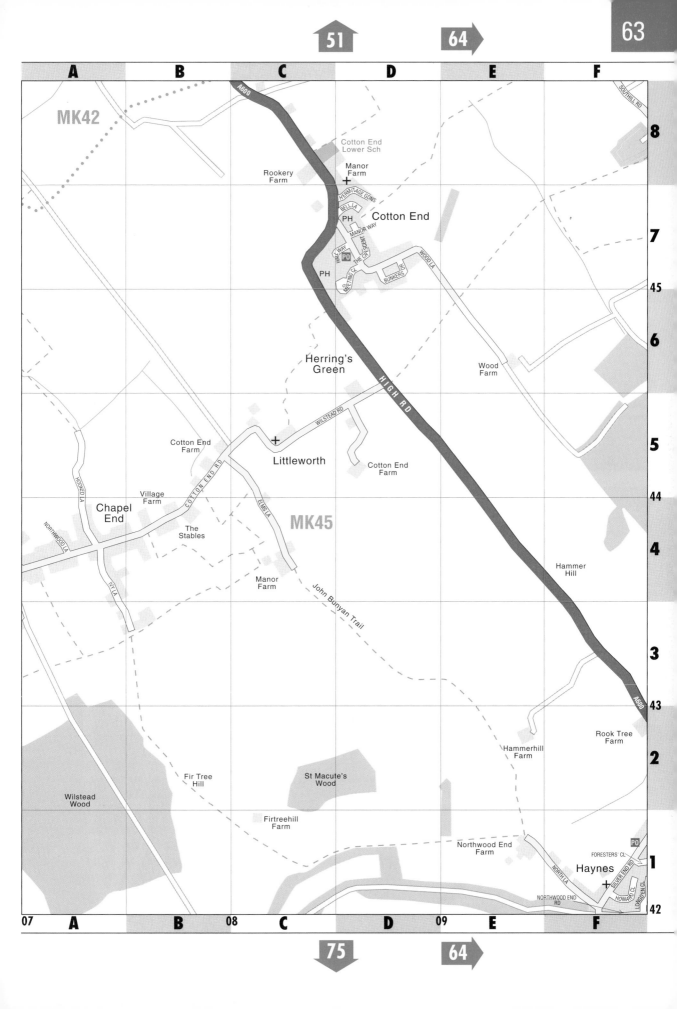

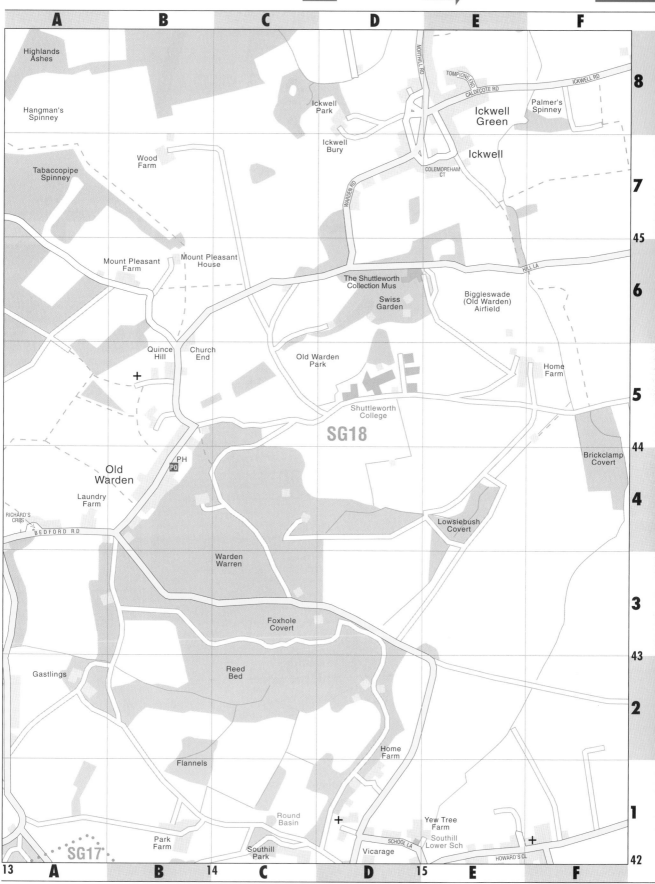

A   B   C   D   E   F

Highlands
Ashes

Hangman's
Spinney

Tabaccopipe
Spinney

Wood
Farm

NORTHILL RD
TOMPIONS END
CALDECOTE RD
ICKWELL RD

Ickwell
Park

Ickwell
Bury

Palmer's
Spinney

Ickwell
Green

Ickwell

COLEMOREHAM
CT

8

7

45

WARDEN RD

HILL LA

Mount Pleasant
Farm

Mount Pleasant
House

The Shuttleworth
Collection Mus

Swiss
Garden

Biggleswade
(Old Warden)
Airfield

6

Quince
Hill

Church
End

Old Warden
Park

Home
Farm

Shuttleworth
College

SG18

5

44

Old
Warden

PH
PO

Brickclamp
Covert

RICHARD'S
CRES
BEDFORD RD

Laundry
Farm

Lowsiebush
Covert

4

Warden
Warren

Foxhole
Covert

3

43

Gastlings

Reed
Bed

2

Flannels

Home
Farm

Round
Basin

Yew Tree
Farm

Southill
Lower Sch

1

SG17

Park
Farm

Southill
Park

SCHOOL LA

Vicarage

HOWARD'S CL

42

13   A   B   14   C   D   15   E   F

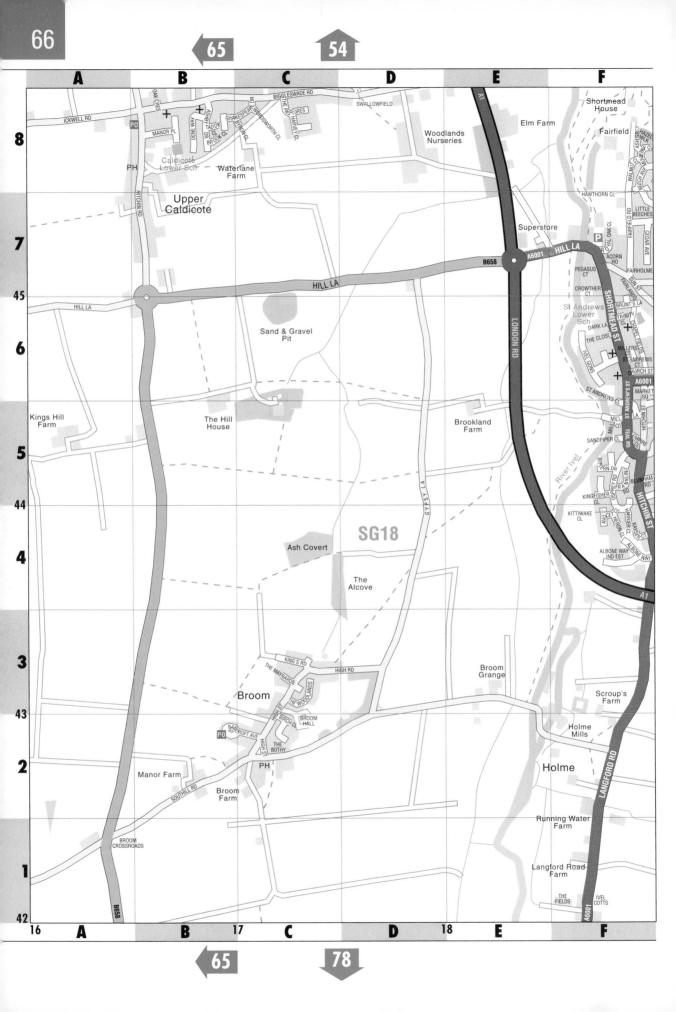

65
54

A   B   C   D   E   F

8

ICKWELL RD
OAK CRES
PO
MANOR PL
Caldicote Lower Sch
Waterlane Farm
Upper Caldicote
DENE WAY
TADDY DR
BROOK CL
BYRON CL
SHAKESPEARE
WORDSWORTH CL
BIGGLESWADE RD
THE PASTURES
HARVEY CL
SWALLOWFIELD
Woodlands Nurseries
Elm Farm
Shortmead House
Fairfield
WALNUT CL
ASH PARK RD
HAZEL WK
BEECH CL
FAIRFIELD RD
HAWTHORN CL
LITTLE BEECHES
CEDAR AVE

7

PH
HITCHIN RD
Superstore
B658
A6001
HILL LA
ROYAL OAK CL
P
ACORN HO
FAIRHOLME
SUN LA
THURLANDS DR
PEGASUS CT
CROWTHER CT

45

HILL LA
HILL LA
Sand & Gravel Pit
LONDON RD
St Andrews Lower Sch
DARK LA
THE CLOSE
CHAPEL FIELDS
BRUNT'S LA
TRINITY
SHORTMEAD ST

6

Kings Hill Farm
The Hill House
Brookland Farm
IVEL GDNS
ST ANDREWS CL
MILLERS CT
ST ANDREWS CT
CHURCH ST
MARKET SQ
MILL LA
EMPIRE
A6001

5

River Ivel
GYPSY LA
SANDPIPER CL
MILL CL
BIRCH DR
OSPREY RD
NUTMEG CL
TEAL RD
HITCHIN ST

44

SG18
KINGFISHER CL
KITTIWAKE CL
AVOCET CL
HERON CL
HARRIER CL
KAVSER CT
BLUNHAM RD

4

Ash Covert
The Alcove
ALBONE WAY IND EST
ALBONE WAY
A1

3

KING'S RD
THE MAYNARDS
HIGH RD
Broom Grange
Scroup's Farm
THE WOODLANDS

Broom
BROOM HALL
Holme Mills

43

PO
BANCROFT AVE
HIGH ST
BIRCH CL
THE BOTHY
LANGFORD RD

2

Manor Farm
SOUTHILL RD
Broom Farm
PH
Holme
Running Water Farm

1

BROOM CROSSROADS
Langford Road Farm
THE FIELDS
IVEL COTTS
A6001

42

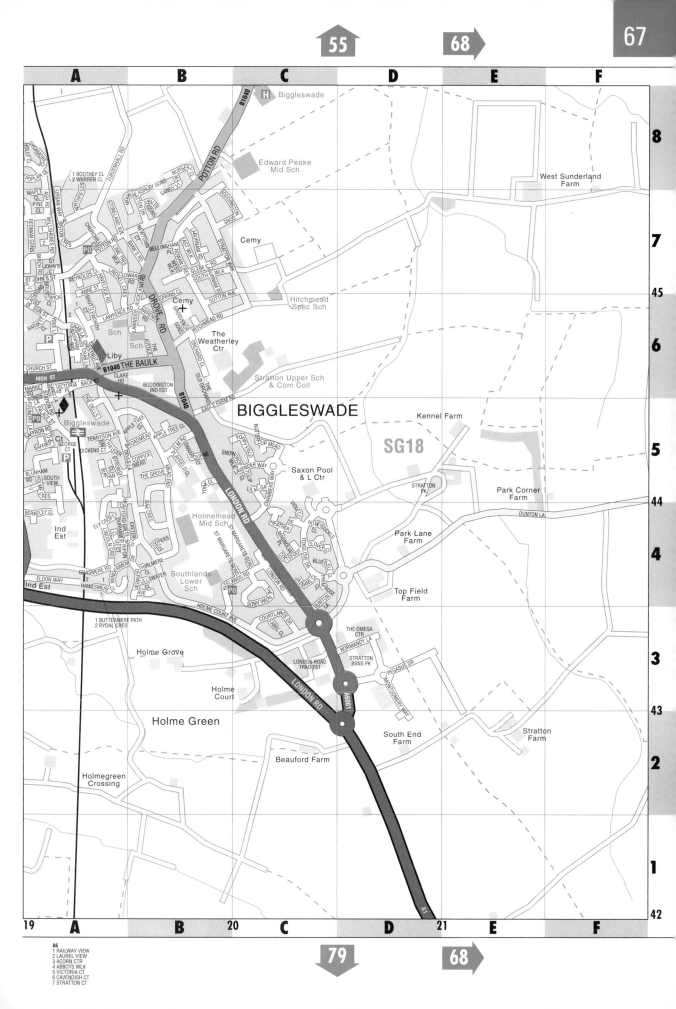

BIGGLESWADE

SG18

West Sunderland Farm

Edward Peake Mid Sch

Cemy

Hitchmead Spec Sch

The Weatherley Ctr

Stratton Upper Sch & Com Coll

Kennel Farm

Saxon Pool & L Ctr

Stratton Pk

Park Corner Farm

Holmemead Mid Sch

Park Lane Farm

Southlands Lower Sch

Top Field Farm

Ind Est

The Omega Ctr

Holme Grove

London Road Trad Est

Stratton Bsns Pk

Pegasus Dr

Holme Court

Holme Green

South End Farm

Stratton Farm

Beauford Farm

Holmegreen Crossing

A6
1 RAILWAY VIEW
2 LAUREL VIEW
3 ACORN CTR
4 ABBOTS WLK
5 VICTORIA CT
6 CAVENDISH CT
7 STRATTON CT

| | A | B | C | D | E | F |

8 Dunton Fen

SG19

Eyeworth

Sunderland Hall Farm

Church Farm

7

45

SUTTON RD

6

CAMBRIDGE RD

Water Works

Newton

Sewage Works

GREENFIELD WAY

Newton Grove Farm

Middlesex Farm

OLD BAKERY YD

KINGS POND CL

MAGDALENE LA

Dunton

5 Dunton Lower Sch

HORSESH CL LA

BOOT LA

PO CHURCH ST

PH

CHAPEL ST

Church Farm

FOX CL

44 BIGGLESWADE RD

HALLSIDE

SPRINGFIELD

HIGH ST

SG18

4 Millow Hall Farm

Millow Lodge Farm

Millow

3 Millow Hill Farm

River Cam or Rhee

43 SG7

Millowbury Farm

Plantation Farm

2

1

Green La

42

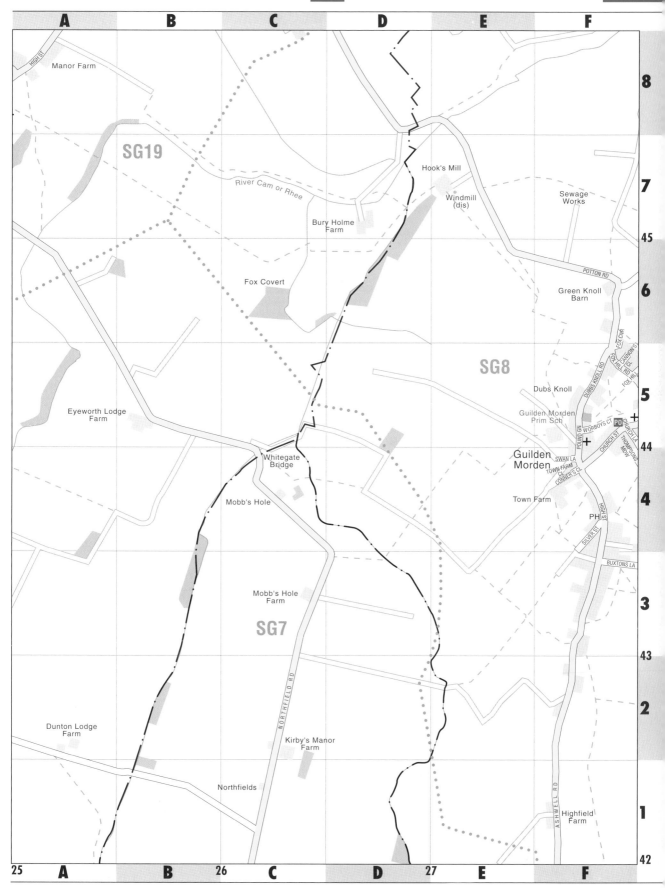

A   B   C   D   E   F

Manor Farm

HIGH ST

SG19

River Cam or Rhee

Hook's Mill

Windmill
(dis)

Sewage
Works

Bury Holme
Farm

POTTON RD

Fox Covert

Green Knoll
Barn

SG8

FOX CNR

DUBBS KNOLL RD

FOX HILL RD

CANNON'S
CL

FOX HILL

Dubs Knoll

Guilden Morden
Prim Sch

PO

CHURCH LA

POUND GN

WORBOYS CT

CHURCH ST

THOMPSON'S
MDW

Eyeworth Lodge
Farm

Guilden
Morden

SWAN LA

TOWN FARM
CL

CONNER'S CL

Whitegate
Bridge

Town Farm

Mobb's Hole

PH

HIGH ST

SILVER ST

BUXTONS LA

Mobb's Hole
Farm

SG7

NORTHFIELD RD

Dunton Lodge
Farm

Kirby's Manor
Farm

ASHWELL RD

Highfield
Farm

Northfields

25   A   B   26   C   D   27   E   F   42

8

7

45

6

5

44

4

43

3

2

1

A   B   C   D   E   F

8

MK43

Lower Wood End Farm

BEANCROFT RD

INGRAM CL 1
OWEN CL 2

DENBIGH CL

Sewage Works

Mast

Motel

Marston Moreteine

BURDOCK CL
PEMBROKE CL

NICHOLLS CL
CHANDLERS CL
BEANCROFT RD
CHURCH RD

LAWSON CL
DENTON DR
PRIMROSE CL

PARISH CL
BEACON
THE MEWS
MORETEYNE RD

HILLSON CL
PO

HOLMES
BEDFORD RD
SCOTCHBROOK RD

PH

BROWNS CL
REYNES CL
ST MARYS CL
CRABTREE RD

7

Moreteyne Farm

Moat Farm

WOBURN RD

MANOR CT

BANK'S CL
BROOK RD
MANOR RD

THE GREEN
CHURCH WLK

Church End Lower Sch

41

Sun Valley

Rock Villa

STATION RD

JUBILEE COTTS

Church Farm Cottages

Millbrook

LC

6

Escheat Farm

Church Farm

5

Vale Farm

A421

40

4

Thrupp End Farm

Marston Crossing

Vehicle Proving Ground

3

Sheeptick End

THRUPP END
SHEEPTICK END
STATION CRES

Allot Gdns

Lidlington

WALNUT
HUDSON
BYE RD
HURST GR

THE GROVE
GREAT FARM CL

MARSTON RD

Haydon Hill

39

Thomas Johnson Lower Sch

LC
PO

CHILTERN CL
GREENSAND RIDGE
WHITEHALL
HIGH ST
OAK GDNS
LOMBARD
MANOR GDNS

THE PADDOCK

CHURCH LA

2

Bye Road Farm

Lidlington

HILL END ROAD LA

Top Farm

Seathill Plantation

MK45

CH

1

BROUGHTON END LA

Bury Ware

Jackdaw Hill

Greensand ridge Walk

John Bunyan Trail

38

98   A   B   99   C   D   00   E   F

A507

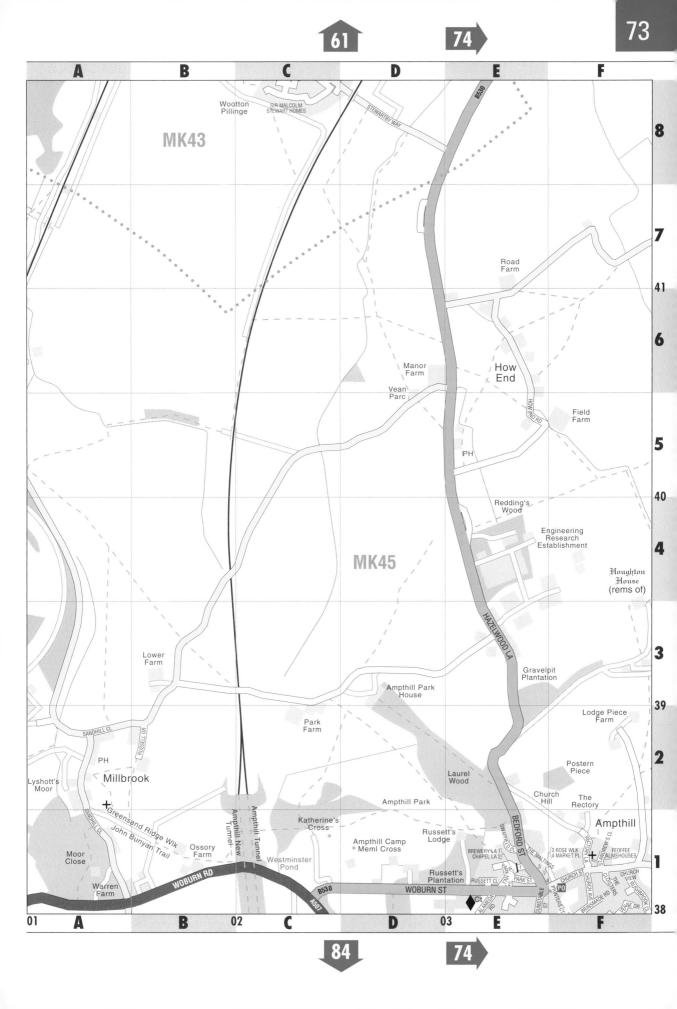

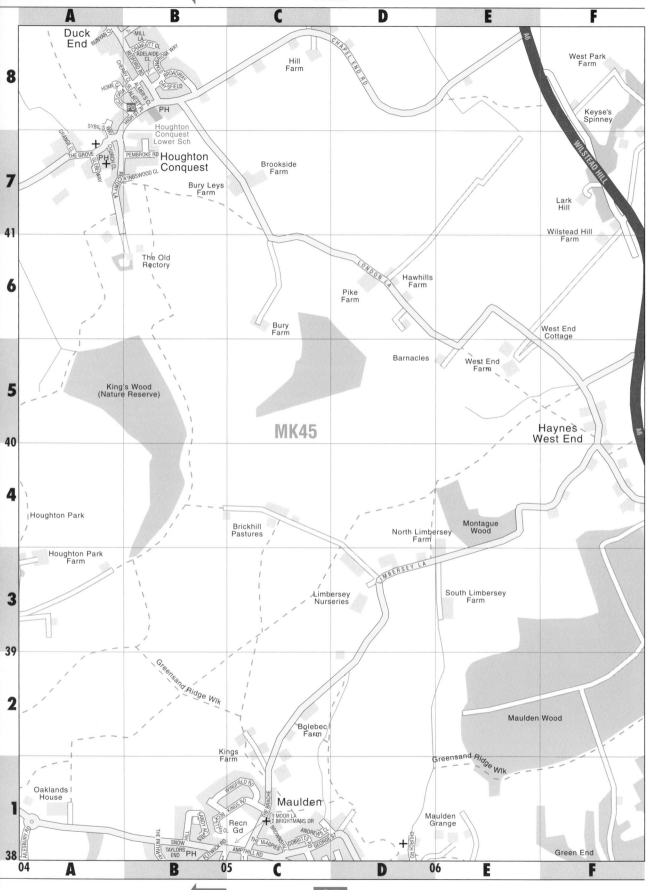

A **B** **C** **D** **E** **F**

8

Duck
End

Hill
Farm

West Park
Farm

Keyse's
Spinney

Houghton
Conquest
Lower Sch

7

Houghton
Conquest

Brookside
Farm

Lark
Hill

Wilstead Hill
Farm

41

Bury Leys
Farm

The Old
Rectory

London La

Hawhills
Farm

6

Pike
Farm

Bury
Farm

Barnacles

West End
Cottage

West End
Farm

5

King's Wood
(Nature Reserve)

MK45

Haynes
West End

40

4

Houghton Park

Brickhill
Pastures

North Limbersey
Farm

Montague
Wood

Houghton Park
Farm

Limbersey La

3

Limbersey
Nurseries

South Limbersey
Farm

39

Greensand Ridge Wlk

2

Bolebec
Farm

Maulden Wood

Greensand Ridge Wlk

Kings
Farm

Oaklands
House

1

Wingfield Rd

Maulden

1 MOOR LA
2 BRIGHTMANS DR

Maulden
Grange

Recn
Gd

Green End

38

04 **A** **B** 05 **C** **D** 06 **E** **F**

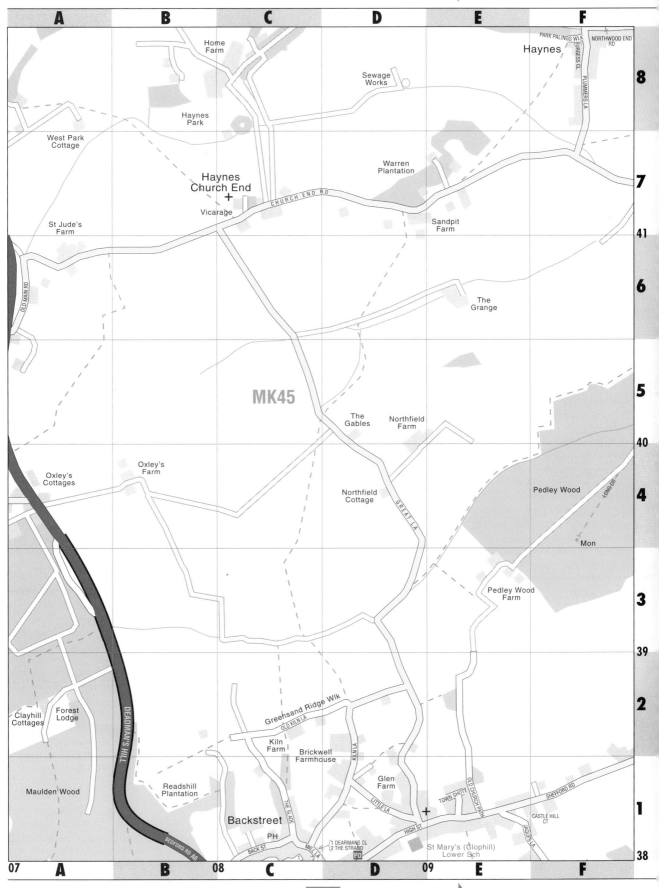

A B C D E F

75 ← 64 ↑

A B C D E F

8

Hill Farm

Pear Tree Farm

A600

PH

HIGH RD

Deadman's Cross

Old Rowney Farm

Greensand Ridge Walk

SG18

Keeper's Warren

NORTHWOOD END RD

Standalone Farm

7

Appley Corner

41

MK45

Wood Farm

Greensand Ridge Wlk

6

John Bunyan Trail

New Rowney Farm

Obelisk

LONG DR

Rowney Warren Wood

A600

SANDY LA

P ✕

Rowney Forest Walk

5

Chicksands Wood

40

Secondlodge Farm

Firstlodge Farm

Penseroso Grove

Druids Grove

4

The Hill

DANGER AREA

Temple Grove

TRENCHARD AVE

MIMROD DR

MOUNTBATTEN WAY

Chicksands

TRENCHARD LA

CHURCHILL DR

NELSON RD

REPTON RD

ROSATA LA

CHICKSANDS AVE

WELLINGTON DR

TEMPLER WAY

Obelisk

Sewage Works

3

SG17

LONG WLK

BEAUMANOR CT

MERCURY PL

Chicksands Priory

KENDALL DR

Sports Island

LEYDENE PL

MEDMENHAM AVE

39

LUFFENHAM PL

ORCHARD DR

WYTON CT

MARESFIELD AVE ←

WASHINGTON AVE

J.F.KENNEDY DR

EISENHOWER PL

OSBORNE AVE

2

Upper Alders

JACKSON PL

TRUMAN PL

TAFT PL

HOOVER LA

CHICKSANDS AVE

A507

River Flint

AMPTHILL RD

PRIORY RD

RECTORY RD

THE GLEBE

Speedsdairy Farm

SHEFFORD RD

Top Farm

Kiln Farm

Beadlow

ELM CL

Nursery

1

Top Farm

Campton Lower Sch

GRANGE GDNS

38

A507

Hotel

CH

10 A B 11 C D 12 E F

75 ← 87 ↓

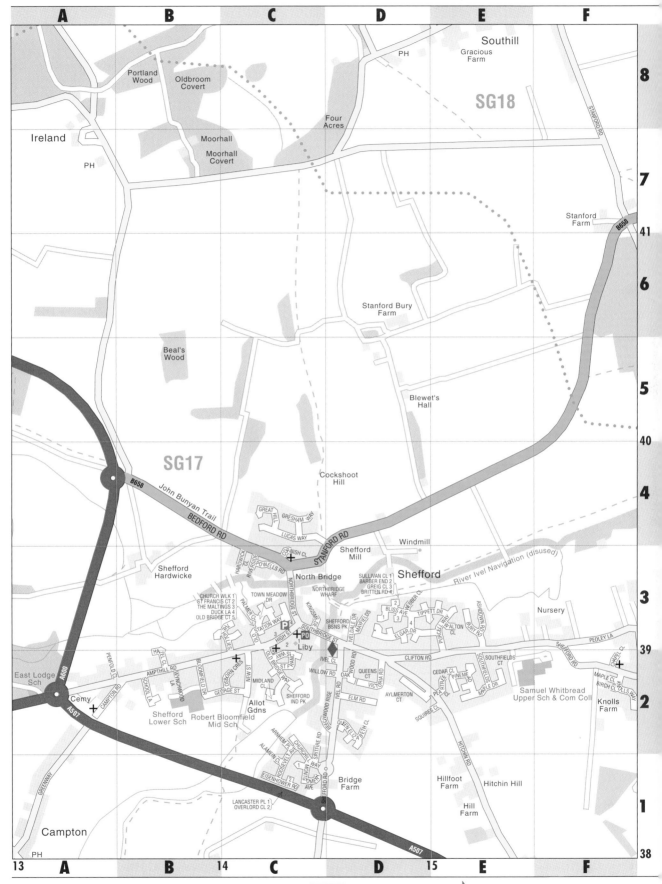

A B C D E F

8

Southill
Gracious
Farm

Portland
Wood
Oldbroom
Covert

SG18

Ireland

PH

Moorhall
Moorhall
Covert

Four
Acres

7

Stanford
Farm

B658

41

Four
Acres

6

Stanford Bury
Farm

Beal's
Wood

5

Blewet's
Hall

40

SG17

4

John Bunyan Trail

B658

BEDFORD RD

Cockshoot
Hill

STANFORD RD

Windmill

Shefford
Mill

River Ivel Navigation (disused)

Shefford
Hardwicke

HARDWICK CL
RIVERSIDE
POWELLS RD
SPANISH CL

North Bridge

NORTHBRIDGE ST

NORTHBRIDGE
WHARF

SULLIVAN CL 1
BARBER END 2
GREIG CL 3
BRITTEN RD 4

Shefford

3

CHURCH WLK 1
ST FRANCIS CT 2
THE MALTINGS 3
DUCK LA 4
OLD BRIDGE CT 5

TOWN MEADOW
DR

PALMER CL

KINGSMEAD

SHEFFORD
BSNS PK

IVELDALE DR

MANFIELDS

BLISS AVE

TIPPETT DR

WEBER CT

ASHDOWN RD

BURY RD

Nursery

PEDLEY LA

STATION WAY

HOLLIES

P

High St

Liby

SOUTHBRIDGE ST

PO

IVEL CL

ELGAR DR

PURCELL WAY

ALTON
CL

Shefford RD

39

HA
FIELD
AMPTHILL RD

SCHOOL LA
BLOOMFIELD DR

OSBORN CRES
LYNN ST
GEORGE ST
WYNCHWOOD
LA

OLD BRIDGE WAY

WILLOW RD

WOOD RD

OAK

QUEENS RD

VICTORIA RD

CLIFTON RD

CEDAR CL
PINE MD

PEAR TREE

SOUTHFIELDS
CT

MAPLE DR

CHPEL CL

MAPLE CL
BIRCH CL
KNOLLS WAY

East Lodge
Sch

A600

PENFOLD CL

CAMPTON RD

Cemy

MIDLAND
CL

Allot
Gdns

SHEFFORD
IND PK

IVEL RD

ELM RD

AYLMERTON
CT

Samuel Whitbread
Upper Sch & Com Coll

Knolls
Farm

2

A507

Shefford
Lower Sch

Robert Bloomfield
Mid Sch

ARNHEM PL
ALAMEIN CL
EISENHOWER RD
ROOSEVELT
CHURCHILL
WAY
SPITFIRE RD
BEECHWOOD RISE
SHEFFORD RD
OMAHA AVE

QUEBEC L
BETH CL

SOUREE CL

HITCHIN RD

Bridge
Farm

Hillfoot
Farm

Hitchin Hill

1

GREENWAY

Campton

LANCASTER PL 1
OVERLORD CL 2

Hill
Farm

PH

A507

38

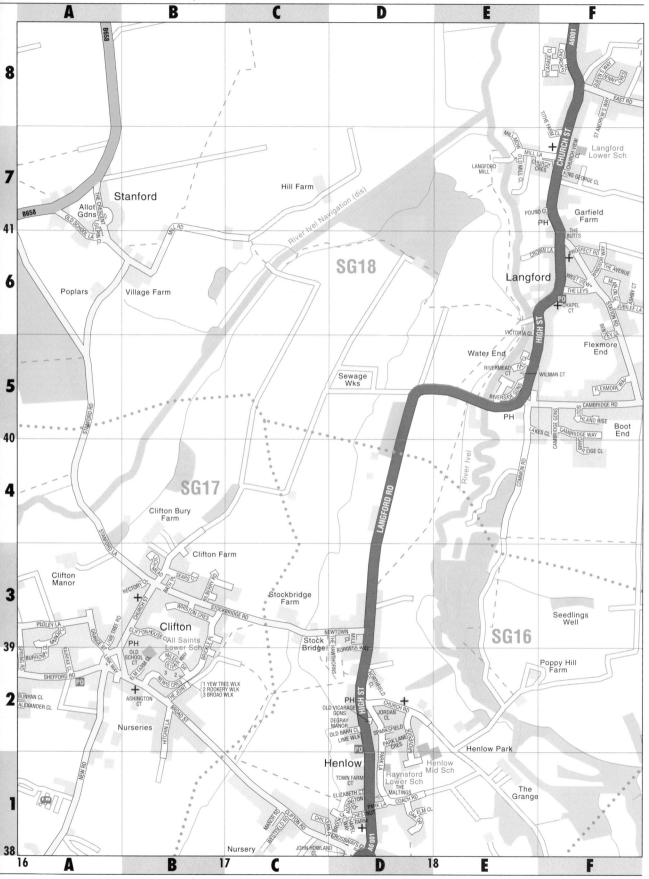

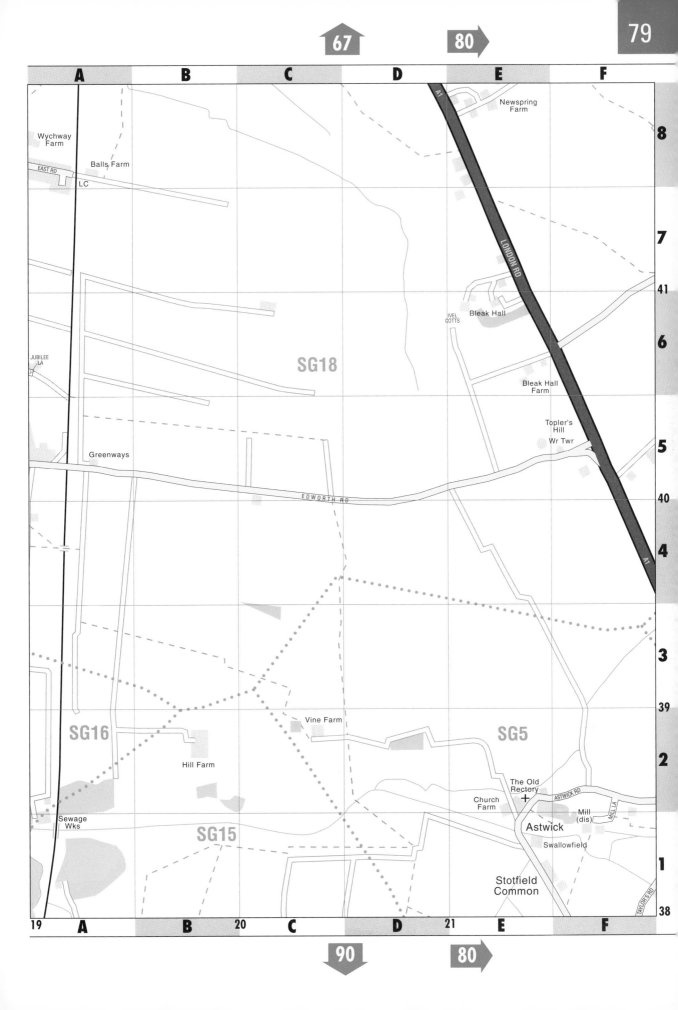

A · B · C · D · E · F

8
7
41
6
5
40
4
3
39
2
1
38

Wychway Farm
EAST RD
Balls Farm
LC
JUBILEE LA
Greenways
SG18
Newspring Farm
LONDON RD
Bleak Hall
IVEL COTTS
Bleak Hall Farm
Topler's Hill
Wr Twr
EDWORTH RD
A1
SG16
Vine Farm
SG5
Hill Farm
The Old Rectory
Church Farm
Sewage Wks
SG15
Astwick
ASTWICK RD
MILL LA
Mill (dis)
Swallowfield
Stotfield Common
TAYLOR'S RD

19 · A · B · 20 · C · D · 21 · E · F

A **B** **C** **D** **E** **F**

8

SG18
Lower Farm

Ash
Plantation

Manor Farm

7
The
Old Rectory

41

6
Manor Farm

+
Edworth

Green La

CHAPEL ST
FRANCIS RD
PH
HIGH ST
HOMEFIELD
THE CLOSE
CHRISTY'S YD
ARNOLDS LA

Hinxworth

Bury End
Farm

Ridge Way

5
Thorns Farm

+

NEW INN RD
ASHWELL RD

40
Dewmead
Farm

Jack's
House

SG7

4
Glebe Farm

Place Farm

Pulter's
Farm

Marshfield

Cuckoo

HINXWORTH RD

Hinxworth
Place

3
Saltmore
Farm

HINXWORTH RD
Capmore
Farm

39

A1

2
Foxhollow

Meadow
Cottages

SG5

LONDON RD

ASTWICK RD

TAYLOR'S RD

Spinney
Farm

Caldecote

+

Caldecote
Manor

1
Ivel Mill

Motel

Taylor's Mill
(dis)

STOTFOLD RD

CALDECOTE RD

ASHWELL RD

A1

38

22 **A** **B** 23 **C** **D** 24 **E** **F**

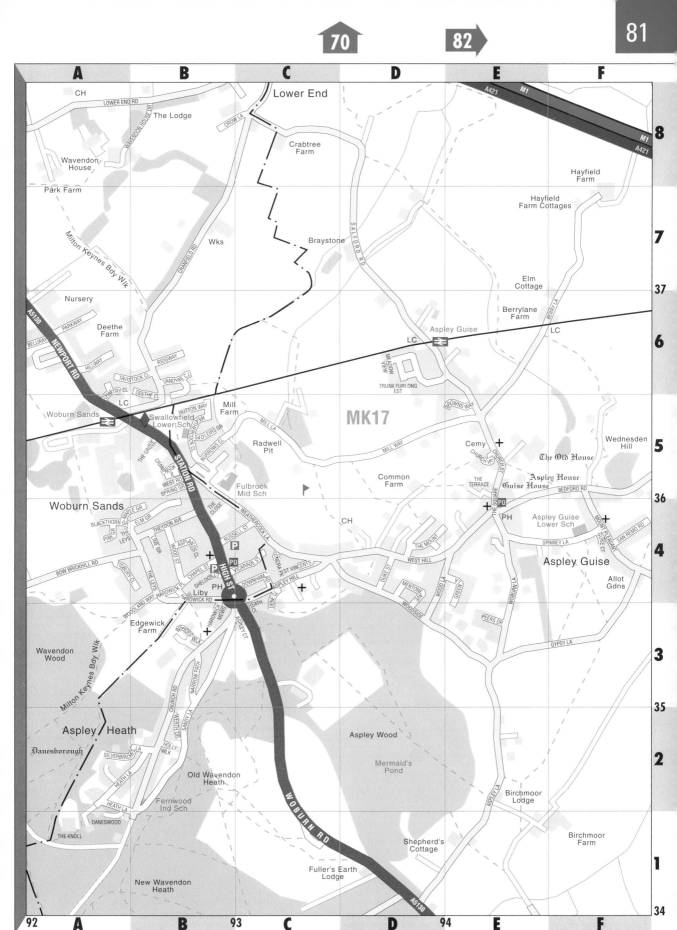

81
71

A B C D E F

8

7

37

6

5

36

4

3

35

2

1

34

Brook Farm

SALFORD RD

BEDFORD RD

M1

A421

A421

13

Charity
Farm

A507

BEDFORD RD

Sewage
Works

Brogborough
Middle Farm

LC

Ridgmont

PH

The Fruit
Farm

Charity
Farm

STATION RD

John Bunyan Trail

M1

Lowhill
Plantation

MK43

Crawley
Hall

BEDFORD RD

Church End

Crawley Park
Farm

Crawley
House

CROW LA

SCHOOL LA

Crawley Park

Husborne Crawley

Husborne Crawley
Lower Sch

PH

Woburn
Experimental
Farm

MILL RD

LYDDS HILL

Castle
Hill

PH

HIGH ST

PH

SL MOUNT

SEGENMORE CL

CHURCH ST

A507

Ridgmont

PO

Ridgmont
Lower Sch

Warren
Farm

EVERSHOLT RD

A507

A4012

Butt
Close

RIDGMONT RD

Stonepit Hill

Sandylane
Plantation

Ridgmont Belt

HORSEPOOL LA

TURNPIKE RD

Crawley Belt

SANDY LA

Crawley
Lodge

Carter's
Grove

Crawleyheath
Farm

Hay Wood

Dean Hills

Background
Plantation

MK17

CRAWLEY RD

The
Log Hut

The
Thornery

A4012

The
Evergreens

Cableway

Dolphinarium

Safari Park

Berryend
Plantation

95 A 96 B C 97 D E F

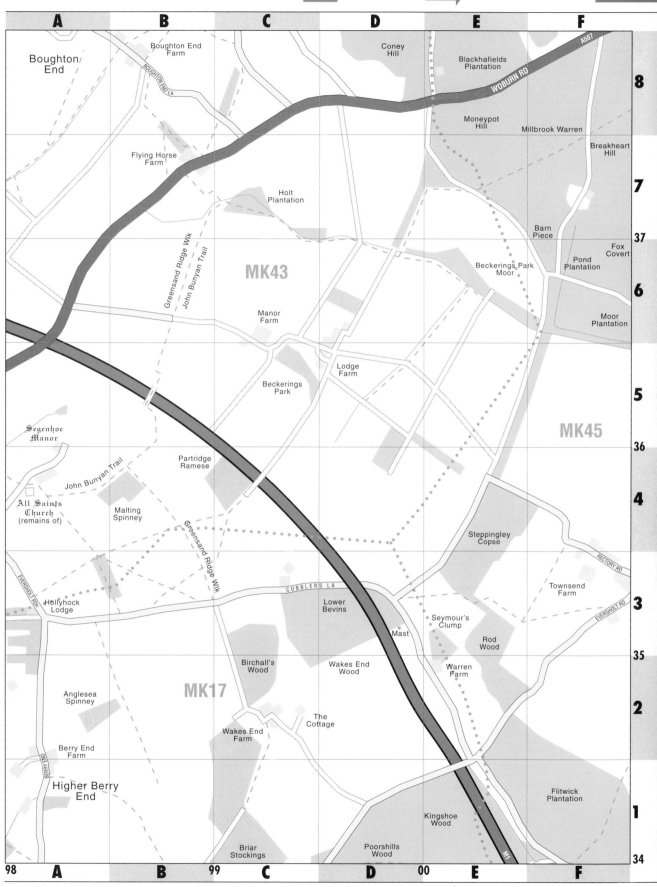

Boughton End

Boughton End Farm

Coney Hill

Blackhafields Plantation

A507

WOBURN RD

8

Moneypot Hill

Millbrook Warren

Flying Horse Farm

Breakheart Hill

7

BOUGHTON END LA

Holt Plantation

37

Barn Piece

Fox Covert

Greensand Ridge Wlk

John Bunyan Trail

MK43

Beckerings Park Moor

Pond Plantation

6

Moor Plantation

Manor Farm

Lodge Farm

Beckerings Park

5

MK45

Segenhoe Manor

36

John Bunyan Trail

Partridge Ramese

All Saints Church (remains of)

Malting Spinney

Greensand Ridge Wlk

Steppingley Copse

4

EVERSHOLT RD

Hollyhock Lodge

COBBLERS LA

Lower Bevins

Seymour's Clump

Townsend Farm

RECTORY RD

3

EVERSHOLT RD

Mast

Rod Wood

35

Birchall's Wood

Wakes End Wood

Warren Farm

Anglesea Spinney

MK17

The Cottage

2

BERRY END

Berry End Farm

Wakes End Farm

Higher Berry End

Flitwick Plantation

1

Kingshoe Wood

Briar Stockings

Poorshills Wood

M1

34

A B C D E F

8

Middle
Piece

Nature
Reserve

Littlepark
Farm

Alameda
Mid Sch

Cooper's
Hill

The
John Crosse
Home

The Firs
Lower Sch

KATHERINE'S
CT

1 KATHERINE'S GDN
2 ARAGON CT
3 LEAFIELD CT

CHANDOS RD

BRIAR CL

LYME RD

ALAMEDA
WLK

GLOUCESTER CT 1
THE CEDARS 2
CEDARS CTYD 3
CEDARS CT 4
LAVENDER CT 5

Russell
Lower
Sch

Liby

7

Fordfield
Farm

Fordfield
House

Fordfield Rd

Station Rd

Ampthill
Ind Est &
Bsns Pk

STATION RD

THE CRESCENT

SIDNEY
RD

HOLLAND RD

THE AVENUE

GLEBE RD

37

AMPTHILL

6

Ampthill
Grange

Redborne Upper Sch
& Com Coll

A507

Sewage
Works

MK45

5

Froghall

THE MEADOWS

Ampthill Rd

CHAUNTRY WAY

A5120

36

Steppingley

H

TRAFALGAR DR

4

Bury Lawn
Sch

Valley
Farm

Sports
Ctr

Kiln
Farm

Beechcroft

Revelstoke

John Bunyan Trail

RECTORY
RD

PH

Eversholt

3

Steppingley

Flitwick

Templefield
Lower
Sch

Woodland
Mid Sch

Steppingley
Road
Trad Est

Waverly
Sch

HIGH ST

Flitwick

PH

Liby

Kingsmoor
Lower Sch

35

Park
Farm

Flitwick
Wood

SEVERN CL 1
COTSWOLD PL 2
CHEVIOT CL 3
WINDRUSH CL 4
PHEASANT WLK 5

Russell
Ctr

2

Wood
Farm

BLENHEIM LINK 6
SYON PATH 7
WOODCOCK WLK 8
LONGLEAT CL 9
BUCKINGHAM MEWS 10
POWIS MEWS 11
SANDRINGHAM RD 12

CHURCH RD

Flitwick
Lower Sch

DUNSTABLE RD

1 HUBBARD CL
2 LOVET RD

WATER
LA

1

Long
Close

Flitwick
Manor
(Hotel)

Flit
Water

A5120

34

01 A B 02 C D 03 E F

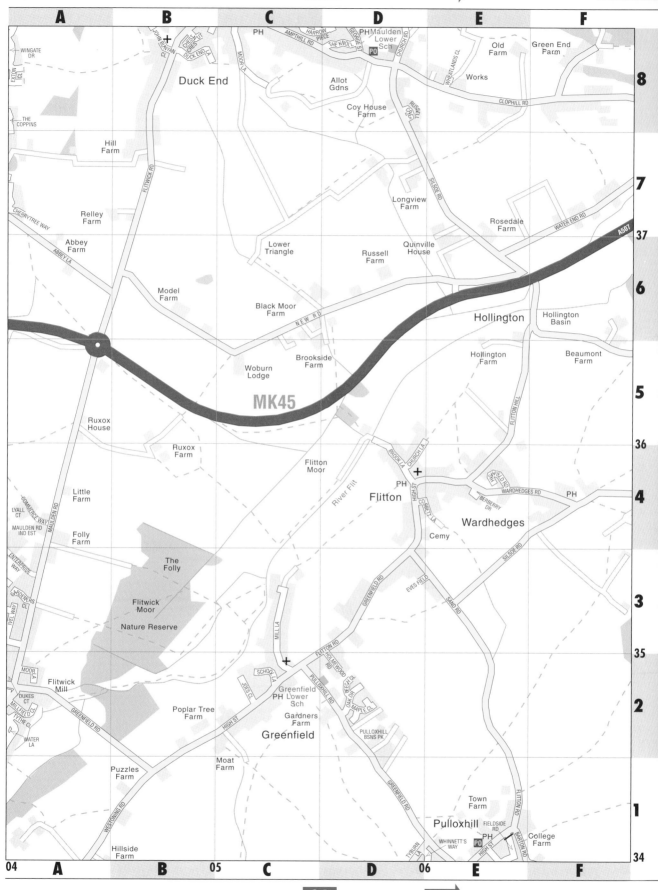

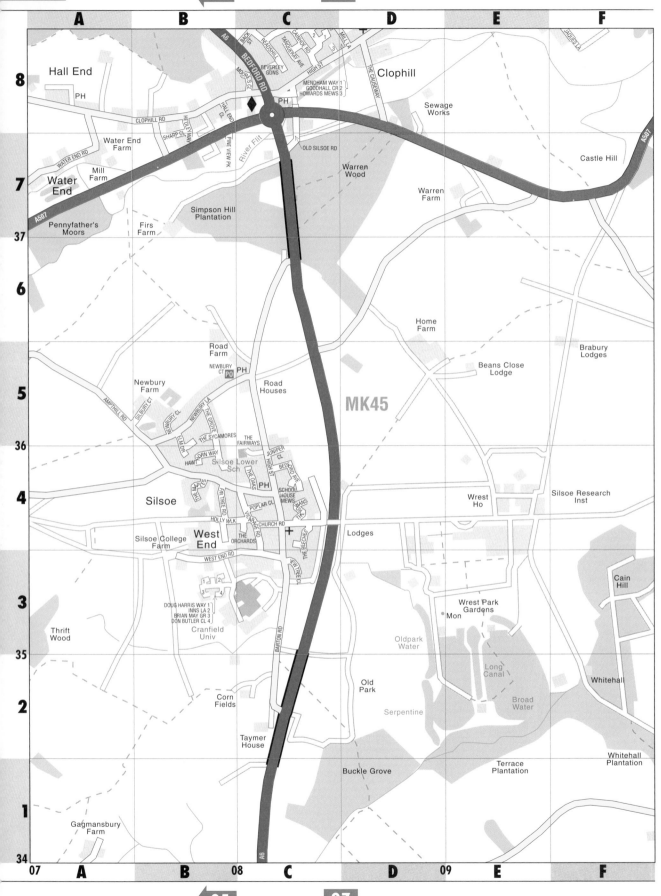

A   B   C   D   E   F

8   **Hall End**   **Clophill**
PH
CLOPHILL RD   Sewage
Water End   Works
Farm   River Flit   Warren
WATER END RD   Mill Farm   PINE VIEW PK   Old Silsoe Rd   Wood   Castle Hill
7   **Water**   Warren
     End   Farm
Pennyfather's   Firs   Simpson Hill
Moors   Farm   Plantation
37

6   Home
                                                         Farm   Brabury
                                                                 Lodges
         Road   Beans Close
         Farm   Lodge
      NEWBURY   PO PH
5   Newbury   CT   Road   **MK45**
     Farm   Houses
     AMPHILL RD
36   THE SYCAMORES   THE FAIRWAYS
              ELM DR   CORN WAY   JUNIPER CL
         HAWT   Silsoe Lower   HIGH ST   Silsoe Research
4   Sch   PH   BEDFORD AVE   Wrest   Inst
     Silsoe   THE OAKS   SCHOOL   Ho
              FIR TREE RD   POPLAR CL   HOUSE
         HOLLY WLK   VICARAGE RD   MEWS
     Silsoe College   **West**   CHURCH RD   Lodges
     Farm   **End**   THE ORCHARDS   KENT TREE CL
3   WEST END RD
              1   2   **Wrest Park**
              3   4   **Gardens**
         DOUG HARRIS WAY 1   Mon
     Thrift   INNS LA 2   Cranfield
     Wood   BRIAN MAY GR 3   Univ   Oldpark
         DON BUTLER CL 4   BARTON RD   Water
35   Long   Whitehall
                                                            Canal
2   Corn   Old
     Fields   Park   Broad
                              Serpentine   Water
     Taymer
     House   Terrace   Whitehall
              Buckle Grove   Plantation   Plantation
1   Gagmansbury
     Farm
34   07   A   08   B   C   09   D   E   F

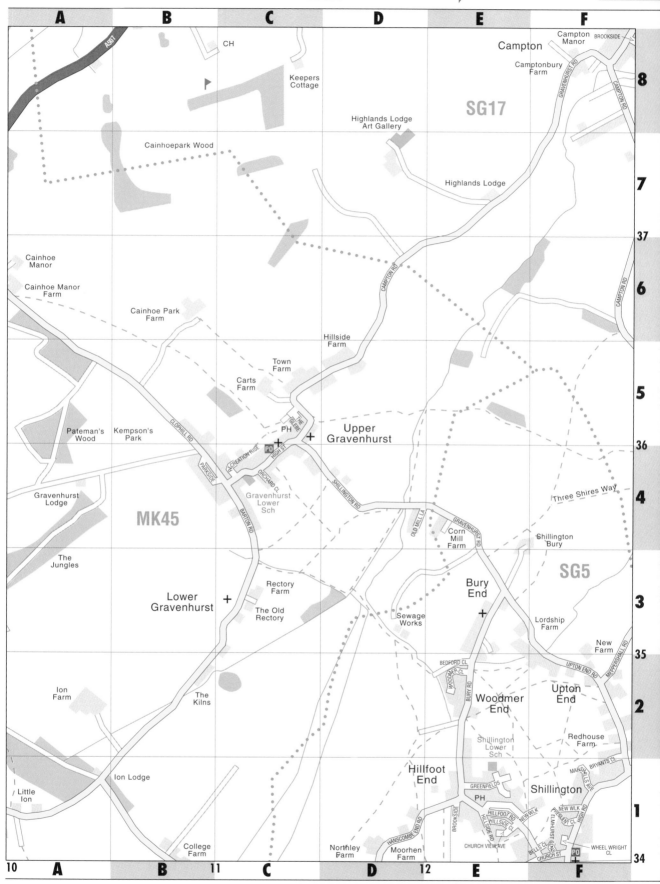

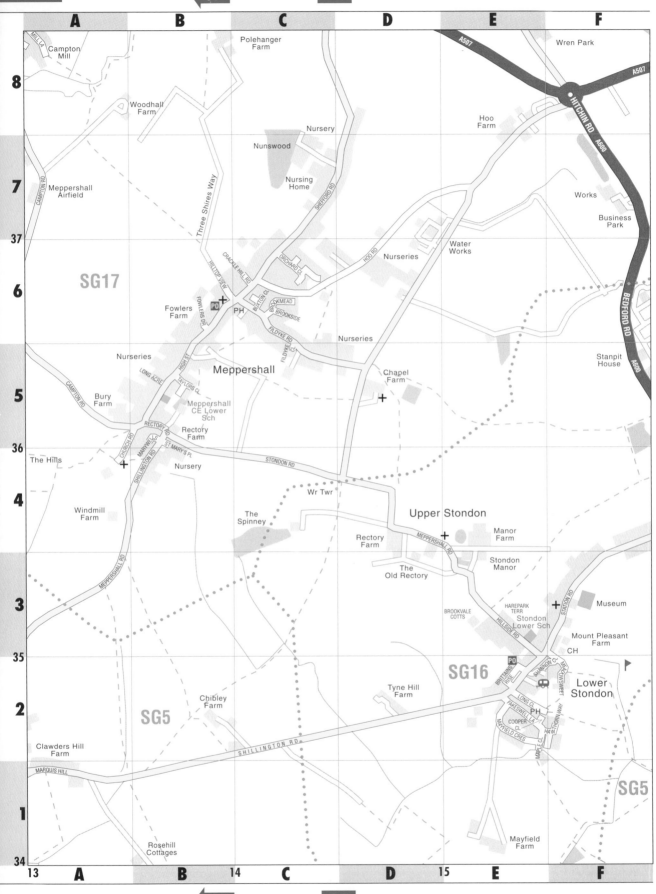

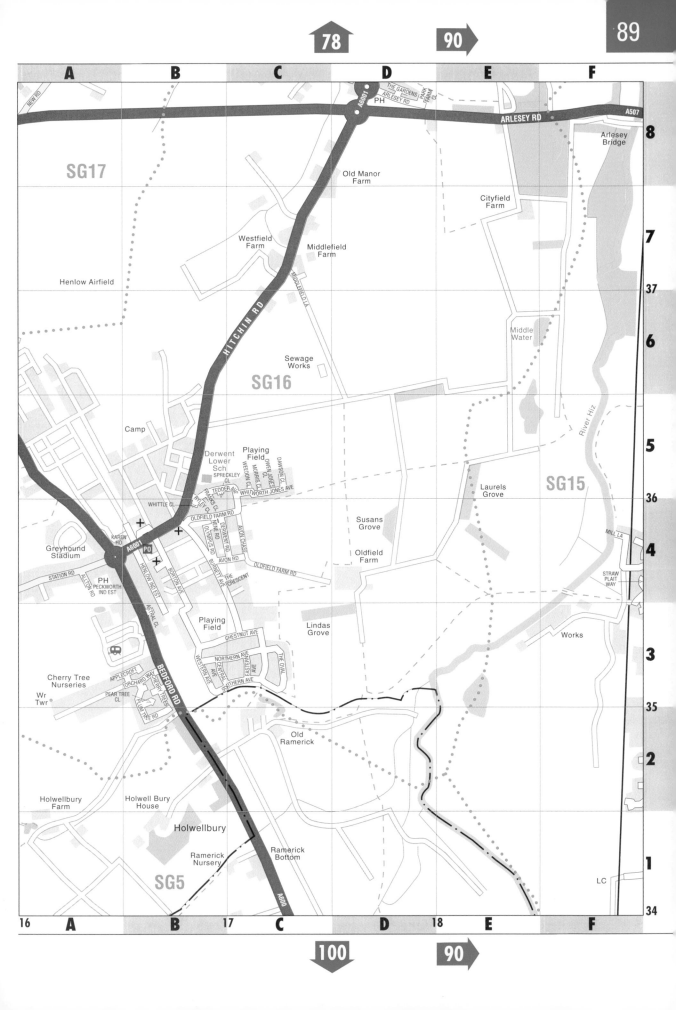

A B C D E F

NEW RD

A507

THE GARDENS
ARLESEY RD
PARK
FARM
CL
PH
A6001
ARLESEY RD

SG17

Arlesey
Bridge

8

Old Manor
Farm

Cityfield
Farm

Westfield
Farm

Middlefield
Farm

7

37

Henlow Airfield

MIDDLEFIELD LA

HITCHIN RD

Middle
Water

6

Sewage
Works

SG16

River Hiz

5

Camp

Derwent
Lower
Sch

Playing
Field

SPRECKLEY CL
WEEDON CL
MORRIS CL
OWEN JONES CL
DAWSON CL
WHITWORTH JONES AVE

Laurels
Grove

SG15

36

WHITTLE CL

TEDDER AVE
BYCE CL
FRANKS CL
OLDFIELD FARM RD
NENE RD
DERWENT RD
OLYMPUS RD
AVON CHASE
AVON RD

Susans
Grove

KAREN HO
A6001
PO

Greyhound
Stadium

BURNETT AVE
THE CRESCENT
OLDFIELD FARM RD

Oldfield
Farm

MILL LA

4

STATION RD
ALTON RD
PH
PECKWORTH
IND EST
HENLOW IND EST

STRAW
PLAIT
WAY

ASTRAL CL
BORTON AVE

Playing
Field

CHESTNUT AVE
NORTHERN AVE
WESTERN AVE
CENTRAL AVE
SOUTHERN AVE
EASTERN AVE
THE OVAL

Lindas
Grove

Works

3

Cherry Tree
Nurseries

APPLECROFT
ORCHARD WAY
PEAR TREE CL
PLUM TREE RD
CHERRY TREE RD

BEDFORD RD

Old
Ramerick

35

Wr
Twr

2

Holwellbury
Farm

Holwell Bury
House

Holwellbury

Ramerick
Bottom

LC

1

Ramerick
Nursery

SG5

A600

34

16 A B 17 C D 18 E F

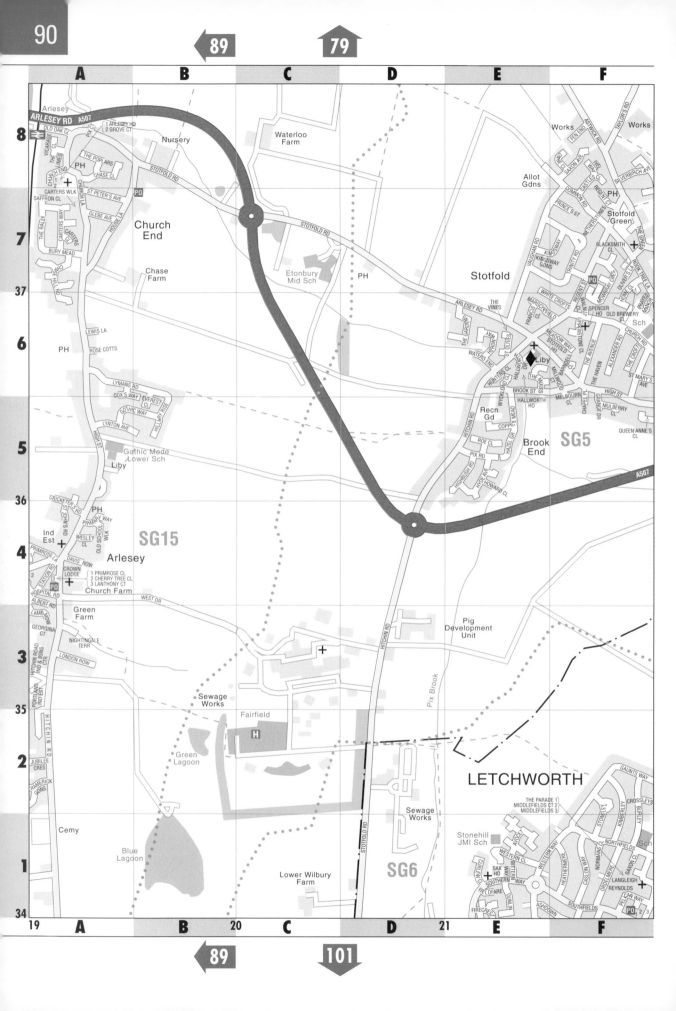

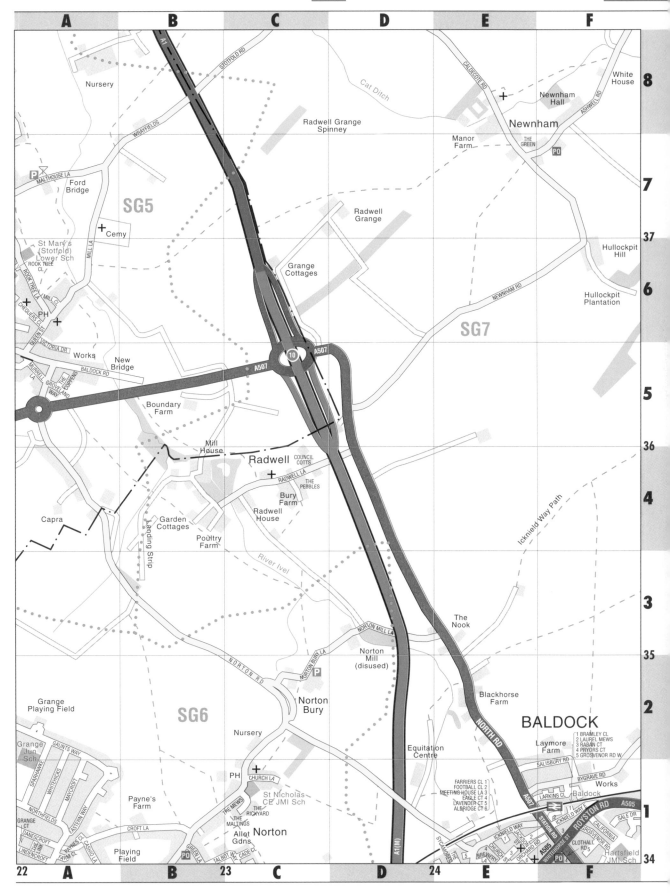

A B C D E F

8 7 37 6 5 36 4 3 35 2 1 34

Nursery

Cat Ditch

CALDECOTE RD

White House

ASHWELL RD

Newnham Hall

+

Newnham

Radwell Grange Spinney

Manor Farm

THE GREEN

PO

STOTFOLD RD

A1

WRAYFIELDS

SG5

MALTHOUSE LA

P

Ford Bridge

Radwell Grange

Hullockpit Hill

NEWNHAM RD

Hullockpit Plantation

SG7

St Mary's (Stotfold) Lower Sch

MILL LA

+ Cemy

ROOK TREE CL

Grange Cottages

ROOK TREE LA

CHEQUERS CL

PH +

QUEENS CL

VICTORIA DR

MURRELL LA

GROVELAND WAY

GROVELAND WAY

Works

BALDOCK RD

New Bridge

A507

10

A507

Radwell

COUNCIL COTTS

Boundary Farm

Mill House

RADWELL LA

+

THE PEBBLES

Bury Farm

Capra

Garden Cottages

Landing Strip

Radwell House

Poultry Farm

River Ivel

Icknield Way Path

The Nook

NORTON MILL LA

A1(M)

Norton Mill (disused)

NORTON RD

NORTON BURY LA

P

Norton Bury

Blackhorse Farm

SG6

Nursery

Grange Playing Field

NORTH RD

BALDOCK

Laymore Farm

1 BRAMLEY CL
2 LAUREL MEWS
3 RABAN CT
4 PRYORS CT
5 GROSVENOR RD W

Grange Jun Sch

GAUNTS WAY

SPARTHANKS

WHITEHICKS

MAYCROFT

EASTERN WAY

NORTHFIELDS

GRANGE CT

PAYNES CL

DANESCROFT

CASHIO LA

LINDENCROFT

Payne's Farm

CROFT LA

PH

CHURCH LA

+

Equitation Centre

SALISBURY RD

FARRIERS CL 1
FOOTBALL CL 2
MEETING HOUSE LA 3
EAGLE CT 4
LAVENDER CT 5
ALBRIDGE CT 6

BYGRAVE RD

Works

LARKINS CL

Baldock

St Nicholas CE JMI Sch

THE MEWS

THE RICKYARD

THE MALTINGS

GREEN LA

PO

TALBOT WAY

CADE CL

Allet Gdns

Norton

A1(M)

SYCAMORES

ICKNIELD WAY

JACKSON ST

BREWERY

CHURCH ST

A505

WHITEHORSE ST

ORCHARD RD

STATION RD

ICKNIELD WAY E

ROYSTON RD

A505

GROSVENOR RD

CALIFORNIA

SALE DR

CLOTHALL RD 5

PO

+

Hartsfield JMI Sch

Playing Field

A 22 B 23 C D 24 E F

Wall Close

Deer Paddock

Redlodge Plantation

Safari Park

8

Cableway

Lower Drakeloe Pond

Star Lodge

Stump Cross

Froxfield

Upper Drakeloe Pond

Woburn Park

Whitnoe Orchard Pond

7

PARK ST

Park Farm

Horse Pond

Charcoal Pond

33

Hotel

Cowhill Belt Pond

Shoulder of Mutton Pond

Duncombe's Breeches Pond

Pipeswell Plantation

Deer Park

Greensand Ridge Wlk

6

Stew Pond

Speedwell Cottages

Basin Pond

Woburn Abbey

Purretts Hill

Speedwell

Basin Bridge

New Pond

5

Speedwell Farm

Coldbath Clump

Lower Hopgarden Pond

The Maze

MK17

32

Cow Pasture Clump

Upper Hopgarden Pond

Milton Wood

4

LONDON RD

Speedwell Belt

Commons Clump

Grange Farm

3

Old Farm

MEAD'S CL

31

Fourteen Acre Spinney

London Entrance Lodge

Church End

2

Milton Lodge

Leys Farm

Cuckoopit Spinney

BATTLESDEN AVE

Milton Bryan

The Manor House

South End

PH

1

MAGS LA

Home Farm

Potsgrove

Grove Wood

A4012

Fountaine's Farm

30

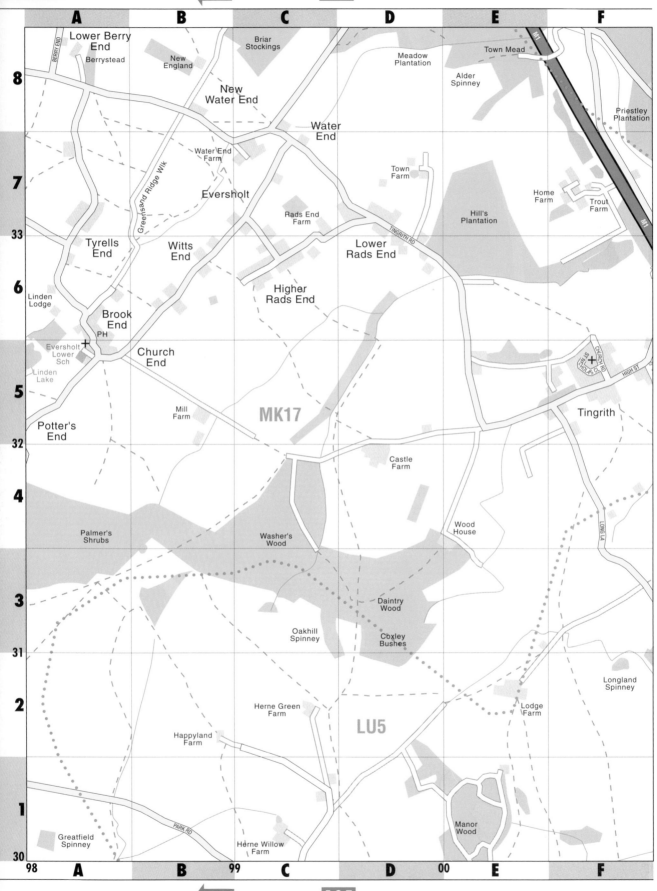

A   B   C   D   E   F

8

Lower Berry End
Berrystead
New England
Briar Stockings
Meadow Plantation
Town Mead
Alder Spinney
Priestley Plantation

New Water End

Water End

7

Water End Farm
Eversholt
Town Farm
Home Farm
Trout Farm

Greensand Ridge Wlk

33

Tyrells End
Witts End
Rads End Farm
Lower Rads End
Hill's Plantation

Tingrith Rd

6

Linden Lodge
Higher Rads End

Brook End
PH

Eversholt Lower Sch

Church End

Church Rd
St Nicholas Cl
High St

5

Linden Lake
Mill Farm
MK17
Tingrith

Potter's End

32

Castle Farm

4

Palmer's Shrubs
Washer's Wood
Wood House
Long La

3

Daintry Wood
Oakhill Spinney
Coxley Bushes

31

Longland Spinney

2

Herne Green Farm
LU5
Lodge Farm

Happyland Farm

1

Park Rd
Manor Wood

Greatfield Spinney
Herne Willow Farm

30

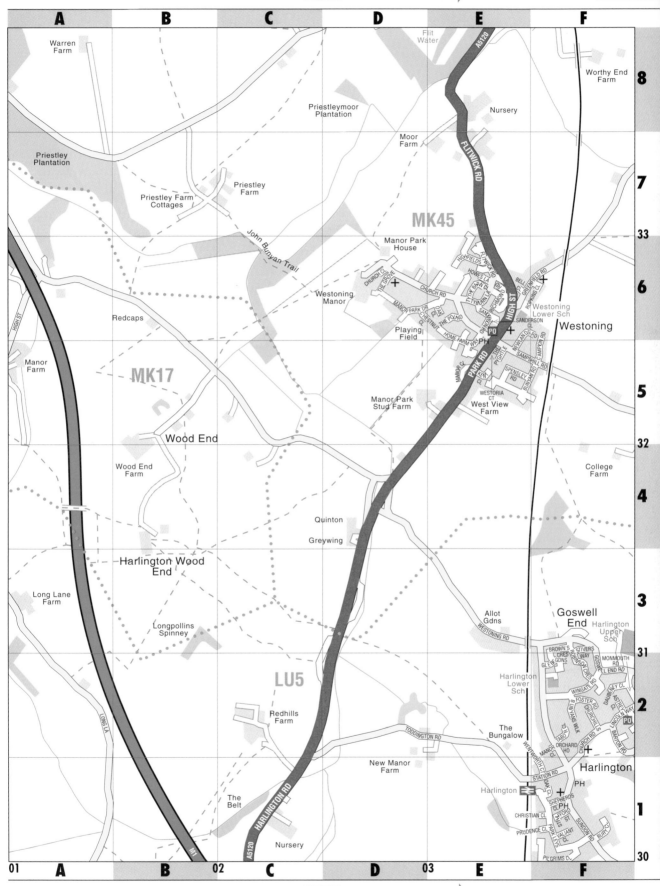

A   B   C   D   E   F

8   7   33   6   5   32   4   3   31   2   1   30

Warren
Farm

Priestley
Plantation

Priestley Farm
Cottages

Priestley
Farm

Priestleymoor
Plantation

Flit
Water

Worthy End
Farm

Nursery

Moor
Farm

John Bunyan Trail

MK45

Manor Park
House

Westoning
Manor

Redcaps

MK17

Manor
Farm

Wood End

Wood End
Farm

Playing
Field

PH

PO

Westoning
Lower Sch

Westoning

HIGH ST

PARK RD

FLITWICK RD

Manor Park
Stud Farm

West View
Farm

College
Farm

Quinton

Greywing

Harlington Wood
End

Long Lane
Farm

Longpollins
Spinney

Allot
Gdns

WESTONING RD

Goswell
End

Harlington
Upper Sch

LU5

Harlington
Lower Sch

The
Bungalow

Harlington

Redhills
Farm

TODDINGTON RD

New Manor
Farm

Harlington

PH

The
Belt

Nursery

HARLINGTON RD

A5120

M1

01   02   03

30

	A	B	C	D	E	F

8

St JAMES CL
TYBURN LA
WHINNETT'S WAY
STANLEY CL
CHURCH RD
HIGH ST
FIELDSIDE RD
1 ORCHARD RD
2 GREENFIELD RD
Pulloxhill Lower Sch
BARTON RD
PH
+ Pulloxhill
Water Twr
BLACKHILL LA

7

The White House

33

Old Farm Cottage
Clayhill Farm
Hill Farm
Higham Bury
Meadhook

6

John Bunyan Trail
Portobello Farm
Portobello Wood
Meadhook Wood

5

MK45
Samshill Farm
Upper Sampshill Farm

32

4

John Bunyan Trail

3

Mill Farm
HARLINGTON RD
Grange Farm
Sharpenhoe Grove
Works
Harlington Mill Nurseries

31

Harlington Upper Sch
Horse-Hill Farm
Horsehill Spinney
Bury Farm

2

GOSWELL END RD
LINCOLN WAY
BRIAN RD
Upper East End Farm
Lower East End Farm
Wateroff
LU5
BARTON RD
Sharpenhoe
PH +
Goswell End
BARTON RD
Willow Farm
Priory Farm
Roberts Farm
SHARPENHOE RD

1

Sharpenhoe Clappers
• Mon

30

Suncote Lodge

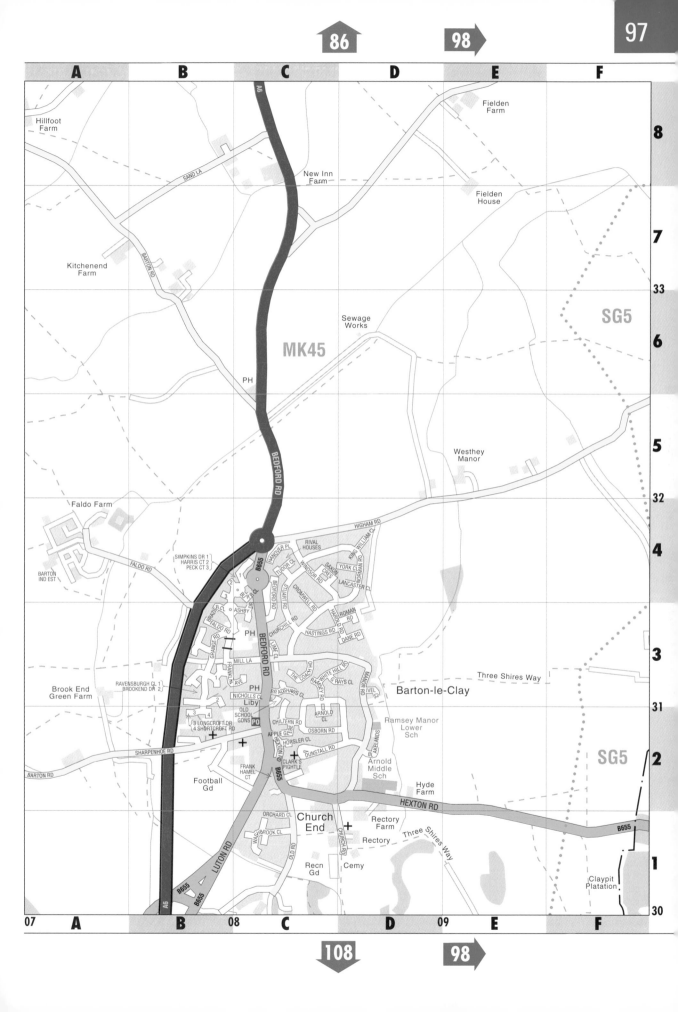

A B C D E F

8
7
33
6
5
32
4
3
31
2
1
30

SG5

MK45

Hillfoot Farm

Fielden Farm

New Inn Farm

Fielden House

Kitchenend Farm

SAND LA

BARTON RD

Sewage Works

PH

BEDFORD RD

A6

Westhey Manor

Faldo Farm

FALDO RD

SIMPKINS DR 1
HARRIS CT 2
PECK CT 3

BARTON IND EST

Higham Rd

HIGHAM RD

RIVAL HOUSES

HANOVER PL

TUDOR CL

WINDSOR RD

SAXON CRES

KING WILLIAM CL

NORMAN CL

YORK CL

LANCASTER CL

STUART RD

BEDFORD RD

CROMWELL RD

CHURCHILL RD

HAROLD RD

ROMAN RD

HASTINGS RD

DANE RD

B655

ASHBY

FALDO RD

GRANGE RD

MILL LA

PH

FRANKLIN AVE

LYME CL

BEDFORD RD

THE COACH

WHITE HILL RD

RAMSEY RD

G RAYS CL

IVEL

MANOR RD

Three Shires Way

Barton-le-Clay

Brook End Green Farm

RAVENSBURGH CL 1
BROOKEND DR 2

PH

NICHOLLS CL

Liby

OLD SCHOOL GDNS

PO

3 LONGCROFT DR
4 SHORTCROFT DR

CHILTERN RD

ARNOLD CL

OSBORN RD

AKELANDS

Ramsey Manor Lower Sch

APPLE CL

HORSLER CL

HEXTON RD

DUNSTALL CL

CLARK'S PIGHTLE

FRANK HAMEL CT

B655

Arnold Middle Sch

SHARPENHOE RD

BARTON RD

Football Gd

Hyde Farm

HEXTON RD

B655

Church End

ORCHARD CL

WASHBROOK CL

OLD RD

CHURCH RD

Rectory Farm

Rectory

Three Shires Way

SG5

Recn Gd

Cemy

LUTON RD

A6

B655

B655

Claypit Platation

07 A B 08 C D 09 E F

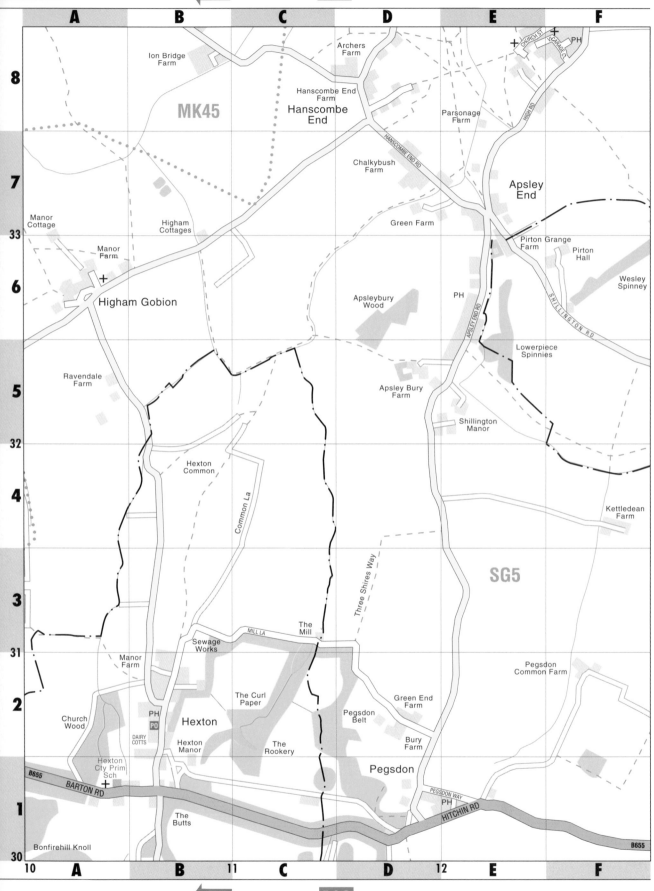

A　B　C　D　E　F

Rosehill Farm

SG16

8

7

33

6

New Wrights Farm

HOLWELL RD

Burge End Farm

Hammonds Farm

Burge End

West Lane Farm

SHILLINGTON RD

BURGE END LA

Rectory Farm

WEST LA

LITTLE LA

ROYAL OAK LA

5

32

COLEMANS CL

FRANKLIN CL

HIGH ST

CROMWELL WAY

BUNYAN CL

Pirton Jun Mix Inf Sch

ST MARY'S CL

CRABTREE LA

PO

Pirton

4

Wr Twr

PRIORS HILL

DANEFIELD RD

POLLARDS WAY

DOCKLANDS

GREAT GN

HAMBRIDGE WAY

Hill Farm

THREE CLOSES

BURY END

Toot Hill

Icknield Way Path

Hill Farm

WALNUT TREE

MALTINGS ORCH

Walnut Tree Farm

3

Knocking Knoll

Icknield Way Path

Wood La

SG5

HITCHIN RD

31

2

Highdown Farm

Tingley Wood

High Down House

Lower Plantation

Highdown Plantation

Punch's Cross

Hanginghill Plantation

Tingley Field Platation

Shrub Wood

B655

1

30

99
89

	A	B	C	D	E	F

SG15

8

New Ramerwick Farm

Riddy Park Farm

North Farm

Holwell

Ickleford Common

Sewage Works

7

GURNEY'S LA

RAND'S CL

RAND'S COTTS

HOLWELL RD

Meadow Farm

Ashcroft Farm

Pestol Farm

RAND'S MDW

PIRTON RD

The Old Rectory

33

Elmdene Farm

Lordship Farm

WATERLOO LA

PH

6

Lower Green Farm

Holme Farm

Snailswell

THE POPLARS

SNAILSWELL LA

Lower Green

ABBIS ORCH

CLAYMORE DR

LONGMEADOW DR

ARLESEY RD

Cadwell Farm

5

Pinchgut Hall

BEDFORD RD

River Hiz

SG5

Pound Farm

RIVER CT

Ickleford Prim Sch

WITTER AVE

32

Ickleford

RAYMOND COTTS

CHAMBERS LA

Cadwell Crossing

4

Hambridge Way

PO

ICKNIELD CL

PH

GREENFIELD LA

WYATT CL

WALNUT WAY

FREEWATERS CL

GREENFIELD CL

GALLEYWOOD

LODGE CT

DUNCOTS CL

ST KATHARINES CL

TURNPIKE LA

MANOR CL

LAUREL WAY

ICKLEFORD BURY

3

Icknield Way Path

RYDER AVE

RYDER WAY

Flour Mill

SG4

Allot Gdns

Mill Way

WESTMILL LA

BESSEMER CL

BILTON RD

CADWELL LA

31

Burford Ray Bridge

WILLOW TREE WAY

Westmill Farm

River Oughton

Our Lady's RC JMI Sch

Sewage Works

Icknield Way

Allot Gdns

BURFORD WAY

PORTER CL

TIMES CL

BEDFORD RD

Strathmore Inf Sch

SHEPHERDS MEAD

OLD HALE WAY

THE MEAD

LAMMAS MEAD

2

WESTMILL LA

TRUEMANS RD

BEECHWOOD

WESTMILL LAWNS

BOW YER'S CL

The Priory Sch

King George V Playing Field

BRAMPTON PARK RD

WILTON RD

STRATHMORE AVE

WHITEHURST AVE

HEATHFIELD RD

BURY MEAD RD

GLOVERS CT

Westmill

RIVER MEAD

MULBERRY

MILESTONE CL

MICHAEL MUIR HO

WELLINGHAM AVE

KING GEORGES CL

DEACONS WAY

BALMORAL RD

STORMONT RD

STRATHMORE CT

1

SWINBURNE AVE

HINE WAY

BINGEN RD

JOHN BARKER PL

SEEDMAN CL

FREEMANS CL

MATTOCKE RD

THE CRESCENT

NORTH PL

NUTLEIGH GR

BEARTON AVE

TA Ctr

BEARTON RD

BEARTON CT

JAMES FOSTER HO

BRAMPTON PARK RD

WHINBUSH RD

ICKLEFORD RD

PERIWINKLE LA

KIWI CT

GROVE RD

ALEXANDRA RD

Oughtonhead Common

KINGS HEDGES

MOSS WAY

REDHILL RD

DUGDALE

Schs

PO

A600

MARK'S CL

30

16	A		B	17	C		D	18	E		F

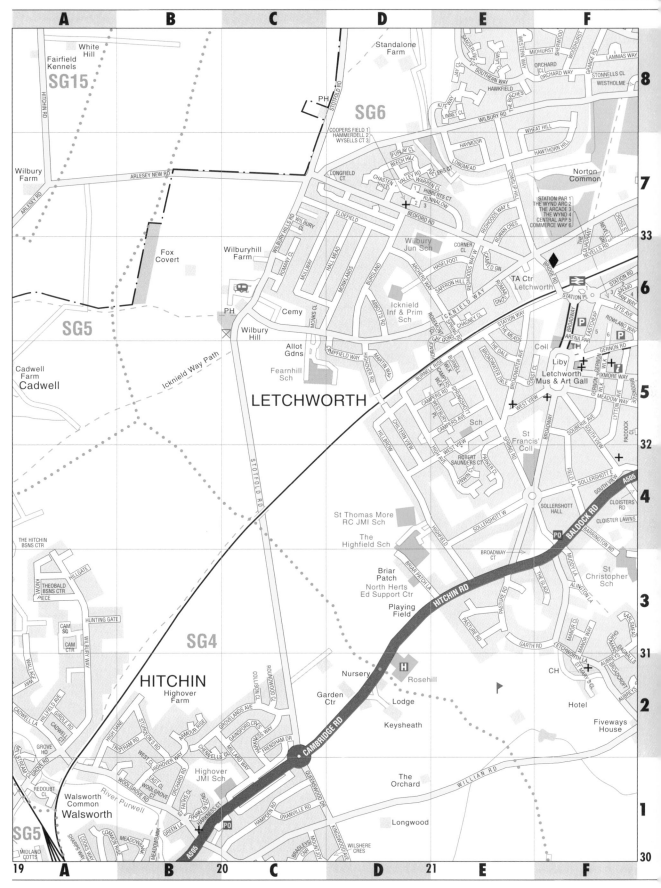

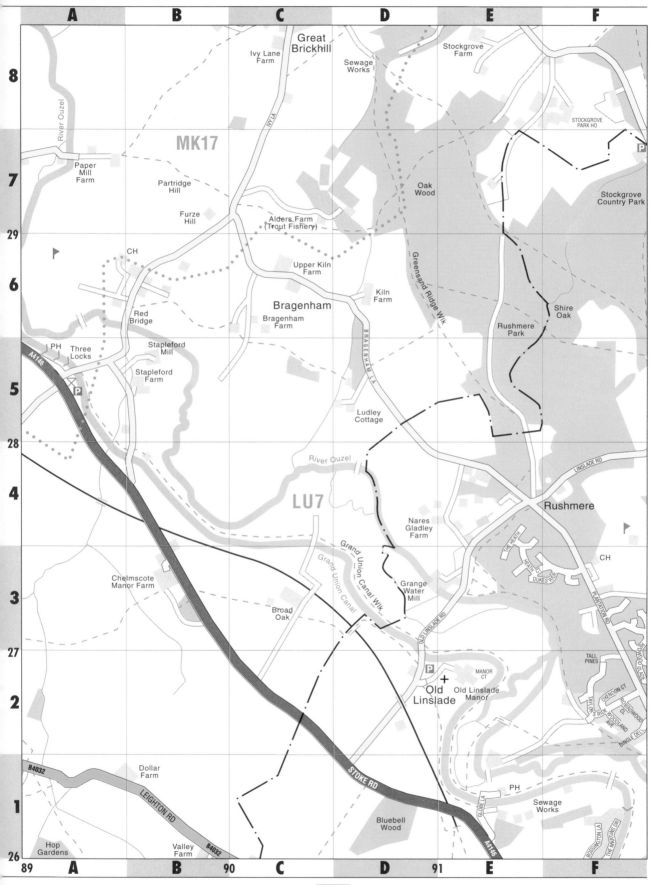

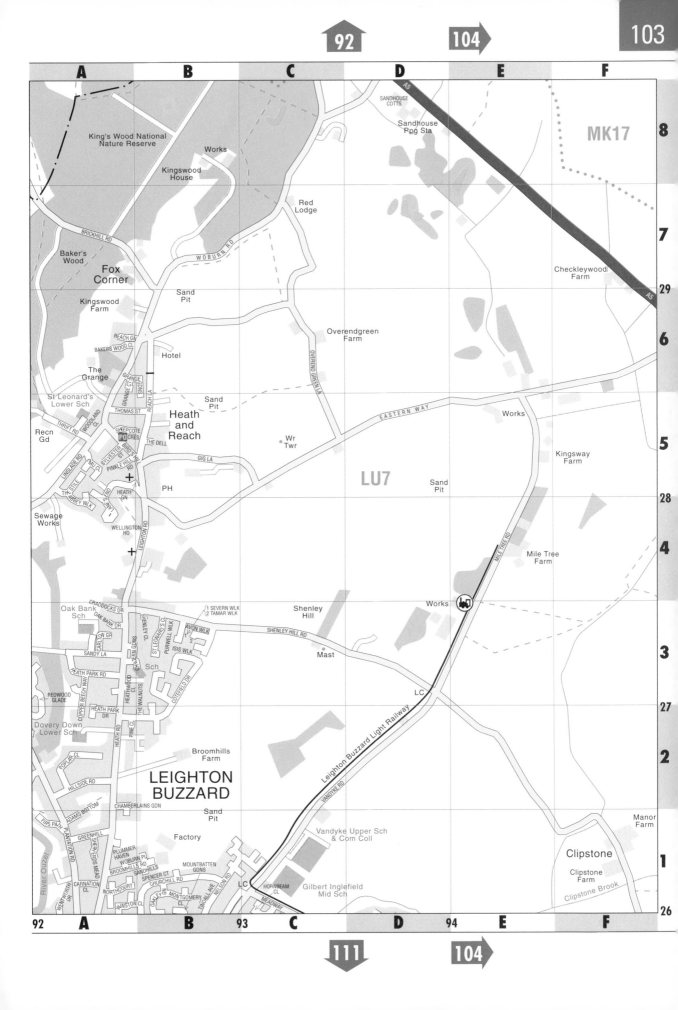

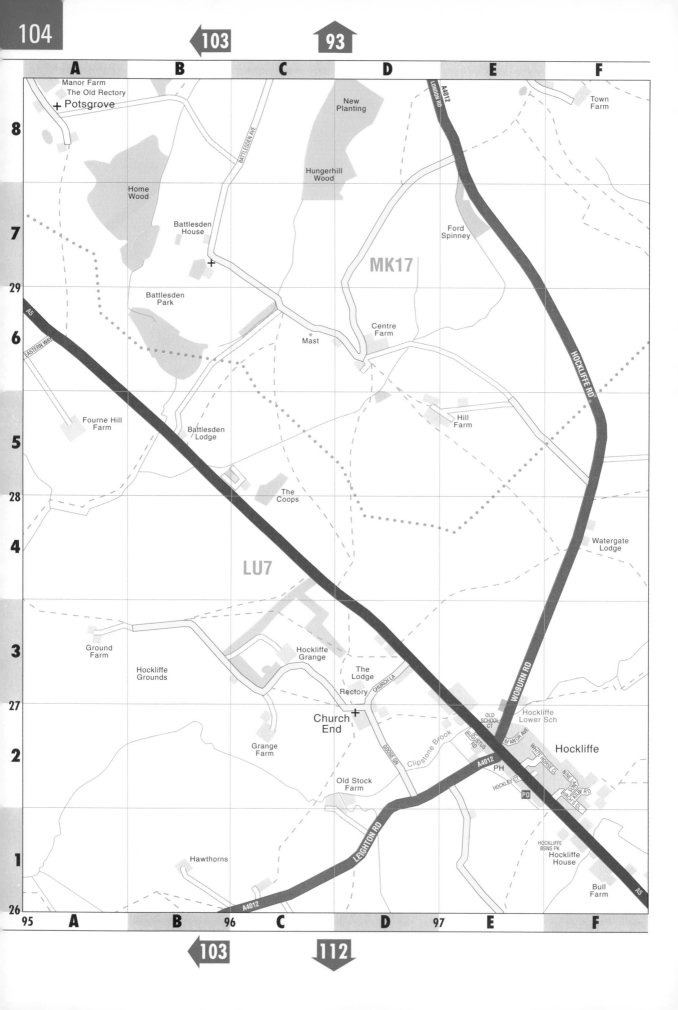

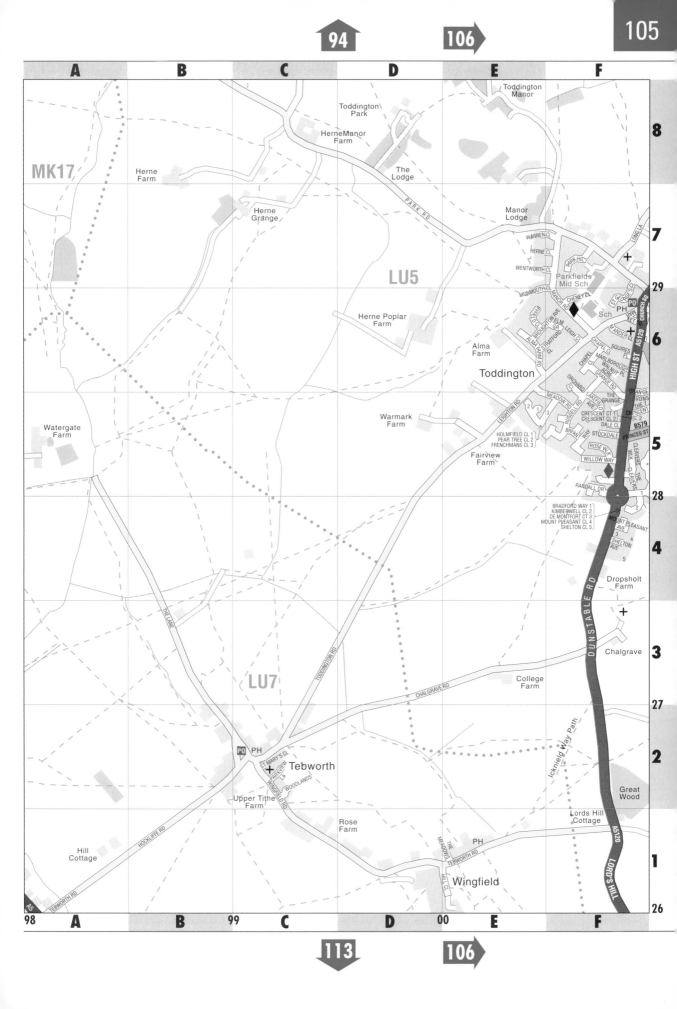

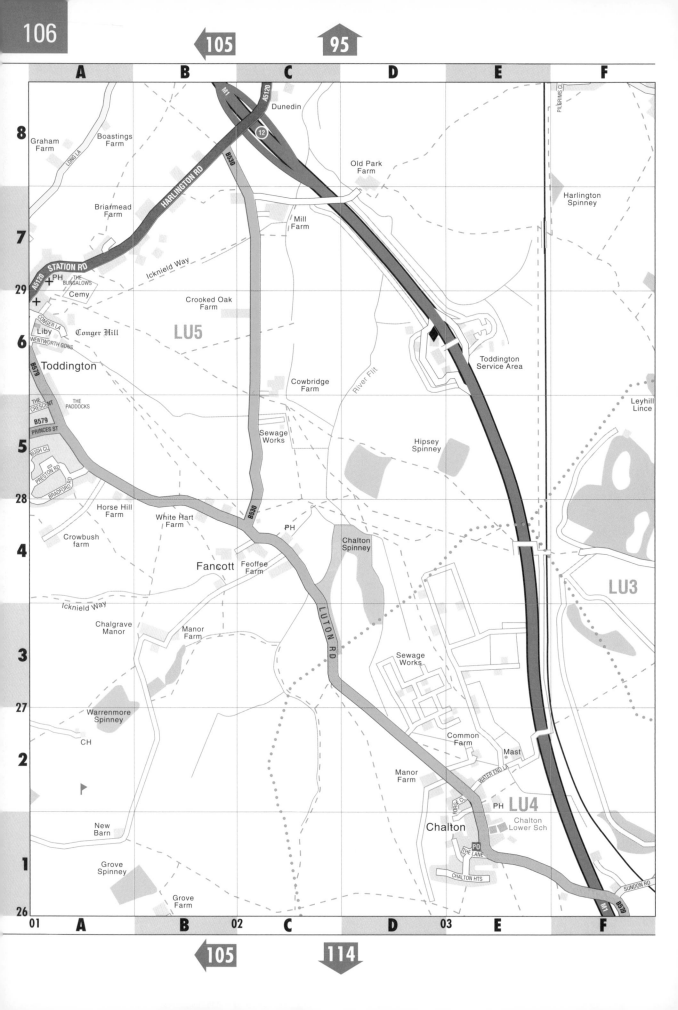

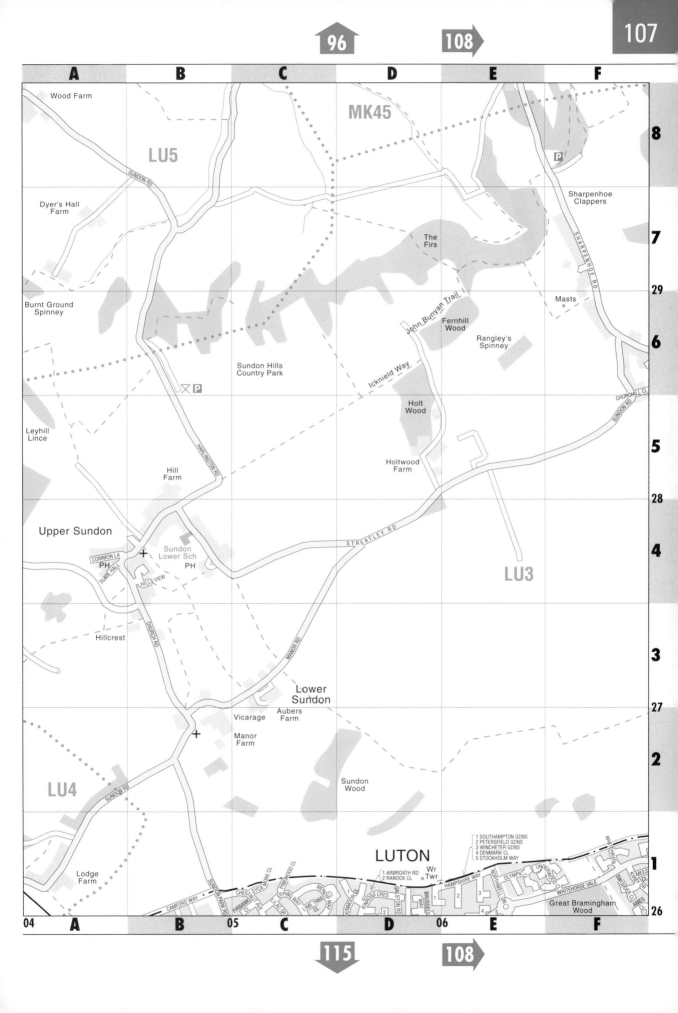

107
97

| | A | B | C | D | E | F |

8

Smithcombe Valley

B655

A6

B655

East Hill

MK45

Leet Wood

Barton Hills

Nature Reserve

Ravensburgh Castle

Smithcombe Hill

Jeremiah's Tree

Bartonhill Cutting

7

Watergutter Hole

Cow Hole

Stonley Wood

29

Top Farm

LUTON RD

6

ST MARGARETS CL

CHURCH RD

CHURCH RD

+ PH

Barton Hill Farm

STANLEY RD

Streatley

5

SHARPENHOE RD

BURY LA

LU3

LU2

Streatley-Bury

28

SHARPENHOE RD

Swedish Cottages

JOHN BUNYAN TRAIL

4

John Bunyan Trail

Icknield Way

BARTON RD

Bury Farm

New Farm

Maulden Firs

3

George Wood

27

Galley Hill

St Margaret's

2

LUTON

Betty Robinson House

Great Bramingham Farm

CH

HAYTON

GATHILL RD

STATHAM

TURNPIKE DR

TURNPIKE DR

1

BURFORD CL

WHITEHORSE VALE

CATISFORD CL

BIRCHWOOD

HAZLESTON CL

IKELTON

DEXTER TOV CL

UNTON CL

CHARNDON CL

QUANTOCK RISE

EDGCOTT CL

ELWINGTON GDNS

FORD WAY

FAIRWAY CL

DANVERS DR

A6

Cardinal Newman High Sch

Warden Hill

ALBURY

KIRBY DR

ALLENDALE

RYEFIELD

FERNHEATH

ASHDALE GDNS

DEXTER CL 1
BALMORE WOOD 2
SPURCROFT 3

CHARD DR

SACOMBE GN

26

| 07 | A | | B | 08 | C | | D | 09 | E | | F |

107
116

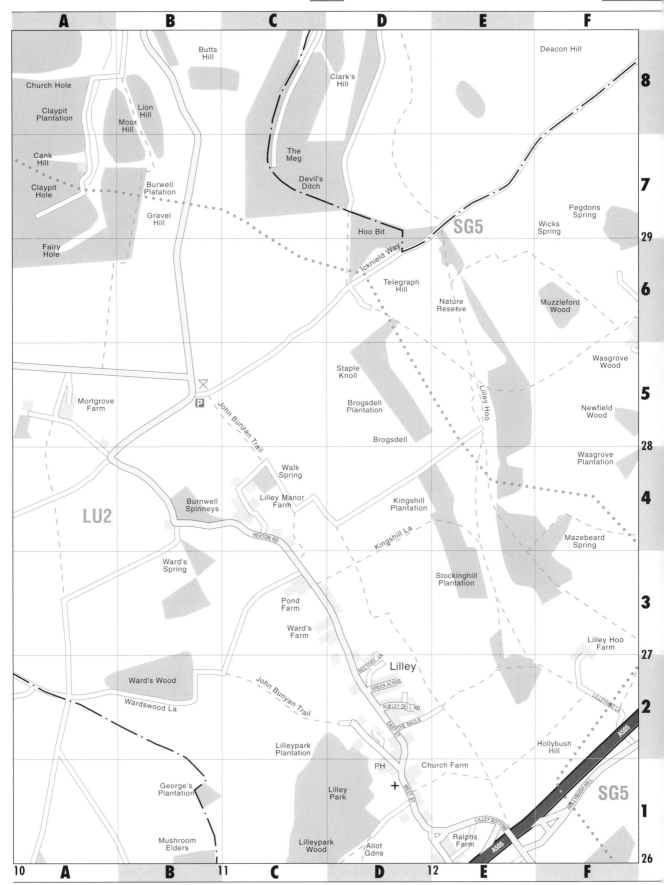

102

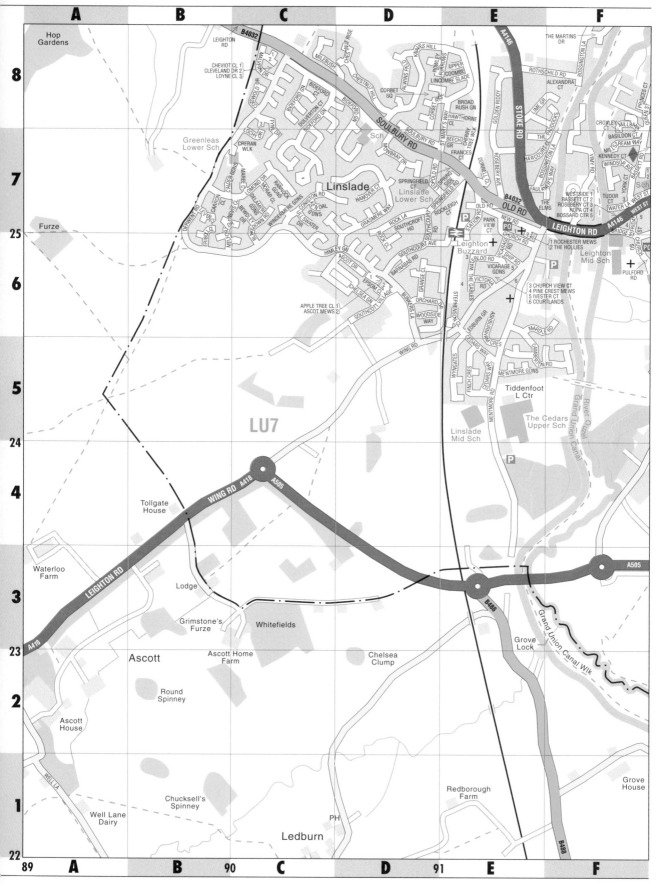

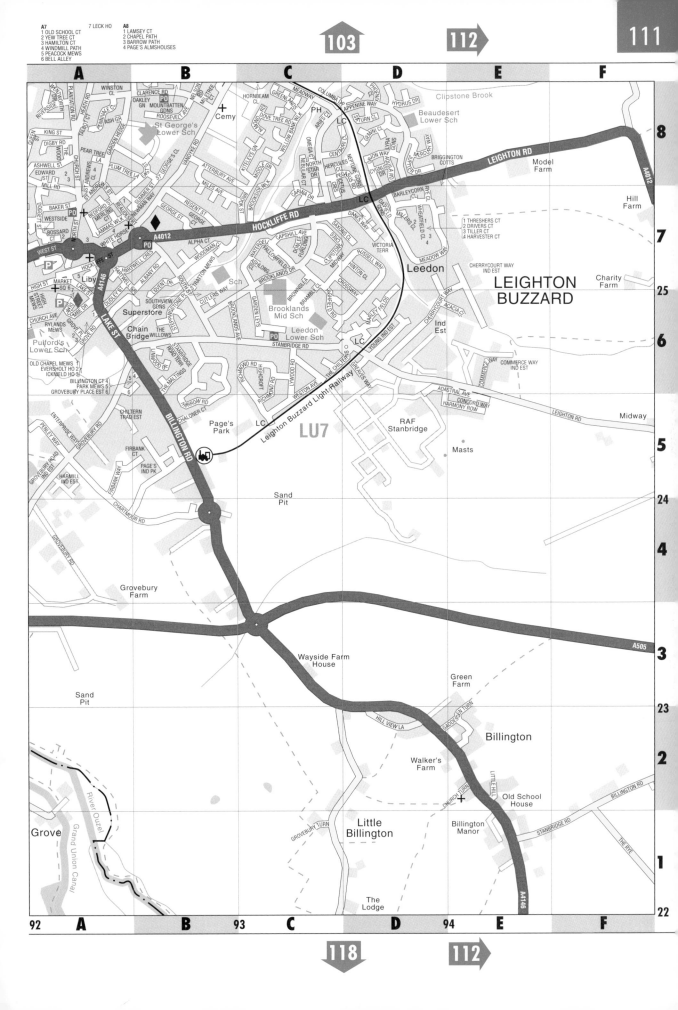

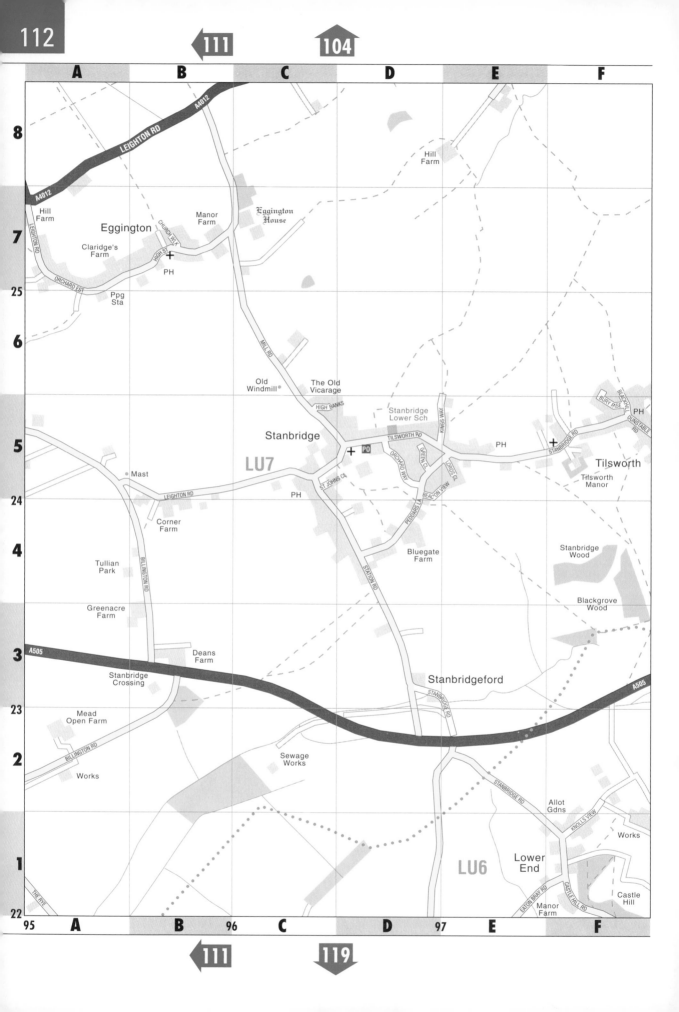

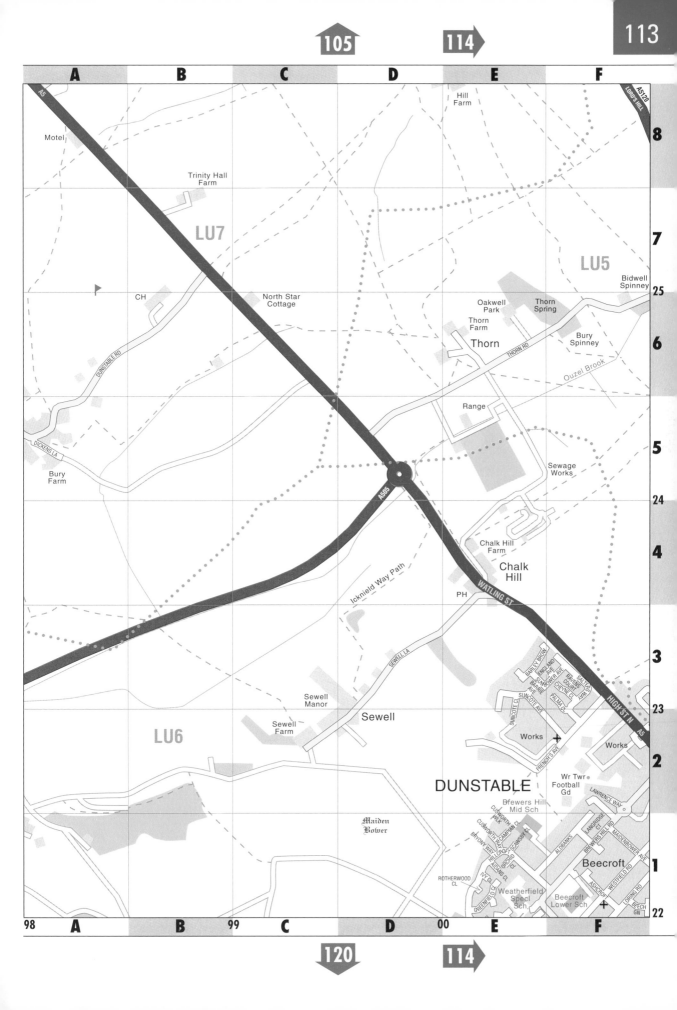

A B C D E F

8

Hill
Farm

Motel

Trinity Hall
Farm

LU7

7

CH

North Star
Cottage

LU5

Bidwell
Spinney

25

DUNSTABLE RD

Oakwell
Park

Thorn
Spring

Thorn
Farm

Thorn

Bury
Spinney

6

THORN RD

DICKENS LA

Ouzel Brook

Bury
Farm

Range

5

Sewage
Works

A505

24

Chalk Hill
Farm

4

Chalk
Hill

Icknield Way Path

PH

WATLING ST

HIGH ST N

A5

3

LORD'S HILL

A5120

SEWELL LA

Sewell
Manor

Sewell

BARLEY BROW
BEECHWOOD AVE
MAYFLOWER AVE
CHEYNE CL
SALTERS
TRAVELL
COURT
PALMA CL

23

Sewell
Farm

SUNCOTE AVE
SUNCOTE CL
SUNCOTE AVE

LU6

Works

Works

2

FRENCH'S AVE

DUNSTABLE

Wr Twr
Football
Gd

LAWRENCE WAY

Maiden
Bower

Bfewers Hill
Mid Sch

CLIFWORTH
WLK
CLIFWORTH CT
CAMPIAN CL
SCAWSBY CL

LANGRIDGE
BFEWERS HILL RD
MAIDENBOWER AVE

1

BRYONY WAY
HILLCROFT
ORCHID
ADKINS CL

ALDBANKS

ASHCROFT
WESTFIELD RD
OPING RD

Beecroft

ROTHERWOOD
CL

Weatherfield
Specl
Sch

Beecroft
Lower Sch

B'ECH
GN

GREENWOOD CT
PT CL

22

98 A B 99 C D 00 E F

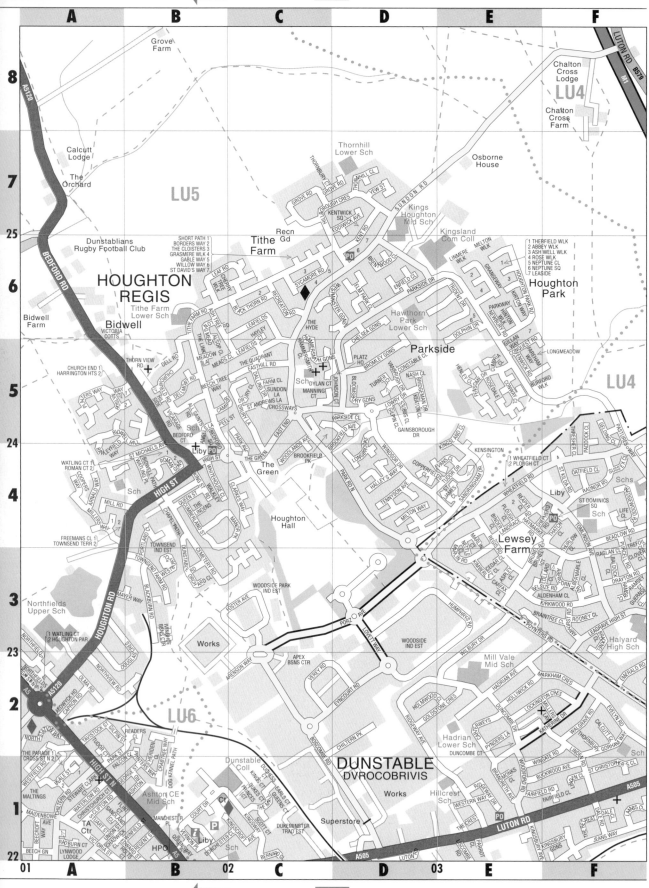

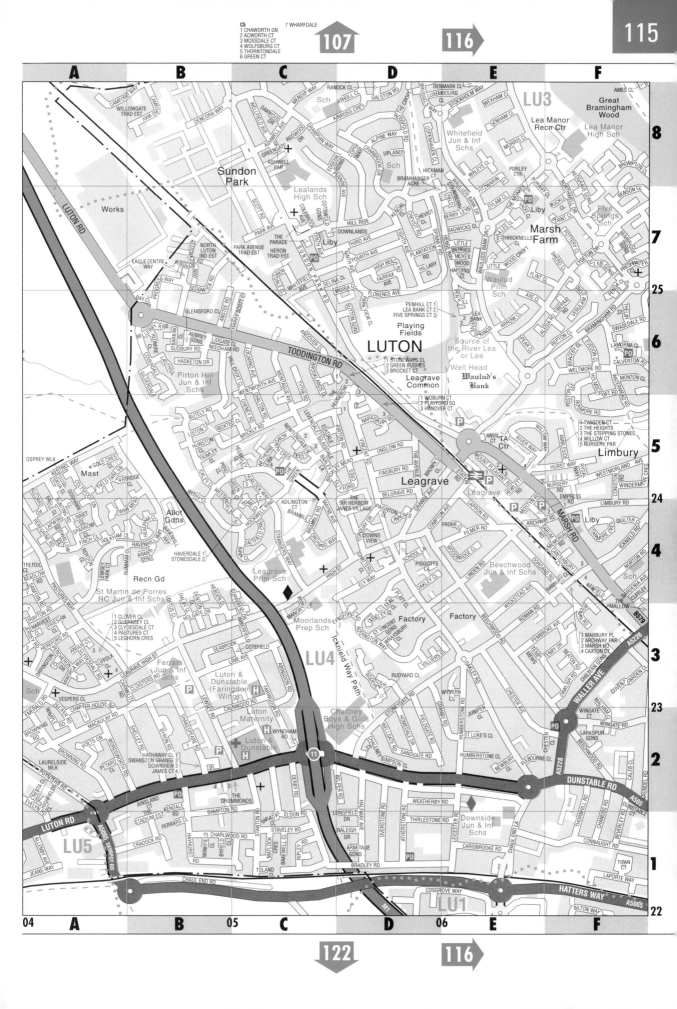

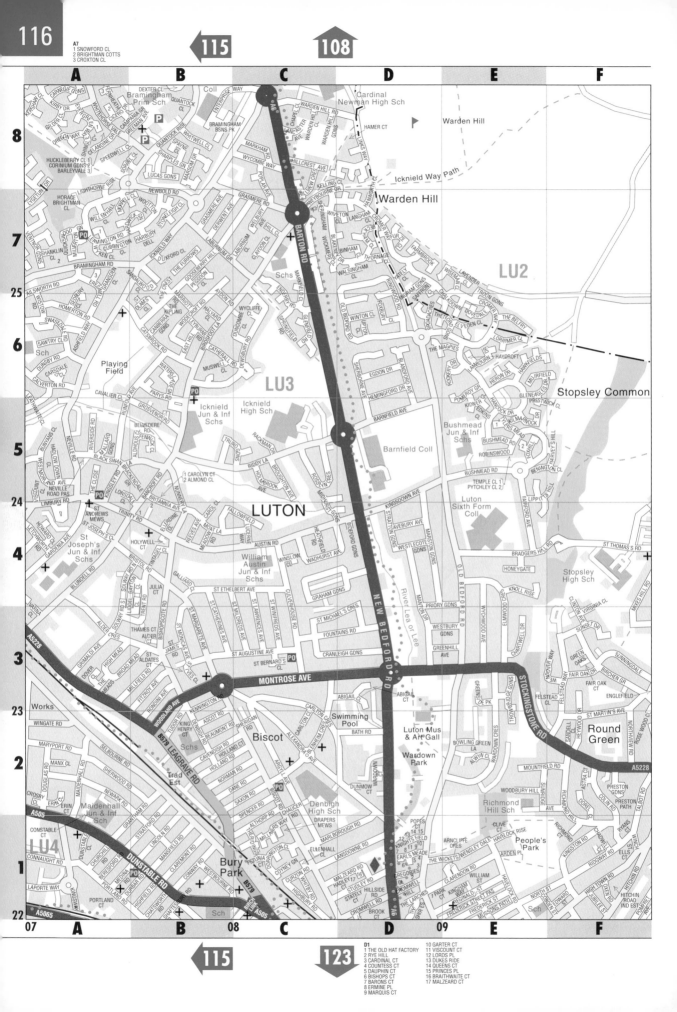

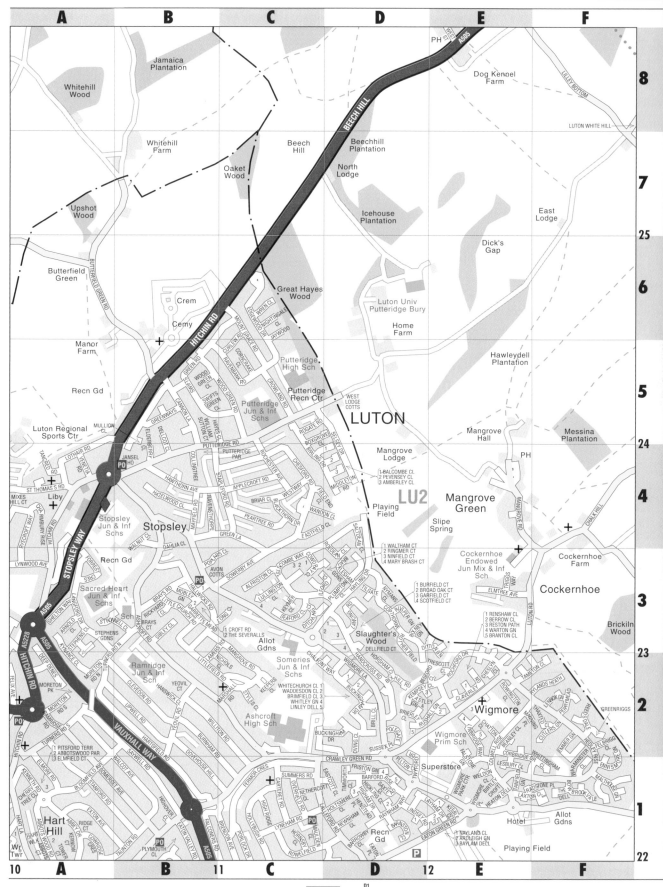

D1
1 CHELSWORTH CL
2 MUTFORD CROFT
3 MELFORD CL
4 PINFORD DELL
5 ALDERTON CL

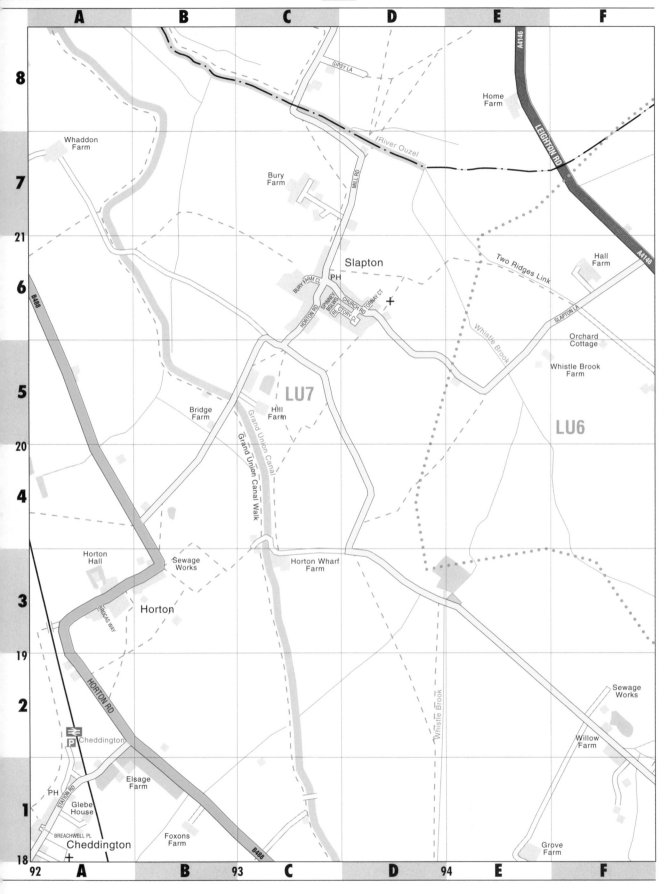

A   B   C   D   E   F

8

7

21

6

5

20

4

3

19

2

1

18

92   A   B   93   C   D   94   E   F

Whaddon Farm

Bury Farm

GIPSY LA

River Ouzel

Home Farm

LEIGHTON RD

A4146

Slapton

PH

Two Ridges Link

Hall Farm

BURY FARM CL

HORTON RD

SPINNEY BALMS

CHURCH RD

TORMAY CT

RECTORY CL

MILL RD

Slapton La

Orchard Cottage

Whistle Brook

Whistle Brook Farm

LU7

LU6

Bridge Farm

Hill Farm

Grand Union Canal

Grand Union Canal Walk

Horton Hall

Sewage Works

Horton Wharf Farm

Horton

BROOK WAY

Whistle Brook

Sewage Works

Willow Farm

HORTON RD

Cheddington

P

STATION RD

Elsage Farm

PH

Glebe House

BREACHWELL PL

Cheddington

Foxons Farm

B488

Grove Farm

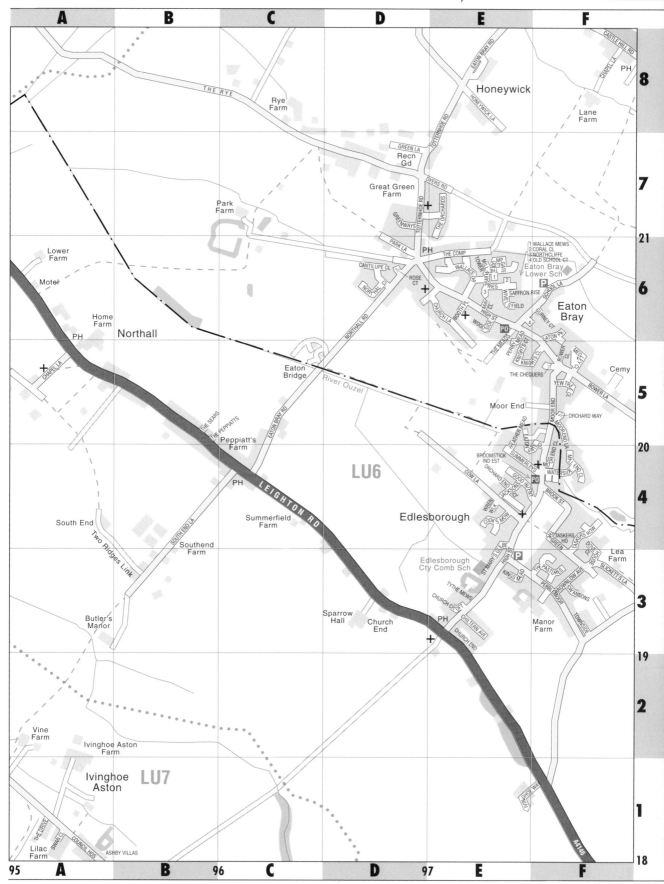

A   B   C   D   E   F

8

Middle
End

Brownlow Rise
Castle Cl
Poplar
Farm

P
Totternhoe Knolls
Nature Reserve

Castle Mill Rd

Saxon Cl 1
Redfield Cl 2
Norman
Way
Weatherby

Green La
Cookfield Cl
Bunhill Cl

Awsombe Cl
Spring Rd
Croft Dr
Beecroft Way
Harmel Cl

Lancot
Lower
Sch

Drovers Way
Worthington
Rank In Pt

7

Totternhoe

Recn
Gd

Dunstable Rd

Harvey Rd
Cl
Gardner's
Mariwa Cr
Beacon Ave
Coombe Dr
The Avenue

Lancot Dr
Oakwell Cl
Totternhoe Rd
Lancot Ave

Melton
Ct

B489
Westdown
Gdns
Meadway
Meadway
Beechwood Ct

21

Church End
Farm
Church Gn
Furlong La
PH
Totternhoe
Lower Sch
Church
End

Allot
Gdns

Brightwell Lane

Ellesmere Ct

Tring Rd

B4541
Whipsnade Rd
Roycrc Cl

Five
Knolls

Pillow
Mounds

Spyondel Cl

The Ride
The Vicarage
Church Rd

Well Head Rd

California
Pascomb
Pit

6

LU6

5

Dunstable Rd
Ware Hill
Cottage

Doolittle Mill
(disused)

Bottom Dr
Manton Rd
Springfield Rd
Icknield Way

Well
Head

London
Gliding Club

CH

20

Bower La

Roseburry
Farm

Wellhead
Farm

P

Robertson
Cnr

4

Bellows
Mill

Harling Rd
Norfolk House
Farm

Harling
House

Tring Rd

Shepherds
Farm

Icknield Way
Farm Cotts

Dunstable Downs

Icknield Way Path

B4541

3

Sluicept's La

Patrick's
Cottage

PH

Icknield Way
Farm

19

Edlesborough
Mills
(disused)

Edlesborough
Hill

B4506

Mast

Sallowspring
Wood

2

Icknield Way

B4540
Dagnall Rd

Valance-end
Farm

P

Sallowsprings

Chute
Farm

1

Tree
Cathedral

Whipsnade
P

18

B489
Willow
Farm

B4506

B4540

98   A   B   99   C   D   00   E   F

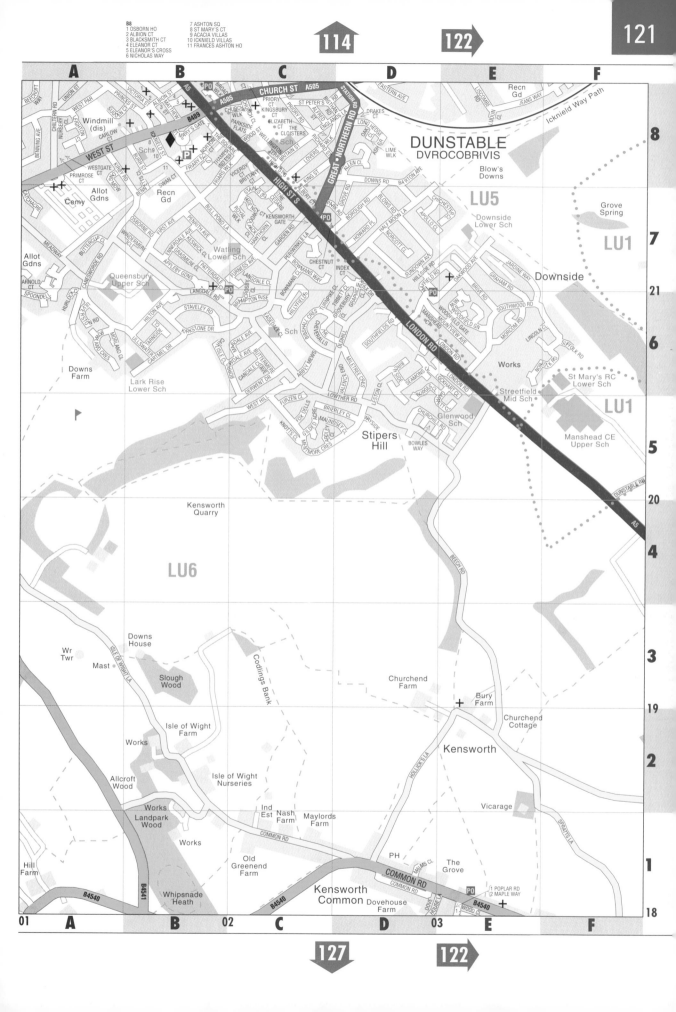

LU5
Skimpot Wood
LU4
Cultivation Terraces
M1
COSGROVE WAY
Foxdell Jun Sch
Works
COULSON CT
BILTON WAY
BILTON WAY
BASINGSWOLD GDNS
WARREN RD
DALLOW RD
KENT RD
HAREFIELD CT
HAREFIELD RD
8

Stanner's Wood
Chaul End Farm
SUMMERFIELD RD
RUNLEY RD

Chaul End
Tunnels

Zouches Farm
Vehicle Compound
Round Wood
WOOD CL
DPTH
BLUEBELL WOOD CL
7

Mast
Twentynine Wood
CH
Bush Wood
Badgerdell Wood
M1
21

Thirty Wood
Blossom Spring
6

Dame Ellen's Wood
LU1
Castlecroft Wood
Brickkiln Farm

Little John's Wood

5

Folly Wood
Manor Farm
COLLINGS WELLS CL
RUSH GN
FOLLY LA
CADRA CL
MANOR CT
LUTON RD
MEADOW CROFT
20

A5
Turnpike Farm
Bury Farm
Cradle Spinney
MEADOW WAY
PH
HEATHFIELD CL
HYDE RD
PO
DELFIELD GDNS
Heathfield Lower Sch
Willowfield Lower Sch
4

Lodge Farm
Gatehouse
DUNSTABLE RD
Garden Centre
MOSSMAN DR
HOLLY FARM CL
HAWTHORN CRES
THE DELL
TAK CRESCENT
ELM AVE
RUSTON RD
FIVE OAKS
Five Oaks Mid Sch
3

Buncer's Wood
Caddington
CROSSLANDS
CULWORTH CL
EDGECOTE CL
THE GLEN
ENSLOW CL
LEDWELL RD
FAIRGREEN
MANOR RD
19

Jockey Farm
MILLFIELD WAY
MANDLE CL
LITTLEGREEN LA
WOODLANDS
Tipplehill Farm
2

LU6
Kensworth House
PH
COTSWOLD BSNS PK
Millfield Farm
Heron Farm
Piper's Farm
MANCROFT RD
Aley Green

MILLFIELD LA
PIPERS LA
Cemy
1

Corner Farm
Lynch Farm
Nurseries
AL3
Cemy
Kensworth Lynch
Hill Farm
A5
18

D7
1 MERSEY PL
2 CHARLOTTES CT
3 CRESTA HO
4 ALMA LINK
5 DUNSTABLE PL
6 PEEL ST

7 PEEL PL
D8
1 THE BARLEYCORN
2 DOWNTON CT
3 BEDFORD GDNS
4 THE MOUNT
5 VILLA CT

6 DEACONS CT
7 ST NINIAN'S CT
8 LANGHAM HO
9 COLLINGDON CT
10 CARDIGAN CT
11 CARDIGAN GDNS

E7
1 WILLIAMSON ST
2 BARBERS LA
3 WALLER STREET MALL
4 CHAPSIDE SQ
5 SMITHS LANE MALL
6 SMITHS SQ

7 THE GALLERY
8 CHURCH ST
9 MELSON SQ

116

124

E8
1 BUTTERWORTH PATH
2 BERKELEY PATH
3 WELBECK RD
4 ALBION ST

F8
1 ENTERPRISE CTR
2 SOUTHLYNN HO
3 HARTWOOD
4 LINDEN CT
5 HYDE HO
6 THE ABBEYGATE BSNS CTR

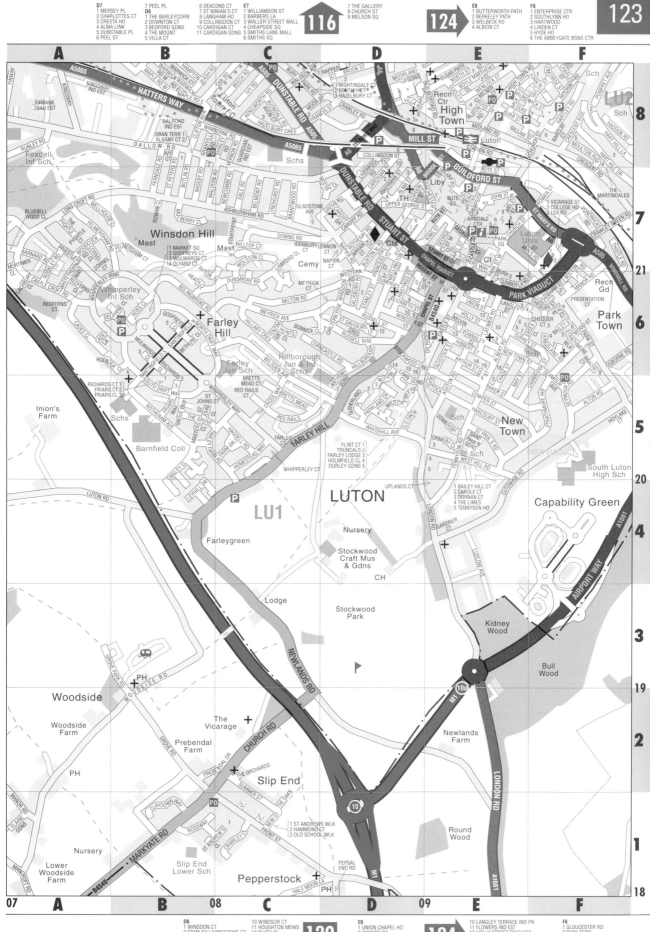

D6
1 WINSDON CT
2 STANLEY LIVINGSTONE CT
3 WELLINGTON CT
4 DUKES CT
5 SPRING PL
6 EBENEZER CT
7 WINDSOR WLK
8 DUMFRIES CT
9 ELIZABETH CT

10 WINDSOR CT
11 HOUGHTON MEWS
12 BLYTH PL
13 BRECON CL
14 HIGH POINT
15 MAPLE CT
16 SMITHS STOCKWOOD CT

129

E6
1 UNION CHAPEL HO
2 OXFORD RD
3 ROBERT ALLEN CT
4 QUEENS CL
5 CHOBHAM WLK
6 ROCHDALE CT
7 ESSEX CT
8 KIRKDALE CT
9 NEW TOWN RD

124

10 LANGLEY TERRACE IND PK
11 FLOWERS IND EST
12 HOLLY STREET TRAD EST
13 HIBBERT STREET ALMSHOUSES
14 JAMES CT
15 TRACEY CT
16 TELMERE IND EST

F6
1 GLOUCESTER RD
2 PARK TERR
3 DES FULLER CT
4 DORSET CT
5 HESWALL CT
6 PARKMEAD
7 KINGSLAND CT
8 OSBORNE CT

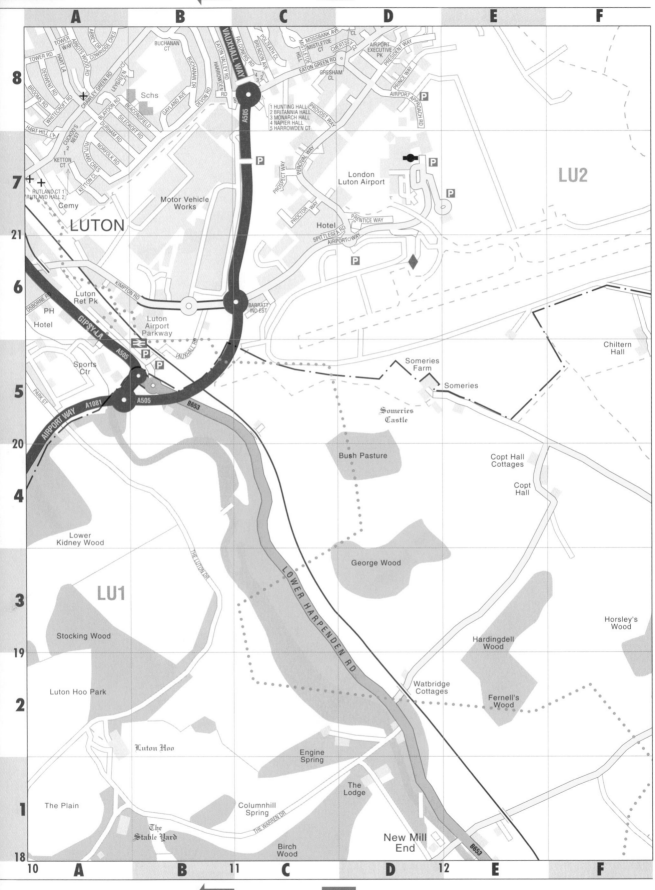

A B C D E F

8

7

21

6

5

20

4

3

19

2

1

18

LU2

Chiltern Hall

LUTON

Motor Vehicle Works

London Luton Airport

1 HUNTING HALL
2 BRITANNIA HALL
3 MONARCH HALL
4 NAPIER HALL
5 HARROWDEN CT.

Hotel

Luton Ret Pk

Luton Airport Parkway

PH Hotel

Sports Ctr

Somaries Farm

Somaries

Someries Castle

Bush Pasture

Copt Hall Cottages

Copt Hall

Lower Kidney Wood

LU1

George Wood

Horsley's Wood

Stocking Wood

Hardingdell Wood

Luton Hoo Park

Watbridge Cottages

Fernell's Wood

Luton Hoo

Engine Spring

The Lodge

The Plain

Columnhill Spring

New Mill End

The Stable Yard

Birch Wood

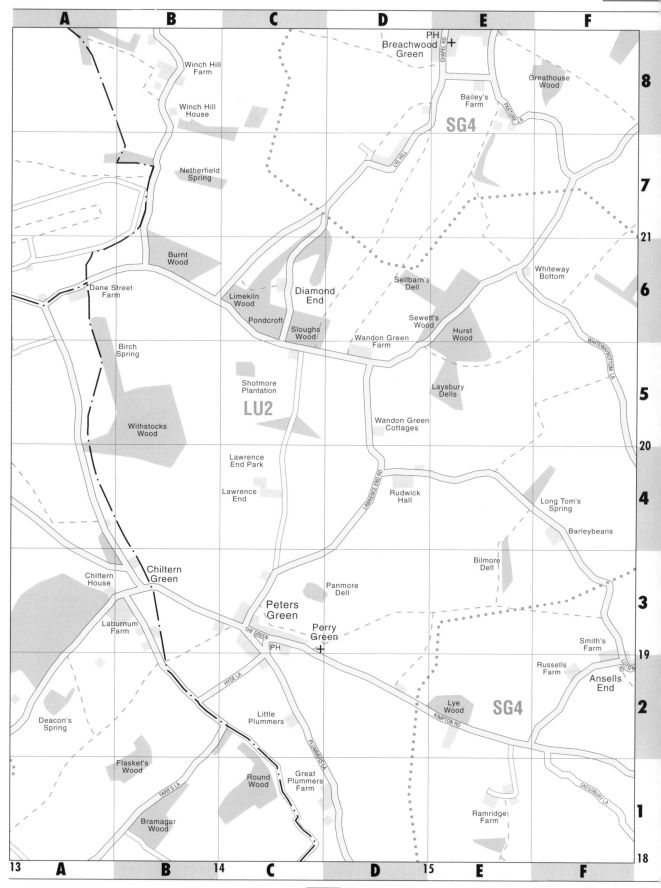

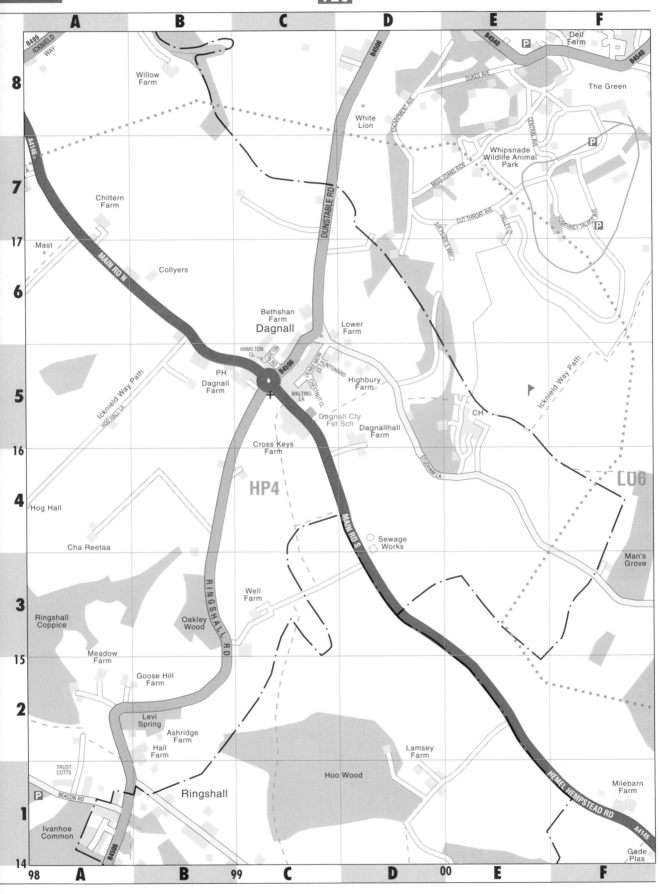

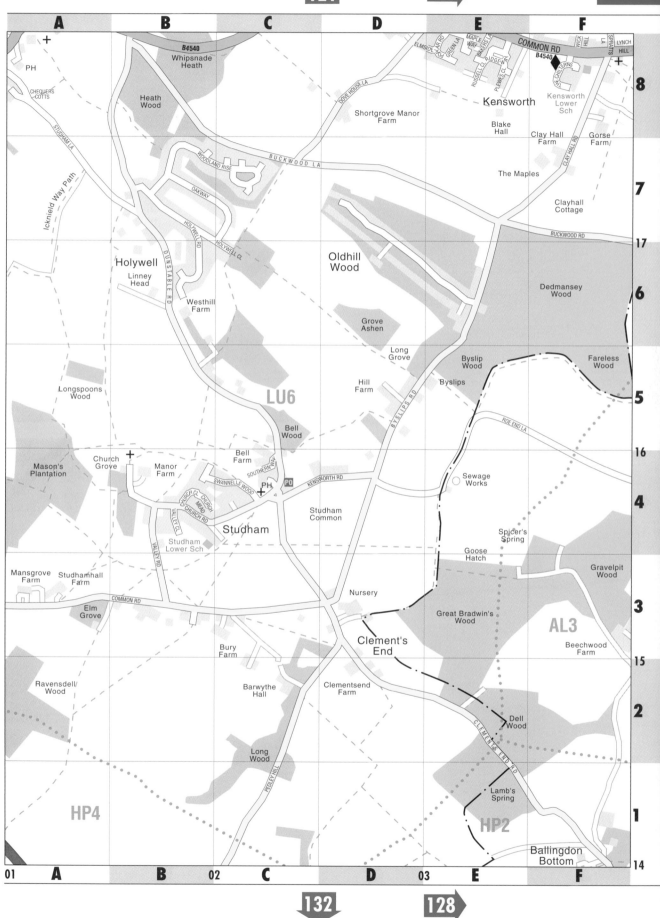

127
122

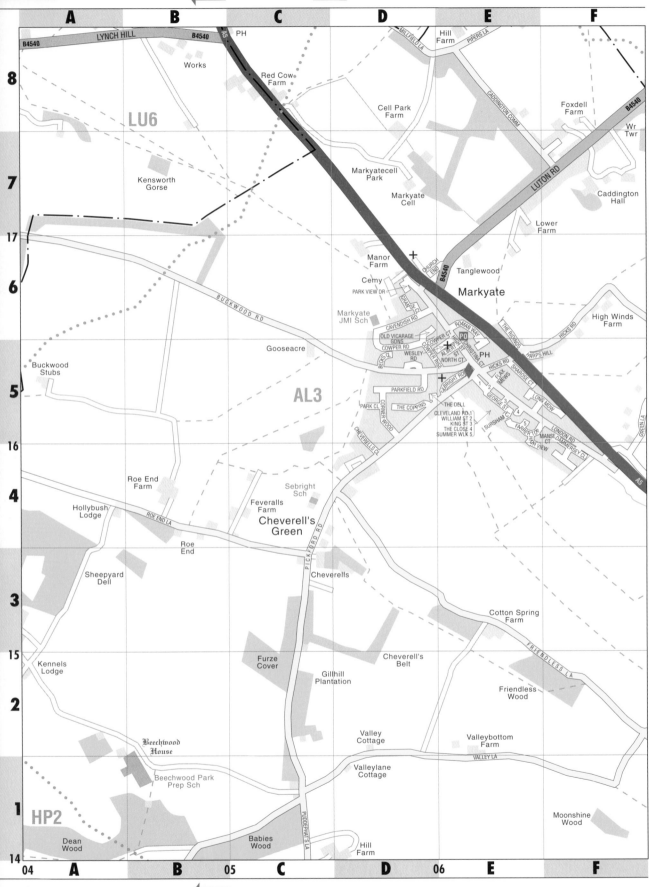

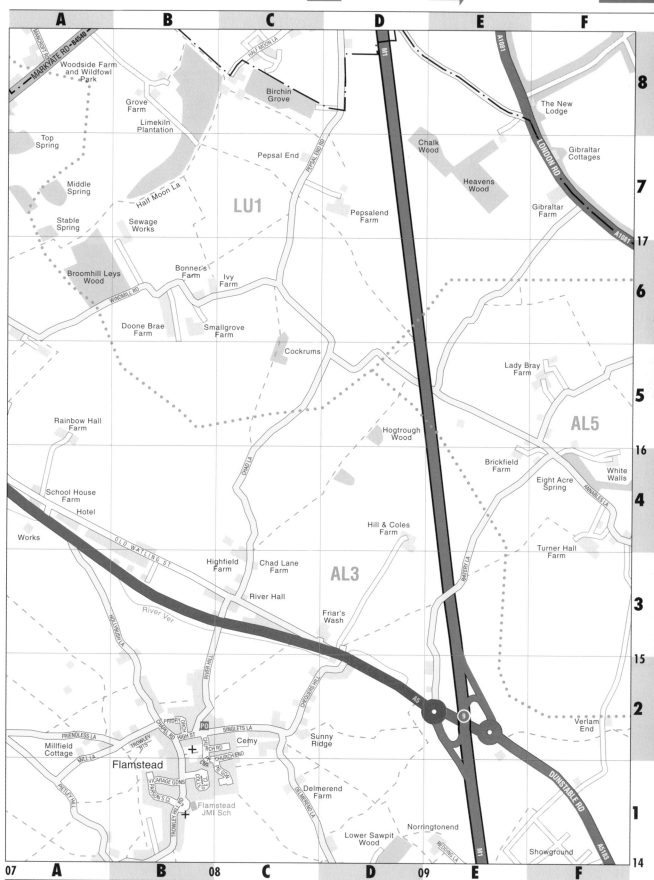

129
124

A **B** **C** **D** **E** **F**

8
Luton Hoo
Home Farm
Hillside
Sewage
Works
East
Hyde
Saw Mill
The Gables
River Lea or Lee
VIADUCT COTTS
SOUTHERN RISE
LOWER HARPENDEN RD
HAMBRO CL
LEE BRIDGE CNR
FAIR'S LA
PH
B653

TARM RD
Tumble
Grove
7
Graves
Wood
LU1
West
Hyde
LU2

LIMETREE AVE
A1081
17
Lady Bute's
Lodge
Circus
Wood
6
LONDON RD

KENNEL LA
Kennels
Farm
Thrales
End
COOTERS END LA
5
Thrales End
Farm
Cooters Hill
Farm

CHAMBERLAINES
SPRING RD
ANNABLES LA
16
THE COMMON
Kinsbourne
Green
PH
PO
PH
KINSBOURNE CRES
LUTON RD
KLONDYKE
Ridgeway
Kings Sch

Long
Spring
Pollard's
Farm
BELMONT RD
KINSBOURNE CL
THE CROSS
CLEVELANDS
VALE CL
GT CLOSE
PENSHURST CL
Cooters End
Farm
AMBROSE LA
4
Dove House
Farm
AL5
TINTERN CL
CROSSPATHS
GREATFIELD
SHEPHERDS WAY
CARPENDERS
TUFFNELLS WAY
REMOLESCROFT
Ridge Ave
LUTON RD

Annables
Farm
KENNESBOURNE
CT
Wood End
JMI Sch
WELLS CL
RIDGEWOOD DR
RIDGEWOOD GDNS
MAYFIELD CL
HOMEDELL
HO
BRAMBLE
CL
ST NICHOLAS
CT
BLOOMFIELD RD
REED
PL
HILLSIDE RD
LAMBOURN
GDNS
3
KINSBOURNE GREEN LA
Faulnkers End
Farm
YEOMANS AVE
ASHLEY GDNS
WOOD END RD
BRACKDALE GR
HASELDEN CL
WOOD END HILL
HIGH RIDGE
WOODLANDS
APPLEWOOD DR
APPLEWOOD CL
Harpenden Rise
OTTERTON CT
ST NICHOLAS
BEECH
CT
BOND
CT
BRIDGE CT
PO
HOLLYBUSH LA
OVERTREES
A1081
15
ROUNDWOOD LA
HOW FIELD
FALCONERS FIELD
ROUNDWOOD PK
THE SPINNEY
ROUNDWOOD GDNS
Park Rise
PARK RISE CL
HARPENDEN RISE
Park Mount
Park Hill
MORETON RD
MORETON END LA
MORETON
PL
Sch
2
Delgarth
Roundwood
Park Sch
St Hilda's
Sch
MEADOWS
ALBERS END LA
MORETON
DOUGLAS RD
CHEPSTOW
TIMBERCROFT
THE
COPPICE
SALISBURY AVE
Roundwood
Prim Sch
CLAYGATE AVE
BROADFIELDS
TANGLEWOOD
AL3
BARNS DENE
HARTWELL GDNS
TOWNSEND LA
TOWNSEND CL
LONGCROFT AVE
MAPLE RD
ROSEBERY AVE
1
Northfield
Spring
Harpenden
Stables
LUTON LA
BADINGHAM DR
PARK AVE
PARK AVE S
ST ANDREW'S
AVE
ROTHAMSTED AVE
ORCHARD AVE
PINDAR RD
KIRKWICK
AVE
14

HARPENDEN

10 **A** **B** **11** **C** **D** **12** **E** **F**

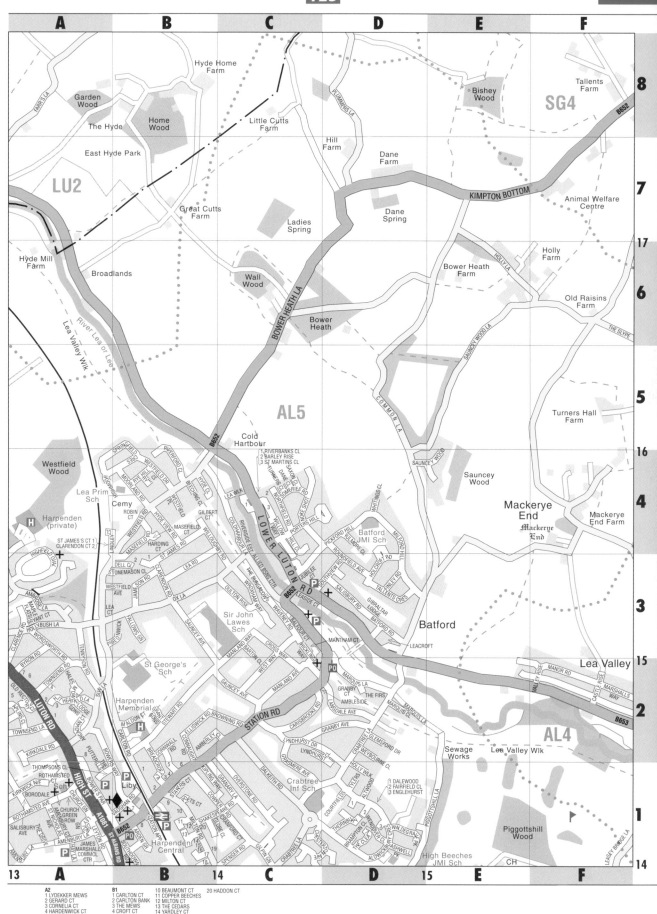

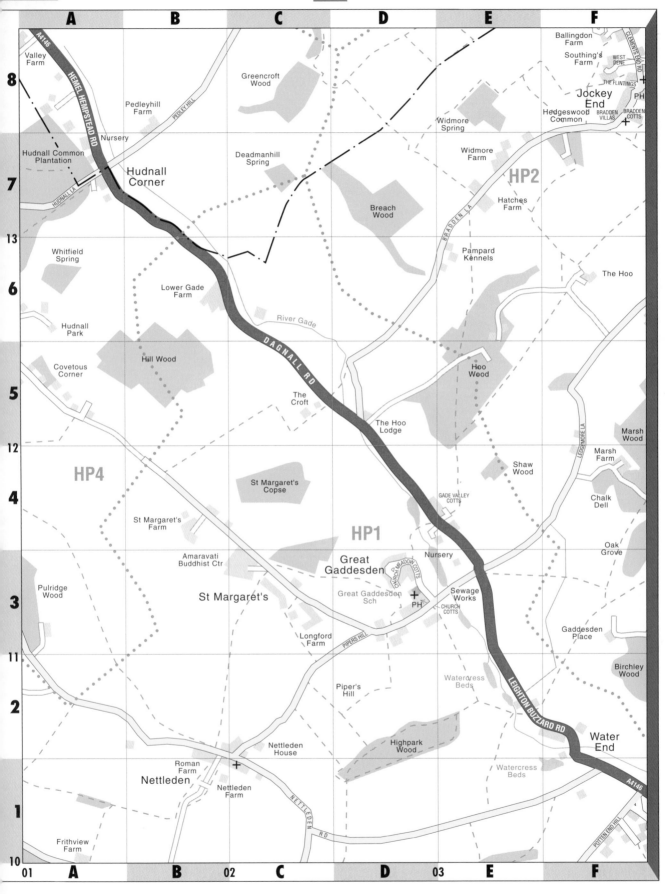

A · B · C · D · E · F

8

7

13

6

5

12

4

3

11

2

1

10

Valley Farm

A4146

HEMEL HEMPSTEAD RD

Hudnall Common Plantation

HUDNALL LA

Pedleyhill Farm

PEDLEY HILL

Nursery

Hudnall Corner

Whitfield Spring

Hudnall Park

Covetous Corner

Lower Gade Farm

Hill Wood

The Croft

DAGNALL RD

River Gade

HP4

St Margaret's Farm

St Margaret's Copse

Amaravati Buddhist Ctr

St Margaret's

Pulridge Wood

Longford Farm

PIPERS HILL

Piper's Hill

Nettleden House

Roman Farm

Nettleden

Nettleden Farm

NETTLEDEN RD

Frithview Farm

Greencroft Wood

Deadmanhill Spring

Breach Wood

The Hoo Lodge

HP1

Great Gaddesden

Great Gaddesden Sch

PH

CHURCH MEADOW COTTS

Nursery

CHURCH COTTS

Highpark Wood

Watercress Beds

Widmore Spring

Widmore Farm

BRADDEN LA

Pampard Kennels

Hoo Wood

Shaw Wood

GADE VALLEY COTTS

Sewage Works

LEIGHTON BUZZARD RD

Watercress Beds

Ballingdon Farm

Southing's Farm

WEST DENE

CLEMENTS END RD

THE FLINTINGS

Jockey End

PH

BRADDEN VILLAS

BRADDEN COTTS

Hedgeswood Common

HP2

Hatches Farm

The Hoo

LEDGEMORE LA

Marsh Wood

Marsh Farm

Chalk Dell

Oak Grove

Gaddesden Place

Birchley Wood

Water End

A4146

POTTEN END HILL

01 · A · B · 02 · C · D · 03 · E · F

Street names are listed alphabetically and show the locality, the Postcode District, the page number and a reference to the square in which the name falls on the map page

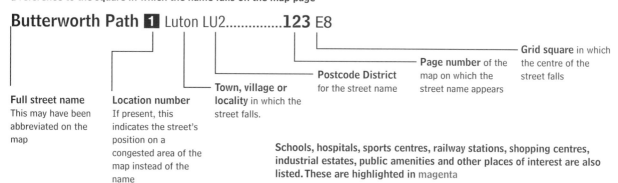

Full street name
This may have been abbreviated on the map

Location number
If present, this indicates the street's position on a congested area of the map instead of the name

Town, village or locality in which the street falls.

Postcode District for the street name

Page number of the map on which the street name appears

Grid square in which the centre of the street falls

Schools, hospitals, sports centres, railway stations, shopping centres, industrial estates, public amenities and other places of interest are also listed. These are highlighted in magenta

Abbreviations used in the index

App	Approach	Cl	Close	Espl	Esplanade	N	North	S	South
Arc	Arcade	Comm	Common	Est	Estate	Orch	Orchard	Sq	Square
Ave	Avenue	Cnr	Corner	Gdns	Gardens	Par	Parade	Strs	Stairs
Bvd	Boulevard	Cotts	Cottages	Gn	Green	Pk	Park	Stps	Steps
Bldgs	Buildings	Ct	Court	Gr	Grove	Pas	Passage	St	Street, Saint
Bsns Pk	Business Park	Ctyd	Courtyard	Hts	Heights	Pl	Place	Terr	Terrace
Bsns Ctr	Business Centre	Cres	Crescent	Ind Est	Industrial	Prec	Precinct	Trad	Trading Est
Bglws	Bungalows	Dr	Drive		Estate	Prom	Promenade	Wlk	Walk
Cswy	Causeway	Dro	Drove	Intc	Interchange	Ret Pk	Retail Park	W	West
Ctr	Centre	E	East	Junc	Junction	Rd	Road	Yd	Yard
Cir	Circus	Emb	Embankment	La	Lane	Rdbt	Roundabout		

Town and village index

Ampthill	84 E6	Cranfield	59 B1	Horton	118 B3
Arlesey	90 A4	Dagnall	126 C6	Houghton Conquest	74 B7
Ascott	110 B2	Dunstable	121 D8	Houghton Regis	114 A6
Aspley Guise	81 F4	Dunton	68 D5	Husborne Crawley	82 A4
Astwick	79 E1	East Hyde	130 F8	Ickleford	100 E4
Astwood	47 A3	Eaton Bray	119 F6	Ickwell	65 E7
Baldock	91 F2	Edlesborough	119 E4	Irchester	7 B7
Barton-le-C	97 D3	Eggington	112 B7	Ivinghoe Aston	119 A1
Bedford	50 D7	Elstow	50 C2	Jockey End	132 F8
Beeston	54 B4	Eversholt	94 B7	Kempston	49 C4
Biddenham	37 C1	Everton	43 C3	Kempston Hardwick	61 D5
Biggleswade	67 C5	Eyeworth	68 F8	Kensworth	121 E2
Billington	111 E2	Felmersham	26 C7	Keysoe	12 B2
Bletsoe	17 C1	Flamstead	129 B1	Kimbolton	6 F5
Blunham	41 E3	Flitton	85 D4	Knotting Green	9 F1
Bolnhurst	19 D4	Flitwick	84 C3	Langford	78 E6
Breachwood Green	125 D8	Gamlingay	44 E6	Lavendon	34 A8
Brogborough	71 D1	Gravenhurst	87 D5	Lea valley	131 F2
Bromham	36 F3	Great Barford	40 F4	Leighton Buzzard	111 E6
Broom	66 C3	Great Gaddesden	132 D3	Letchworth	101 C5
Caddington	122 D3	Great Staughton	13 F6	Lidlington	72 B2
Campton	77 A1	Greenfield	85 C2	Lilley	109 D2
Cardington	51 D4	Guilden Morden	69 F4	Little Barford	32 E6
Carlton	25 B4	Hardmead	46 D4	Little Staughton	13 A2
Caulcott	60 E1	Hargrave	1 E2	Lower Caldecote	54 D2
Chalton	106 E1	Harlington	95 F1	Lower Dean	5 C7
Chawston	31 E5	Harpenden	130 D2	Lower Sundon	107 C3
Cheddington	118 A1	Harrold	24 F6	Luton	123 D4
Chelveston	3 C8	Harrowden	51 A3	Markyate	128 E6
Chicksands	76 E4	Hatley St G	45 F3	Marston Moretaine	72 D8
Church End	90 B7	Haynes	64 A1	Maulden	74 C1
Clapham	37 D7	Haynes Church End	75 B5	Melchbourne	10 D8
Clifton	78 B3	Heath and Reach	103 B5	Meppershall	88 B5
Clophill	86 D8	Henlow	78 D1	Millbrook	73 A2
Cockernhoe	117 F3	Hexton	98 B2	Milton Bryan	93 E1
Cold Brayfield	34 B5	Hinxworth	80 C5	Milton Ernest	27 A5
Colmworth	20 B2	Hitchin	101 B2	Moggerhanger	53 C6
Cople	52 A6	Hockliffe	104 F2	Nettleden	132 B1
Cotton End	63 D7	Holwell	100 B7	Newnham	91 E8
Covington	2 D2	Honeydon	21 B2	Newton Blossomville	34 A4

Newton Bromswold	9 D8	Stewartby	61 C1
North Crawley	58 A6	Stotfold	90 E7
Northall	119 B6	Streatley	108 A5
Oakley	37 A7	Studham	127 C4
Odell	25 C8	Sutton	56 A3
Old Warden	65 B4	Swineshead	11 D8
Pavenham	26 B4	Tebworth	105 C2
Pepperstock	123 C1	Tempsford	42 B8
Pertenhall	12 C8	Thurleigh	18 C1
Peters Green	125 C3	Tilbrook	6 B7
Pirton	99 E4	Tilsworth	112 F5
Podington	7 E2	Tingrith	94 F5
Potton	56 B7	Toddington	105 E6
Pulloxhill	96 E8	Totternhoe	120 B7
Radwell	26 E8	Turvey	34 F6
Ravensden	29 B1	Upper Caldecote	66 B7
Renhold	39 E6	Upper Dean	5 A4
Ridgmont	82 E5	Upper Stondon	88 D4
Ringshall	126 B1	Upper Sundon	107 A4
Riseley	11 A2	Westoning	95 F6
Roxton	31 F1	Wharley End	58 D2
Rushden	8 D8	Whipsnade	120 F1
Salford	70 C3	Wick End	48 B8
Sandy	54 C6	Wilden	29 F3
Sharnbrook	16 B4	Willington	52 B8
Sharpenhoe	96 E2	Wilstead	62 F3
Shefford	77 D3	Wingfield	105 E1
Shillington	87 F1	Woburn	92 F7
Shortstown	51 A2	Woburn Sands	81 A4
Silsoe	86 B4	Woodside	123 A2
Slapton	118 D6	Workhouse End	40 A5
Slip End	123 C2	Wrestlingworth	57 C4
Souldrop	16 B8	Wyboston	32 A5
Southill	77 E8	Wymington	8 B5
St Neots	22 B6	Yelden	4 A2
Stagsden	48 A7		
Stanbridge	112 C5		
Stanford	78 A7		
Steppingley	84 A3		
Stevington	36 B7		

A

Abbey Cl Ampthill MK45 84 F7
Elstow MK42 50 B3
Abbey Dr LU2 117 A1
Abbey Fields MK42 50 B2
Abbey Gr SG19 54 C8
Abbey La MK45 85 A6
Abbey Mews LU6 121 C6
Abbey Mid Sch MK42 50 C3
Abbey Rd MK41 39 A2
Abbey Sq MK43 34 E5
Abbey Way NN10 8 A8
Abbey Wlk
Heath and Reach LU7 103 A4
Houghton Regis LU5 114 E6
Abbeygate Bsns Ctr
The LU2 123 F8
Abbis Orch SG5 100 E5
Abbot Cres MK42 49 D2
Abbots Ct LU2 117 A1
Abbots Wlk 4 SG18 67 A6
Abbots Wood Rd LU2 124 A8
Abbotswood Par LU2 117 A1
Abbotts Rd SG6 101 D6
Abercorn Rd LU4 114 F3
Abigail Cl LU3 116 D3
Abigail Ct LU3 116 D3
Abingdon Rd LU4 115 C3
Acacia Cl LU7 111 E6
Acacia Rd MK42 50 D6
Acacia Villas 9 LU6 121 B8
Ackerman Gdns PE19 22 C2
Ackerman St PE19 22 C2
Acorn Ctr 3 SG18 67 A6
Acorn Ho SG18 66 F7
Acorn Way MK42 50 D5
Acworth Cres LU4 115 C5
Acworth Ct 2 LU4 115 C5
Adams Bottom LU7 103 A1
Adams Cl Ampthill MK45 84 F7
Kempston MK42 49 E1
Adamson Ct MK42 49 D5
Adamson Wlk MK42 49 D5
Adastral Ave LU7 111 E6
Addington Cl
Bedford MK41 39 A1
Henlow SG16 78 D1
Addington Way LU4 115 D3
Addingtons Rd MK44 41 A5
Addison Cl MK42 49 F4
Adelaide Cl MK45 74 B8
Adelaide Sq MK40 38 B1
Adelaide St LU1 123 D7
Adlington Ct LU4 115 C4
Admirals Way PE19 22 A2
Adstone Rd LU1 122 F3
Aelfric Ct MK41 38 C5
Aidans Cl LU6 113 E1
Ailesbury Rd MK45 84 F8
Ailsworth Rd LU3 116 A7
Ainsland Ct LU4 115 B2
Aire Wlk MK41 38 C7
Airport Approach Rd
LU2 124 D8
Airport Executive Pk
LU2 124 D8
Airport Way LU1, LU2 124 A5
Alameda Mid Sch MK45 84 E8
Alameda Rd MK45 84 E8
Alameda Wlk MK45 84 E8
Alamein Ave MK42 50 E6
Alamein Cl SG17 77 C1
Alamein Ct PE19 22 C5
Alban CE Mid Sch MK44 40 F5
Albany Ct LU1 123 B8
Albany Rd Bedford MK40 50 C8
Leighton Buzzard LU7 111 B7
Albermarle Cl LU4 114 F3
Albert Ct LU6 121 C7
Albert Pl Ampthill MK45 84 D6
Houghton Conquest MK45 74 B8
Albert Rd Arlesey SG15 90 A4
Luton LU1 123 E6
Albert St 9 Bedford MK40 38 B1
Markyate AL3 128 E5
Albion Ct
2 Dunstable LU6 121 B8
4 Luton LU2 123 E8
Albion Rd LU2 123 E8
Albion St LU6 121 B8
Albone Way SG18 66 F4
Albone Way Ind Est SG18 66 F4
Alburgh Cl MK42 50 F5
Albury Cl LU3 108 A1
Aldbanks LU6 113 F1
Aldenham Cl Bedford MK41 51 B8
Luton LU4 114 F3
Aldens Mead MK41 38 F4
Alder Cl PE19 22 B6
Alder Cres LU3 116 A3
Alder Ct LU3 116 B3
Alders End La AL5 130 F2
Alders The MK42 49 E3
Alderton Cl 5 LU2 117 D1
Aldgate Cl SG19 56 B7
Aldhous Cl LU3 116 B5
Aldridge Ct SG7 91 E1
Aldwickbury Cres AL5 131 D1
Aldwyck Ct MK42 50 A6
Aldwyck Ho LU5 114 A2
Alesia Rd LU3 115 F6
Alexa Ct MK42 51 A5
Alexander Cl Clifton SG17 78 A2
Alexander Cl *continued*
Stewartby MK43 61 C1
Alexander Rd Stotfold SG5 90 F6
Wrestlingworth SG19 57 B4
Alexandra Ave LU3 116 C2
Alexandra Ct LU7 110 F8
Alexandra Pl 4 MK40 50 B8
Alexandra Rd
Bedford MK40 50 A8
Hitchin SG5 100 F1
Alfred Cope Rd SG19 54 C8
Alfred St Dunstable LU5 121 C8
Irchester NN29 7 A8
Alfriston Cl LU2 117 C3
Alington La SG6 101 F3
Alington Rd PE19 22 E1
All Saints Lower Sch
SG17 78 B2
All Saints Rd Bedford MK40 49 F8
Cople MK44 52 A7
Houghton Regis LU5 114 B5
All Saints Way SG19 54 B8
Allen Cl Bedford MK40 49 F8
Dunstable LU5 121 D8
Allen Ct MK43 60 E1
Allenby Ave LU5 115 A1
Allendale LU3 108 A1
Allhallows Bedford MK40 50 B8
Sandy SG19 54 B8
Allied Bsns Ctr AL5 131 C3
Allton Rd SG16 89 A4
Alma Farm Rd LU5 105 E6
Alma Link 4 LU1 123 D7
Alma St LU1 123 D7
Almer's Cl MK45 74 B8
Almond Cl LU3 116 B4
Almond Dr SG19 44 C5
Almond Rd
Leighton Buzzard LU7 111 C8
St Neots PE19 22 F6
Almonds The MK42 50 A3
Alnwick Cl SG19 54 C8
Alnwick Ct PE19 22 F2
Alpha Ct Kempston MK42 49 D3
Leighton Buzzard LU7 111 B7
Alpine Way LU3 115 D8
Alsop Cl LU5 114 B5
Althorp Cl MK45 84 F3
Althorp Rd LU3 116 C1
Althorpe St MK42 50 B6
Alton Rd LU1 123 F5
Altwood AL5 131 D1
Alwins Field LU7 110 D8
Alwyn Cl LU2 116 E2
Amaravati Buddhist Ctr
HP1 132 C3
Amberley Cl
Harpenden AL5 131 B2
Luton LU2 117 D4
Amberley Gdns MK40 38 D2
Ambleside
Harpenden AL5 131 D2
Luton LU3 115 F5
Ambrose La AL5 130 F4
Amenbury Ct AL5 131 A1
Amenbury La AL5 131 A1
Ames Cl LU3 107 F1
Amhurst Rd LU4 114 F3
Ampthill Ind Est & Bsns Pk
MK45 84 C7
Ampthill Rd Bedford MK42 50 B5
Shefford SG17 76 E2
Silsoe MK45 86 A5
Steppingley MK45 84 D5
Ampthill St MK42 50 C7
Andover Cl LU4 115 C6
Andrew Rd PE19 22 F2
Andrews Cl MK45 74 C1
Angels La LU5 114 B5
Angus Cl LU4 115 A3
Anmer Gdns LU4 115 B4
Annables La AL5 130 A4
Anne St SG18 67 A7
Annes Ct MK42 50 C7
Anson Pl PE19 22 A2
Anstee Rd LU4 115 B6
Anthony Gdns LU1 123 D6
Antonie Farm Cotts MK44 15 F4
Anvil Ct LU3 115 E5
Anvil Ho 8 AL5 131 A2
Apex Bsns Ctr LU5 114 C2
Aplins Cl AL5 131 A2
Apollo Cl LU5 121 D7
Appenine Way LU7 111 D8
Apple Glebe MK45 97 C2
Apple Gr PE19 22 C4
Apple Tree Cl
Biggleswade SG18 67 B5
Leighton Buzzard LU7 110 D6
Appleby Ct PE19 22 E6
Appleby Gdns LU6 121 B7
Applecroft SG16 89 B3
Applecroft Rd LU2 117 C4
Applecross Wlk MK41 39 B3
Applewood Cl AL5 130 E3
Apsley End Rd SG5 98 E6
Aquila Rd LU7 111 D8
Aragon Ct MK45 84 E8
Aragon Pl PE18 6 F5
Aragon Rd MK45 84 F7
Arbour Cl LU3 108 A1
Arbroath Rd LU3 107 D1
Arcade The
15 Bedford MK40 50 B8
Letchworth SG6 101 F6
Arcadian Ct AL5 131 A2
Archers Way SG6 101 D6
Archway Par LU3 115 F4
Archway Rd LU3 115 E4
Arden Gr AL5 131 B1
Arden Pl LU2 116 E1
Arden Wlk MK41 39 B3
Ardleigh Gn LU2 117 E1
Ardley Cl LU6 121 C5
Ardley Hill Lower Sch
LU6 121 C6
Arena Par SG6 101 F6
Arenson Way LU5 114 C2
Argyll Ave LU3 116 C2
Argyll St MK40 38 B2
Aries Ct LU7 111 C8
Arkwright Rd
Bedford MK42 51 A5
Irchester NN29 7 C7
Milton Ernest MK44 27 B5
Arkwright Road Ind Est
MK42 51 A5
Arlesey Ho SG15 90 A8
Arlesey New Rd SG5 101 B7
Arlesey Rd
Church End SG16 89 E8
Henlow SG16 89 D8
Ickleford SG5 100 F5
Arlesey Sta SG15 90 A8
Arlington Ct 14 MK40 38 B1
Armitage Gdns LU4 115 D1
Armour Rise SG4 101 B2
Armstrong Cl MK45 62 F3
Arnald Way LU5 114 A4
Arncliffe Cres LU2 116 E1
Arndale Ctr LU1 123 E7
Arnhem Cl PE19 22 C5
Arnhem Pl SG17 77 C2
Arnold Cl Barton-le-C MK45 97 C2
Luton LU2 117 A3
Arnold Ct LU6 121 A7
Arnold Middle Sch MK45 97 D2
Arnolds La SG7 80 D6
Arran Cl SG19 54 B8
Arran Ct LU1 123 D7
Arrow Cl LU3 115 E6
Arrow Leys MK41 38 F4
Arthur St Ampthill MK45 84 E8
Luton, New Town LU1 123 E6
Arun Cl MK41 38 D5
Arundel Cl MK45 84 D1
Arundel Cres PE19 22 E2
Arundel Ct NN10 8 A8
Arundel Dr MK41 39 A4
Arundel Rd Luton LU4 115 F2
Marston Moretaine MK43 72 C8
Ascot Dr LU7 110 D6
Ascot Mews LU7 110 D6
Ascot Rd LU3 116 B2
Ascott House LU7 110 A2
Asgard Dr MK41 39 D4
Ash Cl Flitwick MK45 84 F2
Irchester NN29 7 A7
Ash Gr Biggleswade SG18 66 F8
Dunstable LU5 121 D8
Leighton Buzzard LU7 111 A8
Ash Rd Biggleswade SG18 67 A7
Luton LU4 123 B8
Ash Tree Rd LU5 114 B6
Ash Well Wlk LU5 114 E6
Ash Wlk MK42 49 F3
Ashburnham Cres LU7 110 E6
Ashburnham Ct MK40 50 A8
Ashburnham Rd
Ampthill MK45 84 E7
Bedford MK40 50 A8
Luton LU1 123 C7
Ashby Ct SG18 78 F6
Ashby Dr Barton-le-C MK45 97 C3
Rushden NN10 8 A8
Upper Caldecote SG18 66 B8
Ashby Villas LU6 119 A1
Ashcroft LU6 113 F1
Ashcroft High Sch LU2 117 C2
Ashcroft Rd LU2 117 B3
Ashdale Ave MK42 49 F5
Ashdale Gdns LU3 108 A1
Ashdown SG6 90 F1
Ashdown Rd SG17 77 E3
Ashfield PE18 6 F5
Ashfield Way LU3 116 A6
Ashington Ct SG17 78 B2
Ashley Gdns
Biggleswade SG18 67 B7
Harpenden AL5 130 D3
Ashlong Cl LU7 111 C7
Ashridge Cl NN10 8 A8
Ashridge Dr MK41 39 C4
Ashton CE Mid Sch LU6 114 B1
Ashton Rd Dunstable LU6 114 B1
Luton LU1 123 E5
Ashton Sq 7 LU6 121 B8
Ashton St Peter CE Sch
LU5 114 C1
Ashwell Ave LU3 115 C8
Ashwell Par LU3 115 C8
Ashwell Pk AL5 131 D1
Ashwell Rd
Guilden Morden SG8 69 F1
Hinxworth SG7 80 E5
Newnham SG7 91 F8
Ashwell St LU7 111 A8
Aspects L Ctr MK41 50 F7
Aspen Ave MK41 38 E4
Asplands Cl MK17 81 B4
Aspley Cl LU4 114 E3
Aspley Ct Bedford MK40 38 A1
Woburn Sands MK17 81 C3
Aspley Guise Lower Sch
MK17 81 F4
Aspley Guise Sta MK17 81 D6
Aspley Hill MK17 81 C4
Aspley La MK17 81 E2
Aspley Rd MK42 50 B6
Astley Gn LU2 117 D2
Aston Rd MK42 51 A5
Astra Ct LU2 116 F2
Astral Cl SG16 89 B3
Astrey Cl MK45 95 F2
Astwick Rd SG5 79 F2
Astwood Cl SG19 56 A8
Astwood Dr MK45 84 D4
Astwood Rd MK43 59 C7
Atherstone Abbey MK41 51 B8
Atherstone Rd LU4 115 D1
Atholl Cl LU3 115 D8
Atholl Wlk MK41 39 B4
Attadale Wlk MK41 39 B4
Atterbury Ave LU7 111 B8
Aubrey Gdns LU4 115 B6
Aubreys SG6 101 F2
Auckland Rd SG18 67 B7
Augustus Rd LU7 104 E2
Austin Canons MK42 50 A6
Austin Cl NN29 7 C8
Austin Rd LU3 116 C4
Avebury Ave LU2 116 D4
Avenells Way SG19 44 D5
Avenue Rd Rushden NN10 8 F5
St Neots PE19 22 F6
Avenue The Ampthill MK45 84 E7
Bedford MK40 50 A8
Biggleswade SG18 67 B6
Bletsoe MK44 17 C1
Blunham MK44 41 D2
Dunstable LU6 120 E7
Flitwick MK45 84 F3
Langford SG18 78 F6
Luton LU4 115 D5
Sandy SG19 54 B7
Stotfold SG5 90 F6
Aviary Wlk MK41 38 C5
Avocet SG6 90 E1
Avocet Cl
Biggleswade SG18 66 F4
Sandy SG19 42 B1
Avon Chase SG16 89 C4
Avon Cotts LU2 117 B3
Avon Ct 17 Harpenden AL5 131 B1
Luton LU1 123 C8
St Neots PE19 22 C3
Avon Dr MK41 38 C5
Avon Rd SG16 89 B4
Avon Rise MK45 84 D2
Avon Wlk LU7 103 B3
Avondale Rd LU1 123 C8
Axe Cl LU3 115 E6
Axis Way PE19 22 B5
Aydon Rd LU3 116 B6
Aylesbury Ct MK41 38 F1
Aylesbury Rd MK41 50 F8
Aylmerton Ct SG17 77 D2
Aylott Cl PE18 5 B4
Aynscombe Cl LU6 120 F8

B

Back La MK44 16 A8
Back St Biggleswade SG18 67 A6
Clophill MK45 75 C1
Luton LU2 123 E8
Badgers Cl MK45 84 E3
Badingham Dr AL5 130 E1
Bagwicks Cl LU3 115 E7
Bailey Hill Ct LU1 123 E5
Bailey St LU1 123 F6
Baileys Villas MK43 26 C8
Baker Ave SG19 56 A8
Baker St Ampthill MK45 84 E8
Leighton Buzzard LU7 111 A7
Luton LU1 123 E5
Baker's La SG19 42 B8
Bakers Cres NN29 7 A8
Bakers La LU6 127 E8
Bakers Wood Cl LU7 103 A6
Bakery Cl MK43 59 B1
Bakery The MK43 36 B7
Bakewell Cl LU4 115 C1
Balcombe Cl LU2 117 D4
Baldock Cl LU4 114 F3
Baldock Rd
Letchworth SG6 101 F4
Stotfold SG5 91 A5
Baldock Sta SG7 91 F1
Baldur Cl MK41 39 D3
Balfour Ct AL5 131 C3
Balham Cl NN10 7 F8
Ballinghall Cl MK41 39 A2
Balliol Lower Sch MK42 49 D3
Balliol Rd MK42 49 D3
Balls La MK44 52 B8
Balmoral Ave MK40 38 D2
Balmoral Cl Flitwick MK45 84 D1
Sandy SG19 42 B1
Balmoral Rd SG5 100 E1
Balmoral Way PE19 22 F2
Balmore Wood LU3 108 B1
Balsall St E 5 MK40 38 B1
Balsall St W MK40 38 B1
Bamburgh Dr MK41 39 A4
Bamford Rd MK42 50 F5
Bamfords La MK43 34 E6
Bamfords Yd MK43 34 E5
Bampton Rd LU4 115 B2
Banbury Cl LU4 115 F4
Bancroft Ave SG18 66 B2
Bancroft Rd LU3 116 B5
Bank Cl LU4 115 C4
Bank's Rd SG18 67 B7
Banks Cl MK43 72 C7
Bar La SG19 45 E3
Barber End SG17 77 D3
Barbers La 2 LU1 123 E7
Barclay Ct LU2 123 F8
Barford Ave MK42 50 D6
Barford Rd Blunham MK44 41 C3
St Neots PE19 22 E2
Willington MK44 40 C7
Barford Rise LU2 117 D1
Barker's La MK41 51 A8
Barkers Cl MK45 84 E6
Barkers Piece MK43 60 D1
Barking Cl LU4 115 B6
Barley Brow LU6 113 E3
Barley Ct PE19 22 D5
Barley La LU4 115 C5
Barley Rd PE19 22 C3
Barley Rise AL5 131 C4
Barley Way MK41 39 A3
Barleycorn Cl LU7 111 D7
Barleycorn The 1 LU3 123 D8
Barleyfield Way LU5 114 A4
Barleyvale LU3 116 A8
Barnabas Rd LU7 110 D6
Barnard Ave MK42 49 C3
Barnard Cl PE19 22 F1
Barnard Rd LU1 123 A7
Barncroft MK43 34 E6
Barndell Cl SG5 90 F6
Barnes Cl PE19 22 E6
Barnes Rd MK43 60 F6
Barnett Cl SG18 67 A6
Barnfield Ave LU2 116 D5
Barnfield Coll
Luton, Farley Hill LU1 123 B5
Luton, Stopsley Common
LU2 116 D5
Luton, Warden Hill LU3 116 B8
Barnhill MK41 39 A2
Barns Dene AL5 130 E2
Barns The MK44 11 A2
Barnstaple Rd MK40 38 E2
Barnston Cl LU2 117 D1
Barnwell Dr NN10 8 A8
Baron Ct PE19 22 B4
Barons Ct 7 LU2 116 D1
Barratt Ind Est LU2 124 C6
Barrie Ave LU6 113 E3
Barringer Way PE19 22 F7
Barrington Rd
Letchworth SG6 101 F4
Rushden NN10 8 C8
Barrow Path 3 LU7 111 A8
Barrowby Cl LU2 117 D1
Barton Ave LU5 121 D8
Barton Cl AL5 131 C3
Barton Ind Est MK45 97 A4
Barton Rd
Barton-le-C MK45 97 B7
Bedford MK42 50 F5
Gravenhurst MK45 87 C4
Harlington MK45 96 A2
Hexton SG5 98 A1
Luton LU3 116 C7
Sharpenhoe MK45 96 F2
Silsoe MK45 86 C3
Bartram Ct MK42 49 C3
Basildon Ct LU7 110 F7
Bassett Ct LU7 110 F7
Bassett Rd LU7 110 F7
Batcheldor Gdns MK43 36 E1
Batford JMI Sch AL5 131 D4
Batford Rd AL5 131 D3
Bath Abbey MK41 51 B8
Bath Pl SG17 78 B3
Bath Rd LU3 116 D2
Battison St MK40 50 B8
Battle Abbey MK41 39 B1
Battlesden Ave MK17 104 C8
Baulk La SG19 45 F3
Baulk The Beeston SG19 54 B6
Biggleswade SG18 67 B6
Clapham MK41 37 F7
Lilley LU2 109 D2
Potton SG19 56 C6
Bay Cl LU4 115 B6
Baylam Dell LU2 117 E1
Beachampstead Rd PE19 13 F6
Beacon Ave LU6 120 E7
Beacon Rd HP4 126 A1
Beacon View LU7 112 D5
Beaconsfield LU2 124 B8
Beaconsfield St MK41 38 B2
Beadlow Rd LU4 114 F4
Beale St LU6 114 A1
Beancroft Rd MK43 60 B1
Beanley Cl LU2 117 E2
Bearton Ct SG5 100 E1
Bearton Gn SG5 100 D1
Bearton Rd SG5 100 E1
Beatrice St MK42 50 A5
Beatty Rd PE19 22 B2
Beauchamp Cl PE19 22 B3
Beauchamp Ct 9 MK40 38 A1
Beauchamp
Mid Sch MK41 38 C5
Beauchamp Rd MK43 61 A7
Beaudesert LU7 111 A7
Beaudesert Lower Sch
LU7 111 D8
Beaufort Way MK41 38 C6
Beaulieu Way MK41 38 E5
Beaumanor Pl SG17 76 E3
Beaumont Ct 10 AL5 131 B1
Beaumont Gdns MK42 49 E3
Beaumont Ho MK40 37 F2

Beaumont Rd
Flitwick MK45 . . . . .84 E3
Luton LU3 . . . . .116 B2
Beaver Cl PE19 . . . . .22 B5
Bec Rd PE19 . . . . .22 E5
Becher Cl MK41 . . . . .39 F5
Beckett Ct 3 MK40 . . . . . . .50 B8
Beckett St MK40 . . . . .50 B8
Becketts Cl MK45 . . . . .74 B1
Beckham Cl LU2 . . . . .116 D7
Becks Cl AL3 . . . . .128 D5
Bedesman La MK42 . . . . . .50 C7
Bedford Ave MK45 . . . . . . .86 C4
Bedford Bsns Ctr MK42 .50 D4
Bedford Cl SG5 . . . . .87 E2
Bedford Coll MK42 . . . . . . .50 B7
Bedford Coll of Physical Ed
MK40 . . . . .38 A1
Bedford Ct LU5 . . . . .114 B5
Bedford Gdns 3 LU2 . . . .123 D8
Bedford High Sch MK40 . .38 B1
Bedford Hospl
(NorthWing) MK40 . . . . .38 D1
Bedford Hospl
(SouthWing) MK42 . . . . .50 B6
Bedford Midland Sta
MK40 . . . . .50 A8
Bedford Modern Sch
MK41 . . . . .37 F3
Bedford Mus MK40 . . . . . . .50 C8
Bedford Rd
Aspley Guise MK17 . . . . . . .81 F5
Barton-le-C MK45 . . . . .97 C3
Brogborough MK43 . . . . . . .82 C8
Cardington MK44 . . . . .51 C5
Caulcott MK43 . . . . .60 E2
Clapham MK41 . . . . .37 F5
Clophill MK45 . . . . .86 C8
Cold Brayfield MK46 . . . . . .34 B5
Cranfield MK43 . . . . .59 C2
Cranfield MK43 . . . . .60 A3
Great Barford SG18 . . . . . . .40 E4
Haynes SG18 . . . . .64 E5
Hitchin SG5 . . . . .100 D2
Hitchin, Westmill SG5 . . . .100 D1
Houghton Conquest MK45 . .62 A1
Houghton Regis LU5 . . . . .114 A6
Kempston MK42 . . . . .49 E4
Kempston Hardwick MK45 . .61 F5
Letchworth SG6 . . . . .101 D7
Lower Stondon SG16 . . . . . .89 B3
Marston Moretaine MK43 . .72 D8
Milton Ernest MK44 . . . . . .27 B3
Moggerhanger MK44 . . . . . .53 B7
Northill SG18 . . . . .53 B2
Ravensden MK44 . . . . .28 E1
Roxton MK44 . . . . .31 E2
Rushden NN10 . . . . .8 D5
Sandy SG19 . . . . .54 B7
Shefford SG17 . . . . .77 B4
Stagsden MK43 . . . . .36 C1
Turvey MK43 . . . . .35 B5
Wick End MK43 . . . . .48 B7
Willington MK44 . . . . .52 B7
Wilstead MK45 . . . . .62 D5
Wilstead, Duck End MK45 . .62 C7
Wootton MK43 . . . . .61 A8
Bedford Road Lower Sch
MK42 . . . . .49 E4
Bedford Sch MK40 . . . . . . .38 C1
Bedford Sq LU5 . . . . .114 B5
Bedford St Ampthill MK45 . .73 E1
Leighton Buzzard LU7 . . . .111 A7
St Neots PE19 . . . . .22 E6
Woburn MK17 . . . . .92 F7
Bedford St Johns Halt
MK42 . . . . .50 B7
Beeby Way MK43 . . . . .25 A3
Beech Ave SG18 . . . . .66 F8
Beech Cl MK45 . . . . .85 D2
Beech Cres NN29 . . . . .7 A7
Beech Ct 5 Bedford MK40 . .38 A1
Harpenden AL5 . . . . .130 F3
Beech Gn LU6 . . . . .114 A1
Beech Gr
Leighton Buzzard LU7 . . . .110 E7
St Neots PE19 . . . . .22 F6
Beech Hill
Letchworth SG6 . . . . .101 D7
Luton LU2 . . . . .117 D8
Beech Hill Prim Sch LU4 116 B1
Beech Rd Dunstable LU6 . .121 E4
Flitwick MK45 . . . . .84 F2
Luton LU1 . . . . .123 C8
Beech Tree Way LU5 . . . .114 B5
Beech Wlk MK42 . . . . .49 F3
Beechdale Rd MK42 . . . . . .50 C5
Beecnes The MK45 . . . . . . .86 C4
Beeching Cl AL5 . . . . .131 B4
Beechside SG19 . . . . .44 C6
Beechwood Cl SG5 . . . . . .100 D2
Beechwood Ct LU6 . . . . . .120 F7
Beechwood Inf Sch LU4 .115 E4
Beechwood Jun Sch
LU4 . . . . .115 E4
Beechwood Park Prep Sch
AL3 . . . . .128 B1
Beechwood Rd LU4 . . . . . .115 E3
Beechwood Rise SG17 . . . .77 D2
Beecroft Lower Sch LU6 113 F1
Beecroft Way LU6 . . . . . . .121 A8
Beeston Gn SG19 . . . . .54 B5
Beezling Cl PE19 . . . . .22 C6
Begwary Cl PE19 . . . . .22 C6
Belam Way SG19 . . . . .42 B1
Belfry Cl MK42 . . . . .50 B4
Belfry Ct SG19 . . . . .54 C7
Belfry The LU2 . . . . .116 E6

Belgrave Rd LU4 . . . . .115 D5
Bell Alley 6 LU7 . . . . .111 A7
Bell Cl MK45 . . . . .95 E6
Bell Foundry Cl SG19 . . . . .44 D5
Bell La MK45 . . . . .63 D7
Bellamy Rd MK43 . . . . .60 F6
Bellerby Rise MK45 . . . . . .115 B6
Bellevue Cl SG19 . . . . .55 F7
Bellingham Pl SG18 . . . . . . .67 B7
Bellway MK17 . . . . .81 A6
Belmont Rd LU1 . . . . .123 C7
Belper Rd LU4 . . . . .115 D2
Belsize Rd LU4 . . . . .114 F3
Belvedere Rd LU3 . . . . . . .116 B5
Belvoir NN10 . . . . .8 C8
Belvoir Wlk MK41 . . . . .39 A4
Bembridge Gdns LU3 . . . .115 F7
Benedict NN10 . . . . .7 F8
Benington Cl LU2 . . . . . . .116 D4
Bennetts Cl Bletsoe MK44 . .17 C1
Dunstable LU6 . . . . .121 B7
Benning Ave LU6 . . . . .121 A8
Benson Cl LU3 . . . . .115 F7
Bentley Cl SG18 . . . . .78 F6
Bentley Ct LU1 . . . . .123 C8
Bents Cl MK41 . . . . .37 D7
Berberry Dr MK45 . . . . .85 E4
Bereford Cl MK44 . . . . .40 F7
Beresford Rd
Bedford MK40 . . . . .50 E8
Luton LU4 . . . . .116 A1
Berkeley Cl SG18 . . . . .67 A4
Berkeley Ct 6 AL5 . . . . . . .131 A2
Berkeley Path 2 LU2 . . . .123 E8
Berkeley Rd MK42 . . . . . . .50 C4
Berkley Ct PE19 . . . . .22 F4
Berkley St PE19 . . . . .22 F4
Bernard Cl LU5 . . . . .114 C1
Berrill St NN29 . . . . .7 A7
Berrow Cl LU2 . . . . .117 E2
Berry Dr MK43 . . . . .36 E2
Berry End MK17 . . . . .83 A1
Berry La MK17 . . . . .81 F6
Berry Leys LU3 . . . . .115 E7
Berwick Way SG19 . . . . . . .54 C8
Besford Cl LU2 . . . . .117 E2
Bessemer Cl SG5 . . . . . . .100 E2
Bethune Cl LU1 . . . . .123 B6
Betony Wlk NN10 . . . . .8 B8
Beverley Cres MK40 . . . . . .37 F1
Beverley Gdns MK45 . . . . .86 C8
Beverley Gr MK41 . . . . .37 E1
Beverley Gr MK42 . . . . .37 E1
Beverley Rd LU4 . . . . .115 F1
Bevery Cl MK43 . . . . .37 A8
Bewcastle Cl MK41 . . . . . . .39 A5
Bewdley Dr LU7 . . . . .110 C7
Bexhill Rd LU2 . . . . .117 D2
Bibshall Cres LU6 . . . . . . .121 C6
Bickerdikes Gdns SG19 . . .54 B8
Biddenham Turn MK40 . . . .37 D1
Biddenham Upper Sch
MK40 . . . . .49 D8
Bideford Cl LU7 . . . . .110 C8
Bideford Gdns LU3 . . . . . .116 D4
Bideford Gn LU7 . . . . .110 C8
Bidwell Hill LU5 . . . . .114 B5
Bidwell Path LU5 . . . . . . .114 B4
Biggleswade Hospl SG18 .67 C4
Biggleswade Rd
Dunton SG18 . . . . .68 B5
Sutton SG19 . . . . .55 E4
Upper Caldecote SG18 . . . .66 C8
Biggleswade Sta SG18 . . . .67 A5
Bigtham Rd LU5 . . . . .121 C8
Bilberry Pl PE19 . . . . .22 C5
Bilberry Rd SG17 . . . . .78 B3
Billington Cl MK45 . . . . . . .84 D3
Billington Ct LU7 . . . . .111 B6
Billington Rd
Billington LU7 . . . . .112 A2
Stanbridge LU7 . . . . .112 B4
Bilsdon Cl NN10 . . . . .7 F8
Bilton Rd SG4 . . . . .100 F2
Bilton Way LU1 . . . . .115 F1
Binder Cl LU4 . . . . .114 E4
Bindon Abbey MK41 . . . . . .51 A8
Bingen Rd SG5 . . . . .100 C1
Binham Cl LU2 . . . . .116 D7
Birch Cl Broom SG18 . . . . . .66 C2
Clifton SG17 . . . . .77 D2
Birch Gr SG19 . . . . .54 B6
Birch Link LU4 . . . . .116 C1
Birch Rd SG18 . . . . .67 A7
Birch Side LU6 . . . . .121 D6
Birch's Cl LU7 . . . . .104 F2
Birchdale Ave MK42 . . . . . .49 F4
Birchen Gr LU2 . . . . .116 F3
Birches The SG6 . . . . .101 E8
Birchfield Rd MK44 . . . . . . .40 E7
Birchmead SG19 . . . . .44 C6
Bird Ct MK45 . . . . .62 E4
Bird's Hill LU7 . . . . .103 A5
Birdsfoot La LU3 . . . . .116 B6
Birkdale Rd MK41 . . . . .38 E5
Birling Dr LU2 . . . . .117 C4
Birse Gn MK41 . . . . .39 B4
Birtley Croft LU2 . . . . .117 E1
Biscot Rd LU3 . . . . .116 C2
Bishops Cl 6 LU3 . . . . . . .116 D1
Bishops Rd Bedford MK41 . .39 B1
St Neots PE19 . . . . .22 F2
Bishops Wlk MK17 . . . . . . .92 F8
Bishopscote Rd LU3 . . . . .116 B3
Bittern Dr SG18 . . . . .66 F5
Bittern Way SG6 . . . . .90 E1
Black Hat Cl MK45 . . . . . . .62 E4

Black Swan La LU3 . . . . . .116 A5
Black Thorn Rd LU5 . . . . .114 C6
Blackbird Cl MK45 . . . . . . .84 D2
Blackbird St SG19 . . . . . . .56 A7
Blackburn Cl MK42 . . . . . . .51 B2
Blackburn Rd LU5 . . . . . . .114 B3
Blackfriars NN10 . . . . .7 F8
Blackhill LU7 . . . . .112 F5
Blackhill La MK45 . . . . .96 E8
Blacksmith Cl
Everton SG19 . . . . .43 C3
Stotfold SG5 . . . . .90 F7
Blacksmith Ct 3 LU6 . . . .121 B8
Blackthorn Dr LU2 . . . . . . .117 C4
Blackthorn Gr MK17 . . . . . .81 A4
Blackwood Rd PE19 . . . . . .22 B3
Blair Way PE19 . . . . .22 B2
Blakedown Rd LU7 . . . . . .110 C7
Blakelands MK45 . . . . .97 D2
Blakeney Dr LU2 . . . . .116 C7
Blakes Way PE19 . . . . .22 B2
Blandford Ave LU2 . . . . . .116 D6
Blaydon Rd Luton LU2 . . .124 A8
Sandy SG19 . . . . .42 C2
Blenheim Cl Rushden NN10 .8 A8
St Neots PE19 . . . . .22 C4
Blenheim Cres LU3 . . . . . .116 C2
Blenheim Link MK45 . . . . . .84 D1
Blenheim Rd MK42 . . . . . . .51 A2
Bliss Ave Cranfield MK43 . .59 C2
Shefford SG17 . . . . .77 D3
Bloomfield Ave LU2 . . . . . .117 A1
Bloomfield Dr MK42 . . . . . .77 B2
Bloomfield Rd AL5 . . . . . . .130 F3
Bloomsbury Cl MK17 . . . . . .92 F6
Bloomsbury Gdns LU5 . . .114 D5
Blows Cl LU1 . . . . .121 D7
Bluebell Cl Bedford MK42 . .50 A4
Biggleswade SG18 . . . . . . .67 C4
Flitwick MK45 . . . . .84 D3
Rushden NN10 . . . . .8 C8
Bluebell Rise NN10 . . . . .8 B8
Bluebell Wood Cl LU1 . . . .123 A7
Blundell Pl MK42 . . . . .50 C4
Blundell Rd LU3 . . . . .116 A4
Blunham Rd
Biggleswade SG18 . . . . . . .66 F5
Moggerhanger MK44 . . . . . .53 C8
Blyth Pl 12 MK41 . . . . . . .123 D6
Blythe Way SG19 . . . . .44 D5
Boddington Gdns SG18 . . .67 B6
Boddington Ind Est SG18 .67 B6
Bodiam Way PE19 . . . . .22 F2
Bodmin Rd MK42 . . . . .115 F3
Bolingbroke Rd LU1 . . . . . .123 B6
Bolney Gn LU2 . . . . .117 D3
Bolton Rd LU1 . . . . .123 F7
Bond Ct AL5 . . . . .130 F3
Bonds La SG18 . . . . .67 A5
Bonnick Cl LU1 . . . . .123 C6
Boot La SG18 . . . . .68 D5
Booth Pl LU6 . . . . .119 E6
Boothey Cl SG18 . . . . .67 A7
Borden La SG18 . . . . .64 C5
Borders Way LU5 . . . . . . .114 C6
Borodale AL5 . . . . .131 A1
Borough Rd LU5 . . . . .121 D7
Borrowdale Ave LU6 . . . . .121 C6
Borton Ave SG16 . . . . .89 B4
Boscombe Rd LU5 . . . . . . .114 C2
Bosmore Rd LU3 . . . . .115 F5
Bossard Ct LU7 . . . . .111 A7
Bossard Ctr LU7 . . . . .110 F7
Bossington La
Leighton Buzzard LU7 . . . .110 F8
Leighton Buzzard,
Linslade LU7 . . . . .110 F7
Boswell Ct 12 MK40 . . . . . .38 B1
Boswell Dr SG5 . . . . .100 E4
Boswell Pl 7 MK40 . . . . . .38 B1
Boteler Gdns MK42 . . . . . .50 F5
Bothy The LU6 . . . . .66 C2
Bottom Dr LU6 . . . . .120 D5
Boughton Dr MK45 . . . . .8 A8
Boughton End La MK43 . . .72 B1
Boulevards 7 MK40 . . . . . .50 B8
Boundary The MK41 . . . . . .39 A2
Bourne End La MK44 . . . . .17 A4
Bourne End Rd
Cranfield MK43 . . . . .59 C4
Kempston MK43 . . . . .48 B1
Bourne Rd MK41 . . . . .10 F2
Bourneside MK41 . . . . .38 D6
Bow Brickhill Rd MK17 . . . .81 A4
Bowbrook Vale LU2 . . . . . .117 F1
Bower Cl LU6 . . . . .119 F5
Bower Heath La AL5 . . . . .131 C6
Bower La LU6 . . . . .119 F5
Bower St MK40 . . . . .50 D8
Bower's Mill PE19 . . . . .22 E5
Bower's Par AL5 . . . . .131 A1
Bowers Cl MK44 . . . . .11 B3
Bowers La MK44 . . . . .11 B3
Bowers Way AL5 . . . . .131 A1
Bowhill MK41 . . . . .38 D7
Bowland Cres LU6 . . . . . . .121 A6
Bowles Way LU6 . . . . .121 D5
Bowling Green La LU2 . . . .116 E2
Bowling Green Rd MK43 . .59 C1
Bowmans Cl LU6 . . . . .121 C6
Bowmans Way LU6 . . . . . .121 C7
Bowyer's Cl SG5 . . . . .100 D1
Box End Rd MK43 . . . . .48 F2
Boxgrove Cl LU2 . . . . .117 C0
Boxgrove Priory MK41 . . . .39 E7
Boxted Cl LU4 . . . . .115 C6
Boyde Gdns MK40 . . . . . . .49 E7
Boyle Cl LU2 . . . . .123 D6

Brace St 17 MK40 . . . . . . .50 B8
Braceby Cl LU3 . . . . .115 F6
Brache Ct LU1 . . . . .123 C6
Brache The MK45 . . . . .74 C1
Bracken Pl MK41 . . . . .39 B1
Brackendale Gr
Harpenden AL5 . . . . .130 D3
Luton LU3 . . . . .116 B5
Bracklesham Gdns LU2 . .117 D3
Brackley Rd MK42 . . . . . . .50 C5
Bracknell Cl LU4 . . . . .114 F4
Bradden Cotts HP2 . . . . . .132 F8
Bradden La HP1, HP2 . . . . .132 E7
Bradden Villas HP2 . . . . . .132 F8
Bradford Rd LU5 . . . . .106 A5
Bradford Way LU5 . . . . . . .105 F5
Bradgate Rd MK40 . . . . . . .38 D1
Bradgers Hill Rd LU2 . . . .116 E4
Bradley Rd LU4 . . . . .115 D1
Bradleys Cnr SG4 . . . . . . .101 C1
Bradshaws Cl MK45 . . . . . .97 C3
Braemar Cl MK40 . . . . .50 A8
Braeside MK41 . . . . .38 F4
Bragenham La MK17 . . . . .102 D5
Braggs La SG19 . . . . .57 C4
Braintree Cl LU4 . . . . .114 F3
Braithwaite Ct 16 LU3 . . .116 D1
Bramble Cl
Harpenden AL5 . . . . .130 D3
Leighton Buzzard LU7 . . . .111 C7
Luton LU4 . . . . .115 C4
Bramble Rd LU4 . . . . .115 C4
Brambles MK45 . . . . .62 F4
Brambling Cl SG19 . . . . . . .42 C2
Bramhanger Acre LU3 . . . .115 D7
Bramingham Bsns Pk
LU3 . . . . .116 B8
Bramingham Prim Sch
LU3 . . . . .116 B8
Bramingham Rd LU3 . . . . .115 F6
Bramley Cl SG7 . . . . .91 F1
Brampton Cl Bedford MK42 50 D3
Harpenden AL5 . . . . .131 D1
Brampton Park Rd SG5 . . .100 E1
Brampton Rise LU6 . . . . . .121 C6
Brancaster Cl MK42 . . . . . .50 F4
Brancker Ave LU5 . . . . .51 A2
Brandreth Ave LU5 . . . . . .114 E1
Brandreth Pl SG19 . . . . . . .54 D6
Brangwyn Gdns MK41 . . . .38 B3
Branton Cl LU2 . . . . .117 E2
Brantwood Rd LU1 . . . . . .123 C7
Braybrook SG19 . . . . .54 A8
Braybrooks Dr SG19 . . . . . .56 A7
Brayes Manor SG5 . . . . . . .90 F6
Brays Ct LU2 . . . . .117 B3
Brays Rd LU2 . . . . .117 B3
Brazier Cl MK45 . . . . .97 B3
Breachwell Pl LU2 . . . . . . .118 A1
Breadcroft La AL5 . . . . . . .131 C1
Breamish Wlk MK41 . . . . . .38 C7
Brecon Cl 13 LU1 . . . . . . .123 D6
Brecon Way MK41 . . . . . . .123 D6
Brendon Ave Bedford MK41 38 E3
Luton LU2 . . . . .117 C1
Brentwood Cl LU5 . . . . . . .114 D6
Brereton Rd MK40 . . . . . . .50 B8
Brett Dr MK43 . . . . .36 F1
Bretts Mead LU1 . . . . .123 C5
Bretts Mead Ct LU1 . . . . .123 C5
Brewers Hill Mid Sch
LU6 . . . . .113 C1
Brewers Hill Rd LU6 . . . . .113 F1
Brewery La Ampthill MK45 .73 E1
Baldock SG7 . . . . .91 E1
Brian May Gr MK45 . . . . . .86 B3
Brian Rd MK45 . . . . .96 A2
Briar Cl Ampthill MK45 . . . .84 E8
Luton LU2 . . . . .117 C4
Briar Patch La SG6 . . . . . .101 D3
Briars The MK42 . . . . .49 F3
Brickfield Rd MK41 . . . . . . .39 B6
Brickhill Cl Blunham MK44 .41 E3
Sandy SG19 . . . . .54 D8
Brickhill Dr MK41 . . . . .38 C4
Brickhill Lower Sch MK41 38 D5
Brickhill Rd
Heath and Reach LU7 . . . .103 A7
Sandy SG19 . . . . .54 D7
Brickle Pl SG17 . . . . .78 B2
Brickly Rd LU4 . . . . .115 C5
Bridge Ct AL5 . . . . .130 F3
Bridge Rd Bedford MK42 . .50 C6
Letchworth SG6 . . . . .101 F6
Bridge St
Leighton Buzzard LU7 . . . .110 F7
Luton LU1 . . . . .123 E8
Turvey MK43 . . . . .34 D5
Bridge View MK40 . . . . . . .50 D8
Bridgeman Dr LU5 . . . . . .114 D5
Bridgend MK43 . . . . .25 B4
Bridle Dr MK41 . . . . .37 C7
Brierley Cl Dunstable LU6 121 D5
Luton LU2 . . . . .117 C0
Briggington Cotts LU7 . . . .111 D8
Brigham Gdns SG18 . . . . . .67 A6
Brightman Cotts 2 LU3 . .116 A7
Brightmans Dr MK45 . . . . .74 B1
Brightwell Ave LU6 . . . . . .120 C7
Brill Cl LU2 . . . . .117 D2
Brimfield Cl LU2 . . . . .117 C0
Brindley Cl SG19 . . . . .42 B1
Brinsmade Rd MK45 . . . . . .73 C1
Bristol Rd LU3 . . . . .116 B4
Britain St LU5 . . . . .121 C8
Britannia Cl LU3 . . . . .116 B4
Britannia Hall LU2 . . . . . . .124 C4
Britannia Rd MK42 . . . . . . .50 B6

Brittains Rise SG16 . . . . . .88 E2
Brittany Ct LU6 . . . . .121 C8
Britten Cl NN9 . . . . .3 C8
Britten Rd SG17 . . . . .77 D3
Brittons Cl MK44 . . . . .16 E3
Brittons La MK17 . . . . .70 C3
Brive Rd LU5 . . . . .121 C6
Brixham Cl MK40 . . . . .38 E2
Broad Ave MK42 . . . . .50 D4
Broad Mead LU3 . . . . .116 A3
Broad Oak Ct LU2 . . . . . . .117 D3
Broad Rush Gn LU5 . . . . . .110 E8
Broad St SG17 . . . . .78 B2
Broad Wlk Clifton SG17 . . .78 B2
Dunstable LU5 . . . . .121 B8
Broad Wlk The PE19 . . . . . .22 E3
Broadacres MK45 . . . . .116 D6
Broadcroft SG6 . . . . .101 F2
Broadfields AL5 . . . . .130 F2
Broadhurst Abbey MK41 . .51 A8
Broadmead SG18 . . . . .67 B5
Broadmead Bsns Pk
MK43 . . . . .61 C2
Broadmead Ind Sch LU1 123 E5
Broadmead Lower Sch
MK43 . . . . .61 C2
Broadmead Rd MK43 . . . . .61 C2
Broadwater Ave SG6 . . . . .101 E5
Broadwater Dale SG6 . . . .101 E5
Broadway
Houghton Conquest MK45 . .74 B8
Letchworth SG6 . . . . .101 F5
Broadway Ct SG6 . . . . . . .101 E5
Broadway The MK40 . . . . . .38 B1
Brocas Way LU7 . . . . .118 A3
Brocket Ct LU4 . . . . .115 D5
Brockwell MK43 . . . . .37 A8
Brockwood Cl SG19 . . . . . .44 D6
Bromham Lower Sch
MK43 . . . . .36 A3
Bromham Rd
Biddenham MK40 . . . . .37 D1
Bromham MK40 . . . . .37 A2
MK43 . . . . .37 A2
Bromham Watermill
MK43 . . . . .37 A2
Bromley Gdns LU5 . . . . . .114 D5
Brompton Cl LU3 . . . . .115 F4
Brook Cl Henlow SG16 . . . .78 D1
Upper Caldecote SG18 . . . .66 B8
Brook Ct LU3 . . . . .116 D1
Brook Farm Cl NN10 . . . . . .8 B5
Brook La Flitton MK45 . . . . .85 D6
Great Barford MK44 . . . . . .41 A5
Harrold MK43 . . . . .24 F6
Newton Blossomville MK43 . .34 B3
Renhold MK41 . . . . .39 B6
Upper Dean PE18 . . . . .5 D7
Brook Rd
Marston Moretaine MK43 . . .72 C4
St Neots PE19 . . . . .22 C4
Brook St Bedford MK42 . . .50 D5
Edlesborough LU6 . . . . . . .119 F4
Hargrave NN9 . . . . .1 E3
Leighton Buzzard LU7 . . . .111 C7
Luton LU2 . . . . .123 D8
St Neots PE19 . . . . .22 B5
Stotfold SG5 . . . . .90 E6
Brook Way MK43 . . . . .36 E2
Brookend Dr MK45 . . . . . . .97 B3
Brookes Rd MK45 . . . . .84 F3
Brookfield Ave LU5 . . . . . .114 C5
Brookfield Pk LU5 . . . . . . .114 C5
Brookfield Rd MK41 . . . . . .38 F2
Brookfields
Pavenham MK43 . . . . .26 C4
Potton SG19 . . . . .56 B7
Brooklands MK42 . . . . .49 B2
Brooklands Ave LU7 . . . . .111 B6
Brooklands Cl LU5 . . . . . . .115 C6
Brooklands Dr LU7 . . . . . .111 C7
Brooklands Mid Sch
LU7 . . . . .111 C6
Brooklands Rd MK44 . . . . . .10 F1
Brookmead SG17 . . . . .88 C6
Brookside Campton SG17 . .87 F8
Great Barford MK44 . . . . . .41 A5
Letchworth SG6 . . . . .101 F5
Meppershall SG17 . . . . . . .88 C6
Renhold MK41 . . . . .39 B7
Shillington SG5 . . . . .87 C1
Brookside Wlk LU7 . . . . . .111 C7
Brookvale Cotts SG16 . . . .88 B3
Broom Crossroads SG18 . .66 A1
Broom Hall MK43 . . . . .66 C2
Broomhills Rd LU7 . . . . . .103 A1
Brooms Rd LU2 . . . . .124 A8
Broomstick Ind Est LU6 . .119 C6
Broughton Ave Luton LU3 116 C5
Toddington LU5 . . . . .105 E6
Broughton Rd MK17 . . . . . .70 C3
Brown's Cl LU4 . . . . .115 D5
Brown's Cres MK45 . . . . . .95 F3
Brown's Sq PE19 . . . . .22 F5
Browney Path MK41 . . . . . .38 C7
Browning Dr PE19 . . . . . . .22 C6
Browning Rd
Harpenden AL5 . . . . .131 C2
Luton LU4 . . . . .115 C4
Brownlow Ave LU6 . . . . . .119 F3
Brownlow Rise LU6 . . . . . .120 A8
Browns Cl MK43 . . . . .72 D7

Browns Way MK17 . . . . .81 E5
Brownshill MK45 . . . . .74 C1
Brownslea LU7 . . . . .111 C7
Broxley Mead LU4 . . . . . .115 D5
Bruce Rd MK42 . . . . .49 D3
Brunel Ct LU4 . . . . .114 E3
Brunel Rd Bedford MK41 . .51 A8
Luton LU4 . . . . .114 E3
Brunswick Cl SG18 . . . . . .67 A6
Brunswick St LU2 . . . . . .123 F8
Brunt's La SG18 . . . . .66 F6
Brussels Way LU3 . . . . . .115 D8
Bruthwaite Gn MK41 . . . .39 C4
Bryans Cres MK16 . . . . . . .58 A6
Bryant Cl AL5 . . . . .131 A3
Bryant Way LU5 . . . . .105 F5
Bryants Cl SG7 . . . . .87 F2
Bryony Cl MK41 . . . . .39 B1
Bryony Way LU3 . . . . .113 E1
Buchanan Ct LU2 . . . . . . .124 B8
Buchanan Dr LU2 . . . . . . .124 B8
Buckfast Ave MK41 . . . . . .38 C5
Buckingham Dr LU2 . . . . .117 D2
Buckingham Mews MK45 .84 D1
Buckle Cl LU3 . . . . .115 F7
Buckley Rd PE19 . . . . .22 E4
Bucks Cl MK43 . . . . .36 F2
Buckwood Ave LU5 . . . . .114 F1
Buckwood La LU6 . . . . . .127 C2
Buckwood Rd AL3 . . . . . .128 C6
Budna Rd SG18 . . . . .53 C4
Buff La SG19 . . . . .45 F1
Bull Pond La LU6 . . . . . .121 B7
Bull St SG19 . . . . .56 A7
Bungalows The
 Harpenden AL5 . . . . . . .131 C3
 Toddington LU5 . . . . . .106 A7
Bunhill Cl LU4 . . . . .120 F8
Bunkers Dr MK45 . . . . . . .63 D7
Bunkers La LU7 . . . . .110 D6
Bunting Rd LU4 . . . . .115 A4
Buntings The
 Bedford MK41 . . . . .38 D4
 Sandy SG19 . . . . .42 C2
Bunyan Cl Clifton SG17 . .78 A2
 Gamlingay SG19 . . . . . . .44 B3
 Houghton Conquest MK45 .74 A8
 Pirton SG5 . . . . .99 D4
Bunyan Ctr MK42 . . . . . . .50 E4
Bunyan Rd Bedford MK42 .50 B5
 Biggleswade SG18 . . . . . .67 A5
 Kempston MK42 . . . . . . .49 E3
 Sandy SG19 . . . . .42 B1
 Westoning MK45 . . . . . . .95 E5
Bunyans Cl LU3 . . . . .116 A5
Bunyans Mead MK42 . . . .50 C3
Bunyans Wlk MK45 . . . . . .95 F2
Burdett's Ct SG19 . . . . . . .56 A7
Bure Cl MK41 . . . . .38 D6
Burfield Ct LU2 . . . . .117 D3
Burford Cl LU3 . . . . .108 A1
Burford Way SG5 . . . . . . .100 D2
Burford Wlk LU4 . . . . . . .114 E5
Burge End La SG5 . . . . . . .99 C5
Burges Cl LU6 . . . . .121 D6
Burgess Cl Haynes MK45 .75 F8
 Kempston MK42 . . . . . . .49 D6
Burgess Way SG16 . . . . . .78 D3
Burghley Cl MK45 . . . . . . .84 C1
Burgoyne Ct SG19 . . . . . . .56 A8
Burgoyne Mid Sch SG19 . .55 F7
Burleigh Pl MK43 . . . . . . .37 A8
Burley SG6 . . . . .90 F2
Burnaby Rd MK40 . . . . . . .38 C1
Burnell Rise SG6 . . . . . . .101 D5
Burnell Wlk SG6 . . . . . . .101 E5
Burnett Ave SG16 . . . . . . .89 B4
Burnham Rd LU2 . . . . . . .117 B2
Burns Ct PE19 . . . . .22 D5
Burnt Cl Luton LU3 . . . . .115 F7
 St Neots PE19 . . . . .22 F3
Burr Cl MK45 . . . . .97 C4
Burr St Dunstable LU6 . . .121 B8
 Luton LU2 . . . . .123 E8
Burr's Pl LU1 . . . . .123 E6
Burridge Cl MK43 . . . . . . .72 D8
Burridge's Cl MK43 . . . . . .36 C7
Burrows Cl Clifton SG17 . .78 A2
 Woburn Sands MK17 . . . .81 B5
Burrsholt MK44 . . . . .52 A5
Bursland SG6 . . . . .101 D6
Burwell Rd PE19 . . . . .22 C6
Bury Cl MK45 . . . . .95 F1
Bury Ct MK41 . . . . .39 B2
Bury End SG5 . . . . .99 D4
Bury Farm Cl LU7 . . . . . .118 C6
Bury Hill SG19 . . . . .56 B7
Bury La LU3 . . . . .108 A5
Bury Lawn Sch MK45 . . . .84 C4
Bury Mead SG15 . . . . .90 A7
Bury Mead Rd SG5 . . . . .100 F1
Bury Park Rd LU1 . . . . . .123 C8
Bury Rd Shefford SG17 . . .77 E3
 Shillington SG5 . . . . .87 E2
Bury Rise LU7 . . . . .112 F5
Bury The MK43 . . . . .26 C4
Bury Wlk MK41 . . . . .39 B2
Bush Cl LU5 . . . . .106 A5
Bushmead Ave MK40 . . . .50 D8
Bushmead Cross MK44 . . .20 C5
Bushmead Cty Jun Sch
 PE19 . . . . .22 A3
Bushmead Gdns PE19 . . .22 B3
Bushmead Inf Sch
 Luton LU2 . . . . .116 E5

Bushmead Inf Sch
 St Neots PE19 . . . . .22 A3
Bushmead Jun Sch LU2 .116 E5
Bushmead Priory MK44 . .20 D6
Bushmead Rd Luton LU2 .116 E5
 St Neots PE19 . . . . .22 A3
Bustard Hill PE18 . . . . .6 D8
Butcher's La SG19 . . . . . . .57 B4
Bute Sq LU1 . . . . .123 E7
Bute St LU1 . . . . .123 E7
Butely Rd LU4 . . . . .115 B5
Butler St MK44 . . . . .28 F1
Butler Way MK42 . . . . . . .49 E5
Butlin Rd LU1 . . . . .123 B7
Buttercup Cl Bedford MK42 50 F4
 Dunstable LU6 . . . . .121 D7
Buttercup Mead SG18 . . .67 C5
Butterfield Green Rd
 LU2 . . . . .117 A6
Buttermere Cl LU6 . . . . .121 C6
Buttermere Cl
 Flitwick MK45 . . . . .84 E2
 Kempston MK42 . . . . . . .49 D3
Buttermere Path SG18 . . .67 A4
Butterworth Path **1** LU2 .123 E8
Butts The Langford SG18 . .78 F4
 Riseley MK44 . . . . .10 E1
Buxton Cl SG17 . . . . .88 C6
Buxton Rd LU1 . . . . .123 D7
Buxtons La SG8 . . . . .69 F3
Buzzard Rd LU4 . . . . .115 A4
Byards Gn SG19 . . . . .55 F8
Bye Rd MK43 . . . . .72 B3
Byfield Cl Luton LU4 . . . .115 E6
 Toddington LU5 . . . . . . .105 E6
Bygrave Rd SG7 . . . . .91 F1
Byng Cl PE19 . . . . .22 B2
Byron Cl Biggleswade SG18 .67 A5
 Upper Caldecote SG18 . .66 C8
Byron Cres Bedford MK40 .37 F2
Byron Pl PE19 . . . . .22 C6
Byron Rd Harpenden AL5 .131 A2
 Luton LU4 . . . . .115 B2
Byslips Rd LU6 . . . . .127 D5

C

Caddington Comm AL3 .128 E8
Cade Cl SG6 . . . . .91 C1
Cades Cl LU1 . . . . .123 A6
Cades La LU1 . . . . .123 A6
Cadia Cl LU1 . . . . .122 E4
Cadwell Ct SG4 . . . . .101 A2
Cadwell La SG4 . . . . .101 A2
Caernarvon Rd PE19 . . . . .22 F1
Cainhoe Rd MK45 . . . . . . .86 C8
Caister Rd MK41 . . . . .39 B4
Calcutt Cl LU5 . . . . .114 F2
Caldecote Rd Ickwell SG18 65 E8
 Newnham SG7 . . . . .91 E8
 St Neots PE19 . . . . .22 E3
Caldecott Rd NN9 . . . . .3 B7
Calder Gdns LU7 . . . . . . .110 B7
Calder Rise MK41 . . . . . . .38 D6
Caleb Cl LU4 . . . . .115 F7
Calnwood Rd LU4 . . . . . .115 C3
Calshot Wlk MK41 . . . . . .39 A5
Calverton Rd LU3 . . . . . .116 A6
Cam Ctr SG4 . . . . .101 A3
Cam Sq SG4 . . . . .101 A3
Camberton Rd LU7 . . . . .110 C5
Cambrian Way MK41 . . . .38 E3
Cambridge Ct SG18 . . . . .78 F4
Cambridge Ct PE19 . . . . .22 F5
Cambridge Gdns
 Langford SG18 . . . . .78 F5
 St Neots PE19 . . . . .22 F5
Cambridge Rd
 Bedford MK42, MK44 . . . .51 A5
 Cardington MK44 . . . . . .51 D6
 Dunton SG18 . . . . .68 D6
 Hitchin SG4 . . . . .101 C2
 Langford SG18 . . . . .78 F5
 Sandy SG19 . . . . .54 C7
Cambridge St Luton LU1 .123 F6
 St Neots PE19 . . . . .22 F5
 Wymington NN10 . . . . . . .8 A7
Cambridge Way SG18 . . .78 F5
Camestone Lower Sch
 MK42 . . . . .49 E4
Camford Ct MK42 . . . . . . .49 D4
Camford Way LU3 . . . . . .107 B1
Camp Dr LU5 . . . . .114 B5
Campania Gr LU3 . . . . . .116 A8
Campbell Cl MK42 . . . . . .49 D3
Campbell Rd MK40 . . . . . .38 D1
Campers Ave SG6 . . . . . .101 E5
Campers Rd SG6 . . . . . . .101 E5
Campers Wlk SG6 . . . . . .101 E5
Campfield Way SG6 . . . . .101 D5
Campian Cl LU6 . . . . .113 C1
Campin Ct MK43 . . . . .60 E1
Campion Cl NN10 . . . . .8 B8
Campion Rd MK45 . . . . . .95 F5
Campion Way MK43 . . . . .34 D3
Campton Lower Sch SG17 76 F1
Campton Rd
 Gravenhurst MK45 . . . . . .87 D6
 Meppershall SG17 . . . . . .87 F6
Canberra Gdns LU3 . . . . .116 B6
Canberra Rd MK42 . . . . . .50 E7
Candale Cl LU6 . . . . .121 C6
Canesworde Rd LU6 . . . .121 D6
Cannock Chase MK41 . . . .39 C4
Cannon La LU2 . . . . .117 B5

Cannon's Cl SG8 . . . . .69 F5
Canons Cl MK43 . . . . .60 F8
Canterbury Cl
 Kempston MK42 . . . . . . .49 E6
 Luton LU3 . . . . .115 F4
Canterbury Rd MK45 . . . .84 E4
Cantilupe Cl LU6 . . . . . . .119 D6
Canvin Way MK40 . . . . . . .50 E5
Capron Rd Dunstable LU5 .114 A2
 Luton LU4 . . . . .115 E4
Capshill Ave LU7 . . . . . . .111 C7
Captains Cl MK44 . . . . . . .17 C1
Capulet Ct PE19 . . . . .22 C3
Cardiff Gr LU1 . . . . .123 D7
Cardiff Rd LU1 . . . . .123 D7
Cardigan Ct **10** LU1 . . . . .123 D8
Cardigan Gdns **11** LU1 . .123 D8
Cardigan St LU1 . . . . .123 D7
Cardinal Ct **3** LU2 . . . . .116 D1
Cardinal Newman
 High Sch LU3 . . . . .108 C1
Cardington Ct MK42 . . . . .50 F5
Cardington Rd
 MK42, MK44 . . . . .50 F6
Carfax Cl LU4 . . . . .114 E3
Carina Dr LU7 . . . . .111 C7
Carisbrooke Rd
 Harpenden AL5 . . . . . . .131 C2
 Luton LU3 . . . . .115 E1
Carisbrooke Way
 Bedford MK41 . . . . .39 A4
 St Neots PE19 . . . . .22 F2
Carlisle Cl Dunstable LU6 .121 B6
 Sandy SG19 . . . . .54 C8
Carlisle Rd MK40 . . . . . . .49 E7
Carlow Ct LU6 . . . . .121 A8
Carlton Bank **2** AL5 . . . .131 B1
Carlton Ct Luton LU3 . . . .116 C2
 Rushden NN10 . . . . .8 A7
Carlton Cres LU3 . . . . . . .116 C2
Carlton Ct **1** AL5 . . . . . .131 B1
Carlton Gdns MK41 . . . . .38 D4
Carlton Gr LU7 . . . . .103 A3
Carlton Lower Sch MK43 .25 A4
Carlton Rd
 Felmersham MK43 . . . . . .25 F7
 Harpenden AL5 . . . . . . .131 B2
 Harrold MK43 . . . . .25 B5
 Turvey MK43 . . . . .34 E7
Carmarthen Way NN10 . . .8 B8
Carmelite Rd LU4 . . . . . .115 A3
Carnaby PE18 . . . . .6 F4
Carnation Cl LU7 . . . . . . .103 A1
Carnegie Gdns LU3 . . . . .116 A8
Carnell Cl MK42 . . . . .49 C2
Carnoustie Dr MK40 . . . . .49 A7
Carol Cl LU3 . . . . .116 B4
Carole Ct LU1 . . . . .123 E5
Carolyn Ct LU3 . . . . .116 B4
Carpenders Cl AL5 . . . . .130 D4
Carrick Rd MK41 . . . . .39 B4
Carriers Way MK43 . . . . . .25 B4
Carron Cl LU7 . . . . .110 B7
Carron Rd MK41 . . . . .38 C7
Carsdale Cl LU3 . . . . .116 A6
Carter Cl MK42 . . . . .50 C6
Carter St SG19 . . . . .54 B8
Carteret Rd LU2 . . . . .117 C1
Carters Cl SG15 . . . . .90 A7
Carters La SG19 . . . . .56 A7
Carters Way SG15 . . . . . . .90 A7
Carters Wlk SG15 . . . . . . .90 A7
Carterweys LU5 . . . . .114 E2
Carthagena Rd SG19 . . . . .55 E5
Cartmel Dr LU6 . . . . .121 B6
Cartmel Priory MK41 . . . .51 B8
Cartwright Cl MK43 . . . . .36 F1
Cashio La MK43 . . . . .91 A1
Caslon Way SG6 . . . . .90 F1
Castle Cl Totternhoe LU6 .120 A8
 Wilstead MK45 . . . . .62 F4
Castle Croft Rd LU1 . . . .123 A6
Castle Ct NN10 . . . . .8 A7
Castle Gdns PE18 . . . . .6 F4
Castle Hill Cl PE19 . . . . . .22 C2
Castle Hill Ct MK45 . . . . .75 F1
Castle Hill Rd LU6 . . . . . .119 F8
Castle La MK40 . . . . .50 C8
Castle Lower Sch MK40 . .38 C1
Castle Rd Bedford MK40 . .50 D8
 Lavendon MK46 . . . . .23 F1
Castle Rise AL4 . . . . .131 F2
Castle St
 Luton, High Town LU1 . . .123 E7
 Luton, New Town LU1 . . .123 E6
Castles LU3 . . . . .90 F8
Catchacre LU6 . . . . .121 A7
Cater St MK42 . . . . .49 E4
Catesby Gn LU3 . . . . .108 A1
Catherall Rd LU3 . . . . . . .116 B6
Catherine Rd MK45 . . . . . .84 E3
Catherines Cl SG19 . . . . .56 A7
Catsbrook Rd LU3 . . . . . .116 B6
Cauldwell Ct
 Bedford MK42 . . . . .50 A6
 Sandy SG19 . . . . .54 C8
Cauldwell Pl MK42 . . . . . .50 B7
Cauldwell St MK42 . . . . . .50 B7
Cauldwell Wlk MK42 . . . .50 A6
Cause End Rd MK43 . . . . .60 F7
Causeway PE19 . . . . .13 F6
Causeway Cl PE19 . . . . . . .13 F6
Causeway The
 Carlton MK43 . . . . .25 B3
 Clophill MK45 . . . . .86 D8

Cavendish Ct
 Bedford MK40 . . . . .37 F2
 6 Biggleswade SG18 . . .67 A5
Cavendish Rd Luton LU3 .116 B2
 Markyate AL3 . . . . .128 D6
Cavendish St MK40 . . . . . .38 B1
Cawdor Cl MK41 . . . . .39 B4
Cawdor Pl PE19 . . . . .22 F2
Caxton Ct LU3 . . . . .115 F4
Caxton Pk MK41 . . . . .39 C3
Caxton Rd MK41 . . . . .39 D3
Cedar Ave
 Biggleswade SG18 . . . . . .66 F7
 Ickleford SG5 . . . . .100 E4
Cedar Cl Ampthill MK45 . .84 F7
 Irchester NN29 . . . . .7 A7
 Luton LU4 . . . . .114 E3
 Rushden NN10 . . . . .8 A8
 Shefford SG17 . . . . .77 E2
Cedar Gdns SG19 . . . . . . .54 B7
Cedar Rd MK42 . . . . .50 D5
Cedars Ctry Pk LU6 . . . . .119 F5
Cedars The Ampthill MK45 .84 E7
 Dunstable LU6 . . . . .121 C7
 18 Harpenden AL5 . . . .131 B1
 Wootton MK43 . . . . .61 A8
Cedars Upper Sch The
 LU7 . . . . .110 F5
Cedars Way LU7 . . . . . . .110 E5
Cedars Wlk MK45 . . . . . . .84 E7
Celandine Dr LU3 . . . . . .116 A8
Cemetery Rd
 Houghton Regis LU5 . . .114 B3
Centauri Cl LU7 . . . . .111 C8
Central App SG6 . . . . . . .101 F6
Central Ave Henlow SG16 .89 B3
 Shortstown MK42 . . . . . .51 A4
 Wharley End MK43 . . . . .58 E2
Cetus Cres LU7 . . . . .111 C7
Chad La AL3 . . . . .129 C4
Chadwell Cl LU2 . . . . . . .116 F1
Chadwick Cl LU6 . . . . . . .114 A1
Chagford Cl MK40 . . . . . . .38 E1
Chagney Cl SG6 . . . . .101 E6
Chainbridge La PE18 . . . . .2 F8
Chalfont Way LU2 . . . . . .117 D2
Chalgrave Rd LU7 . . . . . .105 D3
Chalk Hill LU2 . . . . .117 F4
Chalkdown LU2 . . . . .116 E6
Challney Boys High Sch
 LU4 . . . . .115 D2
Challney Cl LU4 . . . . .115 D2
Challney Girls High Sch
 LU4 . . . . .115 D2
Chaloner Ct LU7 . . . . . . .111 B5
Chalton Hts LU4 . . . . . . .106 E1
Chalton Lower Sch LU4 .106 E1
Chalton Rd LU4 . . . . .115 D1
Chamberlain Way PE19 . .22 F7
Chamberlaines AL5 . . . . .130 A5
Chamberlains Gdn LU3 .103 A2
Chambers La SG5 . . . . . . .100 E4
Chambers Way SG18 . . . .67 C5
Chandler Path MK42 . . . . .49 D5
Chandlers Cl MK43 . . . . . .72 C8
Chandos Ct **13** MK40 . . .38 B1
Chandos Rd Ampthill MK45 .84 E8
 Luton LU4 . . . . .115 F1
Chandos St MK40 . . . . . . .38 B1
Channels End Rd MK44 . .30 C6
Chantry Ave MK42 . . . . . .49 E2
Chantry Cl MK17 . . . . .81 A6
Chantry Piece SG18 . . . . .53 E2
Chantry Prim Sch LU4 . .114 F4
Chantry Rd MK42 . . . . . . .49 E3
Chaomans SG6 . . . . .101 F3
Chapel Cl Bedford MK41 . .39 B1
 Great Barford MK44 . . . . .40 F5
 Honeydon MK44 . . . . . . .21 B2
 Luton LU2 . . . . .116 C8
 Shefford SG17 . . . . .77 F2
 Toddington LU5 . . . . . . .105 F6
 Wrestlingworth SG19 . . . .57 B4
Chapel Cl SG18 . . . . .78 F6
Chapel End Rd MK45 . . . .74 D8
Chapel Field
 Gamlingay SG19 . . . . . . .44 D4
 Great Barford MK44 . . . . .40 F5
Chapel Fields SG18 . . . . . .66 F6
Chapel Hill NN29 . . . . .7 B8
Chapel La Ampthill MK45 . .73 E1
 Cardington MK44 . . . . . .51 E5
 Colmworth MK44 . . . . . . .20 A1
 Northall LU6 . . . . .119 A5
 Souldrop MK44 . . . . .16 A8
 Totternhoe LU6 . . . . . . .119 F8
 Willington MK44 . . . . . . .40 C1
 Wilstead MK45 . . . . .62 F4
Chapel Path
 Houghton Regis LU5 . . .114 B4
 2 Leighton Buzzard LU7 .111 A4
Chapel Pl SG5 . . . . .90 F6
Chapel Pound MK43 . . . . .37 A8
Chapel Rd
 Breachwood Green SG4 . .125 E8
 Flamstead AL3 . . . . .129 B2
 Flitwick MK45 . . . . .84 D3
Chapel St Dunton SG18 . . .68 D5
 Hinxworth SG7 . . . . .80 D6
 Luton, High Town LU1 . . .123 E7
 Luton, New Town LU1 . . .123 E6
 Potton SG19 . . . . .54 A7
 Woburn Sands MK17 . . . .81 B4
Chapel Viaduct LU1 . . . . .123 E7
Chapel Way SG16 . . . . . . .78 D1

Chapelfields MK44 . . . . . .18 D1
Chapman Cl
 Kempston MK42 . . . . . . .49 D6
 Potton SG19 . . . . .56 A7
Chapmans Cl NN29 . . . . . . .7 B8
Chapter House Rd LU4 . .115 A3
Chard Dr LU3 . . . . .108 B1
Charlbury St MK40 . . . . . .38 C1
Charles St LU2 . . . . .123 F8
Charles' St PE19 . . . . .22 F5
Charlottes Ct **2** LU1 . . . .123 D7
Charlwood Rd LU4 . . . . . .115 B1
Charmbury Rise LU2 . . . .117 A4
Charndon Cl LU3 . . . . . . .108 B1
Charnocks Cl SG19 . . . . . .44 D5
Charnwood Ave MK41 . . .39 B3
Chartmoor Rd LU7 . . . . . .111 A4
Chartwell Dr LU2 . . . . . . .116 E3
Chase Cl SG18 . . . . .90 A8
Chase Hill Rd SG15 . . . . . .90 A7
Chase St LU1 . . . . .123 E6
Chase The MK43 . . . . .49 A2
Chasten Hill SG6 . . . . . . .101 D7
Chatsworth Rd LU4 . . . . .116 B1
Chatteris Cl LU4 . . . . . . .115 D4
Chatton Cl LU2 . . . . .117 E2
Chaucer Dr SG18 . . . . .67 A5
Chaucer Pl PE19 . . . . .22 D6
Chaucer Rd Bedford MK40 .37 F1
 Flitwick MK45 . . . . .84 D3
 Luton LU3 . . . . .116 C2
Chaul End La LU4 . . . . . .115 E1
Chaul End Rd
 Caddington LU1 . . . . . . .122 D6
 Luton LU4 . . . . .115 B1
Chauntry Way MK45 . . . . .84 E5
Chaworth Gn **1** LU4 . . . .115 C5
Chawston Cl PE19 . . . . . . .22 C5
Cheapside LU1 . . . . .123 E7
Cheapside Sq **4** LU1 . . . .123 E7
Chelmer Cl MK41 . . . . . . .38 D7
Chelsea Gdns LU5 . . . . . .114 D5
Chelsea Gn LU7 . . . . .110 D6
Chelsworth Cl **1** LU2 . . .117 D1
Cheltenham Cl MK41 . . . .39 B3
Chelveston Base Cres NN9 3 D5
Chelveston Rd NN9 . . . . . . .3 A7
Cheney Cl LU5 . . . . .105 F4
Cheney Rd LU4 . . . . .115 C5
Chennells Cl SG4 . . . . . . .101 B2
Chepstow AL5 . . . . .130 F2
Chepstow Gdns MK41 . . .39 A4
Chequer Ct LU1 . . . . .123 F6
Chequer St LU1 . . . . .123 F6
Chequers Cl
 Marston Moretaine MK43 . .60 D2
 Stotfold SG5 . . . . .91 A6
Chequers Cotts LU6 . . . .127 A8
Chequers Hill
 Flamstead AL3 . . . . .129 C2
 Wilden MK44 . . . . .30 A4
Chequers La MK16 . . . . . .58 B6
Chequers The LU6 . . . . . .119 F5
Cherry Cl MK45 . . . . .74 B8
Cherry Gr SG19 . . . . .44 C5
Cherry Tree Cl
 Arlesey SG15 . . . . .90 A4
 Luton LU2 . . . . .117 A1
Cherry Tree Wlk
 Houghton Regis LU5 . . .114 B6
 Leighton Buzzard LU7 . . .110 E2
Cherry Trees SG16 . . . . . .89 B3
Cherry Wlk MK42 . . . . . . .49 F3
Cherrycourt Way LU7 . . .111 D6
Cherrycourt Way Ind Est
 LU7 . . . . .111 E7
Cherrycroft SG19 . . . . . . .54 D7
Cherrytree Way MK45 . . .85 A7
Chertsey Cl LU2 . . . . .124 D8
Cherwell Rd MK41 . . . . . .38 C5
Chesford Rd LU2 . . . . . . .117 C4
Cheslyn Cl LU2 . . . . .117 E2
Chessington Cl MK41 . . . .51 B8
Chester Ave LU4 . . . . . . .115 E3
Chester Cl LU4 . . . . .115 F2
Chester Rd MK40 . . . . . . .49 E7
Chesterton Ave AL5 . . . .131 D1
Chesterton Ct PE19 . . . . .22 E6
Chesterton Mews MK40 . .37 F1
Chestnut Ave
 Bedford MK40 . . . . .49 F7
 Biggleswade SG18 . . . . . .67 A6
 Bromham MK43 . . . . .36 D3
 Henlow SG16 . . . . .89 C3
 Luton LU3 . . . . .107 C1
Chestnut Cl Ampthill MK45 .84 F8
 Dagnall HP4 . . . . .126 C5
 Westoning MK45 . . . . . . .95 D6
 Wymington NN10 . . . . . . .8 B5
Chestnut Cres MK45 . . . . .85 B8
Chestnut Ct LU6 . . . . . . .121 C7
Chestnut Farm SG16 . . . .78 D1
Chestnut Gdns MK42 . . . .49 E3
Chestnut Gr PE19 . . . . . . .22 F4
Chestnut Hill LU7 . . . . . .110 D8
Chestnut Rise LU7 . . . . . .110 D8
Chestnuts The PE18 . . . . . .6 F5
Chethams MK42 . . . . .50 C7
Cheverall The LU6 . . . . . .121 C6
Cheverells Cl AL3 . . . . . . .128 D4
Cheviot Cl Bedford MK41 .38 E3
 Flitwick MK45 . . . . .84 D2
 Leighton Buzzard LU7 . . .110 C8
 Luton LU3 . . . . .115 D7
Cheviot Rd LU3 . . . . .115 D7
Cheyne Cl LU6 . . . . .113 F3
Cheynes Inf Sch LU3 . . . .115 D8
Chicheley Rd MK16 . . . . . .58 A7

Chichester Cl LU5 . . . . .121 E7
Chicksands Ave SG17 . . . .76 E3
Chillingham Gn MK41 . . . .39 B4
Chiltern Ave Bedford MK41 38 E3
  Edlesborough LU6 . . . . .119 E3
Chiltern Cl Ampthill MK45 . .84 F8
  Flitwick MK45 . . . . .84 D2
  Lidlington MK43 . . . . .72 D2
Chiltern Ct 19 AL5 . . . . . .131 B1
Chiltern Gdns
  Leighton Buzzard LU7 . . . .103 A3
  Luton LU4 . . . . .115 F3
Chiltern Pk LU5 . . . . .114 D2
Chiltern Pl SG16 . . . . .78 C1
Chiltern Rd
  Barton-le-C MK45 . . . . .97 C2
  Dunstable LU6 . . . . .114 A1
Chiltern Rise LU1 . . . . . . .123 D6
Chiltern Trad Est LU7 . . .111 A5
Chiltern View SG6 . . . . . .101 D5
Chilterns The
  Kensworth LU6 . . . . .127 F8
  Leighton Buzzard LU7 . . . .111 D6
Chinnor Rd MK41 . . . . .39 B1
Chobham St LU1 . . . . .123 F6
Chobham Wlk 5 LU1 . . . .123 E6
Christchurch Ct LU6 . . . .114 A1
Christian Cl MK45 . . . . . . .95 F1
Christie Rd MK42 . . . . .50 D6
Christina Ct AL3 . . . . .128 E5
Christy's Yd SG7 . . . . .80 D6
Church Ave Ampthill MK45 .73 F1
  Leighton Buzzard LU7 . . . .111 A6
Church Cl Dunstable LU5 . .121 C8
  Houghton Conquest MK45 . .74 A7
  Milton Ernest MK44 . . . . . .27 B5
  Studham LU6 . . . . .127 B4
  Westoning MK45 . . . . .95 D6
Church Cotts HP1 . . . . . .132 D3
Church Cres SG18 . . . . . . .78 F7
Church Croft LU6 . . . . . . .119 E3
Church End Arlesey SG15 . .90 A8
  Biddenham MK40 . . . . .49 B8
  Edlesborough LU6 . . . . . . .119 E3
  Elstow MK42 . . . . .50 B3
  Everton SG19 . . . . .43 C3
  Felmersham MK43 . . . . . . .26 C8
  Flamstead AL3 . . . . .129 C2
  Gamlingay SG19 . . . . .44 E5
  Houghton Regis LU5 . . . . .114 B5
  Markyate AL3 . . . . .128 D6
  Ravensden MK44 . . . . .29 B1
  Renhold MK41 . . . . .39 D6
  Steppingley MK45 . . . . .84 A3
  Willington MK44 . . . . .52 B8
Church End Farm LU6 . . .120 B7
Church End Lower Sch
  MK43 . . . . .72 D7
Church End Rd MK45 . . . . .75 C7
Church Farm Cl SG19 . . . .55 F3
Church Gn
  Harpenden AL5 . . . . .131 A1
  Milton Ernest MK44 . . . . . .27 B5
  Totternhoe LU6 . . . . .120 B7
Church Green Row AL5 . .131 A1
Church Hill MK17 . . . . .81 E5
Church La Arlesey SG15 . . .90 A7
  Bedford MK41 . . . . .39 B3
  Bolnhurst MK44 . . . . .19 A4
  Cardington MK44 . . . . .51 D4
  Colmworth MK44 . . . . .19 D4
  Covington PE18 . . . . .2 C2
  Eaton Bray LU6 . . . . .119 E6
  Flitton MK45 . . . . .85 D4
  Gamlingay SG19 . . . . .44 E5
  Guilden Morden SG8 . . . . . .69 F5
  Hockliffe LU7 . . . . .104 D3
  Letchworth SG6 . . . . .91 C1
  Lidlington MK43 . . . . .72 C2
  Little Staughton MK44 . . . .13 B2
  Newton Bromswold NN10 . . .9 D8
  Oakley MK43 . . . . .36 F6
  Odell MK43 . . . . .15 D1
  Pavenham MK43 . . . . .26 C4
  Riseley MK44 . . . . .10 F2
  Sharnbrook MK44 . . . . .16 C4
  Stagsden MK43 . . . . .48 A7
  Tilbrook PE18 . . . . .6 B7
  Upper Dean PE18 . . . . .5 B4
  Wrestlingworth SG19 . . . . .57 B3
  Wymington NN10 . . . . .8 B5
  Yelden MK44 . . . . .4 A3
Church Mdw PE19 . . . . . . .22 F5
Church Mead LU6 . . . . . .127 B4
Church Meadow Cotts
  HP1 . . . . .132 D3
Church Path SG19 . . . . . . .54 B7
Church Rd
  Barton-le-C MK45 . . . . .97 D1
  Colmworth MK44 . . . . .20 B1
  Everton SG19 . . . . .43 C3
  Flamstead AL3 . . . . .129 B2
  Flitwick MK45 . . . . .84 D1
  Hargrave NN9 . . . . .1 F1
  Harlington MK45 . . . . .95 F2
  Henlow SG16 . . . . .78 D2
  Kempston MK43 . . . . .49 A4
  Keysoe MK44 . . . . .12 A1
  Leighton Buzzard LU7 . . . .110 E6
  Maulden MK45 . . . . .85 D8
  Meppershall SG17 . . . . .88 A5
  Pulloxhill MK45 . . . . .96 E8
  Silsoe MK45 . . . . .86 C4
  Slapton LU7 . . . . .118 D6
  Slip End LU1 . . . . .123 C2
  Steppingley MK45 . . . . .84 A3
  Stevington MK43 . . . . .36 C7
  Stotfold SG5 . . . . .90 F6

Church Rd continued
  Streatley LU3 . . . . .108 A6
  Studham LU6 . . . . .127 B4
  Tingrith MK17 . . . . .94 F5
  Totternhoe LU6 . . . . .120 B6
  Upper Sundon LU3 . . . . . .107 B3
  Westoning MK45 . . . . .95 C6
  Willington MK44 . . . . .52 B8
  Wilstead MK45 . . . . .62 E4
  Woburn Sands MK17 . . . . .81 B3
  Wootton MK43 . . . . .60 F7
Church Row MK43 . . . . . . .60 E7
Church Sq
  Leighton Buzzard LU7 . . . .110 F6
  Toddington LU5 . . . . .105 F6
Church St Ampthill MK45 . .73 F1
  Aspley Guise MK17 . . . . . . .81 E5
  Baldock SG7 . . . . .91 E1
  5 Bedford MK40 . . . . .50 B8
  Biggleswade SG18 . . . . . . .67 A6
  Clifton SG17 . . . . .78 B3
  Dunstable LU5 . . . . .121 C8
  Dunton SG18 . . . . .68 D5
  Gamlingay SG19 . . . . .44 D5
  Guilden Morden SG8 . . . . . .69 F5
  Hargrave NN9 . . . . .1 E1
  Langford SG18 . . . . .78 F7
  Langford SG18 . . . . .78 F8
  Leighton Buzzard LU7 . . . .111 A8
  Lidlington MK43 . . . . .72 C3
  Luton LU2 . . . . .123 F7
  8 Luton LU1 . . . . .123 E7
  Luton, High Town LU2 . . . .123 F8
  Ridgmont MK43 . . . . .82 F5
  Shillington SG5 . . . . .98 F8
  St Neots PE19 . . . . .22 F5
  Tempsford SG19 . . . . .42 A4
Church Terr MK43 . . . . . . .34 E5
Church Turn LU7 . . . . . . .111 E2
Church View Ampthill MK45 73 F1
  Clapham MK41 . . . . .37 F5
  St Neots PE19 . . . . .22 F5
Church View Ave SG5 . . . .87 E1
Church View Cl SG18 . . . .78 F7
Church View Ct LU7 . . . .110 E6
Church Wlk Cranfield MK43 71 A8
  Dunstable LU5 . . . . .121 C8
  Eggington LU7 . . . . .112 B7
  Harrold MK43 . . . . .25 A6
  Kempston MK42 . . . . .49 C3
  Marston Moretaine MK43 . .72 D7
  Newton Bromswold NN10 . . .9 D8
  North Crawley MK16 . . . . . .58 B6
  Shefford SG17 . . . . .77 C3
  8 St Neots PE19 . . . . .22 E5
Churchfield Rd LU5 . . . . .114 B5
Churchgate MK44 . . . . . . .41 A4
Churchill Cl
  Sharnbrook MK44 . . . . .16 C3
  Stewartby MK43 . . . . .61 B1
  Streatley LU3 . . . . .107 F6
Churchill Dr SG17 . . . . . . .76 F4
Churchill Pl MK41 . . . . . . .40 B1
Churchill Rd
  Barton-le-C MK45 . . . . .97 C3
  Dunstable LU6 . . . . .121 D5
  Leighton Buzzard LU7 . . . .103 B1
  Luton LU4 . . . . .116 A1
  Marston Moretaine MK43 . .72 C8
Churchill Way Sandy SG19 .54 C8
  Shefford SG17 . . . . .77 C1
Churchills 95 F2
Churchville Rd MK42 . . . . .50 B5
Churnet Cl MK41 . . . . .38 D7
Cicero Dr LU3 . . . . .116 A8
Cinques Rd SG19 . . . . . . .44 C6
Cinques The SG19 . . . . . . .44 B6
City La MK44 . . . . .20 C3
Clapham Rd MK41 . . . . . . .37 F4
Clare Ct SG18 . . . . .44 D5
Clare Ho SG18 . . . . .67 A6
Clare Rd MK41 . . . . .38 F5
Claremont Rd LU4 . . . . . .116 B1
Clarence Ct NN10 . . . . .8 A8
Clarence Rd
  Harpenden AL5 . . . . .131 A3
  Leighton Buzzard LU7 . . . .111 A8
Clarendon Ct AL5 . . . . . .131 B3
Clarendon Rd
  Harpenden AL5 . . . . .131 B3
  Luton LU2 . . . . .116 E1
Clarendon St MK41 . . . . . .38 A2
Clark's Pightle MK45 . . . . .97 C2
Clarkes Way LU5 . . . . . . .114 C4
Claverley Gn LU2 . . . . . . .117 E2
Clay Hall Rd LU6 . . . . . . .127 F7
Claydon Cl LU3 . . . . .116 C7
Claydon Ct MK40 . . . . .38 B1
Claydown Way LU1 . . . . . .123 B1
Claygate Ave AL5 . . . . . . .130 E2
Claymore Dr SG5 . . . . . . .100 F5
Cleat Hill MK41, MK44 . . . .38 E7
Cleave The AL5 . . . . .131 D1
Cleavers The LU5 . . . . . . .105 F5
Cleavers Wlk LU5 . . . . . . .105 F5
Cleeve Abbey MK41 . . . . . .39 B1
Clements End Rd LU6 . . .127 E2
Clevedon Rd LU2 . . . . . . .117 B2
Cleveland Dr LU7 . . . . . . .110 C8
Cleveland Rd AL3 . . . . . . .128 E5
Cleveland St MK42 . . . . . . .49 E4
Clifford Cres LU4 . . . . . . .115 D5
Clifton House Cl SG17 . . . .78 B3
Clifton Rd Dunstable LU6 .114 A1
  Henlow SG16 . . . . .78 C1
  Luton LU1 . . . . .123 B8
  Newton Blossomville MK43 .34 A4
  Shefford SG17 . . . . .77 D2

Clinton Ave LU2 . . . . .116 F3
Clipstone Brook
  Lower Sch LU7 . . . . .111 B7
Clipstone Cl MK41 . . . . . . .39 B3
Clipstone Cres LU7 . . . . .111 C7
Clive Ct LU7 . . . . .116 E1
Cloister Lawns SG6 . . . . .101 F4
Cloisters Rd
  Letchworth SG6 . . . . .101 F4
  Luton LU4 . . . . .115 B3
Cloisters The
  Ampthill MK45 . . . . .73 F1
  Bedford MK41 . . . . .39 B1
  Dunstable LU5 . . . . .121 C8
  Houghton Regis LU5 . . . . .114 C6
Clophill Rd
  Gravenhurst MK45 . . . . . . .87 B5
  Maulden MK45 . . . . .85 E8
Close Rd MK43 . . . . .26 E3
Close The
  Biggleswade SG18 . . . . . . .66 F6
  Clapham MK41 . . . . .37 E5
  Great Barford MK44 . . . . . .41 A3
  Hardmead MK16 . . . . .46 D3
  Harpenden AL5 . . . . .130 D4
  Hinxworth SG7 . . . . .80 D6
  Luton LU3 . . . . .116 A5
  Markyate AL3 . . . . .128 E5
  St Neots PE19 . . . . .22 F5
  Tempsford SG19 . . . . .42 C8
  Thurleigh MK44 . . . . .18 C2
  Woburn Sands MK17 . . . . .81 B4
Clothall Rd SG7 . . . . .91 F1
Clovelly Way MK40 . . . . . . .38 F2
Clover Ave MK41 . . . . .39 B1
Clover Cl Biggleswade SG18 67 C4
  Luton LU4 . . . . .115 A3
Clover Dr NN10 . . . . .8 C8
Clover Rd Flitwick MK45 . . .84 D3
  St Neots PE19 . . . . .22 C3
Clyde Cres MK41 . . . . .38 D5
Clydesdale Ct LU4 . . . . . .115 A3
Clydesdale Rd LU4 . . . . . .115 A3
Coach Ho The MK45 . . . . .97 C3
Coach Rd SG16 . . . . .78 D1
Cobbett La MK45 . . . . .85 D4
Cobbitts Rd MK45 . . . . . . .74 C1
Cobblers La MK17 . . . . . . .83 C3
Cobden Sq 10 MK40 . . . . . .38 B1
Cobden St LU2 . . . . .116 F1
Cockernhoe Endowed
  Jun Mix & Inf Sch LU2 .117 E3
Codrington Ct PE19 . . . . . .22 B3
Cody Rd MK41 . . . . .37 D6
Colchester Way MK41 . . . .39 A5
Coldharbour La AL5 . . . . .131 C4
Colebrook Ave LU3 . . . . . .115 C7
Colemans Cl SG5 . . . . .99 D4
Colemoreham Ct SG18 . . . .65 E7
Coleridge Ct
  9 Harpenden AL5 . . . . . .131 B1
  St Neots PE19 . . . . .22 C7
Coles Ct MK41 . . . . .39 A1
Colesden Rd MK44 . . . . . . .31 D5
Colin Rd LU2 . . . . .116 F2
College Cl AL3 . . . . .129 B1
College Dr MK44 . . . . .10 F2
College Ho LU1 . . . . .123 F7
College Rd Bedford MK42 . .50 B5
  Sandy SG19 . . . . .42 C1
  Wharley End MK43 . . . . . . .58 E2
College St MK42 . . . . .50 A5
Colley Cl MK44 . . . . .20 A1
Collie Rd MK42 . . . . .50 E6
Collingdon Ct 9 LU1 . . . .123 D8
Collingdon St LU1 . . . . . .123 D8
Collings Wells Cl LU1 . . .122 E4
Collingtree LU2 . . . . .117 B4
Collingwood Rd PE19 . . . . .22 B2
Collins Pl MK42 . . . . .50 F5
Collison Cl SG4 . . . . .101 C2
Colmworth Gdns PE19 . . . .22 A2
Colmworth Lower Sch
  MK44 . . . . .20 A1
Coltsfoot SG18 . . . . .67 C4
Coltsfoot Gn LU4 . . . . . . .115 A5
Columba Dr LU7 . . . . .111 C8
Columbine Cl MK41 . . . . . .39 C4
Colwell Rise LU2 . . . . .117 E2
Colworth Rd MK44 . . . . . . .16 B4
Comet Dr MK41 . . . . .51 A2
Commerce Way
  Flitwick MK45 . . . . .85 A4
  Leighton Buzzard LU7 . . . .111 E6
  Letchworth SG6 . . . . .101 F6
Commerce Way Ind Est
  LU7 . . . . .111 E6
Commercial Rd MK40 . . . . .50 B8
Common La
  Harpenden AL5 . . . . .131 D5
  Upper Sundon LU3 . . . . . .107 A4
Common Rd
  Kensworth LU6 . . . . .121 D1
  Langford SG18 . . . . .78 C4
  Stotfold SG5 . . . . .90 F7
  Studham LU6 . . . . .127 B3
Common Rise SG4 . . . . . .101 A1
Common The AL5 . . . . . . .130 C4
Comp Gate LU6 . . . . .119 E6
Comp The LU6 . . . . .119 E6
Compass Dr MK42 . . . . . . .51 A3
Compton Ave LU4 . . . . . . .115 D4
Compton Cl Flitwick MK45 .84 D1
  St Neots PE19 . . . . .22 E2
Concord Way LU7 . . . . . . .111 E5
Concorde Cl MK42 . . . . . . .51 A2
Concorde St LU2 . . . . . . .123 F8
Concra Pk MK17 . . . . .81 C4

Conduit Rd MK40 . . . . .50 A8
Conger La LU5 . . . . .106 A6
Coniston Cl Flitwick MK45 .84 C2
  Leighton Buzzard LU7 . . . .110 C7
  Luton LU3 . . . . .115 F1
Connaught Rd
  Harpenden AL5 . . . . .131 B2
  Luton LU4 . . . . .115 F1
Connaught Way MK41 . . . .38 D6
Conner's Cl SG8 . . . . .69 F4
Conquest Rd
  Bedford MK42 . . . . .50 C5
  Houghton Regis LU5 . . . . .114 E5
Constable Ave PE19 . . . . . .22 D5
Constable Cl LU5 . . . . . . .114 D5
Constable Ct LU4 . . . . . . .116 A1
Constable Hill MK41 . . . . .38 A2
Constables Leys PE18 . . . . .6 F5
Conway Cl
  Houghton Regis LU5 . . . . .114 E5
  Rushden NN10 . . . . .8 A8
Conway Cres SG18 . . . . . . .38 C5
Conway Dr MK45 . . . . .84 D1
Conway Pl PE19 . . . . .22 F2
Conway Rd LU4 . . . . .116 B1
Cook's Mdw LU6 . . . . .119 E4
Cookfield Cl LU6 . . . . .120 E8
Cooks Way SG4 . . . . .101 A1
Coombe Dr LU6 . . . . .120 E7
Coombs Cl MK42 . . . . .50 D6
Cooper Cl SG16 . . . . .88 E2
Coopers Cl
  Biggleswade SG18 . . . . . . .67 B4
  Great Barford MK44 . . . . . .40 F5
  Sandy SG19 . . . . .54 B6
Coopers Field SG6 . . . . . .101 D7
Coopers Way LU5 . . . . . . .114 A4
Cooters End La AL5 . . . . .130 F5
Copeland Wlk MK41 . . . . . .39 B3
Copenhagen Cl LU3 . . . . .115 D8
Cople Lower Sch MK44 . . .52 A6
Cople Rd MK44 . . . . .51 E5
Coplowe La MK44 . . . . .17 D1
Coppens The SG5 . . . . . . .91 A5
Copper Beech Way LU7 .103 A3
Copper Beeches 11 AL5 . .131 B1
Copperfields LU4 . . . . . . .115 C3
Copperfields Cl LU4 . . . . .114 D4
Coppice Mead
  Biggleswade SG18 . . . . . . .67 B5
  Stotfold SG5 . . . . .90 E5
Coppice The AL5 . . . . . . .130 F2
Coppins The Ampthill MK45 84 F8
  Markyate AL3 . . . . .128 D5
Copse The MK41 . . . . .39 B2
Copse Way LU3 . . . . .115 D8
Copthorne LU2 . . . . .117 D3
Copthorne Cl MK43 . . . . . .37 A8
Coral Cl LU6 . . . . .119 E6
Corbet Ride LU7 . . . . .110 D8
Corbet Sq LU7 . . . . .110 D8
Corbridge Dr LU2 . . . . . . .117 E1
Corby Cl MK42 . . . . .50 D4
Corfe Pl LU2 . . . . .117 E1
Corfe Rd MK41 . . . . .39 A4
Corinium Gdns LU3 . . . . .116 A8
Corncastle Rd LU1 . . . . . .123 D6
Corncrake Cl LU1 . . . . . . .117 C5
Cornel Cl LU1 . . . . .123 A7
Cornel Ct LU1 . . . . .123 A7
Cornelia Ct 3 AL5 . . . . . .131 A2
Corner Cl Letchworth SG6 .101 E6
  Podington NN29 . . . . .7 E1
Corner Wood AL3 . . . . . . .128 D5
Cornish Cl SG17 . . . . .77 C3
Cornland MK41 . . . . .39 A3
Cornwall Ct PE19 . . . . .22 C4
Cornwall Rd Ampthill MK45 84 F8
  Bedford MK40 . . . . .38 D2
  Harpenden AL5 . . . . .131 B2
Cornwallis Cl AL5 . . . . . . .36 E3
Cornwallis Dr PE19 . . . . . .22 A5
Coronation Rd MK43 . . . . .59 B1
Corunna Cl PE19 . . . . .22 C5
Cosgrove Way LU1 . . . . . .115 D1
Cosmic Ave MK42 . . . . . . .50 A4
Costin St MK40 . . . . .50 B8
Cotefield Cl MK41 . . . . . . .115 C3
Cotefield Dr LU7 . . . . .103 B3
Cotman Cl MK41 . . . . .38 B3
Cotswold Bsns Pk LU1 . .122 D2
Cotswold Cl MK41 . . . . . . .38 F2
Cotswold Dr LU7 . . . . .110 C8
Cotswold Gdns LU3 . . . . .115 C7
Cotswold Pl MK45 . . . . . . .84 D2
Cottage Rd SG19 . . . . .42 B1
Cotton End Lower Sch
  . . . . .63 D8
Cotton End Rd MK45 . . . . .63 A4
Coulson Cl LU1 . . . . .122 F8
Council Cotts Radwell SG7 .91 C4
  Sharnbrook MK44 . . . . .16 F4
Council Hos
  Ivinghoe Aston LU6 . . . . . .119 A1
  Podington NN29 . . . . .7 E1
Countess Cl PE19 . . . . .22 B3
Countess Ct 4 LU2 . . . . . .116 D1
Countess Gdns MK42 . . . . .49 D3
Court Dr LU5 . . . . .114 B1
Court La MK43 . . . . .36 F7
Court Rd MK43 . . . . .71 B8
Court The MK17 . . . . .70 C3
Courtfields AL5 . . . . .131 D1
Courtlands LU7 . . . . .110 E6
Courtlands Dr SG18 . . . . . .67 C3
Covent Garden Cl LU4 . . .115 F3
Coventry Rd MK40 . . . . . . .49 F8

Coverdale LU4 . . . . .115 B6
Cow La LU6 . . . . .119 E4
Cowdray Cl LU2 . . . . .117 C3
Cowper Ct AL3 . . . . .128 D5
Cowper Rd Bedford MK40 . .37 F2
  Harpenden AL5 . . . . .131 C1
  Markyate AL3 . . . . .128 D5
Cowper Rise AL3 . . . . . . .128 D5
Cowper St LU1 . . . . .123 E5
Cowpers Ct PE19 . . . . .22 D6
Cowridge Cres LU2 . . . . . .124 A8
Cowslip Cl NN10 . . . . .8 C8
Cowslip Hill SG6 . . . . . . .101 E7
Cox's Cl Bedford MK40 . . . .49 F7
  Sharnbrook MK44 . . . . .16 B4
Cox's Way SG15 . . . . .90 A6
Coyney Gn LU3 . . . . .116 C1
Crab Apple Way SG19 . . . .44 C5
Crab La SG18 . . . . .67 A6
Crab Tree La SG5 . . . . .99 D4
Crabtree Inf Sch AL5 . . . .131 C1
Crabtree La
  Harpenden AL5 . . . . .131 C1
  Harpenden AL5 . . . . .131 D2
Crabtree Way LU4 . . . . . . .114 B2
Crackle Hill Rd SG17 . . . . .88 C6
Craddock Ct NN29 . . . . .7 B8
Craddocks Dr LU7 . . . . . .103 A3
Cradock Rd LU4 . . . . .115 B1
Cranborne Cl MK41 . . . . . .39 B4
Cranbrook MK17 . . . . .81 B5
Cranbrook Dr LU3 . . . . . . .115 D8
Crancott Cl MK45 . . . . . . .74 B8
Crane Way MK43 . . . . .59 C2
Cranes Cl MK43 . . . . .34 E5
Cranfield Lower Sch
  . . . . .59 B1
Cranfield Rd
  Astwood MK16 . . . . .47 B2
  Salford MK17 . . . . .70 D5
  Woburn Sands MK17 . . . . .81 B7
  Wootton MK43 . . . . .60 E5
Cranfield Univ Silsoe MK45 86 C3
  Wharley End MK43 . . . . . . .58 E2
Cranford Ct AL5 . . . . .131 C1
Cranleigh Gdns LU3 . . . . .116 D3
Crawley Cl LU1 . . . . .123 C1
Crawley Green Inf Sch
  LU2 . . . . .124 B8
Crawley Green Rd
  Luton, Hart Hill LU2 . . . . .124 A8
  Luton, Wigmore LU2 . . . . .117 D1
Crawley Rd Cranfield MK43 59 C3
  Luton LU1 . . . . .123 D8
  Woburn MK17 . . . . .82 A1
Crayton Rd MK45 . . . . .84 E8
Crecy Ct PE19 . . . . .22 C5
Crediton Cl MK40 . . . . .38 E2
Creran Wlk LU3 . . . . .110 C7
Crescent Cl LU5 . . . . .105 F5
Crescent Ct LU5 . . . . .105 F5
Crescent Rd LU2 . . . . .123 F8
Crescent Rise LU2 . . . . . .123 F8
Crescent The
  Ampthill MK45 . . . . .84 E7
  Bedford MK40 . . . . .38 B1
  Beeston SG19 . . . . .54 B5
  Caddington LU1 . . . . .122 F8
  Cotton End MK45 . . . . .63 D7
  Henlow SG16 . . . . .89 C4
  Hitchin SG5 . . . . .100 D1
  Moggerhanger MK44 . . . . .53 C8
  Shortstown MK42 . . . . .51 A3
  St Neots, PE19 . . . . .22 F6
  St Neots, Eaton Socon PE19 .22 C3
  Stanford SG18 . . . . .78 A7
  Stewartby MK43 . . . . .61 C3
  Toddington LU5 . . . . .105 F5
  Wharley End MK43 . . . . . . .58 E2
Cressener Terr 5 PE19 . . . .22 F5
Crest The Dunstable LU5 . .114 E1
  Luton LU3 . . . . .116 B7
Cresta Cl LU5 . . . . .115 A2
Cresta Ho 3 LU1 . . . . .123 F7
Criccieth Way PE19 . . . . . .22 F1
Cricket Cl MK41 . . . . .39 A2
Cricket La MK41 . . . . .39 A2
Cricketer's Rd SG15 . . . . . .90 A4
Crocus Way NN10 . . . . .8 B7
Croft Cl 4 AL5 . . . . .131 B1
Croft Gn LU6 . . . . .120 F8
Croft La SG6 . . . . .91 B1
Croft Rd LU2 . . . . .117 B3
Croft The Bedford MK41 . . .39 A2
  Flitwick MK45 . . . . .84 E3
  Luton LU3 . . . . .115 D8
Crofton Cl MK41 . . . . .38 D4
Crofts The
  Sharnbrook MK44 . . . . .16 E4
  Stotfold SG5 . . . . .90 F6
Cromer Way Luton,
  Stopsley Common LU2 . . .116 E6
  Luton, Warden Hill LU2 . . .116 D7
Cromwell Ct
  Kempston MK42 . . . . .49 E4
  St Neots PE19 . . . . .22 F3
Cromwell Hill LU2 . . . . . .116 D1
Cromwell Rd
  Barton-le-C MK45 . . . . .97 C3
  Bedford MK40 . . . . .49 F7
  Luton LU3 . . . . .116 D1
  St Neots PE19 . . . . .22 F3
Cromwell Way SG5 . . . . . . .99 D4
Crosby Cl Dunstable LU6 . .121 C6
  Luton LU4 . . . . .116 A2

Cross End MK44 ....18 E1
Cross End La MK44 ....18 E2
Cross Hall Rd PE19 ....22 D6
Cross Keys Mall 3 LU19 ....22 E5
Cross St Bedford MK40 ....38 B1
  Covington PE18 ....2 D2
  Letchworth SG6 ....101 F7
  Luton LU2 ....123 E8
Cross St N LU4 ....114 A1
Cross The SG19 ....44 D5
Cross Way AL5 ....131 C3
Cross Way The LU1 ....123 C5
Crosshall Inf Sch PE19 ....22 C6
Crosshall Jun Sch PE19 ....22 C6
Crosslands LU1 ....122 E3
Crossleys SG6 ....90 F2
Crosspaths AL5 ....130 C4
Crossway LU7 ....111 D7
Crossways LU5 ....114 C5
Crossways CI SG16 ....78 D1
Crow La
  Husborne Crawley MK43 ....82 B4
  Woburn Sands MK17 ....81 B8
Crowland Rd LU2 ....117 C5
Crown La SG18 ....78 F6
Crown Lodge SG15 ....90 A4
Crown PI MK42 ....50 B7
Crown Wlk PE19 ....22 B4
Crowther Ct SG18 ....66 F7
Croxley Ct LU7 ....110 F7
Croxton CI 3 LU3 ....116 A7
Cryselco CI MK42 ....49 D2
Cubbington CI LU3 ....116 A4
Cuckoo's Nest LU2 ....124 A7
Cuffley CI LU3 ....115 F4
Culloden CI PE19 ....22 C5
Culver Ho MK40 ....38 A2
Culverhouse Rd LU3 ....116 C3
Culworth CI LU1 ....122 E3
Cumberland St
  Houghton Regis LU5 ....114 B4
  Luton LU1 ....123 E6
Cumberland Way PE19 ....22 F1
Cumbria CI LU4 ....114 E5
Cunningham Way PE19 ....22 A2
Curlew CI SG6 ....90 E1
Curlew Cres MK41 ....38 B4
Curlew Rd MK41 ....117 C5
Curzon Rd LU3 ....116 C1
Cusworth Way LU6 ....113 E1
Cusworth Wlk LU6 ....113 E1
Cut Throat Ave HP4, LU6 ....126 E7
Cut Throat La MK41 ....37 F2
Cutcliffe Gdns MK40 ....49 F8
Cutcliffe Gr MK40 ....49 F8
Cutcliffe PI MK40 ....49 F8
Cutenhoe Rd LU1 ....123 E4
Cutlers Gn LU2 ....117 F2
Cutlers Way LU7 ....111 B6
Cygnus Dr LU7 ....111 D8
Cymbeline Ct 6 MK40 ....38 A1
Cynthia Ct MK43 ....61 A6

D
Daffodil Dr NN10 ....8 B7
Dag La MK44 ....10 F2
Dagnall Cty Fst Sch HP4 126 C5
Dagnall Rd Dunstable LU6 120 D2
  Great Gaddesden HP1 ....132 C5
Dagnalls SG6 ....101 F2
Dahl CI MK42 ....50 C4
Dahlia CI LU2 ....117 B4
Dairy Cotts SG5 ....98 B2
Daisy Croft NN10 ....8 C8
Dalby CI LU4 ....115 B3
Dale CI Bedford MK41 ....39 A3
  Dunstable LU5 ....114 F1
  Toddington LU5 ....105 F5
Dale Rd Dunstable LU5 ....114 F1
  Luton LU1 ....123 C7
Dale The SG6 ....101 E5
Dalewood AL5 ....131 D1
Dalkeith Rd AL5 ....131 C1
Dallas Rd MK42 ....50 A6
Dalling Dr LU5 ....114 C5
Dallow Inf Sch LU1 ....123 C8
Dallow Jun Sch LU1 ....123 C8
Dallow Rd LU1 ....123 B8
Dalroad Ind Est LU1 ....123 B8
Dalton CI LU3 ....108 C1
Dame Alice Harpur Sch
  MK42 ....50 C7
Dame Alice St MK40 ....38 B1
Dammersey CI AL3 ....128 F4
Dane CI Harpenden AL5 ....131 C4
  Stotfold SG5 ....90 F8
Dane La MK45 ....62 C5
Dane Rd Barton-le-C MK45 ....97 D3
  Luton LU2 ....116 C2
Dane St MK40 ....50 B8
Danefield Rd SG5 ....99 C4
Danes Way LU7 ....111 D7
Danescroft SG5 ....91 A1
Daneswood MK17 ....81 A1
Danvers Dr LU3 ....108 C1
Dapifer Dr SG19 ....54 C8
Dark La SG18 ....66 F6
Darlington CI LU3 ....116 A7
Darlow Dr MK40 ....37 D1
Darrington CI PE19 ....22 B3
Dart Rd MK41 ....38 C5

Darwin Rd MK42 ....50 C5
Daubeney CI MK45 ....95 F2
Daubeney Mid Sch MK42 ....49 F3
Dauphin Ct 5 LU2 ....116 D1
Davis Cres SG5 ....99 D4
Davis' Row SG15 ....90 A4
Dawlish Dr MK40 ....38 E1
Dawlish Rd LU4 ....115 F3
Dawson CI SG16 ....89 C5
Day's La MK40 ....37 D1
Daysfield MK45 ....74 B8
De Havilland Ave MK42 ....51 B2
De Montfort Ct LU5 ....105 F4
De Montfort Univ MK41 ....38 F1
De Parys Ave MK40 ....38 C1
Deacon Ave MK42 ....49 C3
Deacon Mews MK43 ....72 C8
Deacons Ct 6 LU2 ....123 D8
Deacons Way SG5 ....100 D1
Deadman's Hill MK45 ....75 B2
Dean CI MK17 ....81 C4
Dean St MK40 ....38 F1
Deans Mdw HP4 ....126 C5
Dearmans CI MK45 ....75 C1
Dearne Villas MK40 ....50 A8
Dearne Wlk MK41 ....38 C5
Deep Denes LU2 ....117 A2
Deep Spinney MK40 ....37 C1
Deepdale Water Gardens
  SG19 ....55 D7
Deeside MK41 ....38 D5
Deethe CI MK17 ....81 B5
Degray Manor SG16 ....78 D2
Delamare CI SG19 ....42 B1
Delamere Gdns LU7 ....110 C7
Delamere Wlk MK41 ....39 B3
Delfield Gdns LU1 ....122 E4
Dell CI AL5 ....131 B3
Dell Rd LU5 ....114 B5
Dell The Caddington LU1 ....122 E3
  Heath and Reach LU7 ....103 B5
  Kempston MK42 ....49 B2
  Luton LU2 ....117 F1
  Markyate AL3 ....128 D5
Dellcot CI LU2 ....117 B4
Dellfield Ct LU2 ....117 D2
Dellmont Rd LU5 ....114 B5
Dells La SG18 ....67 A5
Dells The SG18 ....67 A5
Delmerend La AL3 ....129 C1
Delphine CI LU1 ....123 B6
Denbigh CI MK43 ....72 D8
Denbigh High Sch LU3 ....116 C2
Denbigh Inf Sch LU3 ....116 B2
Denbigh Jun Sch LU3 ....116 B2
Denbigh Rd LU3 ....116 B2
Denbigh Way MK41 ....39 A4
Dencora Way LU3 ....115 B8
Dene CI MK17 ....81 C4
Dene Way SG18 ....66 B8
Denel CI MK45 ....84 E4
Denham CI LU3 ....115 E8
Denmark CI LU3 ....107 E1
Denmark St MK40 ....50 E8
Dennis Ct MK42 ....49 D2
Dennis Rd MK42 ....49 D2
Denny Cres SG18 ....78 F8
Denton CI Irchester NN29 ....7 B8
  Kempston MK42 ....49 D6
  Luton LU3 ....115 B3
Denton Dr MK43 ....72 C7
Dents Rd MK42 ....50 D5
Derby PI MK40 ....38 B1
Derby Rd LU4 ....115 C2
Derwent Ave
  Biggleswade SG18 ....67 B4
  Luton LU3 ....116 B7
Derwent Cotts MK43 ....26 B3
Derwent Dr LU6 ....121 C6
Derwent Lower Sch SG16 89 B5
Derwent PI MK42 ....50 B6
Derwent Rd
  Harpenden AL5 ....130 C4
  Henlow SG16 ....89 B4
  Leighton Buzzard LU7 ....110 B7
  Luton LU2 ....124 A8
Derwent Rise MK42 ....84 E2
Des Fuller Ct 3 LU1 ....123 F6
Devizes Ave MK41 ....39 A5
Devon Rd Bedford MK40 ....38 D2
  Luton LU2 ....124 B8
Devonshire Rd 5 AL5 ....131 B1
Dew Pond Rd MK45 ....84 D1
Dewlands MK43 ....36 F7
Dewsbury Rd LU3 ....116 C6
Dexter CI LU3 ....108 B1
Dickens CI MK43 ....24 F6
Dickens Ct SG18 ....67 A5
Dickens La LU7 ....113 A5
Dickens Rd MK45 ....84 C3
Dickerson CI SG19 ....44 B6
Digby Ct PE19 ....22 B3
Digby Rd LU7 ....111 A8
Dimmock Rd MK43 ....60 F7
Dines CI MK45 ....62 E4
Dingle Dell LU7 ....102 F2
Ditchling CI LU2 ....117 C3
Ditmas Ave MK42 ....49 C2
Ditton Gn LU2 ....117 E3
Docklands SG5 ....99 D4
Dodds CI MK44 ....11 B3
Dog Kennel Path LU6 ....114 B1
Doggett St LU2 ....111 A7
Dolphin Dr LU5 ....114 E6
Dolphins Way LU4 ....44 D6
Don Butler CI MK45 ....86 B3
Donlee Furlong LU7 ....111 C7
Donnelly Dr MK41 ....39 B1

Dorchester CI LU5 ....114 B1
Dorchester Way MK42 ....50 C3
Dordans Rd LU4 ....115 F4
Dorel CI MK42 ....116 F2
Dornan Ct LU1 ....123 E5
Dorrington CI LU3 ....116 C1
Dorset Ct 4 LU1 ....123 F6
Dorsey Dr MK42 ....50 B5
Dothans CI MK44 ....40 F5
Doug Harris Way MK45 ....36 B4
Douglas Cres LU5 ....114 B2
Douglas Rd Bedford MK41 ....38 D6
  Harpenden AL5 ....130 F2
  Luton LU4 ....116 A2
Dove CI SG19 ....42 C2
Dove House CI LU6 ....119 F3
Dove House La LU6 ....127 D8
Dove La MK43 ....25 A6
Dove Rd MK41 ....38 D4
Dove Tree Rd LU7 ....111 C8
Dove Wlk MK45 ....84 E1
Dovedale LU2 ....116 E6
Dovehouse CI
  Bromham MK43 ....36 F2
  St Neots PE19 ....22 F6
Dovehouse Hill LU2 ....117 B1
Dover CI LU3 ....116 A3
Dover Cres MK41 ....39 A5
Dovery Down Lower Sch
  LU7 ....103 A2
Downfield Way LU2 ....49 E5
Downham Rd MK17 ....81 C4
Downlands LU3 ....115 C7
Downs Rd Dunstable LU5 ....121 D8
  Luton LU1 ....123 C7
Downs View LU4 ....115 D4
Downside MK41 ....39 A3
Downside Gdns MK45 ....56 A8
Downside Inf Sch LU4 ....115 C1
Downside Jun Sch LU4 ....115 C1
Downside Lower Sch
  LU5 ....121 C7
Downton Ct 2 LU3 ....123 D8
Downview LU4 ....115 B2
Drake Lower Sch MK42 ....50 B6
Drake Rd PE19 ....22 B2
Drakelow CI MK17 ....92 F8
Drakes Ct SG18 ....121 D8
Drapers Mews LU3 ....116 C1
Drayton CI NN10 ....8 A8
Drayton Rd
  Kempston MK42 ....49 D2
  Luton LU4 ....115 A3
Drewels La PE19 ....33 E4
Drive The Harpenden AL5 ....131 A1
  Ivinghoe Aston LU6 ....119 A1
  Oakley MK43 ....36 F7
  Sharnbrook MK44 ....16 C4
  Wharley End MK43 ....58 D2
Drivers Ct LU7 ....111 D7
Drove Rd Biggleswade SG18 67 B6
  Gamlingay SG19 ....44 B7
Drovers Way LU6 ....120 F8
Drummonds The LU4 ....115 C2
Drury CI LU5 ....114 C5
Drury La LU5 ....114 C5
Dryden Ct PE19 ....22 F5
Dubbs Knoll Rd SG8 ....69 F5
Duchess CI PE19 ....22 A3
Duchess Ct LU5 ....114 C1
Duchess Rd MK42 ....50 F4
Duchy CI NN9 ....3 B8
Duck End La
  Biddenham MK40 ....37 B1
  Maulden MK45 ....85 B8
  Wilstead MK45 ....62 B3
Duck La Shefford SG17 ....77 C3
  St Neots PE19 ....22 F4
  Woburn MK17 ....92 F7
Duck Mill La MK42 ....50 C7
Duckmill Cres MK42 ....50 C7
Dudley CI MK42 ....49 E3
Dudley St Bedford MK40 ....50 E8
  Leighton Buzzard LU7 ....111 A6
  Luton LU2 ....123 E8
Dugdale Ct SG5 ....100 C1
Duke Dr MK41 ....37 D7
Duke St Aspley Guise MK17 ....81 D4
  Bedford MK40 ....50 C8
  Luton LU2 ....123 E8
Dukeminster Trad Est
  LU5 ....114 C1
Dukes Ave LU6 ....126 E8
Dukes Ct Dunstable LU5 ....114 C1
  4 Luton LU2 ....123 D6
  St Neots PE19 ....22 B4
Dukes Ride
  Leighton Buzzard LU7 ....102 F3
  13 Luton LU2 ....116 D1
Dukes Row PE18 ....6 F5
Duloe Brook PE19 ....22 B4
Duloe Rd PE19 ....22 B5
Dulverton Ct LU7 ....110 C8
Dumfries Ct 8 LU1 ....123 D6
Dumfries St LU1 ....123 D6
Duncan Rd MK43 ....58 E2
Duncombe CI LU3 ....116 C6
Duncombe CI LU3 ....122 E2
Duncombe Dr
  Dunstable LU5 ....114 C2
  Leighton Buzzard LU7 ....111 A6
Duncombe St MK42 ....49 F4
Duncots CI SG5 ....100 E3
Dunham CI MK42 ....50 F5
Dunkirk CI MK42 ....50 A5
Dunlin SG6 ....90 E1

Dunmow Ct LU3 ....116 D2
Dunsby Rd LU3 ....116 A6
Dunsmore Rd LU1 ....123 C6
Dunstable CI Flitwick MK45 84 E2
  Luton LU4 ....116 A1
Dunstable Coll LU5 ....114 C1
Dunstable CI LU4 ....115 F2
Dunstable Downs LU6 ....120 E3
Dunstable PI 5 LU1 ....123 D7
Dunstable Rd
  Caddington LU1 ....122 C3
  Dagnall LU6 ....126 C7
  Eaton Bray LU6 ....120 A5
  Flamstead AL3 ....129 F1
  Flitwick MK45 ....84 E1
  Houghton Regis LU5 ....114 B3
  Luton LU1 ,LU4 ....116 F2
  Studham LU6 ....127 B6
  Tilsworth LU7 ....113 A6
  Toddington LU5 ....105 F3
  Totternhoe LU6 ....120 D7
Dunstable St MK45 ....84 E8
Dunstall Rd MK45 ....97 C2
Dunster Gdns MK41 ....39 B5
Dunster Way PE19 ....22 F2
Dunton La
  Biggleswade SG18 ....67 C4
  Biggleswade SG18 ....67 E4
Dunton Lower Sch SG18 .68 D5
Dunvegan Way MK41 ....38 F5
Dunville Rd MK40 ....49 F8
Durbar Rd LU4 ....116 B1
Durham CI
  Biggleswade SG18 ....67 A4
  Flitwick MK45 ....84 E4
Durham Rd LU2 ....124 A7
Durler Ave MK42 ....49 C3
Durley Gdns LU1 ....123 D5
Durrell CI LU7 ....110 E7
Duxford CI LU3 ....116 B7
Dyers Rd LU6 ....119 F2
Dylan Ct LU5 ....114 C5
Dynes PI MK44 ....53 C7
Dynevor CI MK43 ....36 E2
Dynevor Rd MK40 ....38 A1

E
Eagle Centre Way LU4 ....115 B7
Eagle CI LU4 ....115 A4
Eagle Ct SG7 ....91 E1
Eagle Dr MK42 ....84 D2
Eagle Farm Rd SG18 ....67 B5
Eagle Gdns MK41 ....38 B3
Earl Ct PE19 ....22 B4
Earls Ct LU5 ....114 C1
Earls Holme MK42 ....49 D6
Earls Meade LU2 ....116 D1
Earlsmead SG6 ....101 F3
Easby Abbey MK41 ....51 B8
Easedale CI LU6 ....121 C6
Easingwold Gdns LU1 ....122 F8
East Ct SG4 ....101 B1
East Ct Bedford MK41 ....39 A2
  2 St Neots PE19 ....22 F5
East End LU5 ....114 C5
East End La MK44 ....30 B3
East Hill LU3 ....116 B6
East Hills MK43 ....59 B1
East La SG19 ....44 C6
East Lodge Sch SG17 ....77 A2
East Rd Langford SG18 ....78 F8
  Sandy SG19 ....54 B8
  Wharley End MK43 ....58 D2
East Side SG19 ....54 C5
East Sq MK42 ....51 A3
East St Irchester NN29 ....7 B8
  Kimbolton PE19 ....6 F4
  Leighton Buzzard LU7 ....111 B8
  Lilley LU2 ....109 D2
  St Neots PE19 ....22 F5
East Wlk SG18 ....67 B7
Eastcheap SG6 ....101 F6
Eastcote MK42 ....51 A3
Eastcott CI LU2 ....117 D1
Eastcotts Rd MK42 ....50 F5
Eastdale CI MK42 ....50 A4
Eastern Ave
  Dunstable LU5 ....121 D8
  Henlow SG16 ....89 C3
Eastern Way
  Heath and Reach LU7 ....103 D5
  Letchworth SG6 ....91 A1
Eastfield CI LU2 ....117 C4
Easthill Rd LU5 ....114 C5
Eastnor Gdns MK41 ....39 A4
Easton CI MK45 ....84 F3
Easton Rd MK45 ....84 F3
Eastville Rd MK42 ....50 B5
Eaton Bray Lower Sch
  LU6 ....119 F6
Eaton Bray Rd
  Northall LU6 ....119 C5
  Totternhoe LU6 ....119 E8
Eaton Ford Gn PE19 ....22 D5
Eaton Green Rd LU2 ....124 D8
Eaton Pk LU6 ....119 F6
Eaton PI LU2 ....117 D1
Eaton Rd MK42 ....49 E2
Eaton Valley Rd LU2 ....124 B8
Eatongate CI LU6 ....119 F4
Ebble Mead MK41 ....38 D6
Ebenezer St 6 LU1 ....123 D6
Eddiwick Ave LU5 ....114 D7
Eden Way MK41 ....38 D6
Edgcott CI LU3 ....108 B1
Edgcumbe Ct SG19 ....54 C7

Edgecote CI LU1 ....122 E3
Edgehill Gdns LU3 ....115 C8
Edgewood Dr LU2 ....117 C6
Edinburgh CI MK42 ....50 D5
Edinburgh Dr PE19 ....22 C4
Edison Rd MK41 ....39 C3
Edith Cavell Lower Sch
  MK41 ....38 A2
Edkins CI LU2 ....116 E5
Edlesborough Cty Com Sch
  LU6 ....119 E3
Edward Arnold Ct MK42 .49 D5
Edward Peake Mid Sch
  SG18 ....67 C8
Edward Rd Bedford MK42 .50 A6
  Biggleswade SG18 ....67 B7
  Irchester NN29 ....7 B7
  St Neots PE19 ....22 F2
Edward St Dunstable LU6 .114 B1
  Leighton Buzzard LU7 ....111 A8
  Luton LU2 ....116 F1
Edworth Rd SG18 ....79 C5
Egdon Dr LU2 ....116 D6
Egglestone CI MK42 ....49 D4
Eighth Ave MK45 ....115 D7
Eileen Wade Lower Sch
  PE18 ....5 B4
Eisenhower PI SG17 ....76 E2
Eisenhower Rd SG17 ....77 C1
Elaine Gdns LU1 ....123 A1
Eldefield SG6 ....101 D7
Elderberry CI LU2 ....117 B4
Eldon Rd LU4 ....115 C1
Eldon Way SG18 ....67 A4
Eleanor CI MK17 ....92 F7
Eleanor Ct 4 LU6 ....121 B8
Eleanor Wlk MK17 ....92 F7
Eleanor's Cross 5 LU6 ....121 B8
Elgar Dr SG17 ....77 D3
Elgar Path LU2 ....123 E8
Elger CI MK40 ....37 D1
Elizabeth Ct
  Dunstable LU5 ....121 C8
  Henlow SG16 ....78 D1
  9 Luton LU2 ....123 D6
  St Neots PE19 ....22 C4
Elizabeth St LU1 ....123 D6
Elizabeth Way SG19 ....44 C6
Ellenhall CI LU3 ....116 C1
Ellenshaw Ct MK45 ....84 F4
Ellerdine CI LU3 ....116 B4
Ellesmere CI LU6 ....120 C6
Elliot Cres MK41 ....39 B5
Ellis Rd MK41 ....38 D3
Elliswick Rd AL5 ....131 B2
Ells Ct LU2 ....116 F1
Elm Ave LU1 ....122 E3
Elm CI Bedford MK41 ....38 E4
  Campton SG17 ....76 F1
  Hargrave NN9 ....1 F2
  Henlow SG16 ....78 D1
Elm Dr MK45 ....86 B5
Elm Farm CI SG17 ....78 B2
Elm Gr Toddington LU5 ....105 F6
  Woburn Sands MK17 ....81 B4
Elm Lodge PE19 ....22 F3
Elm Park CI LU5 ....114 D6
Elm Rd Biggleswade SG18 .67 B5
  Shefford SG17 ....77 D2
Elm Tree Gr MK44 ....19 C7
Elmfield Ct LU2 ....117 A1
Elmhurst Gdns SG5 ....87 F1
Elmore Rd LU2 ....117 A1
Elms CI MK45 ....84 F7
Elms Ind Est MK41 ....39 D3
Elms La MK45 ....63 C4
Elms The Kempston MK42 .49 E3
  Leighton Buzzard LU7 ....110 E7
Elmsdale Rd MK43 ....61 A8
Elmside LU6 ....127 E8
Elmtree Ave LU2 ....117 E3
Elmtree Rd SG19 ....54 B8
Elmwood MK43 ....34 E6
Elmwood Cres
  Flitwick MK45 ....84 F2
  Luton LU2 ....116 E3
Elstow Lower Sch MK42 ..50 B4
Elstow Moot Hall Mus
  MK42 ....50 B4
Elstow Rd Bedford MK42 ..50 C5
  Kempston MK42 ....49 F4
Elveden CI LU2 ....116 E6
Elvington Gdns LU3 ....108 B1
Ely CI MK45 ....84 E4
Ely Croft SG18 ....67 A4
Ely Way Kempston MK42 ..49 E6
  Luton LU2 ....115 D4
Embankment The MK40 ..50 D8
Emerald Rd LU3 ....115 A3
Emerton Way MK43 ....60 F8
Emery PI PE19 ....22 F7
Emmer Gn LU2 ....117 F2
Emmerton Rd MK42 ....49 D5
Empire CI SG18 ....66 F5
Empress Rd LU3 ....115 E4
Emu CI LU7 ....103 A5
Enderby Rd LU3 ....116 C4
Endsleigh Rd MK42 ....50 B6
Enfield CI LU5 ....114 D6
Engayne Ave SG19 ....42 B1
England Ave LU6 ....113 F3
Englands La LU5 ....121 C8
Englefield CI LU3 ....116 F3
Englehurst AL5 ....131 C4
Ennerdale Ave LU6 ....121 B7
Ennerdale CI MK42 ....49 D3
Ennismore Gn LU2 ....117 F1
Enslow Ct LU1 ....122 E3

Enterprise Ctr 🔲 LU2 ....123 F8
Enterprise Way
Flitwick MK45 ....84 F3
Leighton Buzzard LU7 ..111 A5
Luton LU3 ....116 B8
Epping Way LU3 ....107 C1
Epping Wlk MK41 ....39 B3
Epsom Cl LU7 ....110 D6
Ereswell Rd LU3 ....116 A7
Eriboll Cl LU7 ....110 B6
Erin Cl LU4 ....116 A2
Erin Ct LU4 ....116 A2
Ermine Pl 🔲 LU4 ....116 D1
Escarpment Ave
HP4, LU6 ....126 D8
Eskdale LU3 ....115 C5
Essex Cl LU1 ....123 F6
Essex Ct 🔲 LU1 ....123 E6
Essex Gdns MK42 ....50 D5
Eton Ct MK40 ....38 D2
Etonbury Mid Sch SG15 ...90 C7
Ettrick Dr MK41 ....39 C4
Eugster Ave MK42 ....49 C3
Evans Cl LU5 ....114 A4
Evedon Cl LU3 ....115 F6
Evelyn Rd LU5 ....114 F2
Evelyn Way NN29 ....7 C7
Everard Rd MK41 ....38 F2
Everest Cl SG15 ....90 B5
Evergreen Way LU3 ......116 A8
Eversholt Ho LU7 ....111 A6
Eversholt Lower Sch
MK17 ....94 E1
Eversholt Rd
Ridgmont MK43 ....82 F4
Steppingley MK45 ....83 F3
Everton Hill SG19 ....43 B8
Everton Lower Sch SG19 ..43 C3
Everton Rd Everton SG19 ..43 E3
Potton SG19 ....55 F8
Sandy SG19 ....55 A8
Eves Field MK45 ....85 D3
Evesham Abbey MK41 .....51 B4
Evesham Ct MK41 ....38 C5
Exeter Cl SG18 ....67 A4
Exeter Wlk MK41 ....39 A5
Exton Ave LU2 ....117 A1
Exton Cl MK45 ....85 A8
Eyeworth Rd SG19 ....57 B2
Eyncourt Rd LU5 ....114 D2
Eynesbury Gn PE19 ....22 F4
Eynsford Rd LU4 ....115 D3

F
Fair Oak Ct LU2 ....116 F3
Fair Oak Dr LU2 ....116 F3
Fair Way MK44 ....40 F3
Fairfax Ave LU3 ....115 D7
Fairfax Cl SG17 ....78 A2
Fairfax Ct PE19 ....22 F3
Fairfax Rd MK40 ....49 F7
Fairfield SG19 ....44 D5
Fairfield Cl Dunstable LU5 114 F1
Harpenden AL5 ....131 D1
Fairfield Hospl SG5 .....90 C2
Fairfield Rd
Biggleswade SG18 ....66 F7
Dunstable LU5 ....114 E1
Fairford Ave LU2 ....116 E4
Fairgreen Rd LU1 ....122 F3
Fairholme Bedford MK41 ..38 F3
Biggleswade SG18 ......66 F7
Fairlands SG18 ....66 F7
Fairmead Cres NN10 ......7 F8
Fairway The MK41 ....39 A2
Fairways The MK41 ....86 C4
Fakeswell La SG16 ....88 E2
Falcon Ave MK41 ....38 C4
Falcon Cl Dunstable LU6 114 B1
Sandy SG19 ....42 B1
Falcon Cres MK45 ....84 E1
Falconers Field AL5 ....130 E3
Falconers Rd LU2 ....117 B1
Faldo Rd Barton-le-C MK45 .97 B3
Bedford MK42 ....50 D6
Fallow Dr PE19 ....22 B5
Fallowfield Ampthill MK45 .84 E7
Leighton Buzzard LU7 ...111 C7
Luton LU3 ....116 C4
Fallows Gn AL5 ....131 B3
Falstaff Rd PE19 ....22 C3
Falstone Gn LU2 ....117 E1
Fareham Way LU4 ....114 C5
Faringdon Rd LU4 ....115 C3
Farley Ct LU1 ....123 C5
Farley Farm Rd LU1 .....123 B5
Farley Hill LU1 ....123 C5
Farley Jun Sch LU1 .....123 C6
Farley Lodge LU1 ....123 D5
Farley Way MK43 ....36 C7
Farm Ave AL5 ....130 D4
Farm Cl Ampthill MK45 ..84 D7
Houghton Regis LU5 ....114 C5
Letchworth SG6 ....91 A1
Wyboston MK44 ....31 F6
Farm Gn LU1 ....123 C5
Farm Rd LU1 ....130 B7
Farmbrook LU2 ....116 D7
Farndish Rd NN29 ....7 B7
Farnham Dr NN10 ....7 F8

Farnham Way MK41 ....39 A5
Farr's La LU2 ....125 B1
Farrell Rd LU1 ....60 F7
Farrer St MK42 ....49 E4
Farrer Top AL3 ....128 E5
Farriers Cl SG7 ....91 E1
Farrow Cl LU3 ....108 C1
Farsands MK43 ....36 F8
Faulkner's Way LU7 ....110 E7
Faynes Ct LU5 ....54 C7
Fearnhill Sch SG6 .....101 C5
Fearnley Cres MK42 .....50 A4
Felbrigg Cl LU2 ....117 F2
Felix Ave LU2 ....117 A2
Felmersham Ct LU1 .....123 B7
Felmersham Gravel Pits
Nature Reserve MK43 ..16 C1
Felmersham Rd
Carlton MK43 ....25 C5
Luton LU1 ....123 A7
Radwell MK43 ....26 E7
Felstead Cl LU2 ....116 F3
Felstead Way LU2 ......116 F3
Felton Cl LU2 ....117 D1
Fen End SG5 ....90 F8
Fenlake Rd MK42 ....50 D6
Fensome Dr LU5 ....114 E5
Fenwick Cl LU3 ....116 B5
Fenwick Ct LU5 ....114 E5
Feoffee
Almshouses MK45 ....73 F1
Fermor Cres LU2 ....117 C1
Fern Gdns MK45 ....84 E3
Ferndale 🔲 AL5 ....131 A2
Ferndale Rd LU1 ....123 B7
Fernheath LU3 ....108 A1
Fernlea Cl MK40 ....49 E4
Fernwood Ind Sch MK17 .81 B2
Ferrars Ave PE19 ....22 A4
Ferrars Cl LU4 ....115 B1
Ferrars Inf Sch LU4 ...115 B3
Ferrars Jun Sch LU4 ...115 B3
Festival Rd SG19 ....55 F7
Fetlock Cl MK41 ....37 D7
Field Cottage Rd PE19 ..22 C3
Field End Cl LU2 ....117 C4
Field Fare La LU4 ......115 A5
Field La SG6 ....101 F4
Fieldfare Letchworth SG6 .90 E1
Sandy SG19 ....42 C2
Fieldgate Rd LU4 ......115 D2
Fielding Ct PE19 ....22 C7
Fields Rd MK43 ....61 A6
Fields The SG6 ....66 F1
Fieldside MK41 ....39 B3
Fieldside Rd MK45 ......85 E1
Fildyke Cl SG17 ....88 C5
Fildyke Rd SG17 ....88 C5
Filland Ct SG19 ....54 B6
Filmer Rd LU4 ....115 E4
Finch Cl LU4 ....115 A4
Finch Cres LU7 ....110 E5
Finch Wlk MK45 ....84 E1
Finchale Priory MK41 ...51 B8
Finches The Bedford MK40 .38 A1
Sandy SG19 ....42 C2
Finley Rd AL5 ....131 D3
Finsbury Rd LU4 ....115 D5
Finway LU1 ....123 A8
Fir Tree Cl MK45 ....84 E1
Fir Tree Rd MK45 ....86 B4
Firbank Cl LU3 ....107 C1
Firbank Ct LU7 ....111 B5
Firbank Rd MK42 ....50 C6
Firbank Trad Est LU1 ..123 A8
Firbank Way LU7 ....111 A5
Firecrest SG6 ....90 E1
Firs Lower Sch The MK45 .84 F8
Firs Path LU7 ....103 A1
Firs The Harpenden AL5 .131 D2
Kempston MK42 ....49 F3
First Ave LU6 ....121 B7
Fishers Cl MK44 ....40 E6
Fishers Yd PE19 ....22 E5
Fitzroy Ave LU3 ....116 B3
Fitzwarin Cl LU3 ......115 E8
Five Oaks LU1 ....122 F4
Five Oaks Mid Sch LU1 .122 F3
Five Springs LU3 ......115 E6
Five Springs Ct LU3 ...115 E6
Five Springs Sch LU3 ..115 F7
Flamstead JMI Sch AL3 .129 B1
Flanders Cl MK42 ....50 A5
Flax Mews AL3 ....128 E5
Fleming Cl MK40 ....37 C1
Flexmore Way SG18 .....78 F5
Flint Cl LU3 ....115 E7
Flint Ct Dunstable LU6 ..114 A1
Luton LU1 ....123 D5
Flint Way Bedford MK41 .39 B5
Bedford, Woodside MK41 .39 A4
St Neots PE19 ....22 E2
Flintings The HP2 ......132 F8
Flintwick Rd MK45 ......84 A3
Flitton Hill MK45 ....85 E5
Flitton Rd Greenfield MK45 .85 D3
Pulloxhill MK45 ....85 E1
Flitwick Lower Sch MK45 .84 E2
Flitwick MK45 ....95 E1
Maulden MK45 ....85 B7
Westoning MK45 ....95 E6
Flitwick Sta MK45 ......84 E2
Florence Ave LU3 ......115 D6
Flowerdale Wlk MK41 ...39 B4
Flowers Ind Est 🔲 LU1 .123 E6
Flowers Way LU1 ....123 E7
Folly Farm MK43 ....71 B4

Folly La
Caddington LU1 ....122 E4
North Crawley MK16 ....58 B5
Fontwell Cl MK40 ....38 D1
Foot La MK16 ....3 C8
Football Cl SG7 ....91 E1
Ford Cl PE19 ....22 D5
Ford End Rd MK40 ......49 F7
Ford La MK44 ....31 C1
Ford The MK41 ....37 E5
Fordfield Rd MK45 ......84 B6
Foresters' Cl MK45 ....64 A1
Forge Cl Chalton LU4 ...106 E2
St Neots PE19 ....22 B1
Forge Gdns MK44 ....4 A3
Forrest Cres LU2 ......117 A3
Forty Foot La MK44 .....9 A1
Foster Ave LU5 ....114 C3
Foster Gr SG19 ....54 C6
Foster Hill Rd MK41 ....38 E5
Foster Pl MK42 ....49 E4
Foster Rd
Harlington MK45 ....95 F2
Kempston MK42 ....49 E5
Wootton MK43 ....60 F8
Foster St MK40 ....38 B1
Foster Way MK43 ....60 F8
Foston Cl LU3 ....115 F6
Foundry La SG5 ....67 A5
Foundry Way PE19 ......22 B1
Fountain Gr MK42 ......49 D5
Fountains Rd
Bedford MK41 ....38 F5
Luton LU3 ....116 D3
Fourth Ave LU5 ....115 D7
Fowler Cl MK45 ....49 D5
Fowlers Dr SG17 ....88 B6
Fox Cl SG18 ....68 D5
Fox Cnr SG8 ....69 F5
Fox Dells LU6 ....121 C5
Fox Hill LU6 ....69 F5
Fox Hill Rd SG8 ....69 F5
Foxbrook MK43 ....36 C7
Foxbury Cl LU2 ....116 D6
Foxdell Inf Sch LU1 ...123 A8
Foxdell Jun Sch LU1 ...122 F8
Foxglove Cl Rushden NN10 .8 A8
St Neots PE19 ....22 C5
Foxglove Dr SG18 ......67 C4
Foxglove Way MK42 .....50 E4
Foxhill LU2 ....116 E5
Foxlease MK41 ....38 D5
Frampton Ct MK41 ......38 C5
Frances Ashton Ho 🔲
LU6 ....121 B8
Frances Ct LU7 ....110 E7
Frances Cl SG5 ....90 E6
Francis Groves Cl MK41 .38 D4
Francis Rd SG7 ....80 C6
Francis St LU1 ....123 D8
Franciscan Cl NN10 .....7 F8
Frank Hamel Cl MK45 ..97 C2
Franklin Ave MK45 .....97 B3
Franklin Cl
Marston Moretaine MK43 .60 D2
Pirton SG5 ....99 D4
Franklin Gdns SG4 ....101 B1
Franklin Rd
Biggleswade SG18 ......66 F5
Dunstable LU6 ....120 F8
Franklyn Gdns MK40 ....37 C1
Franks Cl SG16 ....89 B5
Fraser Rd MK44 ....51 C6
Frederick St LU1 ......116 E1
Frederick Street Pas
LU2 ....116 E1
Freeman Ave LU3 ......116 B8
Freemans Cl Hitchin SG5 .100 D1
Houghton Regis LU5 ...114 A4
Freemantle Ct PE19 ....22 B3
Freewaters Cl SG5 .....100 E4
French's Ave LU6 ......113 C2
Frenchmans Cl LU5 ....105 C5
Frensham Dr SG4 ......101 C2
Freshwater Cl LU3 ....115 F7
Friars Cl LU1 ....123 B5
Friars Ct LU1 ....123 B5
Friars Way LU1 ....123 B5
Friars Wlk Dunstable LU6 121 B8
Sandy SG19 ....54 D8
Friary Field LU6 ......121 B8
Friary La LU6 ....121 B8
Friday St LU7 ....110 F7
Friendless La AL3 .....128 F2
Friesian Cl LU4 ....115 A3
Frinton Cl NN10 ....7 F8
Friston Gn LU2 ....117 D1
Froghall Rd MK45 ......84 C5
Frome Cl Bedford MK41 ..38 C5
Luton LU4 ....115 E4
Front St LU1 ....123 C1
Fulbourne Cl LU4 ......115 E2
Fulbrook Mid Sch MK17 .81 B5
Fullers Ct SG6 ....101 E7
Fulmar Rd MK45 ....38 D4
Fulmore Cl AL5 ....131 D4
Furlay Cl SG6 ....101 D7
Furlong La LU6 ....120 C7
Furlong The MK41 .....38 F4
Furness La LU6 ....121 C7
Furness Cl MK41 ....38 F5
Furrows The LU3 ......116 B7
Furze Cl LU7 ....110 D7
Furzedown Ct 🔲 AL5 ..131 B1
Furzefield MK41 ....38 F5
Furzenhall Rd SG18 ....55 A1
Fushia Way NN10 ....8 A8
Fyne Dr LU7 ....110 C8

G
Gable Way LU5 ....114 C6
Gables The LU7 ....110 E6
Gaddesden Row HP2 ...132 E5
Gaddesden Turn LU7 ...111 E2
Gade Valley Cotts HP1 .132 E4
Gadsby St MK40 ....50 E4
Gainsborough Ave PE19 .22 D5
Gainsborough Dr LU5 ..114 D5
Gainsborough Rise MK41 .38 B3
Gainsford Cres SG4 ...101 C2
Gallery The 🔲 LU1 ....123 E7
Galleywood SG5 ....100 D3
Galliard Ct LU3 ....116 B4
Galloway Cl MK42 ......49 C3
Galston Rd LU5 ....115 D8
Gamlingay Village Coll
SG19 ....44 E5
Gamlingay Cty Fst Sch
SG19 ....44 D5
Gamlingay Rd
Gamlingay SG19 ....44 D8
Potton SG19 ....44 C1
Garden Cl MK42 ....49 D6
Garden Fields Ct NN29 ..7 C8
Garden Hedge LU7 .....111 A8
Garden Leys LU7 ......111 C6
Garden Rd LU6 ....121 C7
Gardener Pl MK40 ......37 C1
Gardeners Cl MK45 .....85 A3
Gardenia Ave LU3 .....116 A4
Gardens The Henlow SG16 .89 D8
Stotfold SG5 ....90 E6
Gardner Ct LU1 ....123 E4
Gardner's Cl LU6 .....120 E7
Garfield Ct LU2 ....117 D3
Garfield St MK41 ....38 B2
Garner Ct SG18 ....53 E2
Garnith Cl MK42 ....49 F4
Garrett Ct LU6 ....121 E6
Garretts Mead LU2 ....117 B3
Garter Ct 🔲 LU2 ......116 D1
Garth Rd SG6 ....101 E3
Gatehill Gdns LU3 ....108 B1
Gateshead Cl SG19 .....42 C1
Gaunts Way SG6 ....91 A2
Gayland Ave LU2 ......124 B8
Gayton Cl LU3 ....116 B4
Gazelle Cl PE19 ....22 B5
Gelding Cl LU4 ....114 F5
Geldonia Ct MK40 ......38 D2
Gelt The MK41 ....38 C7
Gemini Cl LU7 ....111 D8
Gentian Cl NN10 ....8 C8
George Ct
Biggleswade SG18 ......67 A5
Leighton Buzzard LU7 ..111 B7
George Pl PE19 ....22 F2
George St Bedford MK40 ..50 E8
Clapham MK41 ....37 D6
Dunstable LU6 ....114 B1
Leighton Buzzard LU7 ..111 B7
Luton LU1 ....123 E7
Markyate AL3 ....128 E5
Maulden MK45 ....74 C1
Shefford SG17 ....77 C2
Woburn MK17 ....92 F6
George St W LU1 ......123 E7
Georgetown Rd SG19 ...42 A1
Georgina Ct SG15 ......90 A3
Gerald Ct MK40 ....37 F1
Gerard Ct 🔲 AL5 ......131 A2
Gernon Rd SG6 ....101 F5
Gery Ct PE19 ....22 C5
Gibbons Rd MK40 ......50 A8
Gibraltar Lodge AL5 ...131 D3
Gifford Rd MK42 ....50 D6
Gig La LU7 ....103 B5
Gilbert Cl MK42 ....49 D6
Gilbert St AL5 ....131 B4
Gilbert Inglefield Mid Sch
LU7 ....103 C1
Gilded Acre LU6 ......121 C5
Gilder Cl LU3 ....116 A8
Gilderdale LU4 ....115 B6
Gillam St LU2 ....123 E8
Gillan Way LU5 ....114 E5
Gilpin Cl
Houghton Regis LU5 ...114 D5
Stanford SG18 ....78 A7
Gilpin Gn AL5 ....131 C1
Gilpin Sq LU6 ....114 A2
Gilwell Cl MK41 ....38 C5
Gipping Cl MK41 ....38 D7
Gipsy La Luton LU1 ....124 A6
Slapton LU7 ....118 D8
Girdle Rd SG4 ....101 A2
Girtford Cres SG19 ....54 B3
Glade The SG6 ....101 F3
Gladstone Ave LU1 ....123 C7
Gladstone Cl SG18 .....67 A6
Gladstone St MK41 .....38 C5
Glaisdale LU4 ....115 C5
Glamis Ct PE19 ....22 E2
Glamis Wlk MK41 ......39 A4
Glastonbury Abbey MK41 .51 B8
Glebe Ave Arlesey SG15 .90 A4
Flitwick MK45 ....84 E2
Glebe Cl SG19 ....54 B8
Glebe Gdns MK45 ......95 F2
Glebe Ho Ampthill MK45 .84 D7
Bedford MK40 ....38 D2
Biggleswade SG18 ......67 B7

Ent-Gra 139

Glebe Rd continued
Sandy SG19 ....54 C8
Glebe Rise MK44 ....16 C4
Campton SG17 ....76 F1
Gravenhurst MK45 .....87 C5
Lavendon MK46 ....34 A8
Glebe Way MK45 ....74 A7
Glemsford Cl LU4 .....115 B6
Glemsford Dr AL5 .....131 D1
Glen The Caddington LU1 .122 E3
Kempston MK42 ....49 D3
Glenariff PE19 ....22 E4
Glenavon Rd MK41 .....39 C4
Gleneagles Dr LU2 ....116 C6
Glenfield Rd LU3 .....116 C6
Glenrose Ave MK41 ....38 C6
Glenwood Sch LU6 ....121 E5
Globe Cl AL5 ....131 B1
Globe La LU7 ....102 C1
Gloucester Ct MK45 ...84 E8
Gloucester Rd
Bedford MK42 ....50 C5
🔲 Luton LU1 ....123 F6
Glovers Ct SG5 ....100 F1
Godfrey La MK45 ......16 E4
Godfreys Cl LU1 ......123 B6
Godfreys Ct LU1 ......123 B6
Godso Cl MK41 ....38 F4
Godwin Cl MK43 ....36 F2
Godwin Way MK43 .....36 F2
Gold Crest Cl LU4 ....115 A5
Gold La AL5 ....37 B1
Gold St Podington NN29 ..7 C2
Riseley MK44 ....10 F2
Goldcrest Way MK41 ..38 B4
Golden Riddy LU7 .....110 E8
Goldington Ave MK40 ..38 D1
Goldington Gn MK41 ...39 A2
Goldington Green
Lower Sch MK41 ......39 B1
Goldington Mid Sch MK41 38 F2
Goldington Rd MK41 ...39 A1
Goldstone Cres LU5 ...114 E2
Good Intent LU6 ......119 E4
Goodhall Cres MK45 ...86 C6
Goodman Rd MK42 .....50 B5
Goodmayes Cl MK42 ...50 F6
Goodrich Ave MK41 ....39 B4
Goose Gn LU7 ....104 D2
Gooseberry Hill LU3 ..116 B7
Gordon St LU1 ....123 D7
Gorham Pl PE19 ....22 D4
Gorham Way LU5 ......114 F2
Gorst Cl SG6 ....101 E5
Gosforth Cl SG19 ......42 C2
Goshawk Cl LU4 ......115 A4
Gostwick Pl MK44 .....52 C8
Gostwick Rd MK42 .....50 C4
Goswell End Rd MK45 ..95 C2
Gothic Mede Lower Sch
SG15 ....90 A5
Gothic Way SG15 ....90 B5
Gower Dr MK40 ....37 C1
Graces Cl MK43 ....59 C3
Grafton Rd MK40 ......50 A8
Graham Gdns LU3 .....116 A4
Graham Rd LU5 ....121 E7
Grampian Way LU3 ....115 C4
Granary La AL5 ......131 C1
Granby Ave AL5 ....131 D2
Granby Cl AL5 ....131 D1
Granby Rd LU4 ....115 E2
Granet Cl MK40 ....37 F1
Grange Ave LU4 ......115 D4
Grange Cl
Houghton Conquest MK45 .74 A7
Irchester NN29 ....7 B7
Leighton Buzzard LU7 ..110 D6
Markyate AL3 ....128 D6
Oakley MK43 ....37 A8
Grange Ct Bromham MK43 .36 E3
Heath and Reach LU7 ..103 A6
Letchworth SG6 ....91 A1
Grange Dr SG5 ....90 F7
Grange Gdns Beeston SG19 54 E5
Campton SG17 ....76 F1
Heath and Reach LU7 ..103 B6
Sharnbrook MK44 ......16 C4
Toddington LU5 ....105 F5
Grange Jun Sch SG6 ..91 A2
Grange La Bromham MK43 .36 E3
Cople MK44 ....52 A5
Grange Rd Ampthill MK45 .84 E7
Barton-le-C MK45 .....97 B3
Bedford MK41 ....39 A1
Blunham MK44 ....41 E5
Felmersham MK43 .....26 C8
Letchworth SG6 ....101 F8
Toddington LU5 ....105 F6
Grange Specl Sch MK42 .49 E5
Grange St SG17 ....78 A3
Grange The
Lower Caldecote SG18 .54 D2
Toddington LU5 ....105 F5
Grange Way Irchester NN29 .7 B7
Willington MK44 ....52 C8
Grangeway
Houghton Regis LU5 ...114 E6
Rushden NN10 ....8 A8
Gransden Cl LU3 ......116 A2
Grant Gdns AL5 ......131 B2
Grantham Rd LU4 .....115 E2
Granville Rd Hitchin SG4 .101 C4
Luton LU1 ....123 B8
Granville St MK42 .....50 A6

Graphic Cl LU6 ....121 D6
Grasmere Ave
  Harpenden AL5 ....131 C1
  Luton LU3 ....116 B7
Grasmere Cl
  Dunstable LU6 ....121 B7
  Flitwick MK45 ....84 E2
  Kempston MK42 ....49 E3
Grasmere Rd
  Biggleswade SG18 ....67 A4
  Luton LU3 ....116 C7
Grasmere Way LU7 ...110 D7
Grasmere Wlk LU5 ...114 C6
Grass Yd PE18 ....6 F4
Gratton Rd MK40 ......49 F8
Gravel Pit Rd MK45 ....84 F2
Gravenhurst Lower Sch
  MK45 ....87 C4
Gravenhurst Rd
  Campton SG17 ....87 F8
  Shillington SG5 ......87 E4
Gray St NN29 ....7 A7
Gray's Rd LU2 ....44 D6
Graylings The MK41 ...38 F4
Grays Cl MK45 ....97 C3
Grays Gr MK44 ....13 E2
Graze Hill MK44 ....28 C2
Great Aldens MK41 ....38 F4
Great Barford Mid Sch
  MK44 ....40 F5
Great Farm Cl MK43 ...72 C3
Great Gaddesden Sch
  HP1 ....132 D3
Great Gn SG5 ....99 D4
Great Hill SG17 ....77 C4
Great La MK45 ....75 D4
Great North Rd
  St Neots PE19 ....22 B2
  Wyboston MK44 ......32 A6
Great Northern Rd LU5 121 D8
Great Portway MK40 ...49 B6
Great Staughton Cty Prim
  Sch PE19 ....13 F6
Greatfield Cl AL5 .....130 C4
Greaves Way LU7 .....111 D6
Grebe Cl MK45 ....84 D2
Green Acres
  Gamlingay SG19 .....44 C5
  Lilley LU2 ....109 D2
Green Bushes LU4 ....115 D6
Green Cl Luton LU4 ...115 C5
  Stanbridge LU7 .....112 D5
Green Ct 6 LU4 ......115 C5
Green End
  Gamlingay SG19 .....44 C5
  Little Staughton MK44 .13 A4
  Workhouse End MK41 .40 A5
Green End Rd
  Great Barford MK44 ...40 E4
  Kempston MK43 ....49 A4
Green Gables PE19 ....22 D4
Green La
  Aspley Guise MK17 ...81 E4
  Clapham MK41 ....37 F6
  Dunstable LU6 ......120 E8
  Eaton Bray LU6 .....119 D2
  Everton SG19 ....43 C3
  Great Staughton PE19 ..13 F6
  Hitchin SG4 ....101 D1
  Kensworth LU6 ......127 E8
  Letchworth SG6 ......91 B1
  Luton LU2 ....117 C4
  Markyate AL3 ....128 F5
  Renhold MK41 ....39 B6
  Swineshead MK44 ....11 C8
Green Milverton LU3 ..116 A7
Green Oaks LU2 ......116 F3
Green The Chelveston NN9 .3 C4
  Edlesborough LU6 ...119 F4
  Great Staughton PE19 ..13 F7
  Harrold MK43 ....25 A6
  Houghton Regis LU5 ..114 C4
  Luton LU4 ....115 C5
  Marston Moretaine MK43 ..72 D7
  Newnham SG7 ....91 E7
  Peters Green LU2 ....125 C3
  Stotfold SG5 ....90 F7
  Turvey MK43 ....34 E5
  Wharley End MK43 ....58 E2
Greenacre Dr NN10 .....8 B8
Greenacres MK41 ......38 E4
Greenfield Ave SG5 ...100 D4
Greenfield Cl LU6 ....113 E1
Greenfield La SG5 ....100 E4
Greenfield Lower Sch
  MK45 ....85 D2
Greenfield Rd Flitton MK45 85 D3
  Flitwick MK45 ....85 A2
  Pulloxhill MK45 ......85 D1
  Westoning MK45 ......95 F6
Greenfield Way SG18 ..68 D5
Greenfields SG5 ....87 E1
Greengate LU3 ....115 C8
Greenhill LU7 ....103 A1
Greenhill Ave LU2 ....116 E3
Greenhill St 13 MK40 .50 B8
Greenlands LU7 ......111 C8
Greenleas Lower Sch
  LU7 ....110 C7
Greenriggs LU2 ......117 F2
Greensand Ridge MK43 .72 B2
Greenshields Rd MK40 .50 E8
Greenside Pk LU2 ....116 E3
Greenview Cl MK42 ....49 C3
Greenway SG17 ....77 A1

Greenways
  Eaton Bray LU6 .....119 D7
  Flitwick MK45 ....84 F3
  Luton LU2 ....117 B5
Gregories Cl LU3 .....116 D1
Greig Cl SG17 ....77 D3
Grenidge Way MK43 ...36 F8
Grenville Way PE19 ...22 B2
Gresham Cl LU2 ......124 D8
Gresham Ct MK40 ......38 D2
Gresham Way SG17 ....77 C4
Greskine Cl MK41 .....39 C4
Greycote MK42 ....51 A2
Greyfriars MK40 ......50 B8
Greys House Sch MK42 .49 D4
Greystoke Wlk MK41 ..38 F4
Grimaldi Ave LU3 ....116 A3
Grisedale Ct MK42 ....49 E2
Groat La SG19 ....44 D8
Grosvenor Gdns
  Biggleswade SG18 ....67 B6
  St Neots PE19 ....22 E6
Grosvenor Rd Baldock SG7 91 F1
Grosvenor Rd W SG7 ...91 F1
Grosvenor St MK42 ....50 C6
Grove Ct Arlesey SG15 .90 A8
  Turvey MK43 ....34 E6
Grove End LU1 ....123 B5
Grove Ho SG4 ....101 A2
Grove Park Rd LU1 ...123 B5
Grove Pl 2 Bedford MK40 .50 C8
  Leighton Buzzard LU7 111 A6
Grove Rd Dunstable LU5 121 D7
  Hitchin SG4 ....100 F1
  Houghton Regis LU5 ..114 C7
  Leighton Buzzard LU7 111 A6
  Luton LU1 ....123 D7
  Slip End LU1 ....123 B2
  Turvey MK43 ....34 E6
Grove The Bedford MK40 .38 C1
  Biggleswade SG18 ....67 B5
  Houghton Conquest MK45 .74 A7
  Lidlington MK43 ......72 C3
  Luton LU1 ....123 B5
  Silsoe MK45 ....86 B5
  St Neots PE19 ....22 E6
  Westoning MK45 ......95 D6
  Woburn Sands MK17 ..81 B5
Grovebury Cl LU6 ....121 D6
Grovebury Rd MK43 ...60 F7
Grovebury Place
  Est LU7 ....111 A6
Grovebury Rd
  Leighton Buzzard LU7 111 A4
  Leighton Buzzard LU7 111 A5
Grovebury Road Ind Est
  LU7 ....111 A5
Grovebury Turn LU7 ..111 C1
Groveland Way SG5 ....91 A9
Grovelands SG4 ....101 C2
Groveside SG16 ....78 D2
Guardian Ind Est LU1 .123 C8
Guernsey Cl LU5 ......115 A3
Guilden Morden Prim Sch
  SG8 ....69 F5
Guildford St LU1 .....123 E7
Guinness Pl MK41 .....51 A8
Guise St MK17 ....81 F4
Gulliver Cl MK42 .....49 D5
Gunnersbury Pk MK41 ..39 B1
Gurney Cl LU4 ....119 F6
Gurney's La SG5 .....100 B7
Gwyn Ct 2 MK40 ......50 B8
Gwyn St 4 MK40 ......50 B8
Gypsy La Aspley Guise MK17 81 F3
  Biggleswade SG18 ....66 D5

H

Hackett Pl MK16 ......58 A6
Haddon Cl NN10 ....8 A8
Haddon Ct 20 AL5 ....131 B1
Haddon Rd LU2 ......123 F8
Haden Cl MK41 ....38 A3
Hadfield Ct MK42 .....50 B6
Hadleigh Rd MK41 .....39 A4
Hadley Ct LU3 ....116 D1
Hadlow Down Cl LU6 ..116 A5
Hadrian Ave LU5 .....114 E2
Hadrian Lower Sch LU5 114 E2
Hagdell Rd LU1 ......123 C5
Hailes Cl MK41 ....38 E5
Hale Lodge MK40 .....38 C2
Halegate MK43 ....60 F8
Hales Mdw AL5 ......131 A2
Half Moon La
  Dunstable LU5 ......121 D7
  Pepperstock LU1 ....129 C8
Halfway Ave LU4 .....115 D1
Halifax Rd MK42 ......51 A2
Hall Ave NN10 ....8 A8
Hall Cl Harrold MK43 ..25 A6
  Sharnbrook MK44 .....16 C4
Hall End Cl MK45 ......86 B8
Hall End Rd MK43 .....60 E7
Hall Mead SG6 ....101 D6
Hall Rd PE19 ....22 E3
Hall Way MK45 ....63 D7
Hallards The PE19 ....22 C6
Halley's Way LU5 ....114 D4
Hallside SG18 ....68 C5
Hallwicks Rd LU2 ....117 B3
Hallworth Dr SG5 .....90 E6
Hallworth Ho SG5 .....90 E6
Halsey Rd MK42 ....49 E5
Halyard Cl LU3 ......116 B6

Halyard High Sch LU4 ..114 F3
Hamble Rd MK41 ....38 D7
Hambling Pl LU6 .....120 F8
Hambridge Way SG5 ...99 D4
Hambro Cl LU2 ....130 F7
Hamer Ct LU2 ....116 D8
Hamilton Cl HP4 .....126 C5
Hamilton Ct 3 LU2 ...111 A7
Hammerdell SG6 .....101 D7
Hammersmith Cl LU5 ..114 C5
Hammersmith Gdns LU5 114 C5
Hammond Ct LU1 .....123 C1
Hammond Rd MK41 ....39 D4
Hampden Cl MK45 .....84 E1
Hampden Ct MK40 .....37 B1
Hampden Rd Flitwick MK45 84 E1
  Hitchin SG4 ....101 C1
Hampshire Way LU3 ..107 C1
Hampton Cl MK45 .....62 F4
Hampton Rd LU4 .....123 B8
Hamsterley MK41 ......39 B4
Hancock Dr LU2 ......116 E5
Handcross Rd LU2 ....117 D2
Handley Page Cl MK43 .58 E2
Hanover Cl PE19 ......22 D5
Hanover Ct
  Leighton Buzzard LU7 110 D7
  Luton LU4 ....115 D5
  Wilstead MK45 ....62 F4
  Wootton MK43 ....60 F8
Hanover Pl MK45 ......97 C4
Hanscombe End Rd SG5 .98 D3
Hanswick Cl LU2 .....117 B2
Hanworth Cl LU2 .....116 D7
Harbury Dell LU3 ....116 B7
Harcourt Cl LU7 .....110 E7
Harcourt St LU1 .....123 E5
Hardenwick Cl 4 AL5 .131 A2
Harding Cl Bedford MK42 .50 E6
  Luton LU3 ....115 E7
Harding Ct MK45 ......84 B4
Hardmead Rd MK45 ....34 A3
Hardwick Cl SG17 .....77 C3
Hardwick Gn LU3 .....116 B7
Hardwick Hill MK45 ...61 F7
Hardwick Mews MK17 ..81 B3
Hardwick Pl MK17 .....81 B4
Hardwick Rd
  Bedford MK42 ....50 C6
  St Neots PE19 ....22 E3
  Woburn Sands MK17 ..81 B4
Hardy Pl PE19 ....22 D6
Harefield Ave MK42 ...50 A4
Harefield Cl LU1 .....122 F8
Harefield Rd LU1 ....122 F8
Harepark Terr SG16 ...88 E3
Harewood Rd MK42 ....50 C4
Hargood Ct PE19 ......22 B3
Hargreaves Ct MK42 ...50 C4
Harkness Cl SG4 .....101 B1
Harkness Way SG4 ...101 C2
Harland Rd PE19 ......22 F6
Harlech Ct PE19 ......22 F2
Harlech Rd MK41 ......38 F4
Harlestone Cl LU3 ...108 A1
Harling Rd LU6 ......120 B4
Harlington Lower Sch
  MK45 ....95 F2
Harlington Rd
  Sharpenhoe MK45 .....96 C3
  Toddington LU5 .....106 B7
  Upper Sundon LU3 ...107 B5
Harlington Sta LU5 ...95 E1
Harlington Upper Sch
  MK45 ....95 F3
Harmill Ind Est LU7 ..111 A5
Harmony Row LU7 ....111 E5
Harold Rd MK45 ....97 C3
Harpenden Central Sta
  AL5 ....131 B1
Harpenden Cl MK41 ...39 A1
Harpenden Hospl (private)
  AL5 ....131 A4
Harpenden
  Memorial Hospl AL5 .131 B2
Harpenden Prep Sch
  AL5 ....130 F2
Harpenden Rise AL5 ..130 F3
Harps Hill AL3 ......128 E5
Harpur Ctr 9 MK40 ...50 B8
Harpur Sq 16 MK40 ...50 B8
Harpur St MK40 ....50 B8
Harrier Cl SG18 ......66 F4
Harrier Way MK42 .....49 E2
Harriers The SG19 ....42 B1
Harrington Dr MK41 ...38 E4
Harrington Hts LU5 ..114 A5
Harris Cl MK42 ....49 E4
Harris Ct MK45 ....97 B4
Harrold Lower Sch MK43 .24 C1
Harrold Odell Ctry Pk
  MK43 ....25 B7
Harrold Priory MK41 ..39 B1
Harrold Priory Mid Sch
  MK34 ....24 F6
Harrold Rd MK46 ......24 C1
Harrow Piece MK45 ...85 C8
Harrow Rd LU7 ....111 B5
Harrowden Ct LU2 ....124 C8
Harrowden La
  Bedford MK42 ....50 E4
  Harrowden MK42, MK41 .51 B4
Harrowden Mid Sch
  MK42 ....50 E5
Harrowden Rd
  Bedford MK42 ....50 F4
  Luton LU2 ....124 C8

Harry Scott Ct LU2 ...115 C6
Hart Hill Dr LU2 ....123 F8
Hart Hill La LU2 ....123 F8
Hart Hill Prim Sch LU2 123 F8
Hart La LU2 ....124 A8
Hart Wlk LU2 ....117 A1
Harter Ave MK43 ......71 B7
Harter Rd MK42 ....49 D2
Hartington St MK41 ...38 B2
Hartland Ave MK40 ....38 E1
Hartley Rd LU2 ......123 F8
Hartop Cl MK41 ....38 F4
Hartsfield JMI Sch SG7 91 F1
Hartsfield Rd LU2 ...117 B2
Hartshill MK41 ....38 E3
Hartwell Cres LU7 ...111 B7
Hartwell Dr MK42 .....49 E6
Hartwell Gdns AL5 ...130 E1
Hartwell Gr LU7 .....111 A7
Hartwood 3 LU2 .....123 F8
Harvest Cl LU4 ......115 A3
Harvester Ct LU7 ....111 D7
Harvey Cl SG18 ....66 C8
Harvey Rd Bedford MK41 .39 E7
  Dunstable LU6 ......120 D7
  Rushden NN10 ....8 B7
Harvey St PE19 ....22 E4
Harvey's Hill LU2 ...116 F5
Haselfoot SG6 ....101 E6
Hasketon Dr LU4 .....115 B6
Haslingden Cl AL5 ...130 D3
Hassett St MK40 ......50 B8
Hastings Rd
  Barton-le-C MK45 ....97 C3
  Kempston MK42 ....49 D2
Hastings St LU1 .....123 D6
Hatch La MK44 ....19 A6
Hatfield Ave MK43 ....71 B7
Hatfield Cl MK45 .....84 F3
Hatfield Cres
  Bedford MK41 ....38 F1
  Flitwick MK45 ....84 F3
Hatfield Rd MK45 .....84 F3
Hathaway Cl Luton LU4 115 B2
  St Neots PE19 ....22 C3
Hatley Rd Gamlingay SG19 45 B4
  Potton SG19 ....56 E7
Hatters Way LU1 .....123 B8
Havelock Cl
  Gamlingay SG19 .....44 C5
  Sandy SG19 ....42 B1
Havelock Rd
  Biggleswade SG18 ....67 A7
  Luton LU2 ....116 E1
Havelock Rise LU2 ...116 E1
Havelock St MK40 .....50 A7
Haven The SG5 ....90 F6
Haverdale LU4 ....115 C4
Hawes Cl MK45 ....84 E3
Hawesmere Cl SG18 ...67 A4
Hawk Cl MK45 ....84 D2
Hawk Dr MK41 ....38 B6
Hawkesford Way PE19 ..22 F7
Hawkfield SG6 ....101 E8
Hawkfields LU2 ......116 E6
Hawkins Rd MK42 .....50 C5
Hawthorn Ave LU3 ....116 D6
Hawthorn Cl Ampthill MK45 84 F7
  Biggleswade SG18 ....66 F8
  Dunstable LU6 ......121 C7
  Turvey MK43 ....34 E6
Hawthorn Cres LU1 ..122 E3
Hawthorn End SG19 ...44 C5
Hawthorn Hill SG5 ...101 F7
Hawthorn Park Lower Sch
  LU5 ....114 D6
Hawthorn Rd PE19 ....22 E6
Hawthorn Way
  Lower Stondon SG16 ..88 F2
  Silsoe MK45 ....86 B4
Hawthorne Ave MK40 ..49 F7
Hawthorne Cl LU7 ....110 E8
Hawthorns The
  Cranfield MK43 ......59 B1
  Henlow SG16 ....78 D3
Hay Cl NN10 ....8 B8
Hay La AL5 ....131 A1
Haycroft LU2 ....116 E6
  Wootton MK43 ....61 A6
Hayes Cl LU2 ....117 C5
Haylands Way MK41 ...38 F2
Hayley Ct LU5 ....114 C6
Hayling Dr LU2 ......117 D3
Haylock Cl MK42 ......49 D2
Haymarket Rd LU4 ...114 E4
Haymoor SG6 ....101 E7
Haynes Lower Sch MK45 64 A1
Haynes Rd MK42 ......50 C5
Hayton Cl LU3 ....108 B2
Hazel Cl SG17 ....77 B2
Hazel Gr SG5 ....90 E5
Hazel Wlk SG18 ....66 F8
Hazelbury Cres LU1 ..123 C8
Hazelbury Ct LU1 ....123 C8
Hazeldene Lower Sch
  MK41 ....38 E3
Hazelwood Cl LU2 ....117 B4
Hazelwood La MK45 ...73 E3
Hazelwood Rd MK42 ...50 D5
Heacham Cl LU4 ......115 B4
Heath Cl Luton LU1 ..123 B6
  Woburn Sands MK17 ..81 C3
Heath Ct LU7 ....102 F3
Heath Gn LU7 ....103 A5
Heath La MK17 ....81 A2

Heath Park Dr LU7 ...103 A3
Heath Park Rd LU7 ...103 A3
Heath Rd Gamlingay SG19 44 B4
  Leighton Buzzard LU7 103 A2
Heath The LU7 ....102 E4
Heather Dr LU5 ....67 C4
Heather Gdns MK41 ...39 B1
Heather Mead LU6 ...119 E4
Heathermere SG6 .....90 F1
Heathfield MK41 ......39 A3
Heathfield Cl LU1 ...122 F4
Heathfield Lower Sch
  LU1 ....122 E4
Heathfield Rd Hitchin SG5 100 F1
  Luton LU1 ....116 C4
Heathwood Cl LU7 ....103 A3
Heathwood Lower Sch
  LU7 ....103 B3
Heaton Dell LU2 .....117 E1
Hebden Cl LU4 ....115 B4
Hedgerow The LU4 ...115 D6
Hedley Rise LU2 .....117 F2
Hedley Way MK45 ......86 B8
Heights The LU3 ....115 E5
Helen Ho MK42 ....50 B6
Helford Cl MK41 ......38 D6
Helmsley Ave MK41 ...39 A3
Helmsley Cl LU4 .....115 C5
Hemel Hempstead Rd
  HP4 ....126 F1
Hemingford Dr LU2 ..116 D6
Hempsals PE19 ....22 C6
Hen Brook PE19 ......22 F4
Henderson Way MK42 ..49 F4
Henge Way LU3 ......115 E7
Henley Cl LU5 ....114 E5
Henlow Ind Est SG16 ..89 B4
Henlow Mid Sch SG16 ..78 D1
Henson Cl MK43 ......58 E2
Henstead Pl LU2 .....117 D1
Herbrand Rd MK42 ....51 A4
Hercules Cl LU7 .....111 C8
Hereford Gr SG18 .....67 B4
Hereford Rd Bedford MK42 50 E4
  Luton LU4 ....115 A3
Hermitage Gdns MK45 .63 D7
Herne Cl LU5 ....105 F7
Heron Cl Biggleswade SG18 66 F4
  Sandy SG19 ....54 B6
Heron Dr LU2 ....116 E6
Heron Hts MK41 ....39 A2
Heron Rd MK45 ....84 E1
Heron Trad Est LU3 ..115 C7
Heron Way SG5 ....90 E6
Herons Mead MK42 ....36 F2
Heronscroft MK41 .....38 F2
Heswall Ct 5 LU1 ....123 F6
Hever Cl NN10 ....8 C8
Hewlett Rd LU3 ......115 D8
Hexton Cty Prim Sch SG5 98 A1
Hexton Rd
  Barton-le-C MK45 ....97 C2
  Barton-le-C, Church End
  MK45 ....97 D2
  Lilley LU2 ....109 C4
Heywood Dr LU2 .....116 F2
Hibbert St LU1 ......123 E6
Hibbert Street
  Almshouses 13 LU1 ..123 E6
Hibberts Ct SG6 .....101 E7
Hickling Cl Bedford MK40 .49 F7
  Luton LU2 ....117 D1
Hickling Way AL5 ....131 C3
Hickman Ct LU3 .....115 D8
Hicks Rd AL3 ....128 F6
High Ave SG6 ....101 E4
High Banks LU7 ......112 C5
High Beech Rd LU3 ..115 D7
High Beeches JMI Sch
  AL5 ....131 D1
High Dane SG4 ....101 A2
High Elms MK43 ....25 A1
High Mead LU3 ....116 A3
High Point 14 LU1 ...123 D6
High Rd Beeston SG19 ..54 B5
  Broom SG18 ....66 D3
  Cotton End MK45 .....63 D5
  Shillington SG5 ......98 E8
High Rd The
  Felmersham MK43 ....26 C8
  Harrowden MK42 .....51 A4
High Ridge
  Harpenden AL5 ......130 E3
  Luton LU2 ....117 C1
High St Arlesey SG15 ..90 A5
  Bedford MK40 ....50 C8
  Biggleswade SG15 ....67 A6
  Blunham MK44 ....41 E3
  Broom SG18 ....66 C3
  Carlton MK43 ....25 A3
  Chelveston NN9 ....3 C8
  Clophill MK45 ....75 D1
  Cranfield MK43 ......59 B1
  Dunton SG18 ....68 D5
  Eaton Bray LU6 .....119 E6
  Edlesborough LU6 ...119 E3
  Eggington LU7 ......112 B7
  Elstow MK42 ....50 B4
  Eyeworth SG19 ....68 F8
  Flamstead AL3 ......129 B2
  Flitton MK45 ....85 C4
  Flitwick MK45 ....84 E3
  Gravenhurst MK45 ....87 C4
  Great Barford MK44 ...41 A4
  Greenfield MK45 .....85 C2
  Guilden Morden SG8 ..69 F4
  Guilden Morden, Eyeworth
  SG19 ....69 A8

Hig–Ken 141

High St *continued*
Harpenden AL5 131 A1
Harrold MK43 24 F6
Henlow SG16 78 D2
Hinxworth SG7 80 D6
Houghton Conquest MK45 74 B8
Houghton Regis LU5 114 B4
Irchester NN29 7 B8
Kempston MK42 49 C3
Kimbolton PE18 6 F4
Langford SG18 78 F6
Leighton Buzzard LU7 111 A7
Lidlington MK43 72 C2
Little Staughton MK44 13 B1
Lower Dean PE18 5 C7
Luton LU4 115 C4
Markyate AL3 128 E5
Meppershall SG17 88 B5
North Crawley MK16 58 B6
Oakley MK43 36 F8
Odell MK43 25 C8
Pavenham MK43 26 B3
Pirton SG5 99 D4
Podington NN29 7 E2
Pulloxhill MK45 85 E1
Ridgmont MK43 82 F5
Riseley MK44 11 A2
Roxton MK44 31 E2
Sandy SG19 54 C7
Sharnbrook MK44 16 D4
Shefford SG17 77 C3
Silsoe MK45 86 C4
Souldrop MK44 16 B8
St Neots PE19 22 B8
St Neots PE19 22 E5
Stagsden MK43 48 A6
Stotfold SG5 90 F6
Sutton SG19 56 A3
Swineshead MK44 11 D8
Thurleigh MK44 18 C2
Tilbrook PE18 6 B6
Tingrith MK17 94 F5
Toddington LU5 105 F6
Turvey MK43 34 E5
Upper Dean PE18 5 B4
Westoning MK45 95 E6
Wilden MK44 29 F3
Woburn MK17 92 F7
Woburn Sands MK17 81 B4
Wrestlingworth SG19 57 B3
Wymington NN10 8 B5
Yelden MK44 4 A2
High St N LU6 114 A1
High St S LU6 121 C7
High Street Mews LU7 111 A6
High Top Barns MK44 4 A2
High Town Rd LU2 116 F1
High View Bedford MK41 39 A3
Markyate AL3 128 E5
High Wood Cl LU1 122 F7
Higham Dr LU2 117 D1
Higham Park Rd NN10 9 A5
Higham Rd
Barton-le-C MK45 97 D4
Chelveston NN9 3 B7
Highbury Gr MK41 37 E6
Highbury Rd LU3 116 C1
Highbush Rd SG5 90 E5
Highcroft LU7 111 C6
Highfield Bedford MK41 38 C5
Letchworth SG6 101 E4
Highfield Cres MK43 71 C1
Highfield Oval AL5 131 A4
Highfield Rd Flitton MK45 85 E4
Kempston MK42 49 E3
Leighton Buzzard LU7 111 C6
Luton LU4 116 B1
Oakley MK43 27 B1
Highfield Sch The SG6 101 D4
Highfields MK45 95 E6
Highfields Cl LU5 115 A2
Highlands MK45 84 E3
Highlands Lodge
Art Gallery SG17 87 D7
Highmoor AL5 131 A4
Highover Cl LU2 117 B1
Highover JMI Sch SG4 101 C1
Highover Rd SG6 101 D5
Highover Way SG4 101 B1
Highway The MK42 51 A3
Hill Cl Harpenden AL5 131 C4
Luton LU3 116 C7
Wingfield LU7 105 E1
Hill Cres MK43 71 C1
Hill Croft Cl LU4 115 C6
Hill End House La MK43 72 B2
Hill La Biggleswade SG18 66 F7
Ickwell SG18 65 F6
Upper Caldecote SG18 66 C7
Hill Milford AL5 131 D3
Hill Pickford AL5 131 D4
Hill Rise Bedford MK41 38 B2
Kempston MK42 49 B2
Luton LU3 115 D7
Hill Side LU5 114 B5
Hill The MK44 41 E3
Hill View SG19 54 C5
Hill View La LU7 111 D2
Hillary Cl LU3 115 D7
Hillary Cres LU1 123 C6
Hillary Rise SG15 90 B5
Hillborough Cres LU5 114 C7
Hillborough Inf Sch LU1 123 C6
Hillborough Jun Sch
LU1 123 C6
Hillborough Rd LU1 123 D6
Hillbrow SG6 101 D5
Hillcrest MK43 59 C2
Hillcrest Ave LU2 116 C8
Hillcrest Sch LU5 114 E1
Hillcroft LU6 113 E1
Hillesden Ave MK42 50 B4
Hillfield Ave SG4 101 A2
Hillfoot Rd SG5 87 E1
Hillgate SG4 101 A3
Hillgrounds Rd MK42 49 D6
Hills Cl MK44 31 E1
Hills Lower Sch The
MK41 38 E3
Hills View LU3 107 B4
Hillside NN9 3 B8
Hillside Cl SG5 87 E1
Hillside Rd Dunstable LU5 121 D7
Harpenden AL5 130 F3
Leighton Buzzard LU7 103 A2
Luton LU3 116 D1
Shillington SG5 87 E1
Upper Stondon SG16 88 E3
Hillson Cl MK43 72 D8
Hilltop Ct LU1 123 C7
Hilltop View SG17 88 B6
Hillview Cres LU2 116 C8
Hillway MK17 81 A6
Hillyfields LU6 121 C6
Hilton Ave LU6 121 B6
Himley Gn LU7 110 D6
Hindburn Cl MK41 38 D6
Hine Way SG5 100 C1
Hinksley Rd MK45 84 F3
Hinton Cl LU7 111 D7
Hinton Wlk LU5 114 E6
Hinwick Hall Coll of F Ed
NN29 7 C1
Hinwick Rd NN29 7 A2
Hinxworth Rd
Hinxworth SG7 80 C3
Hinxworth SG7 80 F4
Hitchin Bsns Ctr The
SG4 101 A3
Hitchin La SG17 78 B2
Hitchin Rd Arlesey SG15 90 A2
Henlow SG16 89 C6
Hexton SG5 98 E1
Letchworth SG6 101 E3
Luton LU2 117 A4
Pirton SG5 99 E2
Shefford SG17 77 E1
Stotfold SG5 90 E5
Upper Caldecote SG18 66 B7
Hitchin Road Ind & Bsns Ctr
SG15 90 A3
Hitchin Road Ind Est
LU2 116 F1
Hitchin St SG18 66 F5
Hitchmead Rd SG18 67 B6
Hitchmead Spec Sch
SG18 67 C6
Hitherfield La AL5 131 A2
Hives The PE19 22 D4
Hockley Ct LU7 104 E2
Hockliffe Bsns Pk LU7 104 F1
Hockliffe Lower Sch
LU7 104 E2
Hockliffe Rd Bedford MK42 50 D6
Hockliffe LU7 104 F6
Leighton Buzzard LU7 111 C7
Tebworth LU7 105 B1
Hockliffe St LU7 111 A7
Hockwell Ring LU4 115 C4
Hodder Rd MK41 38 C7
Hog Hall La HP4 126 A5
Hogarth Cl MK41 38 B2
Hogarth Pl PE19 22 D5
Holcroft Rd AL5 131 D3
Holden Cl MK40 37 C1
Holford Way LU3 108 B1
Holgate Dr LU4 115 B3
Holkham Cl LU4 115 A4
Holland Ct LU3 116 C2
Holland Rd Ampthill MK45 84 E7
Luton LU3 116 B2
Hollick's La LU6 121 D2
Hollies The
Kempston MK42 49 F3
Leighton Buzzard LU7 110 E7
Shefford SG17 77 C3
Hollies Wlk MK43 60 F8
Hollis La MK44 29 F2
Holliwick Rd LU5 114 E2
Holly Cl SG18 67 A8
Holly Farm Cl LU1 122 E3
Holly La AL5 131 E6
Holly St LU1 123 E6
Holly Street Trad Est 12
LU1 123 E6
Holly Wlk Harpenden AL5 131 D1
Silsoe MK45 86 B4
Woburn Sands MK17 81 B2
Hollybush Hill SG5 109 F1
Hollybush La
Flamstead AL3 129 B3
Harpenden AL5 131 A3
Hollybush Rd
Flitwick MK45 84 F2
Luton LU2 117 C1
Holm Oak Gn MK44 51 D4
Holmbrook Ave LU3 116 C5
Holme Cl MK43 72 D8
Holme Court Ave SG18 67 B3
Holme Cres SG18 67 A5
Holmemead Mid Sch
SG18 67 B4
Holmewood Rd MK45 85 D2
Holmfield Cl Luton LU1 123 D5
Toddington LU5 105 E5
Holmscroft Rd LU3 115 F6
Holmwood Cl LU5 114 D2
Holts Ct LU6 114 B1
Holtsmere Cl LU2 117 D1
Holwell Rd Holwell SG5 100 C7
Pirton SG5 99 E6
Holywell Cl LU6 127 C6
Holywell Ct LU3 116 B4
Holywell Mid Sch MK43 59 B1
Holywell Rd LU6 127 B6
Home Cl
Houghton Conquest MK45 74 A8
Luton LU4 115 C4
Renhold MK41 39 B6
Sharnbrook MK44 16 D3
Stotfold SG5 90 F7
Wilstead MK45 62 E3
Home Farm Cl SG19 42 B8
Home Farm Way MK45 95 E5
Home Rd MK43 48 F3
Homebrook Ho MK42 50 C7
Homedale Dr LU4 115 D2
Homedell Ho AL5 130 E3
Homefield SG7 80 D6
Homefield Rd MK44 31 E5
Homerton Rd LU3 116 A6
Homestead Way LU1 123 C5
Honey Hill SG19 44 D4
Honey Hill Gdns MK40 49 E7
Honey Hill Rd MK40 49 E7
Honeydon Ave PE19 22 C5
Honeydon Rd MK44 20 C2
Honeygate LU2 116 E4
Honeysuckle Cl SG18 67 C4
Honeysuckle Way MK41 39 B1
Honeywick La LU6 119 E8
Honiton Way MK40 38 E2
Hoo Cl MK43 60 F8
Hoo La MK43 60 E3
Hoo Rd SG17 88 D6
Hoo St LU1 123 E5
Hoo The MK42 49 B2
Hooked La MK45 63 A5
Hookhams La MK41 39 B6
Hooper Cl MK42 49 C2
Hoover Pl SG17 76 E2
Hope Rd MK42 50 B4
Horace Brightman
Cl LU3 116 A7
Horace Gay Gdns SG6 101 E6
Hornbeam Cl
Leighton Buzzard LU7 111 C8
Podington NN29 7 E2
Hornbeams The MK42 49 F4
Horne La Bedford MK40 50 B8
Potton SG19 56 A7
Hornes End Rd MK45 84 E1
Hornsby Cl LU2 117 C1
Horsefair La MK43 25 C8
Horsepool La MK43 82 A3
Horseshoe Cl SG18 68 D5
Horsham Cl LU2 117 D2
Horsler Cl MK45 97 C2
Horslow St SG19 56 A7
Horton Rd Horton LU7 118 A2
Slapton LU7 118 C6
Hospital Rd SG15 90 A4
Hotch Croft MK43 59 C3
Houghton Cl MK45 84 E7
Houghton Conques Lower Sch
MK45 74 B8
Houghton House (rems of)
MK45 73 F4
Houghton Mews 11 LU1 123 D6
Houghton Par LU6 114 A2
Houghton Park Rd LU5 114 E6
Houghton Rd
Bedford MK42 50 B6
Houghton Regis LU5 114 A3
Houghton Regis
Lower Sch LU5 114 A4
House La SG15 90 A7
How End Rd MK45 73 E5
How Field AL5 130 E3
Howard Ave MK40 49 F8
Howard Cl
Cardington MK44 51 E4
Haynes MK45 63 F1
Luton LU3 116 A4
Stotfold SG5 90 E5
Wilstead MK45 62 E3
Howard Ct MK45 84 E1
Howard Ctr 8 MK40 50 B8
Howard Pl Bedford MK40 49 F8
Dunstable LU5 121 D7
Howard Rd PE19 22 C1
Howard Road Ind Est
PE19 22 C1
Howard St Bedford MK40 50 C8
Kempston MK42 49 F4
Howard's Cl SG18 65 F1
Howards Mews MK45 86 C8
Howbury St MK40 50 D8
Howden Gdns MK40 37 C1
Howes La MK45 95 E6
Howitt's Gdns PE19 22 F2
Howitt's La PE19 22 F3
Howland Pl MK17 92 F7
Hoylake Ct LU1 123 F5
Hubbard Cl MK45 84 E1
Huckleberry Cl LU3 116 A8
Hudnall Rd HP4 132 A7
Hudson Cl MK43 72 B3
Hudson Rd MK41 39 C3
Hulme Cl MK42 49 E4
Humber Ave MK41 38 D5
Humberley Cl PE19 22 F3
Humberstone Cl LU4 115 E2
Humberstone Rd LU4 115 E2
Humphrey Talbot Ave
LU6 126 F7
Humphrys Rd LU5 114 E3
Hunston Cl LU4 115 B5
Hunters Cl SG5 90 E6
Hunters Way PE18 6 F5
Hunters Yd MK44 11 B3
Hunting Gate SG4 101 A3
Hunting Hall LU2 124 C8
Huntingdon Rd
Kempston MK42 49 D3
St Neots PE19 22 F7
Huntingdon St PE19 22 F6
Huntingdonshire
Regional Coll PE19 22 F6
Hunts Cl LU1 123 C6
Hunts Field MK44 40 F5
Hunts La MK43 26 B8
Hunts Path MK43 37 A8
Huntsmans Cl HP4 126 C5
Huntsmans Way MK44 27 B5
Hurlock Cl LU6 121 A6
Hurlock Way LU4 115 C5
Hurst Gr Bedford MK40 49 F8
Lidlington MK43 72 B3
Hurst Way LU3 115 F5
Husborne Crawley
Lower Sch MK43 82 B4
Hutton Way MK17 81 B5
Hyacinth Way NN10 8 B7
Hyde Ave SG5 90 E5
Hyde Cl AL5 131 B4
Hyde Ho 5 LU2 123 F8
Hyde La LU2 125 C2
Hyde Rd LU1 122 F4
Hyde The LU5 114 C6
Hyde View Rd AL5 131 B4
Hydrus Dr LU7 111 D8

I

Ibbett Cl MK43 49 A2
Ibbetts Yd 4 PE19 22 E5
Ickleford Bury SG5 100 E3
Ickleford Prim Sch SG5 100 E4
Ickleford Rd SG5 100 F1
Ickley Cl LU4 115 B5
Icknield Cl SG5 100 E4
Icknield Gn SG6 101 E6
Icknield High Sch LU3 116 C5
Icknield Ho LU7 111 A6
Icknield Inf & Prim Sch
SG6 101 D6
Icknield Inf Sch LU3 116 B5
Icknield Jun Sch LU3 116 B5
Icknield Lower Sch LU6 121 B8
Icknield Rd LU3 115 F4
Icknield St LU6 121 B8
Icknield Villas 10 LU6 121 B8
Icknield Way Baldock SG7 91 E1
Dunstable LU6 120 B1
Dunstable, Well Head LU6 120 D5
Letchworth SG6 101 E6
Luton LU3 116 B7
Icknield Way E SG7 91 F1
Icknield Way
Farm Cotts LU6 120 D3
Ickwell Rd Northill SG18 53 D1
Upper Caldecote SG18 66 A8
Iddesleigh Rd MK40 49 F7
Idenbury Ct LU1 123 C7
Ilford Cl LU2 117 D3
Imberfield LU4 115 C3
Index Ct LU6 121 D7
Index Dr LU6 121 D7
Ingle Ct PE19 22 F6
Ingram Cl MK43 72 C8
Ingram Gdns LU2 116 D7
Inkerman Rise PE19 22 C5
Inkerman St LU1 123 D7
Inns La MK45 86 B3
Instow Ct MK40 38 E2
Interchange Ret Pk MK42 49 F2
Irchester Jun & Inf Schs
NN29 7 A8
Irchester Rd NN29 7 B4
Ireton Cl PE19 22 F3
Irthing Cl MK41 38 D6
Irvine Ct MK41 38 D5
Irwin Rd MK40 38 E1
Isis Rd MK41 38 C5
Isis Wlk LU7 103 B3
Isle Of Wight La LU6 121 A3
Ison Cl MK40 49 D8
Itchen Cl MK41 38 C5
Ivel Cl Barton-le-C MK45 97 D3
Bedford MK41 38 D6
Langford SG18 78 E5
Shefford SG17 77 D2
St Neots PE19 22 C4
Ivel Cotts SG18 66 F1
Ivel Gdns SG18 66 F6
Ivel Rd Sandy SG19 54 C6
Shefford SG17 77 D2
Ivel View SG19 54 D6
Ivel Way Flitwick MK45 85 A3
Stotfold SG5 90 F8
Iveldale Dr SG17 77 D3
Ivester Ct LU7 110 E6
Ivinghoe Bsns Ctr LU5 114 B3
Ivinghoe Way LU6 119 E1
Ivy Cl Dunstable LU6 113 E1
Tempsford SG19 42 B8
Ivy Ct LU1 123 B8
Ivy La
Heath and Reach MK17 102 C8
Wilstead MK45 63 A4
Ivy Rd Bedford MK42 50 D6
Luton LU1 123 C8

J

J F Kennedy Dr SG17 76 E2
Jacey Ct MK42 49 D6
Jack's La MK43 34 F5
Jackman Cl MK43 36 F1
Jackson Pl SG17 76 E2
Jackson St SG7 91 E1
Jacksons Cl LU6 119 E4
Jacobs Cl SG19 56 A8
James Ct Luton LU4 115 B2
14 Luton, New Town LU1 123 E6
St Neots PE19 22 F2
James Foster Ho SG5 100 E1
James Marshall
Commercial Ctr AL5 131 A1
James St 10 Bedford MK40 50 B8
Irchester NN29 7 B7
Jameson Rd AL5 131 B3
Jansel Ho LU2 117 B4
Jaques La MK45 75 E1
Jardine Way LU5 121 E7
Jasmine Cl Bedford MK41 39 C4
Biggleswade SG18 67 C4
Jasmine Gdns NN10 8 B7
Jay Cl SG6 101 E8
Jays The SG19 42 C2
Jaywood LU2 117 C6
Jeans Way LU5 114 F1
Jellicoe Pl PE19 22 A2
Jenkins Cl PE19 22 B2
Jenkyn Rd MK43 60 E6
Jennings Cl SG19 55 F8
Jersey Rd LU4 115 A3
Jillifer Rd LU4 115 A2
Joes Cl MK45 85 C2
John Barker Pl SG5 100 C1
John Bunyan Cl MK45 85 B8
John Bunyan Upper Sch
& Com Coll MK42 50 E4
John Clover Ind Est MK42 49 C4
John Donne CE Lower Sch
MK44 41 E3
John Gibbard Lower Sch
MK44 16 D4
John Howland Cl SG16 78 D1
John St LU1 123 E7
Johnson Cl
Biddenham MK40 37 C1
Marston Moretaine MK43 72 C8
Johnson Ct LU5 114 D5
Joint The SG17 78 B2
Jordan Cl SG16 78 D2
Jowitt Ave MK42 49 F4
Jubilee Cotts MK43 72 D6
Jubilee Cres SG15 90 A2
Jubilee Ct AL5 131 C3
Jubilee Gdns SG18 67 B7
Jubilee La SG18 78 F6
Jubilee St LU2 116 F1
Judith Gdns
Kempston MK42 49 D3
Potton SG19 56 B8
Julia Ct LU3 116 B4
Julius Gdns LU3 115 F7
Juniper Cl Luton LU4 115 E2
Silsoe MK45 86 C4
Juniper Wlk MK42 49 F2
Jupiter Dr LU7 111 D8
Jutland Rise PE19 22 C5

K

Karen Ho SG16 89 A4
Katherine Dr LU5 114 F2
Katherine's Ct MK45 84 E8
Katherine's Gdn MK45 84 E8
Kathie Rd MK42 50 D5
Kayser Ct SG18 66 F4
Keaton Cl LU5 114 D5
Keats Cl MK40 37 F2
Keats Ct PE19 22 C6
Keats Ho 15 AL5 131 B1
Keats Rd MK45 84 D3
Keeble Cl LU2 117 E1
Keeley Farm Ct MK43 48 F1
Keeley La MK43 48 E1
Keepers Cl LU2 117 C2
Kelling Cl LU2 116 C8
Kelvin Ave MK42 50 C5
Kelvin Cl LU1 123 E6
Kempsey Cl LU2 117 D2
Kempston Ct MK43 61 E5
Kempston Hardwick
Gypsy Site MK45 61 F5
Kempston Hardwick Sta
MK43 61 D6
Kempston Rd MK42 50 A6
Kempston Rural Lower Sch
MK43 49 B4
Kendal Cl LU3 115 D7
Kendal Dr MK45 84 E2
Kendal Gdns LU7 110 C7
Kendale Rd LU4 115 B2
Kendall Dr SG17 76 F3
Kendall Rd MK42 49 D3
Kenilworth Cl PE19 22 C3
Kenilworth Rd LU1 123 C8
Kenilworth Wlk MK41 39 A4
Kennedy Ct LU7 110 F7

Kennedy Rd MK42 . . . . . . .50 C5
Kennel La AL5 . . . . .130 A5
Kennell Hill MK44 . . . . . . .16 D3
Kennet Rise MK41 . . . . . . .38 C6
Kenneth Ct LU2 . . . . .117 A1
Kenneth Way MK45 . . . . . .62 B6
Kennington Rd LU3 . . . . . .116 B3
Kensington Cl LU5 . . . . . . .114 E4
Kensworth Gate LU6 . . . . .121 C7
Kensworth Lower Sch
  LU6 . . . . .127 F8
Kensworth Rd LU6 . . . . . . .127 D4
Kent Ave MK42 . . . . .50 C5
Kent Cl MK45 . . . . .95 E5
Kent Rd
  Houghton Regis LU5 . . . . .114 D7
  Luton LU1 . . . . .122 F8
Kentmere Cl MK42 . . . . . . .49 D3
Kentwick Sq LU5 . . . . .114 D7
Kenworth Cl MK41 . . . . . . .38 B2
Kernow Ct LU2 . . . . .117 A1
Kershaw Cl LU3 . . . . .116 A8
Kershope Cl MK41 . . . . . . .39 C3
Kestrel Rd Bedford MK41 . .38 C4
  Flitwick MK45 . . . . .84 D1
Kestrel Way Luton LU4 . . . .115 A5
  Sandy SG19 . . . . .42 B2
Keswick Cl LU6 . . . . .121 B7
Ketton Cl LU2 . . . . .124 A7
Ketton Ct LU2 . . . . .124 A7
Keymer Cl LU2 . . . . .117 C3
Keysoe Rd Riseley MK44 . . .11 B1
  Thurleigh MK44 . . . . .18 D3
Keysoe Row E MK44 . . . . . .19 D8
Keysoe Row W MK44 . . . . .19 B7
Keyston Rd PE18 . . . . .2 D2
Kidner Cl LU2 . . . . .116 E5
Kielder Path MK41 . . . . . . .39 B4
Kilby Rd LU7 . . . . .104 F2
Kilmarnock Dr LU2 . . . . . . .116 E5
Kiln La LU7 . . . . .75 D2
Kilpin Gn MK16 . . . . .58 B6
Kilpin Cl MK42 . . . . .50 D6
Kimberley Gn 90 F2
Kimberley Cl LU4 . . . . .114 E3
Kimberwell Cl LU5 . . . . . . .105 F4
Kimble Dr MK41 . . . . .51 A8
Kimbolton Ave MK42 . . . . .38 D2
Kimbolton Cl MK41 . . . . . . .38 E3
Kimbolton Ct MK40 . . . . . . .38 D2
Kimbolton Overhills
  Cty Prim Sch PE18 . . . . . .6 F5
Kimbolton Rd
  Bedford MK40, MK41 . . . . .38 D4
  Chelveston NN9 . . . . .3 D8
  Pertenhall MK44 . . . . .12 D7
  St Neots PE19 . . . . .22 A8
  Wilden MK44 . . . . .19 D4
Kimbolton Sch
  Kimbolton PE18 . . . . .6 E5
  Kimbolton PE18 . . . . .6 F4
Kimpton Bottom SG4 . . . . .131 E7
Kimpton Rd
  Luton LU1, LU2 . . . . .124 A6
  Peters Green LU2, SG4 . . . .125 E2
King Edward Rd MK41 . . . .39 A1
King George Cl MK43 . . . . .78 F7
King Georges Cl SG5 . . . . .100 D5
King Henry Ct LU3 . . . . . . .116 B2
King St Clapham MK41 . . . .37 D6
  Dunstable LU5 . . . . .121 C8
  Houghton Regis LU5 . . . . .114 B4
  Kempston MK42 . . . . .49 E4
  Leighton Buzzard LU7 . . . .111 A8
  Luton LU1 . . . . .123 E7
  Markyate AL3 . . . . .128 E5
  Potton SG19 . . . . .56 A7
King William Cl
  Barton-le-C MK45 . . . . . . .97 D4
  Kempston MK42 . . . . .49 C4
King William Rd MK42 . . . .49 C4
King's Pl MK42 . . . . .50 B6
King's Rd Broom SG18 . . . . .66 C3
  Flitwick MK45 . . . . .84 F2
  Sandy SG19 . . . . .54 C7
  St Neots PE19 . . . . .22 F6
King's Wood National
  Nature Reserve LU7 . .103 A8
Kingfisher Cl
  Bedford MK41 . . . . .38 D3
  Biggleswade SG18 . . . . . . .66 F5
  Sandy SG19 . . . . .42 C2
Kingfisher Rd MK45 . . . . . .84 D1
Kinghamway LU2 . . . . .116 E1
Kings Cl MK44 . . . . .10 F2
Kings Ct Dunstable LU5 . . .114 C1
  Flitwick MK45 . . . . .84 F2
Kings Hedges SG5 . . . . . . .100 C1
Kings Houghton
  Mid Sch LU6 . . . . .114 D7
Kings Mead LU6 . . . . .119 E3
Kings Pond Cl SG18 . . . . . .68 D5
Kings Rd Maulden MK45 . . .74 C1
  St Neots PE19 . . . . .22 B3
Kings Sch AL5 . . . . .130 F4
Kings Way LU7 . . . . .112 D5
Kingsbrook Rd MK42 . . . . .50 C7
Kingsbury Ave LU5 . . . . . . .114 E1
Kingsbury Ct LU5 . . . . .121 C8
Kingsbury Gdns LU5 . . . . . .114 F1
Kingscroft Ave LU5 . . . . . .114 C1
Kingsdown Ave LU2 . . . . . .116 D5
Kingsland Cl LU4 . . . . .114 E4
Kingsland Com Coll LU5 . .114 E6

Kingsland Ct 7 LU1 . . . . . .123 F6
Kingsland Rd LU1 . . . . .123 F6
Kingsley Ct SG19 . . . . .54 B8
Kingsley Rd Bedford MK40 .50 C8
  Luton LU3 . . . . .116 A5
Kingsmede SG17 . . . . .77 C3
Kingsmoor Cl MK45 . . . . . .84 F3
Kingsmoor Lower Sch
  MK45 . . . . .84 F3
Kingston Ct MK42 . . . . .50 A6
Kingston Rd LU2 . . . . .116 F1
Kingsway Bedford MK42 . . .50 C7
  Dunstable LU5 . . . . .114 C1
  Luton LU4 . . . . .116 A1
  Stotfold SG5 . . . . .90 F7
Kingsway Gdns SG5 . . . . . .90 F7
Kingsway Ind Est LU1 . . . .123 A8
Kingswood Ave SG4 . . . . . .101 D1
Kingswood Cl MK45 . . . . . .74 B7
Kingswood Way MK40 . . . .49 B6
Kinloch Ct 6 AL5 . . . . .131 B1
Kinmoor Cl LU3 . . . . .107 D1
Kinross Cres LU3 . . . . .115 D8
Kinsbourne Cl AL5 . . . . . . .130 C4
Kinsbourne Cres AL5 . . . . .130 D4
Kinsbourne Green La
  AL5 . . . . .130 B3
Kipling Pl PE19 . . . . .22 D5
Kipling The LU3 . . . . .116 B6
Kipling Way AL5 . . . . .131 B1
Kirby Dr LU3 . . . . .116 A8
Kirby Rd LU6 . . . . .121 A8
Kirkdale Ct 8 LU1 . . . . .123 E6
Kirkstall Cl MK42 . . . . .50 C3
Kirkstone Dr LU6 . . . . .121 B6
Kirkwick Ave AL5 . . . . .131 A1
Kirkwood Rd LU4 . . . . .114 F3
Kirton Way LU5 . . . . .114 E6
Kite Way SG6 . . . . .101 E8
Kitelands Rd SG18 . . . . . . .67 C4
Kiteleys Gn LU7 . . . . .111 C8
Kittiwake Cl SG18 . . . . .66 F4
Kiwi Ct SG5 . . . . .100 F1
Klondyke AL5 . . . . .130 A5
Knaresborough Ct PE19 . .22 F1
Knarsdale Wlk MK41 . . . . . .39 B4
Knaves Hill LU7 . . . . .110 D8
Kneller Cl MK41 . . . . .38 A2
Knights Ave MK41 . . . . .37 D7
Knights Cl Eaton Bray LU6 .119 F5
  St Neots PE19 . . . . .22 A4
Knights Ct LU6 . . . . .119 E5
Knights Field LU2 . . . . .116 E1
Knoll Rise LU2 . . . . .116 E4
Knoll The Maulden MK45 . . .85 D8
  Woburn Sands MK17 . . . . .81 A1
Knolls The SG19 . . . . .54 B5
Knolls View LU6 . . . . .112 F1
Knolls Way SG17 . . . . .77 F2
Knotting La MK44 . . . . .10 C1
Knotting Rd MK44 . . . . .10 A4
Knotts Cl LU6 . . . . .121 C5
Knowl Piece SG4 . . . . .101 A3
Kym Rd PE19 . . . . .22 C4
Kymbrook Lower Sch
  MK44 . . . . .19 C7
Kynance Cl LU2 . . . . .117 A2

L

Laburnam Rd SG18 . . . . . . .67 B7
Laburnum Ave MK40 . . . . .49 F7
Laburnum Cl LU3 . . . . .116 C7
Laburnum Gr LU3 . . . . .116 B7
Laburnum Lower Sch
  SG19 . . . . .54 B7
Lachbury Cl LU1 . . . . .123 A6
Lady Way PE19 . . . . .22 B4
Lady Zia Wernher Sch
  LU2 . . . . .117 B3
Ladybridge Terr MK43 . . . .34 E5
Ladyhill LU4 . . . . .115 B6
Lake St LU7 . . . . .111 A6
Lakefield Ave LU5 . . . . . . .105 F5
Lakes Cl SG18 . . . . .78 E5
Lakeview MK43 . . . . .60 E1
Lalleford Rd LU2 . . . . .117 D1
Lamb Mdw SG5 . . . . .90 A3
Lambourn Dr LU2 . . . . .116 E6
Lambourn Gdns AL5 . . . . . .130 F3
Lambourn Way MK41 . . . . .38 D6
Lambs Cl LU5 . . . . .114 F1
Lamers Rd LU2 . . . . .117 B2
Lammas Mead SG5 . . . . . .100 E2
Lammas Way
  Ampthill MK45 . . . . .84 B6
  Letchworth SG6 . . . . .101 F8
  St Neots PE19 . . . . .22 E6
Lammas Wlk LU7 . . . . .111 A7
Lamorna Cl LU3 . . . . .115 F6
Lamsey Ct 1 LU7 . . . . .111 A8
Lancaster Ave
  Bedford MK42 . . . . .50 C5
  Luton LU2 . . . . .116 C8
Lancaster Cl MK45 . . . . . . .97 D4
Lancaster Pl SG17 . . . . . . .77 C1
Lancaster Rd MK42 . . . . . . .51 A2
Lanchester Cl MK41 . . . . . .37 E6
Lanchester Rd MK43 . . . . .58 D2
Lancing Rd LU2 . . . . .117 D1
Lancot Dr LU6 . . . . .120 F8
Lancot Lower Sch LU6 . . .120 E8
Lancotbury Cl LU6 . . . . . . .120 C7

Landrace Rd LU4 . . . . .114 E4
Landseer Wlk MK41 . . . . . .38 A2
Lane The Chalton LU4 . . . .106 E1
  Tebworth LU7 . . . . .105 B3
  Wyboston MK44 . . . . .31 F6
Lane's End LU7 . . . . .103 A4
Langdale MK41 . . . . .38 E3
Langdale Ave AL5 . . . . . . .131 D2
Langdale Cl LU6 . . . . .121 C7
Langdale Gr LU6 . . . . .121 B6
Langford Dr LU2 . . . . .117 A3
Langford Lower Sch SG18 78 F7
Langford Rd SG18 . . . . .78 E7
Langford Rd
  Biggleswade SG18 . . . . . . .66 F2
  Henlow SG16 . . . . .78 D4
Langham Ct LU2 . . . . .116 D7
Langham Ho 8 LU1 . . . . . .123 D8
Langleigh SG6 . . . . .90 F1
Langley St LU1 . . . . .123 E6
Langley Terrace Ind Pk
  LU1 . . . . .123 E6
Langridge Ct LU6 . . . . .113 F1
Langwood Cl PE19 . . . . . . .22 C6
Lansbury Cl PE19 . . . . .22 E4
Lansdowne Rd
  Bedford MK40 . . . . .38 A1
  Luton LU3 . . . . .116 D1
Lansdowne Terr MK40 . . . .38 A1
Lanthony Ct SG15 . . . . .90 A4
Laporte Way LU4 . . . . .115 F1
Lapwing Rd LU4 . . . . .115 A4
Larch Cl NN29 . . . . .7 A7
Larches The
  Kempston MK42 . . . . .49 F3
  Luton LU2 . . . . .116 D1
Lark Rise Lower Sch
  LU6 . . . . .121 B6
Larkins Cl SG7 . . . . .91 F1
Larks Rise SG19 . . . . .42 C2
Larkspur Gdns LU4 . . . . . .115 F2
Larkway Bedford MK41 . . . .38 C4
  Flitwick MK45 . . . . .84 D2
Latimer Rd LU1 . . . . .123 E6
Launton Cl LU3 . . . . .108 B1
Laurel Cl PE19 . . . . .22 F4
Laurel Mews SG7 . . . . .91 F1
Laurel View 2 SG18 . . . . . .67 A6
Laurel Way SG5 . . . . .100 E3
Laurelside Wlk LU5 . . . . . .115 A2
Lavender Cl LU2 . . . . .116 E1
Lavender Ct Ampthill MK45 .84 E7
  Baldock SG7 . . . . .91 E1
Lavender Way
  Biggleswade SG18 . . . . . . .67 C5
  Rushden NN10 . . . . .8 C8
Lavenham Dr MK40 . . . . . .37 C1
Lawford Cl LU1 . . . . .123 C7
Lawn Gdns LU1 . . . . .123 D6
Lawns The SG19 . . . . .43 C3
Lawnside SG18 . . . . .67 B6
Lawnside Lower Sch
  SG18 . . . . .67 B6
Lawrence End Rd LU2 . .125 D4
Lawrence Rd
  Biggleswade SG18 . . . . . . .67 A6
  St Neots PE19 . . . . .22 C5
Lawrence St MK40 . . . . . . .49 F7
Lawrence Way LU6 . . . . . . .113 F2
Laws Cl MK45 . . . . .34 C6
Laxton Cl Luton LU2 . . . . . .117 E1
  St Neots PE19 . . . . .22 C4
Laycock Abbey MK41 . . . . .51 B8
Layham Dr LU2 . . . . .117 E1
Lea Bank LU3 . . . . .115 E6
Lea Bank Ct LU3 . . . . .115 E6
Lea Ct AL5 . . . . .131 A3
Lea Manor High Sch
  LU3 . . . . .115 F8
Lea Manor Recn Ctr LU3 115 F8
Lea Prim Sch AL5 . . . . . . .131 B4
Lea Rd Ampthill MK45 . . . .84 F8
  Harpenden AL5 . . . . .131 B3
  Luton LU1 . . . . .123 F7
Lea Wlk AL5 . . . . .131 C4
Leacroft AL5 . . . . .131 D3
Leaf Rd LU5 . . . . .114 B6
Leafield LU3 . . . . .115 F4
Leafield Ct AL5 . . . . .84 E8
Leafields LU5 . . . . .114 C5
Leagrave High St LU4 . . . .115 B3
Leagrave Prim Sch LU4 . .115 B3
Leagrave Rd LU4 . . . . .116 B2
Leagrave Sta LU4 . . . . .115 C3
Lealands High Sch LU3 . . .115 C8
Leamington Rd LU3 . . . . . .116 A7
Leasey Bridge La AL4 . . . .131 F1
Leaside LU5 . . . . .114 E6
Leaside Ct AL5 . . . . .131 C3
Leasway MK41 . . . . .84 F8
Leathwaite Cl LU3 . . . . . . .116 A6
Leck Ho 6 LU7 . . . . .111 A7
Ledburn Gr 7 LU7 . . . . . . .110 E6
Ledgemore La HP2 . . . . . . .132 F5
Ledwell Rd LU1 . . . . .122 F3
Lee Bridge Cnr LU2 . . . . . .130 F7
Lee Cl MK40 . . . . .37 C1
Lee Ct PE19 . . . . .22 E5
Lee Farm Cotts MK44 . . . .15 E6
Leedon Lower Sch LU7 . . .111 C6
Leeds Smith Dr SG19 . . . .54 C8
Lees Cl SG18 . . . . .68 D5
Leghorn Cres LU4 . . . . . . .115 A3
Leicester Rd LU4 . . . . .115 A3
Leigh Cl LU5 . . . . .105 F6
Leigh Ct MK40 . . . . .38 B1
Leighfield Cl MK41 . . . . . . .39 C3

Leighton Buzzard
  Light Railway LU7 . . .103 C1
Leighton Buzzard Rd
  HP1 . . . . .132 E2
Leighton Buzzard Sta
  LU7 . . . . .110 E6
Leighton Ct Bedford MK41 .38 C5
  Dunstable LU5 . . . . .121 A8
Leighton Mid Sch LU7 . . .110 F6
Leighton Rd Ascott LU7 . . .110 A3
  Eggington LU7 . . . . .112 A7
  Heath and Reach LU7 . . . .103 B4
  Leighton Buzzard LU7 . . . .102 B1
  Leighton Buzzard LU7 . . . .110 F7
  Leighton Buzzard,
  Eggington LU7 . . . . .112 B8
  Northall LU6 . . . . .119 C4
  Stanbridge LU7 . . . . .112 B5
  Toddington LU5 . . . . .105 E5
Leighton St MK17 . . . . .92 E6
Leith Rd MK42 . . . . .50 F5
Lely Cl MK41 . . . . .38 A3
Lennon Ct LU1 . . . . .123 D7
Lennox Gn LU2 . . . . .117 F2
Leopold Rd LU7 . . . . .110 D7
Lesbury Cl LU2 . . . . .117 E1
Leston Cl LU6 . . . . .121 D5
Letchworth La SG6 . . . . . .101 C3
Letchworth Mus
  & Art Gall 101 F5
Letchworth Rd LU3 . . . . . .116 A4
Letchworth Sta SG6 . . . . .101 F6
Levellers La PE19 . . . . .22 F3
Leven Cl LU7 . . . . .110 B7
Leven Wlk MK41 . . . . .38 C7
Levendale LU4 . . . . .115 C5
Lewes Gdns MK41 . . . . . . .39 A5
Lewis La LU5 . . . . .90 A6
Lewsey Park Ct LU4 . . . . . .115 A4
Lewsey Rd LU4 . . . . .115 B2
Ley Side MK43 . . . . .36 F2
Leyburne Rd LU3 . . . . .116 B6
Leydene Pl SG17 . . . . .76 E3
Leygreen Cl LU2 . . . . .124 A8
Leyhill Dr LU1 . . . . .123 B4
Leys Ave SG6 . . . . .101 F6
Leys Rd PE19 . . . . .22 E6
Leys The Ampthill MK45 . . .84 F7
  Langford SG18 . . . . .78 F6
  Woburn Sands MK17 . . . . .81 A4
Leyton Gn AL5 . . . . .131 A1
Leyton Rd AL5 . . . . .131 A1
Library Rd LU1 . . . . .123 E7
Library Wlk MK41 . . . . .38 F4
Lichfield SG6 . . . . .67 A4
Lichfield Cl MK42 . . . . .49 E5
Liddel Cl LU3 . . . . .116 B3
Lidgate Cl LU4 . . . . .115 B6
Lidlington Sta MK43 . . . . . .72 B3
Life Cl LU4 . . . . .114 F4
Lighthorne Rise LU3 . . . . .116 A7
Lilac Gr Biggleswade SG18 .67 C5
  Luton LU3 . . . . .107 C1
Lilac Wlk MK42 . . . . .49 F3
Lilleshall Dr MK42 . . . . . . .50 C3
Lilley Bottom LU2 . . . . .117 F8
Lilleyhoo La LU2 . . . . .109 F2
Lily Cl MK42 . . . . .50 F4
Limbersey La MK45 . . . . . .74 D3
Limbury Rd LU3 . . . . .115 F4
Lime Ave LU4 . . . . .115 C3
Lime Cl Barton-le-C MK45 . .97 C3
  Bromham MK43 . . . . .36 C1
  Flitwick MK45 . . . . .84 F2
Lime Gr
  Leighton Buzzard LU7 . . . .110 E8
  St Neots PE19 . . . . .22 F6
  Woburn Sands MK17 . . . . .81 B4
Lime St MK40 . . . . .50 B8
Lime Tree Cl LU3 . . . . .107 C5
Lime Tree Rd SG17 . . . . . .78 A3
Lime Tree Wlk MK45 . . . . .67 A7
Lime Wlk Dunstable LU5 . .121 D8
  Henlow SG16 . . . . .78 D2
Limes The Arlesey SG15 . . .90 A8
  Luton LU1 . . . . .123 E5
Limetree Ave LU1 . . . . .130 A7
Linacres LU4 . . . . .115 A4
Linbridge Way LU2 . . . . . .117 E2
Linclare Pl PE19 . . . . .22 C4
Lincoln Cl Dunstable LU5 . .121 F6
  Flitwick MK45 . . . . .84 E4
Lincoln Cres SG18 . . . . . . .67 A4
Lincoln Ct MK40 . . . . .50 E8
Lincoln Rd Kempston MK42 49 D2
  Luton LU4 . . . . .116 B1
  Shortstown MK42 . . . . .51 A2
Lincoln Way MK45 . . . . . . .96 A2
Lincombe Slade LU7 . . . . .110 E8
Lincroft Cranfield MK43 . . .59 B1
  Oakley MK43 . . . . .37 A7
Lincroft Mid Sch MK43 . . .37 A7
Linden Cl LU5 . . . . .114 F1
Linden Ct Bedford MK40 . . .38 A2
  4 Luton LU2 . . . . .123 F8
Linden Rd Bedford MK40 . .38 A1
  Dunstable LU5 . . . . .114 F2
  Luton LU4 . . . . .115 E4
Lindencroft SG6 . . . . .91 A1
Lindens The LU5 . . . . .114 B4
Lindisfarne Cl Sandy SG19 54 C8
  St Neots PE19 . . . . .22 F1
Lindisfarne Priory MK41 . .51 B8
Lindley Cl AL5 . . . . .131 A4
Lindsell Cres SG18 . . . . . . .67 A7
Lindsey Rd LU2 . . . . .117 D1
Link Rd NN10 . . . . .8 B7

Link The
  Houghton Regis LU5 . . . . .114 B5
  Letchworth SG6 . . . . .91 A1
Link Way SG17 . . . . .78 A3
Links The MK42 . . . . .49 E3
Links Way LU2 . . . . .116 C8
Linkway MK41 . . . . .39 A2
Linley Cl PE19 . . . . .117 D2
Linley Rd PE19 . . . . .22 E3
Linmere Wlk LU5 . . . . .114 E6
Linnet Cl Letchworth SG6 .101 E8
  Luton LU4 . . . . .115 A4
  Sandy SG19 . . . . .42 C2
Linnet Way MK41 . . . . .38 C4
Linslade Lower Sch LU7 . .110 D7
Linslade Mid Sch LU7 . . . .110 E8
Linslade Rd LU7 . . . . .102 F4
Linwood Gr LU7 . . . . .111 B6
Lippitts Hill LU2 . . . . .116 E5
Lipscombe Dr MK45 . . . . . .84 E1
Liscombe Rd LU5 . . . . .121 E8
Liston Cl LU4 . . . . .115 B5
Litchfield MK44 . . . . .11 A2
Little Beeches LU3 . . . . . . .66 F7
Little Berries LU3 . . . . .115 F7
Little Church Rd LU2 . . . . .117 B3
Little End PE19 . . . . .22 B2
Little End Road Ind Est
  PE19 . . . . .22 B2
Little Grove Pl MK40 . . . . .50 C8
Little Headlands MK41 . . . .38 F4
Little Heath SG19 . . . . .44 C4
Little Hill LU7 . . . . .111 E2
Little La Clophill MK45 . . . .75 D1
  Pirton SG5 . . . . .99 D5
Little Portway MK40 . . . . . .49 B6
Little Spinney MK43 . . . . . .59 C3
Little Staughton Rd MK44 20 C3
Little Townsend MK42 . . . .50 B4
Little Wood Croft LU3 . . . .115 E7
Littledale St MK42 . . . . . . .49 F5
Littlefield Rd LU2 . . . . .117 B2
Littlegreen La LU1 . . . . . . .122 E3
Liverpool Rd LU1 . . . . .123 D7
Livingstone Lower Sch
  MK41 . . . . .38 A2
Locarno Ave LU4 . . . . .115 C6
Lochy Dr LU7 . . . . .110 C7
Lockhart Cl LU6 . . . . .121 E6
Lockington Cres LU5 . . . . .114 F2
Lodge Ave MK42 . . . . .49 C3
Lodge Cl MK44 . . . . .16 C4
Lodge Ct SG5 . . . . .100 E4
Lodge Gdns AL5 . . . . .131 A2
Lodge Rd Cranfield MK43 . .71 A7
  Rushden NN10 . . . . .8 A8
  Sharnbrook MK44 . . . . . . .16 C4
Lodge The MK41 . . . . .37 D6
Lodge The Nature Reserve
  SG19 . . . . .54 F4
Loftus Cl LU4 . . . . .115 B3
Lollard Cl LU4 . . . . .114 E3
Lombard St MK43 . . . . .72 C2
Lombardy Cl MK41 . . . . . . .38 E4
Lomond Dr LU7 . . . . .110 C7
London Coll of Dance
  MK40 . . . . .38 A1
London End Irchester NN29 .7 B8
  Milton Ernest MK44 . . . . . .27 B4
  Woburn MK17 . . . . .92 F6
London La
  Houghton Conquest MK45 . .74 D6
  Riseley MK44 . . . . .10 F1
London Luton Airport
  LU2 . . . . .124 D7
London Rd Astwick SG18 . .79 E7
  Bedford MK42 . . . . .50 D6
  Biggleswade SG18 . . . . . . .67 C4
  Dunstable LU6 . . . . .121 D6
  Luton LU1 . . . . .129 F7
  Luton, New Town LU1 . . . .123 E4
  Markyate AL3 . . . . .128 E5
  Sandy SG19 . . . . .54 B7
  Woburn MK17 . . . . .93 B3
London Road Ind Est
  SG19 . . . . .42 A1
London Road Trad Est
  SG18 . . . . .67 C3
London Row SG15 . . . . . . .90 A3
Long Acre SG17 . . . . .88 B5
Long Cl
  Lower Stondon SG16 . . . . .88 E2
  Luton LU2 . . . . .117 C3
Long Croft Rd LU1 . . . . . . .123 A7
Long Dr MK45 . . . . .76 A5
Long Hedge LU5 . . . . .121 D8
Long La Gamlingay SG19 . .45 B6
  Tingrith LU5 . . . . .95 A2
Long Mdw Dunstable LU6 .121 A8
  Markyate AL3 . . . . .128 F5
Long Mead LU5 . . . . .114 B6
Long Wlk SG17 . . . . .76 D3
Longbournes MK43 . . . . . .59 C2
Longbrooke LU5 . . . . .114 D4
Longcroft Ave AL5 . . . . . . .130 F1
Longcroft Rd MK45 . . . . . .97 B2
Longden Cl MK45 . . . . .64 C1
Longfellow Ave PE19 . . . . .22 D2
Longfield Ct SG6 . . . . .101 D7
Longfield Dr LU5 . . . . .115 D1
Longfield Rd SG18 . . . . . . .54 B8
Longholme Way
  MK40, MK41, MK42 . . . . . .50 E7
Longleat MK41 . . . . .39 B1
Longmead LU5 . . . . .84 D1
Longmead SG6 . . . . .101 E7
Longmeadow LU5 . . . . . . .114 E5
Longmeadow Dr SG5 . . . .100 F5

Lonsdale CI LU3 ....116 B5
Lord's Hill LU5 ....105 F1
Lords CI LU7 ....112 E5
Lords PI 12 LU2 ....116 D1
Lordsmead MK43 ....59 C2
Loring Rd Dunstable LU6 .113 F1
Sharnbrook MK44 ....16 B4
Lorraine Ct MK41 ....39 A1
Lorraine Rd MK43 ....60 F8
Lorrimer CI LU2 ....116 E6
Loseby CI NN10 ....8 A8
Lothair Rd LU2 ....117 A4
Lottings Way PE19 ....22 C6
Lovat Wlk LU2 ....49 E3
Lovell Rd Bedford MK42 .50 F5
Oakley MK43 ....37 B6
Lovent Dr LU7 ....111 B7
Loveridge Ave MK42 ....49 D6
Lovers' Wlk LU5 ....121 C8
Lovet Rd MK45 ....84 E1
Lovett Way LU5 ....114 D3
Lower End Rd MK17 ....81 A8
Lower Farm Rd MK43 ....37 C4
Lower Harpenden Rd
  LU1, LU2 ....124 C3
Lower Luton Rd AL5 .131 C3
Lower Shelton Rd MK43 .60 D2
Lowry Dr LU4 ....114 D5
Lowry Rd PE19 ....22 C6
Lowther Rd Bedford MK41 .38 E5
Dunstable LU6 ....121 D5
Loyne CI LU7 ....110 C8
Lucas Ct MK40 ....37 C1
Lucas Gdns LU3 ....116 B8
Lucas Way SG17 ....77 C4
Lucerne Way LU3 ....116 C4
Ludlow Ave LU1 ....123 E4
Ludlow Wlk MK41 ....39 A4
Ludun CI LU5 ....121 E8
Luffenham PI SG17 ....76 D3
Luke PI MK42 ....50 C4
Luke St PE19 ....22 E4
Lullington CI LU2 ....117 C3
Lune Wlk MK41 ....38 C5
Lunedale CI MK42 ....49 E3
Lurke St MK40 ....50 C8
Luton Airport Parkway Sta
  ....124 B5
Luton Dr The LU1 ....124 B3
Luton & Dunstable Hospl
  LU4 ....115 C2
Luton & Dunstable Hospl
  (Faringdon Wing)
  LU4 ....115 C3
Luton Ind Coll LU1 ....123 E7
Luton La AL3 ....130 B1
Luton Maternity Hospl
  LU4 ....115 C2
Luton Mus & Art Gall
  LU3 ....116 D2
Luton Rd Barton-le-C MK45 .97 B1
Caddington LU1 ....123 A4
Chalton LU4 ....106 C3
Cockernhoe LU2 ....117 E3
Dunstable LU5 ....114 E1
Harpenden AL5 ....130 D4
Luton LU4 ....115 A7
Markyate AL3 ....128 F7
Peters Green SG4 ....125 F2
Streatley LU3 ....108 A6
Wilstead MK45 ....62 E3
Luton Regional Sports Ctr
  LU2 ....117 A5
Luton Ret Pk LU1 ....124 A6
Luton Sixth Form Coll
  LU2 ....116 E4
Luton Sta LU2 ....123 E8
Luton Town FC LU1 ....123 C8
Luton Univ LU1 ....123 F7
Luton Univ,Putteridge Bury
  LU2 ....117 D6
Luton White Hill LU2 .117 F8
Luxembourg CI LU3 .115 D8
Lyall CI MK45 ....84 F2
Lyall Ct MK45 ....85 A4
Lych Mead SG17 ....78 B3
Lydds Hill MK43 ....82 E5
Lydekker Mews 1 AL5 .131 A2
Lydford CI MK40 ....38 E1
Lye Hill SG4 ....125 D7
Lygetun Dr LU2 ....115 F7
Lymans Rd SG15 ....90 A6
Lyme Rd MK45 ....84 E8
Lymington Gdns MK41 .39 C4
Lynch Hill LU6 ....128 A8
Lyndhurst CI MK45 .131 C2
Lyndhurst Dr AL5 ....131 C2
Lyndhurst Rd LU1 ....123 C7
Lyneford Way NN10 ....7 F8
Lyneham Ct LU2 ....117 C1
Lynn CI MK42 ....50 C2
Lynton Ave SG15 ....90 A5
Lynton Gr MK42 ....50 B4
Lynwood Ave LU2 ....117 A3
Lynwood Lodge LU6 .114 A1
Lyon CI MK42 ....49 E2
Lyra Gdns LU7 ....111 D8
Lytham PI MK40 ....49 B6
Lytton Ave SG6 ....101 F5
Lywood Rd LU7 ....111 C6

M

Mabel Rd MK42 ....50 B5
Macaulay Rd LU4 ....115 A2
Maddison Ho PE19 ....22 E6
Magdalene CI SG18 ....68 D5

Magnolia CI MK42 ....49 F2
Magnolia Dr NN10 ....8 B7
Magnolia PI LU5 ....67 C4
Magpies The Luton LU2 .116 E6
Maulden MK45 ....74 C1
Mags La MK42 ....49 D5
Mahew Ct MK42 ....49 D5
Maidenbower Ave LU6 .113 F1
Maidenhall Inf Sch LU4 .116 A2
Maidenhall Jun Sch LU4 116 A2
Maidenhall LU4 ....116 A2
Main Rd Astwood MK16 .47 A3
Biddenham MK40 ....49 C8
Main Rd N HP4 ....126 A6
Main Rd S HP4 ....126 D4
Main St SG19 ....45 F3
Maitland St MK40 ....50 B8
Malakand Rd MK42 ....50 A5
Malaunay PI SG19 ....54 C7
Malcote Ct MK40 ....37 C5
Malden Ho PE19 ....22 E6
Maldon Ct AL5 ....131 B2
Malham CI Flitwick MK45 .84 E2
Luton LU4 ....115 F2
Mall The LU5 ....114 C1
Mallard Gdns LU3 ....116 A5
Mallard Hill MK41 ....38 C4
Mallard La PE19 ....22 F4
Mallow The LU3 ....115 F3
Malmesbury Abbey MK41 .51 A8
Malms CI LU6 ....121 D1
Malthouse Gn LU2 ....117 F1
Malthouse La SG5 ....91 A7
Malting CI MK43 ....59 A1
Maltings Orch SG5 ....99 D3
Maltings The
  Ampthill MK45 ....73 E1
  Dunstable LU6 ....114 A1
  Henlow SG16 ....78 D1
  Leighton Buzzard LU7 .111 B6
  Shefford SG17 ....77 C3
  St Neots PE19 ....22 C5
Maltings Way SG6 ....41 A5
Malvern Ave MK41 ....38 F2
Malvern CI MK45 ....84 D2
Malvern Dr LU7 ....110 C8
Malvern Rd LU1 ....123 B7
Malzeard Ct 17 LU3 ....116 D1
Malzeard Rd LU3 ....116 D1
Manchester PI LU5 ....114 B1
Manchester St LU1 ....123 E7
Mancroft Rd LU1 ....122 E2
Mander CI LU5 ....105 F6
Mangrove Rd
  Cockernhoe LU2 ....117 E4
  Luton LU2 ....117 C2
Manland Ave MK42 ....131 C2
Manland Way AL5 ....131 C3
Manning Ct LU5 ....114 C5
Manning PI LU2 ....117 E2
Manor Ave LU7 ....104 E2
Manor CI Bromham MK43 .37 A4
  Carlton MK43 ....25 A3
  Clifton SG17 ....78 A3
  Great Staughton PE19 .13 F6
  Harlington MK45 ....95 F2
  Ickleford SG5 ....100 E3
  Irchester NN29 ....7 B8
  Kempston MK42 ....49 D4
  Langford SG18 ....78 E4
  Letchworth SG6 ....101 F3
  Salford MK17 ....70 D3
  Westoning MK45 ....95 E5
  Wilden MK44 ....29 F3
Manor Ct Caddington LU1 .122 F4
  Leighton Buzzard LU7 .102 E2
  Marston Moretaine MK43 .72 C7
Manor Dr MK42 ....49 D4
Manor Farm CI LU4 ....115 C3
Manor Farm Way MK44 .16 C3
Manor Hospl MK40 ....49 B8
Manor House CI PE19 .22 C2
Manor La NN10 ....8 A5
Manor Lodge MK42 ....49 D4
Manor Park Dr MK45 .95 D6
Manor Pk LU5 ....114 C4
Manor PI SG18 ....66 B8
Manor Rd
  Barton-le-C MK45 ....97 D3
  Bedford MK41 ....39 A2
  Biddenham MK40 ....49 B8
  Caddington LU1 ....122 F2
  Gamlingay SG19 ....44 D6
  Henlow SG16 ....78 C1
  Kempston Hardwick MK43 .61 D6
  Lea valley AL4 ....131 F2
  Lower Sundon LU3 ....107 C3
  Luton LU1 ....123 F6
  Marston Moretaine MK43 .72 C7
  Rushden NN10 ....8 B8
  Sandy SG19 ....54 B8
  Toddington LU5 ....105 F6
  Wootton MK43 ....61 A7
Manor The SG19 ....56 B8
Manor Way
  Cotton End MK45 ....63 D7
  Flitwick MK45 ....84 D2
  Letchworth SG6 ....101 F3
  Potton SG19 ....56 B8
Manorbier Rd MK41 ....38 F5
Manse Ct AL3 ....128 E1
Mansfield Rd LU4 ....116 B1
Manshead CE Upper Sch
  LU1 ....121 F5
Manshead Ct LU5 ....121 D6
Mansion La MK43 ....24 F6

Manton CI MK45 ....84 F8
Manton Ctr The MK41 .38 A3
Manton Dr LU2 ....116 D3
Manton La MK41 ....38 A3
Manton Rd LU6 ....120 D5
Manx CI LU4 ....116 A2
Maple CI Biggleswade SG18 67 A7
  Clifton SG17 ....77 F2
  Lower Stondon SG16 ....88 E2
  Pulloxhill MK45 ....85 D2
Maple Ct Gamlingay SG19 ..44 C5
  18 Luton LU1 ....123 D6
Maple Dr SG17 ....77 E2
Maple Flats AL5 ....131 A3
Maple Gdns MK44 ....11 A3
Maple Gr MK17 ....81 B4
Maple Rd Harpenden AL5 .130 F1
  Sandy SG19 ....42 C1
Maple Rd E LU4 ....123 B8
Maple Rd W LU4 ....123 B8
Maple Way Cranfield MK43 .71 A8
  Kensworth LU6 ....121 E1
Maple Wood NN10 ....8 B7
Maples The
  Kempston MK42 ....49 E3
  Silsoe MK45 ....86 B4
Marbury PI LU3 ....115 F4
Marchioness Way PE19 .22 B4
Mardale Ave LU6 ....121 C6
Mardale CI MK42 ....49 E4
Mardle CI LU1 ....122 E2
Mardle Rd LU2 ....110 E6
Maree CI LU7 ....110 C7
Maresfield Ave SG17 ....76 F2
Mareth Rd MK42 ....50 E6
Margaret Beaufort Mid Sch
  MK44 ....11 B3
Margetts Rd MK42 ....49 F4
Marigold Way MK42 ....50 F4
Marina CI MK42 ....50 A6
Marina Dr LU6 ....120 E7
Mark Rutherford Rd
  MK42 ....50 D6
Mark Rutherford Upper
  Sch & Com Coll MK41 .39 A5
Market PI Ampthill MK45 .73 E1
  Woburn MK17 ....92 F7
Market Sq
  Biggleswade SG18 ....67 A6
  Leighton Buzzard LU7 ....111 A7
  Luton LU1 ....123 B6
  Potton SG19 ....56 A7
  Sandy SG19 ....54 C7
  Toddington LU5 ....105 F6
Markfield CI LU3 ....116 C7
Markham Cres LU5 ....114 F2
Markham Rd LU1 ....116 C8
Markyate JMI Sch AL3 .128 D6
Markyate Rd LU1 ....123 B1
Marlborough Lower Sch
  MK40 ....49 F8
Marlborough Pk MK42 ....49 C3
Marlborough PI LU5 ....105 F6
Marlborough Rd
  Bedford MK40 ....49 F8
  Luton LU1 ....116 D1
Marley Fields LU7 ....111 D6
Marlin Ct LU4 ....114 E4
Marlin Rd LU4 ....114 E3
Marlow Way MK41 ....38 C6
Marlowe Ct PE19 ....22 D6
Marne St MK42 ....50 A5
Marquis CI
  Harpenden AL5 ....131 D2
  St Neots PE19 ....22 B4
Marquis Ct 9 Luton LU2 .116 D1
  Woburn MK17 ....92 F7
Marquis Hill SG5 ....88 A1
Marquis La AL5 ....131 D2
Marriott Rd LU3 ....116 B6
Marriotts CI MK43 ....26 B8
Marschefield SG5 ....90 E6
Marsh Ho LU3 ....115 F4
Marsh La MK44 ....27 B5
Marsh Rd LU3 ....115 F4
Marsh The MK43 ....25 A3
Marshall CI MK42 ....49 D5
Marshall Ct MK41 ....39 A1
Marshall Rd Luton LU2 .117 C2
  St Neots PE19 ....22 F5
Marshalls Ave SG5 ....87 F1
Marshalls Way AL4 ....131 F2
Marsom Gr LU3 ....116 B8
Marston Gdns LU2 ....116 D4
Marston Hill MK43 ....59 F2
Marston Rd MK43 ....72 C3
Marston Thrift
  (Nature Reserve) MK43 .71 E8
Marston Vale Mid Sch
  MK43 ....61 C1
Martham CI MK40 ....49 D7
Martham Ct AL5 ....131 C3
Martin CI MK41 ....38 D4
Martin Rd MK41 ....84 D1
Martin Way SG6 ....101 D5
Martindales The LU2 ....123 F7
Martins Dr The LU7 ....102 F1
Mary Bassett Lower Sch
  LU7 ....110 F7
Mary Brash Ct LU2 ....117 C3
Maryland Coll MK17 ....92 F4
Maryport Rd LU4 ....116 A2
Maryville Rd MK42 ....50 B5
Marywells SG17 ....88 B5
Masefield CI MK42 ....49 C6
Masefield Ct AL5 ....131 B4
Masefield Rd AL5 ....131 B4
Massey CI MK42 ....49 E4

Masters CI LU1 ....123 B5
Matlock Cres LU4 ....115 C1
Matthew St LU6 ....121 B8
Mattocke Rd SG5 ....100 C1
Maulden Rd Ind Est
  MK45 ....85 A4
Maulden CI LU2 ....117 C1
Maulden Lower Sch
  MK45 ....85 D8
Maulden Rd MK45 ....85 A4
Maundsey CI LU6 ....121 D7
Maurice CI PE18 ....6 F5
May CI LU6 ....119 E6
May Rd MK43 ....34 E6
May St LU1 ....123 E5
Maycroft SG6 ....91 A1
Mayer Way LU5 ....114 A3
Mayes CI MK44 ....29 F2
Mayfield CI
  Harpenden AL5 ....130 E3
  Kempston MK42 ....49 E5
Mayfield Cres SG16 ....88 E2
Mayfield Ct SG19 ....54 B7
Mayfield Rd
  Dunstable LU5 ....121 D7
  Luton LU1 ....117 A4
Mayfields SG17 ....77 D3
Mayhew CI MK43 ....36 E1
Maynards The SG18 ....66 C3
Mayne Ave LU4 ....115 C4
Mead End SG18 ....67 B5
Mead The SG5 ....100 F2
Mead's CI MK17 ....93 E2
Meadow CI PE19 ....22 F5
Meadow Croft LU1 ....122 F4
Meadow La Bedford MK44 .51 D7
  Houghton Regis LU5 ....114 B5
Meadow Piece MK45 ....76 A8
Meadow Rd Luton LU3 ....116 A4
  Toddington LU5 ....105 F5
Meadow View MK17 ....81 D6
Meadow Way
  Ampthill MK45 ....84 D7
  Caddington LU1 ....122 E4
  Leighton Buzzard LU7 .111 D7
  Letchworth SG6 ....101 F5
  Stotfold SG5 ....90 F6
Meadowbank SG4 ....101 B1
Meadows The
  Flitwick MK45 ....84 D5
  Stewartby MK43 ....61 C1
  Wingfield LU7 ....105 E1
Meadowsweet
  Lower Stondon SG16 ....88 F2
  St Neots PE19 ....22 B6
Meadowsweet Dr MK42 .50 E4
Meadowview Rd MK42 ....49 C3
Meads CI LU5 ....114 C5
Meads Prim Sch The
  LU3 ....116 A6
Meads The
  Eaton Bray LU6 ....119 E5
  Letchworth SG6 ....101 E6
  Luton LU3 ....116 A3
Meadway Bedford MK41 ....39 A2
  Dunstable LU6 ....121 A7
  Harrold MK43 ....25 A7
  Leighton Buzzard LU7 .111 C8
Meadway Ct LU6 ....120 F7
Medallion Ct 4 PE19 ....22 F5
Medbury La MK42 ....50 C2
Medina Rd LU4 ....116 A1
Medley CI LU6 ....119 F5
Medlows AL5 ....130 E2
Medmenham Ave SG17 .76 F2
Medusa Way SG19 ....42 B1
Medway CI MK45 ....84 D2
Medway Ct MK41 ....38 D5
Mees CI LU3 ....107 F1
Meeting CI MK45 ....63 D7
Meeting House La SG7 .91 E1
Meeting La SG19 ....56 A7
Melbourn CI SG5 ....90 F4
Melbourne St MK42 ....50 B7
Melchbourne Rd MK44 ....9 F4
Melford CI 3 LU2 ....117 D1
Melfort Dr LU7 ....110 B6
Melrose Dr MK42 ....50 C3
Melson Sq 9 LU1 ....123 E7
Melson St LU1 ....123 E7
Melton Ct LU6 ....120 F7
Melton Wlk LU5 ....114 E6
Memorial La Bletsoe MK44 .17 C1
  Felmersham MK43 ....26 C4
Memorial Rd LU3 ....115 F4
Mendham Way MK45 ....86 C8
Mendip CI MK45 ....84 D2
Mendip Cres MK41 ....38 F3
Mendip Way LU3 ....107 C1
Mentmore CI MK40 ....49 B6
Mentmore Cres LU6 ....121 C5
Mentmore Gdns LU7 ....110 E5
Mentmore Rd LU7 ....110 E5
Mentone Ave MK17 ....81 D4
Mepham Rd MK43 ....60 F8
Meppershall CE Lower Sch
  SG17 ....88 B6
Meppershall Rd
  Meppershall SG17 ....88 A3
  Upper Stondon SG16 ....88 D4
Merchant La
  Cranfield MK43 ....59 A1
  Wharley End MK43 ....58 F2
Mercury PI SG17 ....76 D3
Mercury Way LU7 ....111 D8
Merlin Dr SG19 ....42 B2
Merlin Gdns MK41 ....38 C4

Merlins Ct LU7 ....111 A7
Mersey CI MK45 ....84 D2
Mersey PI 1 LU1 ....123 D7
Mersey Way MK41 ....38 C5
Merton Ho MK40 ....38 B1
Merton Rd MK40 ....38 D2
Mews The
  3 Harpenden AL5 ....131 B1
  Letchworth SG6 ....91 C1
Meyrick Ave LU1 ....123 C6
Meyrick Ct LU1 ....123 D6
Mickle Hill PE18 ....2 D7
Middle Gn LU7 ....111 C8
Middlefield Cty Prim Sch
  PE19 ....22 F2
Middlefield Ind Est SG19 .42 D1
Middlefield La SG16 ....89 C7
Middlefields SG6 ....90 F1
Middlefields Ct SG19 ....90 F1
Middleham SG19 ....54 C8
Middleton Rd LU2 ....117 D4
Midhurst SG6 ....101 F8
Midhurst Gdns LU3 ....116 C4
Midland CI SG17 ....77 C2
Midland Cotts SG4 ....101 A1
Midland Rd Bedford MK40 .50 B8
  Luton LU2 ....123 C8
  Sandy SG19 ....54 B8
Midway LU7 ....111 C7
Milburn CI LU3 ....108 B1
Milburn Rd MK41 ....39 B4
Mile Rd MK42 ....50 D4
Mile Tree Rd LU7 ....103 E4
Milebush LU7 ....110 C8
Miles Ave LU7 ....111 B7
Miles Dr SG17 ....78 B2
Milestone Rd SG5 ....100 D2
Miletree Cres LU6 ....121 C6
Miletree Ct LU7 ....111 B8
Milford Hill AL5 ....131 C4
Mill CI Biggleswade SG18 .66 F5
  Henlow SG16 ....78 D3
  Stotfold SG5 ....91 A6
Mill End LU6 ....119 F4
Mill Est NN10 ....8 B7
Mill Hill Keysoe MK44 ....12 B2
  Thurleigh MK44 ....18 B1
Mill Hill Rd PE19 ....22 C5
Mill La Arlesey SG15 ....89 F4
  Astwick SG5 ....79 F1
  Barton-le-C MK45 ....97 C3
  Biggleswade SG18 ....66 F5
  Campton SG17 ....88 A8
  Clophill MK45 ....75 C1
  Everton SG19 ....43 D1
  Flamstead AL3 ....129 A1
  Greenfield MK45 ....85 C3
  Hexton SG5 ....98 C3
  Houghton Conquest MK45 .62 B3
  Kempston MK42 ....49 C4
  Keysoe MK44 ....12 B2
  Langford SG18 ....78 E7
  Odell MK43 ....25 D8
  Pavenham MK43 ....26 B3
  Potton SG19 ....55 F8
  Salford MK17 ....70 C3
  Sandy SG19 ....54 B6
  St Neots PE19 ....22 F8
  Stotfold SG5 ....91 A6
  Tempsford SG19 ....42 A7
  Turvey MK43 ....34 D7
  Woburn Sands MK17 ....81 C5
Mill Mdw SG18 ....78 E7
Mill Rd Colmworth MK44 ....30 C7
  Cranfield MK43 ....59 C2
  Houghton Regis LU5 ....114 A4
  Husborne Crawley MK43 ..82 D5
  Leighton Buzzard LU7 .111 A8
  Sharnbrook MK44 ....16 F3
  Slapton LU7 ....118 D7
  Stanbridge LU7 ....112 C6
  Stanford SG18 ....78 B7
  Thurleigh MK44 ....28 B7
Mill Rise MK43 ....34 D5
Mill St Bedford MK40 ....50 C8
  Gamlingay SG19 ....44 D5
  Luton LU1 ....123 C8
Mill Tower LU6 ....119 E6
Mill Vale Mid Sch LU5 .114 C2
Mill Way MK17 ....81 B5
Millard Way LU4 ....101 C1
Millards CI Cranfield MK43 .59 C2
  Flitwick MK45 ....84 D3
Millbrook Rd MK42 ....50 B6
Millbrook Sta MK45 ....72 F6
Miller Rd MK42 ....50 B5
Millers CI LU7 ....111 D7
Millers Ct SG18 ....66 F6
Millers Lay LU5 ....54 F6
Millers Way LU5 ....114 A4
Millfield MK43 ....36 F2
Millfield CI Cranfield MK43 .59 B2
  Letchworth MK45 ....85 A2
Millfield La LU1 ....122 C2
Millfield Rd LU3 ....116 B3
Millfield Way LU1 ....122 D3
Milliners Way LU3 ....116 C1
Mills Wlk SG19 ....54 C8
Millstream CI SG4 ....101 A4
Millwood Ct SG5 ....90 F4
Millwright Way MK45 ....84 D4
Milne Row MK40 ....37 F1

Milner Ct LU2 . . . .**123** E8
Milton Ave PE19 . . . .**22** D6
Milton Ct **12** AL5 . . . .**131** B1
Milton Ernest Lower Sch
 MK44 . . . .**27** B5
Milton Rd Bedford MK40 . . . .**37** F1
 Clapham MK41 . . . .**37** C7
 Flitwick MK45 . . . .**84** D3
 Harpenden AL5 . . . .**131** B1
 Luton LU1 . . . .**123** C6
Milton Way LU5 . . . .**114** D4
Milverton Gn LU3 . . . .**116** A7
Minden Cl MK45 . . . .**84** E4
Minden Ct LU2 . . . .**22** C5
Minorca Way LU4 . . . .**115** A3
Miss Joans Ride
 HP4, LU6 . . . .**126** E7
Mistletoe Ct LU2 . . . .**124** C8
Mistletoe Hill LU2 . . . .**124** C8
Mitchell Ct MK42 . . . .**51** A3
Mitchell Rd MK43 . . . .**58** E2
Mitford Cl MK41 . . . .**39** A4
Mitre Cl MK41 . . . .**39** B1
Mixes Hill Ct LU2 . . . .**117** A4
Mixes Hill Rd LU2 . . . .**116** F4
Mixies The SG5 . . . .**90** E6
Moakes The LU3 . . . .**115** E7
Moat La LU3 . . . .**116** B4
Mobbs Cl MK42 . . . .**49** D5
Mobley Gn LU2 . . . .**117** B3
Moggerhanger Lower Sch
 MK44 . . . .**53** C7
Moira Ct LU3 . . . .**115** D7
Molescroft AL5 . . . .**130** D4
Molivers La MK43 . . . .**36** F3
Molly Moore Ave MK42 . . . .**49** D3
Monarch Hall LU2 . . . .**124** C8
Monarch Rd PE19 . . . .**22** B4
Monklands SG6 . . . .**101** D6
Monks Cl Dunstable LU5 . . .**114** E1
 Letchworth SG6 . . . .**101** C6
Monks Row MK43 . . . .**26** B3
Monkshill MK41 . . . .**39** A3
Monmouth Cl
 Bedford MK42 . . . .**50** D5
 Toddington LU5 . . . .**105** E6
Monmouth Rd MK45 . . . .**95** F2
Monoux Pl SG19 . . . .**54** C7
Monoux Rd MK43 . . . .**61** A6
Montagu Ct PE19 . . . .**22** E4
Montagu Gdns PE18 . . . .**6** F5
Montagu Sq PE19 . . . .**22** E4
Montagu St PE19 . . . .**22** E4
Montague Ave LU5 . . . .**115** C6
Montgomery Ave SG17 . . . .**77** C1
Montgomery Cl
 Leighton Buzzard LU7 . . . . .**103** B1
 Stewartby MK43 . . . .**61** C1
Montgomery Ct MK42 . . . . . .**50** A5
Montgomery Way SG18 . . . .**67** D3
Monton Cl LU3 . . . .**115** F6
Montrose Ave LU3 . . . .**116** C3
Moor End LU6 . . . .**119** F5
Moor End Cl LU6 . . . .**119** F4
Moor End La
 Eaton Bray LU6 . . . .**119** F5
 Felmersham MK43 . . . .**16** F1
Moor End Rd MK43 . . . .**26** F8
Moor La Bedford MK42 . . . . .**50** D4
 Flitwick MK45 . . . .**85** A2
 Maulden MK45 . . . .**85** C8
Moor Pl PE19 . . . .**13** E1
Moor St LU1 . . . .**123** C8
Moor The MK43 . . . .**25** A4
Moore's Cl MK45 . . . .**86** C8
Moores Wlk **7** PE19 . . . .**22** C5
Moorland Gdns LU2 . . . . . .**123** D8
Moorland Rd AL5 . . . .**131** B4
Moorlands Prep Sch
 LU4 . . . .**115** C3
Morar Cl LU7 . . . .**110** C7
Morcom Rd LU5 . . . .**121** E6
Mordaunt Cl MK43 . . . .**34** E6
Moreteyne Rd MK43 . . . .**72** D8
Moreton Ave AL5 . . . .**130** F2
Moreton End Cl AL5 . . . . . .**130** F2
Moreton End La AL5 . . . . . .**130** F2
Moreton Pk LU2 . . . .**117** A2
Moreton Pl AL5 . . . .**130** F3
Moreton Rd N LU2 . . . .**117** A2
Moreton Rd S LU2 . . . .**117** A2
Morgans MK45 . . . .**62** F3
Moriston Rd MK41 . . . .**38** C6
Morland Cl LU6 . . . .**121** A6
Morland Way MK41 . . . .**38** B3
Morrell Cl LU3 . . . .**116** A7
Morris Cl Henlow SG16 . . . . .**89** C5
 Luton LU3 . . . .**115** E8
Morris Gdns MK45 . . . .**84** D7
Morris Wlk MK44 . . . .**31** F6
Mortimer Cl LU1 . . . .**123** A7
Mortimer Rd MK42 . . . .**49** D6
Moss La MK42 . . . .**50** C1
Moss Way SG5 . . . .**100** C1
Mossbank Ave LU2 . . . .**124** C8
Mossdale Ct **3** LU4 . . . .**115** C5
Mossman Dr LU1 . . . .**122** E4
Mostyn Rd LU3 . . . .**115** E4
Moulton Ave MK42 . . . .**50** E6
Moulton Rise LU2 . . . .**123** F8
Mount Dr MK41 . . . .**39** A3
Mount Grace Rd LU2 . . . . .**117** C6
Mount Pleasant
 Aspley Guise MK17 . . . .**81** F4
 Ridgmont MK43 . . . .**82** F3

Mount Pleasant Ave LU5 .**105** F4
Mount Pleasant Cl LU5 . . .**105** F4
Mount Pleasant Rd
 Clapham MK41 . . . .**37** D6
 Luton LU3 . . . .**115** E5
Mount The
 Aspley Guise MK17 . . . .**81** D4
 4 Luton LU2 . . . .**123** D8
Mountbatten Ct PE19 . . . . .**22** C4
Mountbatten Dr SG18 . . . . .**67** B7
Mountbatten Gdns LU7 . . .**103** B1
Mountbatten Pl MK41 . . . . .**39** B1
Mountbatten Way SG17 . . . .**76** E4
Mountfield Rd LU2 . . . .**116** E2
Mountfort Cl PE19 . . . .**22** F3
Mountjoy SG4 . . . .**101** C1
Mountview Ave LU5 . . . . . .**121** E6
Mowbray Cl MK43 . . . .**36** E3
Mowbray Cres SG5 . . . .**90** F7
Mowbray Dr LU7 . . . .**110** D7
Mowbray Pl MK44 . . . .**40** C1
Mowbray Rd MK42 . . . .**50** C4
Mowhills MK43 . . . .**24** F6
Moxes Wood LU3 . . . .**115** E7
Muddy La SG6 . . . .**101** F3
Muirfield Biddenham MK40 . .**49** B6
 Luton LU2 . . . .**116** E6
Mulberry Cl
 Biggleswade SG18 . . . .**66** F8
 Luton LU1 . . . .**123** D7
 Stotfold SG5 . . . .**90** F5
Mulberry Way SG5 . . . .**100** D2
Mulberry Wlk MK42 . . . .**49** F3
Mullein Cl PE19 . . . .**22** C5
Mullion Cl LU2 . . . .**117** B5
Mullway LU3 . . . .**101** C6
Muntjac Cl PE19 . . . .**22** B5
Murdock Rd MK41 . . . .**38** A4
Murfitt Way SG19 . . . .**44** D6
Murrell Cl MK43 . . . .**34** E6
Murrell Ct PE19 . . . .**22** F7
Murrell La SG5 . . . .**91** A1
Musgrave Way **6** PE19 . . . . .**22** F5
Mussons Path LU2 . . . .**116** E1
Muswell Cl LU3 . . . .**116** B6
Muswell Rd MK42 . . . .**50** B5
Mutford Croft **2** LU2 . . . . .**117** D1
Myers Rd SG19 . . . .**56** A8
Myrtle Rd MK42 . . . .**50** D5

N

Nags Head La NN9 . . . .**1** F2
Nagshead La MK44 . . . .**32** A5
Napier Ct LU1 . . . .**123** D7
Napier Hall LU7 . . . .**124** C8
Napier Rd Bedford MK41 . . . .**39** D3
 Luton LU1 . . . .**123** D7
Nappsbury Rd LU4 . . . .**115** D5
Narrow Path MK17 . . . .**81** B3
Naseby Pl MK45 . . . .**84** E4
Naseby Rd LU1 . . . .**123** B7
Nash Cl LU5 . . . .**114** D5
Nash Rd MK42 . . . .**50** E6
Navigation Wharf PE19 . . . .**22** E5
Nayland Cl LU2 . . . .**117** C1
Naylor Ave MK42 . . . .**49** E2
Neale Rd MK43 . . . .**60** F8
Neale Way MK43 . . . .**60** F8
Neath Abbey MK41 . . . .**51** B8
Nebular Ct LU7 . . . .**111** C8
Needham Rd LU4 . . . .**115** B6
Needwood Rd MK41 . . . .**39** C3
Nelson Rd Chicksands SG17 .**76** F4
 Dagnall HP4 . . . .**126** C5
 Leighton Buzzard LU7 . . . . .**103** B1
 St Neots PE19 . . . .**22** B2
Nelson St MK40 . . . .**49** F7
Nene Rd Flitwick MK45 . . . . .**84** D2
 Henlow SG16 . . . .**89** B4
 St Neots PE19 . . . .**22** C4
Neotsbury Rd MK45 . . . .**84** F8
Neotsbury Rd MK45 . . . .**84** F8
Neptune Cl LU5 . . . .**114** E6
Neptune Gdns LU7 . . . .**111** D8
Neptune Sq LU5 . . . .**114** E6
Nethercott Cl LU2 . . . .**117** C1
Netherstones SG5 . . . .**90** F7
Nettle Cl LU4 . . . .**114** E4
Nevell's Gn SG6 . . . .**101** F6
Nevells Rd SG6 . . . .**101** F6
Nevern Gdns MK40 . . . .**37** C1
Neville Cl MK43 . . . .**36** E2
Neville Cres MK43 . . . .**36** F2
Neville Rd LU3 . . . .**116** A5
Neville Road Pas LU3 . . . . .**116** A5
Nevis Cl LU7 . . . .**110** C7
New Bedford Rd LU3 . . . . .**116** D3
New Inn Rd SG7 . . . .**80** D5
New Rd Bromham MK43 . . . . .**36** E1
 Clifton SG17 . . . .**78** A1
 Clifton SG17 . . . .**78** A1
 Colmworth MK44 . . . .**29** F8
 Great Barford MK44 . . . .**41** B5
 Harrold MK43 . . . .**24** E6
 Leighton Buzzard LU7 . . . . .**110** E7
 Maulden MK45 . . . .**85** C6
 Sandy SG19 . . . .**54** D5
New St Irchester NN29 . . . . . .**7** B8
 Luton LU1 . . . .**123** E6
 Shefford SG17 . . . .**77** C2
 Slip End LU1 . . . .**123** C1
 St Neots PE19 . . . .**22** B1
New Street Ct NN29 . . . .**7** B8
New Town Rd **9** LU1 . . . . .**123** E6

New Town St LU1 . . . .**123** E6
New Wlk Shillington SG5 . . .**87** E1
 Shillington SG5 . . . .**87** F1
New Woodfield Gn LU5 . . .**121** E6
Newark Ave MK41 . . . .**39** A5
Newark Rd LU4 . . . .**116** A2
Newbold Rd LU3 . . . .**116** B7
Newbury Cl
 Kempston MK42 . . . .**49** D4
 Luton LU4 . . . .**115** E2
 Silsoe MK45 . . . .**86** B5
Newbury Ct MK45 . . . .**86** B5
Newbury La MK45 . . . .**86** B5
Newbury Rd LU5 . . . .**114** E6
Newcombe Rd LU1 . . . .**123** C7
Newis Cres SG17 . . . .**78** B2
Newlands Rd Luton LU1 . . .**123** C3
 Westoning MK45 . . . .**95** E6
Newman Way LU7 . . . .**111** B8
Newmans Dr AL5 . . . .**130** F2
Newnham Ave MK41 . . . .**50** F8
Newnham Cl LU2 . . . .**117** D1
Newnham Mid Sch MK41 . . .**38** E2
Newnham Rd
 Bedford MK40 . . . .**50** C8
 Newnham SG7 . . . .**91** E6
 Newnham SG7 . . . .**50** C8
Newport Pagnell Rd
 MK43 . . . .**47** D5
Newport Rd
 Hardmead MK16 . . . .**46** C2
 Woburn MK17 . . . .**92** F8
 Woburn Sands MK17 . . . .**81** A6
Newstead Way MK41 . . . .**38** F5
Newton Blossomville
 CE First Sch MK43 . . . .**34** B4
Newton Rd Bedford MK42 . . .**50** C5
 Chelveston NN9 . . . .**3** B3
 Rushden NN10 . . . .**8** F8
 Turvey MK43 . . . .**34** E5
Newton Way LU4 . . . .**54** C8
Newtondale LU4 . . . .**115** C5
Newtown Henlow SG16 . . . . .**78** D3
 Kimbolton PE19 . . . .**6** F5
 Potton SG19 . . . .**55** F7
 St Neots PE19 . . . .**22** B8
Newtown Ct SG18 . . . .**67** B7
Newtown La PE19 . . . .**22** B8
Nicholas Way **6** LU5 . . . . .**121** B8
Nicholls Cl
 Barton-le-C MK45 . . . .**97** C3
 Marston Moretaine MK43 . . .**72** C8
Nicholls Rd MK42 . . . .**50** D6
Nichols Cl LU2 . . . .**117** C2
Nightingale Cl LU2 . . . .**117** C6
Nightingale Ct LU3 . . . . . .**123** C8
Nightingale Terr SG15 . . . . .**90** A3
Nimrod Dr SG17 . . . .**76** E4
Nine Lands LU7 . . . .**104** F2
Ninfield Ct LU2 . . . .**117** C3
Ninth Ave LU3 . . . .**115** D7
Nith Wlk MK41 . . . .**38** C7
Nodders Way MK40 . . . .**37** C1
Noke Shot AL5 . . . .**131** C4
Norcott Cl LU5 . . . .**121** D7
Norfolk Cl MK41 . . . .**38** D6
Norfolk Rd Dunstable LU5 . .**121** F6
 Luton LU2 . . . .**124** A7
 Turvey MK43 . . . .**34** E5
Norman Cl MK44 . . . .**40** F5
Norman Rd
 Barton-le-C MK45 . . . .**97** C4
 Luton LU3 . . . .**116** B2
 Sharnbrook MK44 . . . .**16** D3
Norman Way
 Dunstable LU6 . . . .**120** E8
 Irchester NN29 . . . .**7** C8
Normandy Cl MK42 . . . .**50** A5
Normandy La SG18 . . . .**67** D3
Normans Cl SG6 . . . .**90** F1
Norse Rd MK41 . . . .**39** D4
North Crawley Fst Sch
 MK16 . . . .**58** B6
North Cl AL3 . . . .**128** C5
North Dr MK42 . . . .**51** A3
North Drift Way LU1 . . . . .**123** B6
North End MK42 . . . .**51** A3
North Hertfordshire Coll
 . . . .**101** F5
North Herts
 Ed Support Ctr
 SG6 . . . .**101** D3
North La Gamlingay SG19 . . .**44** B6
 Haynes MK45 . . . .**63** F1
North Par **2** MK40 . . . .**38** B1
North Pl SG5 . . . .**100** D1
North Rd SG7 . . . .**91** E2
North St
 Leighton Buzzard LU7 . . . . .**111** A7
 Luton, Hart Hill LU2 . . . . . .**116** E1
 Luton, High Town LU2 . . . . .**123** E8
North Star Dr LU7 . . . .**111** C8
North Station Way LU6 . . .**114** A2
Northall Cl LU6 . . . .**119** D6
Northall Rd LU6 . . . .**119** D6
Northampton Rd
 Bromham MK43 . . . .**36** B3
 Bromham MK43 . . . .**36** D3
Northbridge Wharf SG17 . .**77** C3
Northcliffe LU6 . . . .**119** D6
Northcote AL5 . . . .**131** A3
Northcourt LU1 . . . .**103** A1
Northcroft SG19 . . . .**54** C7
Northdale Cl MK42 . . . .**50** A4
Northern Ave SG16 . . . .**89** C3

Northfield Cl
 Gamlingay SG19 . . . .**44** D6
 Henlow SG16 . . . .**78** D2
Northfield Rd
 Guilden Morden SG7 . . . .**69** C2
 Harpenden AL5 . . . .**131** C4
 Wyboston MK44 . . . .**21** F1
Northfields
 Biggleswade SG18 . . . .**67** A7
 Dunstable LU5 . . . .**114** A3
 Letchworth SG6 . . . .**90** F1
Northfields Inf Sch SG6 . . .**90** F1
Northfields Upper Sch
 LU5 . . . .**114** A3
Northill CE Lower Sch
 SG18 . . . .**53** D2
Northill Rd Cople MK44 . . . .**52** D3
 Ickwell SG18 . . . .**65** D8
Northview Rd
 Houghton Regis LU5 . . . . . .**114** A2
 Luton LU2 . . . .**116** F2
Northway Cl MK42 . . . .**50** D6
Northwell Dr LU3 . . . .**115** F2
Northwood End Rd MK45 . . .**74** E2
Northwood La MK45 . . . .**63** A4
Norton Bury La SG6 . . . .**91** C2
Norton Cl LU6 . . . .**121** B8
Norton Mill La SG6 . . . .**91** D3
Norton Rd Letchworth SG6 . .**91** C2
 Luton LU3 . . . .**115** F2
 Stotfold SG5 . . . .**91** A4
Norton Road Prim Sch
 LU3 . . . .**115** F4
Nunnery La LU3 . . . .**116** B5
Nurseries The LU6 . . . .**119** E6
Nursery Cl
 Biggleswade SG18 . . . .**67** B8
 Dunstable LU6 . . . .**121** A8
Nursery Dr SG19 . . . .**54** A8
Nursery Gdns MK41 . . . .**38** D4
Nursery Par LU3 . . . .**115** E5
Nursery Rd Luton LU3 . . . .**115** F5
 St Neots PE19 . . . .**22** F4
Nutleigh Gr SG5 . . . .**100** D1
Nutwood Cl MK41 . . . .**39** C3
Nymans Cl LU2 . . . .**117** D3

O

Oak Bank Dr LU7 . . . .**103** A3
Oak Bank Dr LU7 . . . .**103** A3
Oak Cl Dunstable LU5 . . . .**121** D8
 Harlington MK45 . . . .**95** F1
 Irchester NN29 . . . .**7** A7
 Sandy SG19 . . . .**54** B8
 Westoning MK45 . . . .**95** E6
 Wootton MK43 . . . .**61** A8
Oak Cres Biggleswade SG18 .**67** B4
 Potton SG19 . . . .**55** F7
 Upper Caldecote SG18 . . . . . .**66** B8
Oak Dr Henlow SG16 . . . .**78** D1
 Pulloxhill MK45 . . . .**85** D2
Oak Gdns LU3 . . . .**115** B8
Oak Rd Bedford MK42 . . . . . .**50** E5
 Flitwick MK45 . . . .**84** F2
 Luton LU4 . . . .**123** C8
Oakcroft MK43 . . . .**48** A6
Oakham Cl NN10 . . . .**8** A8
Oaklands Rd MK40 . . . .**38** D2
Oakley Cl LU4 . . . .**115** D4
Oakley Gn LU7 . . . .**103** B1
Oakley Lower Sch MK43 . . .**37** A7
Oakley Rd Bromham MK43 . . .**37** A4
 Clapham MK41 . . . .**37** C6
 Luton LU4 . . . .**115** E3
Oakpits Way NN10 . . . .**8** C8
Oaks The Silsoe MK45 . . . . . .**86** C4
 Slip End LU1 . . . .**123** C1
Oaktree Rd MK45 . . . .**84** F7
Oakway LU6 . . . .**127** B7
Oakwell Cl LU6 . . . .**120** F7
Oakwood Ave LU5 . . . .**121** E2
Oakwood Dr LU3 . . . .**115** C8
Oakwood Rd SG17 . . . .**77** D2
Oatfield Cl LU4 . . . .**114** F4
Oatfield Gdns LU7 . . . .**111** D7
Oban Terr LU1 . . . .**123** B8
Oberon Ct MK40 . . . .**38** A1
Ockendon Cl PE19 . . . .**22** B3
Odell Cl MK42 . . . .**49** D6
Odell Rd Odell MK43 . . . .**25** A8
 Sharnbrook MK44 . . . .**16** B2
Odin Cl MK41 . . . .**39** D4
Offa Rd MK42 . . . .**50** B5
Old Bakery Yd SG18 . . . .**68** D5
Old Barn Cl SG16 . . . .**78** D2
Old Barns The MK40 . . . .**49** B8
Old Bedford Rd
 Luton LU2 . . . .**116** E4
 Luton, Warden Hill LU2 . . . .**116** D6
 Potton SG19 . . . .**55** F7
Old Brewery Cl SG5 . . . .**90** F7
Old Bridge Ct SG17 . . . .**77** C2
Old Bridge Way SG17 . . . . .**77** C2
Old Chapel Mews LU7 . . . .**111** A6
Old Chapel The PE19 . . . . . .**22** B2
Old Church Path MK45 . . . . .**75** E1
Old Ford End Rd MK40 . . . . .**49** E7
Old Hale Way SG5 . . . .**100** E2
Old Harrowden Rd MK42 . . .**51** A3
Old Hat Factory The **1**
 LU2 . . . .**116** D1
Old Kiln La MK45 . . . .**75** D2
Old Linslade Rd LU7 . . . . . .**102** D3
Old Main Rd MK45 . . . .**75** A6
Old Market Ct PE19 . . . .**22** E5
Old Mews MK41 . . . .**38** A2

Old Mill Cl SG18 . . . .**78** E7
Old Mill La MK45 . . . .**87** D4
Old Oak Cl SG15 . . . .**90** A8
Old Orch LU1 . . . .**123** D6
Old Orchard The SG18 . . . . .**67** B6
Old Rd Barton-le-C MK45 . . .**97** C1
 Leighton Buzzard LU7 . . . . .**110** E7
Old Rd The MK43 . . . .**16** D1
Old Rectory Cl AL5 . . . .**131** A2
Old School Ct Clifton SG17 .**78** B2
 Eaton Bray LU6 . . . .**119** E6
 Hockliffe LU7 . . . .**104** E2
 1 Leighton Buzzard LU7 . . .**111** A7
Old School Gdns
 Barton-le-C MK45 . . . .**97** C3
 St Neots PE19 . . . .**22** C2
 Wootton MK43 . . . .**60** F7
Old School La SG18 . . . .**78** A7
Old School Wlk
 Arlesey SG15 . . . .**90** A4
 Slip End LU1 . . . .**123** C1
Old School Yd PE19 . . . .**22** F4
Old Silsoe Rd MK45 . . . .**86** C8
Old Station Cl MK44 . . . .**41** D2
Old Station Way SG17 . . . . .**77** C3
Old Vicarage Gdns
 Henlow SG16 . . . .**78** D2
 Markyate AL3 . . . .**128** D6
Old Watling St AL3 . . . .**129** B3
Old Way MK44 . . . .**17** C1
Oldfield Farm Rd
 Henlow SG16 . . . .**89** B4
 Henlow SG16 . . . .**89** C4
Oldfield Rd MK40 . . . .**49** E8
Oldhill LU6 . . . .**121** D6
Oldways Rd MK44 . . . .**28** F1
Oliver Cl MK40 . . . .**38** B1
Oliver St MK45 . . . .**84** F7
Oliver's La SG5 . . . .**90** F7
Olivier Way SG17 . . . .**78** B2
Olma Rd LU5 . . . .**114** A2
Olyard Ct LU1 . . . .**123** B6
Olympic Cl LU3 . . . .**107** E1
Olympus Rd SG16 . . . .**89** B4
Ombersley Rd MK42 . . . .**50** B6
Omega Ct LU7 . . . .**111** C8
Omega Ctr The SG18 . . . . . .**67** D3
Onley Ct SG19 . . . .**54** D6
Onslow Rd LU4 . . . .**115** D5
Openshaw Way SG6 . . . . . .**101** F6
Orchard Ave AL5 . . . .**130** F1
Orchard Cl
 Barton-le-C MK45 . . . .**97** C1
 Bedford MK41 . . . .**38** E3
 Biggleswade SG18 . . . .**67** B6
 Bromham MK43 . . . .**37** A4
 Cranfield MK43 . . . .**59** A1
 Gravenhurst MK45 . . . .**87** C4
 Houghton Regis LU5 . . . . . .**114** B3
 Letchworth SG6 . . . .**101** F8
 Meppershall SG17 . . . .**88** C6
 St Neots PE19 . . . .**22** C5
 Toddington LU5 . . . .**105** F6
Orchard Dr
 Chicksands SG17 . . . .**76** F2
 Leighton Buzzard LU7 . . . . .**110** D6
Orchard End LU6 . . . .**119** E4
Orchard Est LU7 . . . .**112** A7
Orchard Ho MK45 . . . .**95** F2
Orchard La MK43 . . . .**24** F7
Orchard Pl NN29 . . . .**7** A8
Orchard Rd Baldock SG7 . . . .**91** E1
 Beeston SG19 . . . .**54** C5
 Hitchin SG4 . . . .**101** B1
 Pulloxhill MK45 . . . .**96** E8
 St Neots PE19 . . . .**22** C4
Orchard St MK42 . . . .**49** F3
Orchard The **10** F2
Orchard Way
 Cranfield MK43 . . . .**59** A1
 Eaton Bray LU6 . . . .**119** F5
 Flitwick MK45 . . . .**84** F2
 Great Barford MK44 . . . .**41** A4
 Letchworth SG6 . . . .**101** F8
 Lower Stondon SG16 . . . .**89** B3
 Luton LU4 . . . .**115** C4
 North Crawley MK16 . . . .**58** A6
 Stanbridge LU7 . . . .**112** D5
Orchards The
 Eaton Bray LU6 . . . .**119** E7
 Silsoe MK45 . . . .**86** C4
 Slip End LU1 . . . .**123** C2
Orchid Cl Dunstable LU6 . . .**113** E1
 St Neots PE19 . . . .**22** C6
Ordelmere SG6 . . . .**90** F1
Oregon Way LU3 . . . .**116** A8
Orion Way LU7 . . . .**111** D8
Ormesby Way MK40 . . . .**49** E2
Ormsby Cl LU1 . . . .**123** E5
Orpington Cl LU4 . . . .**115** A3
Orwell Cl MK41 . . . .**38** C5
Osborn Cres SG17 . . . .**77** C2
Osborn Ho **1** LU6 . . . .**121** B8
Osborn Rd MK45 . . . .**97** C2
Osborne Ave SG17 . . . .**76** E2
Osborne Ct **8** LU1 . . . .**123** F6
Osborne Rd
 Dunstable LU6 . . . .**121** B7
 Luton LU1 . . . .**123** F6
Osier Ct PE19 . . . .**22** C6
Osier Link LU7 . . . .**84** F7
Osprey Cl MK42 . . . .**49** E2
Osprey Rd
 Biggleswade SG18 . . . .**66** F5
 Flitwick MK45 . . . .**84** E2
Osprey Wlk LU4 . . . .**115** A5
Ossary Pl MK45 . . . .**84** E4
Ossory Way MK42 . . . .**50** B6

Otter Way PE19 . . . 22 B5
Otter Wlk MK41 . . . 38 C5
Otterton Cl AL5 . . . 130 F3
Oughtonhead Jun & Inf Schs
SG5 . . . 100 C1
Oulton Ct MK41 . . . 38 D5
Oulton Rise AL5 . . . 131 C3
Our Lady's RC JMI Sch
SG5 . . . 100 E2
Ouse Rd Bedford MK41 . . . 39 A2
St Neots PE19 . . . 22 C4
Ouseland Rd MK40 . . . 49 E7
Ouseley Cl LU4 . . . 115 D3
Oval The SG16 . . . 89 C3
Overdale MK41 . . . 39 A3
Overend Green La LU7 . . . 103 C6
Overfield Rd LU2 . . . 117 C1
Overlord Cl SG17 . . . 77 C1
Overstone Rd
Harpenden AL5 . . . 131 C1
Luton LU4 . . . 115 D1
Overtrees AL5 . . . 130 F3
Oving Cl LU2 . . . 117 D2
Owen Cl Kempston MK42 . . 49 D3
Marston Moretaine MK43 . . . 72 C8
Owen Jones Cl SG16 . . . 89 C5
Ox La AL5 . . . 131 B3
Oxen Rd LU2 . . . 116 F1
Oxendon Ct LU7 . . . 102 F2
Oxford Rd 2 LU1 . . . 123 E6
Oxford St NN10 . . . 8 A7

P

Padbury Ho 4 MK40 . . . 38 A1
Paddock Cl Clapham MK41 . 37 D7
Letchworth SG6 . . . 101 F5
Luton LU4 . . . 114 F5
Paddock The
Biddenham MK40 . . . 49 D8
Lidlington MK43 . . . 72 C2
St Neots PE19 . . . 22 D5
Paddocks The
Bromham MK43 . . . 36 F1
Flitwick MK45 . . . 84 D5
Leighton Buzzard LU7 . . . 110 F8
Potton SG19 . . . 55 F7
Toddington LU5 . . . 106 A5
Page's Almshouses 4
LU7 . . . 111 A8
Page's Ind Pk LU7 . . . 111 B5
Paignton Cl LU4 . . . 115 D4
Paines Mill PE19 . . . 22 E6
Palace St SG18 . . . 67 A5
Palma Cl LU6 . . . 113 F3
Palmer Cl SG17 . . . 77 A2
Palmerston St MK41 . . . 38 B2
Parade The
Dunstable LU6 . . . 114 A1
Letchworth SG6 . . . 90 F1
Luton LU3 . . . 115 C7
Paradine Rd MK42 . . . 50 D6
Park Ave Bedford MK40 . . . 38 C2
Houghton Regis LU5 . . . 114 C5
Luton LU3 . . . 115 C7
Totternhoe LU6 . . . 120 B8
Park Ave N AL5 . . . 130 F1
Park Ave S AL5 . . . 130 F1
Park Avenue Trad Est
LU3 . . . 115 C7
Park Cl Markyate AL3 . . . 128 D5
Moggerhanger MK44 . . . 53 B6
Park Cres MK43 . . . 61 C1
Park Ct Luton LU2 . . . 116 D1
Sandy SG19 . . . 54 C6
Park Farm Cl SG16 . . . 89 D8
Park Hill Ampthill MK45 . . . 73 E1
Harpenden AL5 . . . 130 F2
Toddington LU5 . . . 105 F7
Park La Blunham MK44 . . . 41 E3
Eaton Bray LU6 . . . 119 D6
Henlow SG16 . . . 78 D1
Kimbolton PE18 . . . 6 F2
Sharnbrook MK44 . . . 16 E5
Park Lane Cres SG16 . . . 78 D2
Park Leys MK45 . . . 95 F1
Park Mews
Leighton Buzzard LU7 . . . 111 A6
Sandy SG19 . . . 54 C7
Park Mount AL5 . . . 130 F3
Park Palings Wlk MK45 . . . 75 F8
Park Rd Dunstable LU5 . . . 121 C7
Kempston MK42 . . . 49 F5
Melchbourne MK44 . . . 10 D8
Moggerhanger MK44 . . . 53 B7
Roxton MK44 . . . 31 E2
Sandy SG19 . . . 54 C7
St Neots PE19 . . . 22 F7
Stevington MK43 . . . 36 D6
Toddington LU5 . . . 105 D7
Westoning MK45 . . . 95 E5
Park Rd N
Bedford MK41 . . . 38 B2
Houghton Regis LU5 . . . 114 D4
Park Rd W MK41 . . . 38 B2
Park Rise AL5 . . . 130 E3
Park Rise Cl AL5 . . . 130 E3
Park Sq LU1 . . . 123 E7
Park St Ampthill MK45 . . . 73 E1
Dunstable LU6 . . . 114 A1
Luton LU1 . . . 123 F6
Woburn MK17 . . . 93 A7
Park St W LU1 . . . 123 E7
Park Terr 2 LU1 . . . 123 F6
Park Viaduct LU1 . . . 123 F6
Park View MK44 . . . 41 D3
Park View Cl LU3 . . . 115 D6
Park View Ct
Leighton Buzzard LU7 . . . 110 E7
St Neots PE19 . . . 22 D5
Park View Dr AL3 . . . 128 D6
Park Way PE19 . . . 22 F7
Parker Cl SG6 . . . 101 E4
Parkfield Rd AL3 . . . 128 D5
Parkfields Mid Sch LU5 . 105 F7
Parkland MK43 . . . 36 D3
Parkland Dr LU1 . . . 123 D5
Parkmead 6 LU1 . . . 123 F6
Parkside Gravenhurst MK45 87 B4
Milton Ernest MK44 . . . 27 B5
Parkside Cl LU5 . . . 114 D5
Parkside Dr LU5 . . . 114 D6
Parkside Flats LU6 . . . 121 C8
Parkstone Cl MK41 . . . 38 E6
Parkview La LU7 . . . 105 C2
Parkway
Houghton Regis LU5 . . . 114 E6
Woburn Sands MK17 . . . 81 A6
Parmiter Way MK45 . . . 84 D7
Parrish Cl MK43 . . . 72 D8
Parrot Cl LU5 . . . 114 E1
Parson's Cl AL3 . . . 129 B1
Parsonage Cl MK43 . . . 37 A7
Parsons Rd NN29 . . . 7 B8
Partridge Cl LU4 . . . 115 A5
Partridge La MK43 . . . 36 D1
Partridge Piece
Cranfield MK43 . . . 59 C3
Sandy SG19 . . . 42 B2
Parys Rd LU3 . . . 116 B6
Pascomb Rd LU6 . . . 120 F8
Pasture La SG4 . . . 125 E8
Pasture Rd SG6 . . . 101 E3
Pastures Ct LU4 . . . 115 A3
Pastures The
Edlesborough LU6 . . . 119 F3
Stewartby MK43 . . . 61 C1
Upper Caldecote SG18 . . . 66 C8
Pastures Way LU4 . . . 115 A4
Pathway The MK45 . . . 74 B1
Patterdale Cl LU6 . . . 121 B7
Patteshull Ct 1 MK40 . . . 50 B8
Paul Waller Ave MK42 . . . 51 B3
Paulsons Cl MK44 . . . 11 A2
Pavenham Rd
Felmersham MK43 . . . 26 C7
Pavenham MK43 . . . 26 F3
Stevington MK43 . . . 25 D4
Pax Hill MK41 . . . 38 E4
Payne Rd MK43 . . . 60 F7
Paynes Cl SG6 . . . 91 A1
Peach Ct LU1 . . . 123 F6
Peach's Cl MK43 . . . 25 A6
Peacock Mews 5 LU7 . . . 111 A7
Peakes End MK45 . . . 84 A3
Pear Tree Cl
Bromham MK43 . . . 36 D1
Lower Stondon SG16 . . . 89 B3
Pear Tree La LU7 . . . 111 A8
Pear Tree View MK42 . . . 50 C2
Pearcey Rd MK42 . . . 50 C5
Pearmain Cl MK41 . . . 38 F1
Peartree Cl Shefford SG17 . 77 E2
Toddington LU5 . . . 105 E5
Peartree Rd LU2 . . . 117 C4
Peashill La MK44 . . . 40 F6
Pebblemoor LU6 . . . 119 F3
Pebbles The SG7 . . . 91 C4
Peck Ct MK45 . . . 97 B4
Peckworth Ind Est SG16 . . 89 A4
Peddars La LU7 . . . 112 D4
Pedley Hill HP4, LU6 . . . 127 C1
Pedley La SG17 . . . 77 F3
Peel Pl 7 LU1 . . . 123 D7
Peel St 6 Bedford MK40 . . . 38 B1
Houghton Regis LU5 . . . 114 B5
6 Luton LU1 . . . 123 D7
Peel's Pl SG19 . . . 54 D7
Peer Rd PE19 . . . 22 B4
Peers Dr MK17 . . . 81 E3
Pegasus Ct SG18 . . . 66 F7
Pegasus Dr SG18 . . . 67 D3
Pegasus Rd LU7 . . . 111 D8
Pegsdon Cl LU3 . . . 116 B7
Pegsdon Way SG5 . . . 98 E1
Pelican Way SG6 . . . 90 F1
Pemberley Ave MK40 . . . 38 C2
Pemberley La MK40 . . . 38 C1
Pembroke Ave Luton LU4 . 115 F3
St Neots PE19 . . . 22 F2
Pembroke Cl MK43 . . . 72 D8
Pembroke Rd MK45 . . . 74 B7
Pembroke St MK40 . . . 50 D8
Penda Cl LU3 . . . 115 F7
Pendennis Rd MK41 . . . 39 A4
Penfold Cl SG17 . . . 77 A2
Penhill LU3 . . . 115 E6
Penhill Ct LU3 . . . 115 E6
Penlee Cl MK41 . . . 38 F1
Penley Way LU7 . . . 111 A5
Pennine Ave LU3 . . . 115 D8
Pennine Rd MK41 . . . 38 E3
Pennine Rise MK45 . . . 84 D2
Pennivale Cl LU7 . . . 111 A8
Penrith Ave LU6 . . . 121 B7
Penrwyn Ct PE19 . . . 22 F1
Penshurst Cl AL5 . . . 130 D4
Pentelowes The PE18 . . . 2 D2
Pentland Cl SG19 . . . 54 B8
Pentland Rise MK41 . . . 38 E3
Penwright Cl MK42 . . . 49 D5
Peppercorns La PE19 . . . 22 C2
Peppiatts The LU6 . . . 119 B5
Pepsal End Rd LU1 . . . 129 C7
Percheron Dr LU4 . . . 115 A3
Percival Way LU2 . . . 124 C7
Peregrine Rd LU4 . . . 115 A4
Periwinkle La
Dunstable LU6 . . . 121 C7
Hitchin SG5 . . . 100 F1
Perkins Rd MK41 . . . 39 C2
Perring Cl MK44 . . . 16 C4
Perry Mead LU6 . . . 119 E6
Perrymead LU2 . . . 117 F2
Pershore Cl MK41 . . . 38 E5
Pertenhall Rd MK44 . . . 12 B4
Petard Cl LU4 . . . 115 A2
Petersfield Gdns LU3 . . . 107 E1
Petley Cl MK45 . . . 84 E1
Petteril Wlk MK41 . . . 38 C7
Petunia Ct LU3 . . . 116 C1
Pevensey Cl LU2 . . . 117 D4
Pevensey Gr MK45 . . . 84 C1
Pevensey Rd MK41 . . . 39 A3
Pheasant Wlk MK45 . . . 84 D2
Philip Gdns PE19 . . . 22 F2
Philip Larkin Ho MK40 . . . 50 A8
Phillpotts Ave MK40 . . . 38 E1
Phipps Cl MK45 . . . 62 F3
Phoenix Cl LU7 . . . 111 D8
Phoenix Sq PE19 . . . 22 E6
Pickering Cl SG19 . . . 54 C8
Pickford Hill AL5 . . . 131 C3
Pickford Rd AL3 . . . 128 C3
Pie Cnr AL3 . . . 129 B1
Pie Gdn AL3 . . . 129 C1
Pietley Hill AL3 . . . 129 A1
Pigeonwick AL5 . . . 131 B3
Piggotts La LU4 . . . 115 D4
Piggottshill La AL5 . . . 131 E1
Pilcroft St MK42 . . . 50 C7
Pilgrims Cl Flitwick MK45 . . 84 E3
Harlington MK45 . . . 95 F1
Pilgrims Way MK42 . . . 50 C4
Pillinge Rd MK43 . . . 61 C1
Pinchmill Cl MK44 . . . 16 C3
Pinchmill Lower Sch
MK43 . . . 26 C8
Pinchmill Way MK44 . . . 16 C3
Pine Cl Biggleswade SG18 . . 67 A7
Irchester NN29 . . . 7 A7
Leighton Buzzard LU7 . . . 103 A2
Rushden NN10 . . . 8 A8
Pine Crest Mews LU7 . . . 110 E6
Pine Gr MK17 . . . 81 A4
Pine View Pk MK45 . . . 86 B7
Pinemead SG17 . . . 77 E2
Pines The Ampthill MK45 . . 84 E8
Kempston MK42 . . . 49 F3
Pinewood Cl LU3 . . . 107 C1
Pinford Dell 4 LU2 . . . 117 D1
Pinkle Hill Rd LU7 . . . 103 A5
Pinsent Ave MK43 . . . 36 E1
Pioneer Pk MK42 . . . 50 B5
Pipers Croft LU6 . . . 120 F7
Pipers Hill HP1 . . . 132 D3
Pipers La AL3, LU1 . . . 122 F1
Pipit Cl MK45 . . . 84 E2
Pipit Gr SG19 . . . 42 B2
Pipit Rise MK41 . . . 38 D4
Pirton Hill Inf Sch LU4 . . 115 B6
Pirton Hill Jun Sch LU4 . 115 B6
Pirton Jun Mix Inf Sch
SG5 . . . 99 D4
Pirton Rd Holwell SG5 . . . 100 A7
Luton LU4 . . . 115 D5
Pitsdean Rd PE19 . . . 33 F3
Pitsford Terr LU2 . . . 117 A1
Pix Ct SG15 . . . 90 A8
Pix Rd SG5 . . . 90 E5
Pixmore Way SG6 . . . 101 F5
Plaiters Cl MK43 . . . 26 B3
Plaiters Way LU5 . . . 114 A5
Plane Tree Cl SG19 . . . 44 C6
Planes The MK42 . . . 49 E3
Plantation Rd
Leighton Buzzard LU7 . . . 102 F3
Luton LU3 . . . 115 D7
Platt Cl LU4 . . . 115 D4
Platz Ho LU5 . . . 114 D5
Playfield Cl SG18 . . . 67 B5
Playford Sq LU4 . . . 115 D5
Pleasance The AL5 . . . 130 D4
Pleasent Pl SG19 . . . 54 C7
Plewes Cl LU6 . . . 127 E8
Plough Cl Cranfield MK43 . . 71 A8
Luton LU4 . . . 114 E4
Plough Ct LU4 . . . 114 E4
Plover Way MK41 . . . 38 B4
Plum Tree La LU7 . . . 111 A8
Plum Tree Rd SG16 . . . 89 B2
Plummer Haven LU7 . . . 103 A1
Plummers La Haynes MK45 75 F8
Peters Green LU2 . . . 125 C2
Plumpton Cl LU2 . . . 117 D3
Plymouth Cl LU2 . . . 117 B1
Podington Rd NN10 . . . 8 A4
Poets Ct AL5 . . . 131 B1
Poets Gn LU4 . . . 115 A2
Pokas Cotts NN9 . . . 3 C8
Polam Sch MK40 . . . 38 A1
Polegate LU2 . . . 117 D2
Polhill Ave MK40, MK41 . . . 38 E2
Pollards Cl MK45 . . . 62 E3
Pollards Way SG5 . . . 99 D4
Polo Field Way MK42 . . . 50 A2
Polzeath Cl LU2 . . . 124 C8
Pomeroy Gr LU2 . . . 116 E6
Pomfret Ave LU2 . . . 116 F1
Pond Cl LU4 . . . 115 B5
Pondwick Rd AL5 . . . 130 E2
Pondwicks Rd LU1 . . . 123 F7
Pope Cl MK45 . . . 84 E1
Pope Rd PE19 . . . 22 E4
Popes Ct LU2 . . . 116 D1
Popes Way MK43 . . . 60 E7
Popham Cl PE19 . . . 22 A3
Poplar Ave Bedford MK41 . . 38 E4
Luton LU3 . . . 116 C8
Poplar Cl
Biggleswade SG18 . . . 67 A8
Irchester NN29 . . . 7 A7
Leighton Buzzard LU7 . . . 103 A2
Roxton MK44 . . . 31 E1
Rushden NN10 . . . 8 A8
Silsoe MK45 . . . 86 C4
Poplar Gr SG19 . . . 54 B7
Poplar Rd LU6 . . . 127 E8
Poplars Cl LU2 . . . 117 B3
Poplars The Arlesey SG15 . . 90 A8
Flitwick MK45 . . . 84 E3
Ickleford SG5 . . . 100 F5
Poppy Cl NN10 . . . 8 C8
Poppy Field SG18 . . . 67 C5
Poppyfields MK41 . . . 39 C4
Porlock Dr LU2 . . . 117 C1
Porters Hill AL5 . . . 131 C4
Portland Cl Bedford MK41 . 39 A2
Houghton Regis LU5 . . . 114 B4
Portland Ct LU4 . . . 116 A1
Portland Ind Est SG15 . . . 90 A3
Portland Rd LU4 . . . 116 A1
Portman Cl SG5 . . . 100 D2
Portnall Pl MK43 . . . 59 B1
Porz Ave LU5 . . . 114 D3
Postley Rd MK42 . . . 49 E2
Potten End Hill HP1 . . . 132 F1
Potter Way MK42 . . . 50 C4
Potters Cross MK43 . . . 61 A8
Pottery Cl LU3 . . . 115 F7
Potton Lower Sch SG19 . . 55 F7
Potton Rd
Biggleswade SG18 . . . 67 A7
Biggleswade SG18 . . . 67 B8
Everton SG19 . . . 43 D2
Gamlingay SG19 . . . 44 D3
Guilden Morden SG8 . . . 69 F6
Potton SG19 . . . 43 F3
Sandy SG19 . . . 55 B6
St Neots PE19 . . . 22 F2
Wrestlingworth SG19 . . . 57 B4
Poulter Cl 6 MK40 . . . 50 B8
Pound Cl Blunham MK44 . . . 41 E4
Langford SG18 . . . 78 F7
Pound Gn SG8 . . . 69 F5
Pound La Kimbolton PE18 . . . 6 F4
North Crawley MK16 . . . 58 B7
Pound The MK45 . . . 95 E6
Pounds Cl MK43 . . . 59 B1
Powells Rd SG17 . . . 77 C3
Power Ct LU1 . . . 123 F7
Powers Cl SG19 . . . 42 B1
Powis Mews MK45 . . . 84 D1
Powis Pl PE19 . . . 22 F1
Powis Rd MK41 . . . 39 B4
Poynters Rd LU4 . . . 114 E3
Prebend St MK40 . . . 50 B7
Prebendal Dr LU1 . . . 123 B2
Prentice Gdns MK42 . . . 49 F6
Prentice Way LU2 . . . 124 D7
Presentation Ct LU1 . . . 123 F6
Preservine Wlk MK41 . . . 37 E5
President Way LU2 . . . 124 D8
Preslent Cl SG5 . . . 87 F1
Preston Cl MK45 . . . 84 E8
Preston Gdns LU2 . . . 116 F2
Preston Path LU2 . . . 116 F2
Preston Rd Bedford MK40 . . 49 F8
Toddington LU5 . . . 106 A5
Prestwick Cl LU2 . . . 116 E5
Priestleys LU1 . . . 123 A7
Primary Way SG15 . . . 90 A4
Primrose Cl Arlesey SG15 . 90 A4
Biggleswade SG18 . . . 67 C4
Flitwick MK45 . . . 84 D2
Marston Moretaine MK43 . . . 72 C7
Primrose Ct LU6 . . . 121 A8
Primrose La SG15 . . . 90 A4
Prince Cl PE19 . . . 22 B5
Prince Philip Ave MK43 . . 58 D2
Prince Way LU2 . . . 124 D8
Prince's St SG5 . . . 90 F7
Princes Ct Dunstable LU5 . 114 C1
Leighton Buzzard LU7 . . . 110 F8
Princes Pl 15 LU2 . . . 116 D1
Princes Rd MK43 . . . 36 E2
Princes St 8 Bedford MK40 38 B1
Dunstable LU6 . . . 121 A8
Toddington LU5 . . . 106 A5
Princess St Bedford MK40 . 38 B1
Clapham MK41 . . . 37 D6
Luton LU1 . . . 123 D7
Prinknash Rd MK41 . . . 38 E5
Printers Ct MK45 . . . 73 F1
Printers Way LU6 . . . 114 B1
Priors Cl NN10 . . . 7 F8
Priors Hill SG5 . . . 99 C4
Priory Bsns Pk MK44 . . . 51 C6
Priory Cl Harrold MK43 . . . 25 A6
Turvey MK43 . . . 35 B5
Priory Ct 1 Bedford MK40 . . 38 B1
Dunstable LU5 . . . 121 C8
Priory Ctry Pk MK41 . . . 51 A7
Priory Gdns LU2 . . . 116 D4
Priory La PE19 . . . 22 E5
Priory Lower Sch MK40 . . 50 A8
Priory Mall 2 PE19 . . . 22 E5
Priory Mews PE19 . . . 22 E6
Priory Mid Sch LU5 . . . 121 C8
Priory Orch AL3 . . . 129 B2
Priory Park Inf Sch PE19 . 22 F6
Priory Rd Campton SG17 . . . 76 F1
Dunstable LU5 . . . 121 C8
St Neots PE19 . . . 22 E6
Priory Sch The SG5 . . . 100 E2
Priory St MK40 . . . 50 B8
Priory The PE19 . . . 22 E5
Proctor Cl MK42 . . . 49 D5
Proctor Way LU2 . . . 124 C7
Progress Way Elstow MK42 50 B4
Luton LU4 . . . 115 B7
Prospect Ave NN29 . . . 7 A7
Prospect Rd SG18 . . . 78 F6
Prospect Row 3 PE19 . . . 22 F5
Prospect Way LU2 . . . 124 C7
Provost Way LU2 . . . 124 C8
Prudden Cl MK42 . . . 50 B4
Prudence Cl MK45 . . . 95 F1
Pryors Ct SG7 . . . 91 F1
Puddephat's La AL3 . . . 128 C1
Pulford Rd LU7 . . . 110 F6
Pulford's Lower Sch
LU7 . . . 111 A6
Pulloxhill Bsns Pk MK45 . . 85 D2
Pulloxhill Lower Sch
MK45 . . . 96 E8
Pulloxhill Rd MK45 . . . 85 D2
Purbeck Cl MK41 . . . 39 A2
Purcell Rd LU4 . . . 114 F3
Purcell Way SG17 . . . 77 E3
Purley Ctr LU3 . . . 115 E7
Purway Cl LU3 . . . 115 E7
Purwell Wlk LU7 . . . 103 B3
Putnoe Hts MK41 . . . 38 F4
Putnoe La MK41 . . . 38 E4
Putnoe Lower Sch MK41 . 39 A3
Putnoe St MK41 . . . 39 A4
Putteridge High Sch
LU2 . . . 117 C5
Putteridge Inf Sch LU2 . . 117 C5
Putteridge Jun Sch LU2 . 117 C5
Putteridge Par LU2 . . . 117 B4
Putteridge Rd LU2 . . . 117 C4
Putteridge Recn Ctr LU2 117 C5
Putterills The AL5 . . . 131 A1
Pyghtle Ct LU1 . . . 123 A7
Pyghtle The Luton LU1 . . . 123 A7
Turvey MK43 . . . 34 E6
Westoning MK45 . . . 95 E5
Pym's Way SG19 . . . 42 B1
Pyms Cl MK44 . . . 40 F5
Pynders La LU5 . . . 114 E2
Pytchley Cl LU2 . . . 116 E5

Q

Quadrant The
Houghton Regis LU5 . . . 114 C5
Letchworth SG6 . . . 101 F6
Quantock Cl Bedford MK41 38 E2
Luton LU3 . . . 116 B8
Quantock Rise LU3 . . . 108 B1
Quantocks The MK45 . . . 84 D2
Quantrelle Ct MK42 . . . 51 A3
Queen Alexandra Rd
MK41 . . . 39 A1
Queen Anne's Cl SG5 . . . 90 F5
Queen Elizabeth Cl SG17 . 77 D2
Queen St Bedford MK40 . . . 38 B1
Houghton Regis LU5 . . . 114 B4
Leighton Buzzard LU7 . . . 110 F8
Stotfold SG5 . . . 91 A6
Queen's Cl MK40 . . . 37 D1
Queen's Cres MK41 . . . 38 F3
Queen's Ct 11 MK40 . . . 38 B1
Queen's Dr MK41 . . . 38 F3
Queen's Rd SG19 . . . 54 B7
Queen's Way SG18 . . . 78 F8
Queens Cl Flitwick MK45 . . . 84 F2
4 Luton LU1 . . . 123 E6
Northill SG18 . . . 53 E1
Oakley MK43 . . . 36 F8
Queens Cres MK41 . . . 37 D7
Queens Ct
Dunstable LU5 . . . 114 C1
14 Luton LU2 . . . 116 D1
Shefford SG17 . . . 77 D2
St Neots PE19 . . . 22 B3
Queens Gdns PE19 . . . 22 B4
Queens Park Lower Sch
MK40 . . . 49 F8
Queens Rd Ampthill MK45 . . 84 F8
Colmworth MK44 . . . 20 B2
Queensbury Cl MK40 . . . 49 F8
Queensbury Upper Sch
LU6 . . . 121 B7
Queensway
Dunstable LU5 . . . 114 B1
St Neots PE19 . . . 22 F7
Queenswood Dr SG4 . . . 101 C1
Quenby Way MK43 . . . 36 F1
Quickswood LU3 . . . 116 A7
Quilter Cl LU3 . . . 115 F4

R

Raban Ct SG7 . . . 91 F1
Race Meadows Way MK42 49 F2
Rackman Dr LU3 . . . 116 C5
Radburn Ct LU6 . . . 114 A1
Radnor Rd LU4 . . . 114 F4
Radnor Wlk MK41 . . . 39 B3
Radstone Pl LU2 . . . 117 E1
Radwell La SG7 . . . 91 C4

Radwell Rd
Felmersham MK43 . . . . .26 D8
Milton Ernest MK44 . . . . . . .26 A6
Raglan Cl LU4 . . . . .114 F3
Raglan Gn MK41 . . . . .39 A4
Railton Rd MK42 . . . . .49 D1
Railway Cotts
Kempston Hardwick MK45 . .61 F4
Oakley MK43 . . . . .37 A8
Railway View 1 SG18 . . . . .67 A6
Rainbow Specl Sch MK43 36 D3
Raleigh Cl PE19 . . . . .22 A2
Raleigh Gr LU4 . . . . .115 D1
Raleigh Lower Sch MK42 .50 B6
Raleigh St MK40 . . . . .49 F7
Rally The SG15 . . . . .90 A7
Ram Yd MK40 . . . . .50 C8
Ramerick Gdns SG15 . . . . .90 A2
Ramillies Cl MK42 . . . . . . .49 F7
Ramridge Inf Sch LU2 . . .117 B2
Ramridge Jun Sch LU2 . .117 B2
Ramridge Rd LU2 . . . . . . .117 A2
Ramsay Cl MK41 . . . . .38 B3
Ramsey Cl Kempston MK42 49 D2
Luton LU4 . . . . .114 F3
Ramsey Ct LU4 . . . . .114 F3
Ramsey Manor Lower Sch
MK45 . . . . .97 D2
Ramsey Rd MK45 . . . . .97 C3
Rand's Cl SG5 . . . . .100 B7
Rand's Cotts SG5 . . . . . . .100 B7
Rand's Mdw SG5 . . . . .100 B7
Randall Dr LU5 . . . . .105 F5
Randalls Cl MK43 . . . . .36 F2
Rannock Gdns LU7 . . . . . .110 C7
Ranock Cl LU3 . . . . .115 D8
Ranworth Wlk MK40 . . . . . .49 D7
Rapper Cl MK42 . . . . .123 D8
Raunds Rd NN9 . . . . .3 C8
Raven Wlk MK45 . . . . .84 E2
Ravenbank Rd LU2 . . . . . .117 C5
Ravenhill Way LU4 . . . . . .115 B4
Ravensburgh Cl MK45 . . . .97 B3
Ravenscourt LU6 . . . . . . .113 F3
Ravensdale CE Lower Sch
MK44 . . . . .29 B1
Ravensden Rd
Renhold MK41 . . . . .39 B7
Wilden MK44 . . . . .29 D3
Ravensthorpe LU2 . . . . . .117 B4
Ray's Cl MK42 . . . . .50 C7
Raymond Cotts SG5 . . . . .100 E4
Raynham Way LU2 . . . . . .117 D1
Raynsford Lower Sch
SG16 . . . . .78 D1
Reach Gn LU7 . . . . .103 A6
Reach La LU7 . . . . .103 B5
Readers Cl LU6 . . . . .114 B2
Readshill MK45 . . . . .86 C8
Reaper Cl LU4 . . . . .114 E4
Recreation Rd LU5 . . . . . .114 C6
Recreation Rise MK45 . . . .87 C4
Rectory Cl Carlton MK43 . . .25 A4
Clifton SG17 . . . . .78 B3
Slapton LU7 . . . . .118 D6
Rectory Ct SG19 . . . . .54 D7
Rectory La Ampthill MK45 . .73 F1
Houghton Conquest MK45 . .74 A7
Lilley LU2 . . . . .109 D2
Rectory Rd Campton SG17 .76 F1
Meppershall SG17 . . . . . . .88 B5
Steppingley MK45 . . . . . . .83 F3
Red Lion St MK43 . . . . .59 B1
Red Rails LU1 . . . . .123 C5
Red Rails Ct LU1 . . . . .123 C5
Redborne Upper Sch
& Com Coll MK45 . . . . .84 E6
Reddall Cl MK42 . . . . .50 F5
Redding Cl NN10 . . . . .8 A7
Reddings La AL3 . . . . .129 E1
Rede Cl MK41 . . . . .38 C6
Redferns Cl LU1 . . . . .123 A6
Redferns Ct LU1 . . . . .123 A6
Redfield Cl LU6 . . . . .120 E8
Redgrave Gdns LU3 . . . . .115 F7
Redhill Rd SG5 . . . . .100 D1
Redhoods Way E SG6 . . . .101 E7
Redhoods Way W SG6 . . . .101 E6
Redman Gdns SG18 . . . . . .67 A7
Redmire Cl LU4 . . . . .115 B6
Redoubt Cl SG4 . . . . .101 A1
Redwood Cl NN29 . . . . .7 A7
Redwood Dr LU3 . . . . .115 C8
Redwood Glade LU7 . . . . .103 A3
Redwood Gr MK42 . . . . . . .50 C6
Reed Pl AL5 . . . . .130 F4
Reedsdale LU2 . . . . .117 F2
Reeves Ave LU3 . . . . .116 B4
Regency Ct LU6 . . . . .121 C7
Regent Cl Bedford MK41 . . .38 C6
St Neots PE19 . . . . .22 B4
Regent Ct 1 Bedford MK40 .38 A1
Stotfold SG5 . . . . .90 F7
Regent St Dunstable LU6 .114 B1
Leighton Buzzard LU7 . . . .111 B7
Luton LU1 . . . . .123 E4
Stotfold SG5 . . . . .90 F7
Regents Mews MK40 . . . . .49 C8
Reginald St LU2 . . . . .116 E1
Regis Rd LU4 . . . . .114 E4
Rendlesham Wlk MK41 . . . .39 C3
Renhold Lower Sch MK41 39 D6
Renhold Rd MK44 . . . . .29 E1
Renshaw Cl LU2 . . . . .117 E2
Repton Cl Bedford MK41 . . .38 F4

Repton Cl continued
Luton LU3 . . . . .115 F6
Repton Rd SG17 . . . . .76 E4
Reston Path LU2 . . . . .117 E2
Restormel Cl MK41 . . . . . . .38 F5
Retreat The LU5 . . . . .114 F1
Reynes Cl MK43 . . . . .72 D7
Reynes Dr MK43 . . . . .37 A8
Reynolds SG6 . . . . .90 F1
Reynolds Cl Bedford MK41 .38 A2
Biggleswade SG18 . . . . . . .67 A7
Wharley End MK43 . . . . . . .58 E2
Reynolds Ct PE19 . . . . .22 D6
Rhineland Way MK41 . . . . .38 D6
Ribble Way MK41 . . . . .38 C6
Ribocon Way LU4 . . . . . . .115 B7
Richard St LU5 . . . . .121 C8
Richard's Cres SG18 . . . . .65 A4
Richards Cl LU1 . . . . .123 B6
Richards Ct LU1 . . . . .123 B5
Richbell Ct MK40 . . . . .38 B1
Richmond Cl Bedford MK40 .38 D1
St Neots PE19 . . . . .22 F1
Richmond Ct LU2 . . . . . . .116 F1
Richmond Hill LU2 . . . . . .116 F2
Richmond Hill Sch LU2 . .116 E2
Richmond Rd
Bedford MK40 . . . . .38 D1
Leighton Buzzard LU7 . . . .111 C6
Westoning MK45 . . . . .95 E6
Rickyard Cl LU2 . . . . .117 B3
Rickyard The SG6 . . . . . . .91 C1
Riddy La LU3 . . . . .116 C5
Ride The LU6 . . . . .120 B6
Ridge Ave AL5 . . . . .130 E4
Ridge Ct LU2 . . . . .117 A1
Ridge Rd MK42 . . . . .49 B2
Ridgeway Harpenden AL5 130 E4
Kensworth LU6 . . . . .127 E8
St Neots PE19 . . . . .22 F3
Ridgeway Ave LU5 . . . . . .114 D2
Ridgeway Bsns Pk The
SG19 . . . . .53 E8
Ridgeway Dr LU5 . . . . . . .114 E1
Ridgeway Specl Sch
MK42 . . . . .49 C2
Ridgeway The
Bedford MK41 . . . . .39 A4
Blunham MK44 . . . . .53 E8
Flitwick MK45 . . . . .84 E4
Potton SG19 . . . . .56 A7
Ridgewood Dr AL5 . . . . . .130 E4
Ridgewood Gdns AL5 . . . .130 E4
Ridgmont Lower Sch
MK43 . . . . .82 F4
Ridgmont Rd MK43 . . . . . . .82 D4
Ridgmont Sta MK43 . . . . . .82 F7
Ridgmount St MK42 . . . . . .50 B6
Ridgway MK17 . . . . .81 B6
Ridgway Rd
Brogborough MK43 . . . . . . .71 C1
Luton LU2 . . . . .116 F1
Ridings The Luton LU3 . . .116 F1
Markyate AL3 . . . . .128 E6
Ringmer Ct LU2 . . . . .117 C3
Ringshall Rd HP4 . . . . . . .126 B3
Ringwood Cl MK42 . . . . . . .49 F4
Ringwood Rd LU2 . . . . . . .116 D7
Ripley Rd LU4 . . . . .115 C1
Ripon Cl MK42 . . . . .49 E6
Ripon Ct SG18 . . . . .67 A4
Risborough Ct MK41 . . . . . .38 F1
Risborough Rd MK41 . . . . .38 F1
Riseley Lower Sch MK44 . .10 F2
Riseley Rd MK44 . . . . .12 A3
Risings The MK41 . . . . .39 A3
Rival Houses MK45 . . . . . .97 C4
River Cl SG5 . . . . .100 F4
River Hill AL3 . . . . .129 B2
River La MK44 . . . . .27 B4
River Mead SG5 . . . . .100 C2
River Rd PE19 . . . . .22 C4
River Row MK43 . . . . .26 B3
River St MK40 . . . . .50 B8
River Terr PE19 . . . . .22 E5
River Way LU3 . . . . .115 E5
Riverbanks Cl AL5 . . . . . .131 C4
Riverfield Dr MK41 . . . . . . .39 B1
Riverford Cl AL5 . . . . .131 A4
Riverhead Gdns SG19 . . . .54 B6
Rivermead Ct SG18 . . . . . .78 E5
Riverside
Leighton Buzzard LU7 . . . .111 A8
Shefford SG17 . . . . .77 C3
Riverside Cl MK42 . . . . . . .50 A6
Riverside Est AL5 . . . . . . .131 C4
Riverside Gdns SG18 . . . . .78 E5
Riverside Rd LU3 . . . . .116 A5
Riverside View MK44 . . . . .27 A5
Riversmead PE19 . . . . .22 E6
Riverview Way MK42 . . . . .49 C4
Robert Allen Ct 3 LU1 . . .123 E6
Robert Bloomfield
Mid Sch SG17 . . . . .77 B2
Robert Bruce Mid Sch
MK42 . . . . .49 D4
Robert Hunt Gdns SG19 . . .54 B7
Robert Peel Lower Sch
SG19 . . . . .54 C8
Robert Saunders SG6 101 E4
Roberts Dr MK43 . . . . .60 E2
Robertson Cnr LU6 . . . . . .120 F4
Robin Cl Flitwick MK45 . . . .84 E2
Sandy SG19 . . . . .42 B1
Robin Ct AL5 . . . . .131 B4
Robin Hill MK41 . . . . .38 C4
Robins Folly MK44 . . . . . . .28 E7
Robinson Cres MK45 . . . . .95 F2

Robinson Ct SG19 . . . . . . .44 D6
Robinswood LU2 . . . . .116 E5
Robinswood Cl LU7 . . . . . .102 F2
Rochdale LU2 . . . . .116 E5
Rochdale Cl 6 LU1 . . . . . .123 E6
Rochester Ave LU2 . . . . . .117 C4
Rochester Mews LU7 . . . .110 E7
Rochford Dr LU7 . . . . .117 E2
Rock Cl LU7 . . . . .110 D6
Rock La LU7 . . . . .110 D7
Rockbeck St MK42 . . . . . . .49 E4
Rockingham Ct NN10 . . . . . .8 A8
Rockingham Wlk MK41 . . . .39 B3
Rockleigh Ct LU7 . . . . .110 E7
Rockley Rd LU1 . . . . .123 A7
Rodean Ct MK40 . . . . .38 D2
Rodeheath LU4 . . . . .115 D3
Rodney Cl LU4 . . . . .114 F3
Roe Cl SG5 . . . . .90 E5
Roe End La AL3 . . . . .128 B4
Roe Gn PE19 . . . . .22 B5
Roebuck Cl LU1 . . . . .123 B6
Roecroft Lower Sch SG5 .90 F6
Roedean Cl LU2 . . . . .117 D3
Roff Ave MK42 . . . . .38 B2
Rogate Rd LU2 . . . . .117 C5
Roise Cl 3 MK40 . . . . .38 B1
Roise St MK40 . . . . .38 B1
Roman Ct LU5 . . . . .114 B4
Roman Gdns
Houghton Regis LU5 . . . . .114 B4
Letchworth SG6 . . . . .101 E6
Roman Rd
Barton-le-C MK45 . . . . .97 D3
Luton LU5 . . . . .115 E3
Roman View SG19 . . . . . . .54 D6
Roman Way Flitwick MK45 .84 F4
Irchester NN29 . . . . .7 B7
Markyate AL3 . . . . .128 E6
Romany Cl SG6 . . . . .101 C6
Romney Ct PE19 . . . . .22 C5
Romney Wlk MK41 . . . . . . .38 B3
Romsey Way MK42 . . . . . . .50 C3
Ronald Cl MK41 . . . . .38 E2
Rondini Ave LU3 . . . . .116 B3
Rook Tree Cl SG5 . . . . .91 A6
Rook Tree La SG5 . . . . .91 A6
Rookery Dr LU2 . . . . .116 E6
Rookery Rd MK44 . . . . .31 F8
Rookery The SG19 . . . . . . .42 C2
Rookery Wlk SG17 . . . . . . .78 B2
Rooksmead MK41 . . . . .38 C4
Rooktree Way MK45 . . . . . .64 A1
Roosevelt Ave
Leighton Buzzard LU7 . . . .111 B8
Shefford SG17 . . . . .77 C1
Ropa Ct LU7 . . . . .110 F7
Rope Wlk MK42 . . . . .50 C7
Ropkins Cl MK45 . . . . .95 F6
Rosamond Rd MK40 . . . . . .38 E1
Rosata La SG17 . . . . .76 E4
Rose Cotts SG15 . . . . .90 D8
Rose Cl Eaton Bray LU6 . .119 D6
Irchester NN29 . . . . .7 B8
St Neots PE19 . . . . .22 C4
Rose La SG18 . . . . .67 A6
Rose Wlk Ampthill MK45 . . .73 F1
Houghton Regis LU5 . . . . .114 E6
Toddington LU5 . . . . .105 F5
Rose Wood Cl LU2 . . . . . .116 F3
Rosebay Cl MK45 . . . . .84 D3
Rosebery Ave
Harpenden AL5 . . . . .130 F1
Leighton Buzzard LU7 . . . .110 E7
Rosebery Ct LU7 . . . . .110 F7
Roseby Way MK41 . . . . . . .51 A8
Rosedale LU5 . . . . .114 E5
Rosedale Cl LU3 . . . . .115 C7
Rosedale Way MK42 . . . . . .49 E4
Rosehill Hospl SG6 . . . . . .101 D2
Rosemary Dr MK43 . . . . . . .36 F2
Rosemont Cl SG6 . . . . . . .101 E6
Roslyn Way LU5 . . . . .114 A5
Ross Cl LU1 . . . . .123 B6
Rossendale Wlk MK41 . . . .39 B4
Rossfold Rd LU3 . . . . .115 D8
Rosslyn Cres LU3 . . . . . . .116 C5
Rossway LU1 . . . . .123 B1
Rothamsted Ave AL5 . . . . .131 A1
Rothamsted Ct AL5 . . . . . .131 A1
Rothbury Cl SG19 . . . . .42 C2
Rothbury Ct MK41 . . . . .39 B4
Rother Cl MK41 . . . . .38 D5
Rother Field LU2 . . . . .117 D3
Rotheram Ave LU1 . . . . . .123 B5
Rotherwood Cl LU6 . . . . . .113 E1
Rothesay Rd LU1 . . . . .123 D7
Rothsay Gdns MK40 . . . . . .38 D1
Rothsay Pl MK40 . . . . .50 D8
Rothsay Rd MK40 . . . . .50 D8
Rothschild Rd LU7 . . . . . . .110 F8
Rotten Row MK44 . . . . .10 F2
Roundfield Ave AL5 . . . . . .131 D3
Roundmead MK41 . . . . .39 A2
Roundwood Cl SG4 . . . . . .101 C4
Roundwood Gdns AL5 . . . .130 E2
Roundwood La AL5 . . . . . .130 D3
Roundwood Park Sch
AL5 . . . . .130 E2
Roundwood Pk AL5 . . . . . .130 E3
Roundwood Prim Sch
AL5 . . . . .130 E2
Rousbury Rd MK44 . . . . . . .61 C1
Rowallan Dr MK41 . . . . . . .38 E5
Rowan Cl LU1 . . . . .123 B7
Rowan Cres
Biggleswade SG18 . . . . . . .67 B7
Letchworth SG6 . . . . .101 E7
Rowan Ct SG19 . . . . .54 B8

Rowan Gdns SG19 . . . . . . .44 C5
Rowan Way MK43 . . . . .71 A8
Rowans The
Kempston MK42 . . . . .49 F3
Silsoe MK45 . . . . .86 C4
Rowelfield LU2 . . . . .117 C1
Rowington Cl LU2 . . . . . . .117 E2
Rowland Way SG6 . . . . . . .101 F6
Rowlands The SG18 . . . . . .67 C4
Rowlandson Way MK41 . . .38 F4
Rowley Furrows LU7 . . . . .110 E8
Rowney Forest Walk
SG17 . . . . .76 F5
Roxhill Rd MK43 . . . . .59 F3
Roxton Lower Sch MK44 . .31 E3
Roxton Rd
Great Barford MK44 . . . . . .41 B7
Roxton MK44 . . . . .31 E3
Royal Cl PE19 . . . . .22 B4
Royal Oak La SG18 . . . . . . .66 F7
Royal Oak La SG5 . . . . . . .99 D4
Royal Wlk LU6 . . . . .121 C7
Royce Cl LU4 . . . . .120 F7
Royce Ct PE19 . . . . .22 D5
Royce Rd MK43 . . . . .58 D3
Roydon Cl LU4 . . . . .115 A4
Royle Gdns MK42 . . . . .50 F5
Royston Ct SG19 . . . . .56 A7
Royston Rd SG7 . . . . .91 F1
Royston St SG19 . . . . .56 A7
Rudyard Cl LU4 . . . . .115 D3
Rueley Dell Rd LU2 . . . . . .109 D2
Ruffs Furze MK43 . . . . .36 F7
Runfold Ave LU3 . . . . .116 A5
Runham Cl LU4 . . . . .115 A4
Runley Rd LU1 . . . . .122 F7
Runnalow SG6 . . . . .101 E7
Rush Ct MK40 . . . . .38 C1
Rushall Gn LU2 . . . . .117 C2
Rushbrook Cl MK45 . . . . . .73 F1
Rushden Hospl NN10 . . . . . .8 B8
Rushden Rd
Milton Ernest MK44 . . . . . .27 B5
Newton Bromswold NN10 . . .9 C7
Wymington NN10 . . . . .8 A6
Rushmoor Sch MK40 . . . . .37 F2
Rushmore Cl LU1 . . . . .122 E4
Rusper Gn LU2 . . . . .117 D3
Russell Ave MK40 . . . . .50 E8
Russell Cl LU6 . . . . .127 E8
Russell Cres MK45 . . . . . . .85 D8
Russell Ct PE19 . . . . .22 F6
Russell Dr Ampthill MK45 . .84 F7
Willington MK44 . . . . .40 C1
Russell Gr MK45 . . . . .73 B2
Russell Rd LU5 . . . . .105 F5
Russell Rise LU1 . . . . .123 D6
Russell St Luton LU1 . . . . .123 D6
St Neots PE19 . . . . .22 E6
Woburn Sands MK17 . . . . . .81 C4
Russell Way
Leighton Buzzard LU7 . . . .111 D7
Wootton MK43 . . . . .60 F6
Russet Cl MK43 . . . . .61 B1
Russett Cl MK45 . . . . .73 E1
Ruthin Cl LU1 . . . . .123 D5
Rutland Cres LU2 . . . . .124 A7
Rutland Ct LU2 . . . . .124 A7
Rutland Gdns SG19 . . . . . .54 D7
Rutland Hall LU2 . . . . .124 A7
Rutland Rd MK40 . . . . .50 A8
Ryans Cl LU2 . . . . .116 F1
Rycroft Ave PE19 . . . . .22 F6
Rydal Cres SG18 . . . . .67 A4
Rydal Way LU3 . . . . .115 F5
Ryder Ave SG5 . . . . .100 D3
Ryder Way SG5 . . . . .100 D3
Rye Cl Harpenden AL5 . . . .131 B4
Leighton Buzzard LU7 . . . .111 D7
Rushden NN10 . . . . .8 C8
Rye Cres MK44 . . . . .52 A6
Rye Hill Harpenden AL5 . . .131 B4
2 Luton LU2 . . . . .116 D1
Rye The LU6 . . . . .119 C8
Ryecroft Way LU2 . . . . . . .117 A4
Ryefield LU3 . . . . .108 A1
Ryeland Heath LU2 . . . . . .117 F2
Rylands Heath LU2 . . . . . .117 F2
Rylands Mews LU7 . . . . . .111 A6
Ryley Cl SG16 . . . . .89 B5
Ryswick Rd MK42 . . . . .50 A5
Ryton Cl Bedford MK41 . . . .38 C6
Luton LU1 . . . . .123 B6

S

Sabel Cl SG18 . . . . .67 C3
Sacombe Gn LU3 . . . . .108 B1
Sacred Heart Inf Sch
LU2 . . . . .117 A3
Sacred Heart Jun Sch
LU2 . . . . .117 A3
Saddle Cl MK41 . . . . .37 C7
Sadleirs Gn MK17 . . . . .81 B5
Saffron Cl Arlesey SG15 . . .90 A7
1 Bedford MK40 . . . . .50 B8
Luton LU2 . . . . .116 D7
Saffron Ct SG18 . . . . .67 A5
Saffron Gdns SG5 . . . . .67 A5
Saffron Hill SG6 . . . . .101 E6
Saffron Rd SG18 . . . . .67 A5
Saffron Rise LU6 . . . . .119 E6
St Alban Rd MK40 . . . . .38 D2
St Albans St MK45 . . . . . . .84 E4
St Albans Rd AL5 . . . . .131 B1
St Aldates Ct LU2 . . . . . . .116 B3
St Andrew's Ave AL5 . . . .130 F1

St Andrew's Cl
Ampthill MK45 . . . . .73 F1
Slip End LU1 . . . . .123 B1
St Andrew's Sch MK40 . . .38 C2
St Andrew's St
Biggleswade SG18 . . . . . . .66 F6
Leighton Buzzard LU7 . . . .111 A8
St Andrew's Way SG18 . . .78 F8
St Andrews Cl
Biggleswade SG18 . . . . . . .66 F5
Flitwick MK45 . . . . .84 E4
Leighton Buzzard LU7 . . . .111 A7
St Andrews Ct SG18 . . . . . .66 F6
St Andrews La
Houghton Regis LU5 . . . . .114 C5
Kimbolton PE18 . . . . .6 F4
St Andrews Lower Sch
SG18 . . . . .66 F6
St Andrews Mews LU3 . . .116 A4
St Andrews Rd MK40 . . . . .38 C2
St Andrews Wlk LU1 . . . . .123 C1
St Ann's Rd LU1 . . . . .123 F7
St Anselm Pl PE19 . . . . . . .22 E6
St Augustine Ave LU3 . . .116 C3
St Augustine's Rd MK40 . .38 D2
St Bede's RC Mid Sch
MK40 . . . . .38 A1
St Bernard's Cl LU3 . . . . .116 C3
St Catherines Ave LU3 . . .116 B3
St Christopher Sch SG6 .101 F3
St Christopher's Cl LU5 . .114 F1
St Christopher's Lower Sch
LU5 . . . . .114 F2
St Cuthbert's St 1 MK40 . .50 C8
St Cuthberts Ct 3 MK40 . .50 C8
St David's Way LU5 . . . . . .114 D6
St Dominics Sq LU4 . . . . .114 F4
St Edmond Rd MK40 . . . . . .38 D2
St Ethelbert Ave LU3 . . . .116 C4
St Faiths Cl SG4 . . . . .101 B1
St Francis' Coll SG6 . . . . .101 E4
St Francis Ct SG17 . . . . . . .77 C3
St Francis Way SG17 . . . . .77 C2
St George's Cl
Leighton Buzzard LU7 . . . .111 B8
Toddington LU5 . . . . .105 F6
St George's Lower Sch
LU7 . . . . .111 B8
St George's Rd MK40 . . . . .38 C2
St George's Sch AL5 . . . . .131 B2
St Gregory's RC Mid Sch
MK40 . . . . .37 E1
St Helena Rd MK42 . . . . . . .50 D5
St Helenas Gdn MK42 . . . . .50 B4
St Hilda's Sch AL5 . . . . . . .130 F2
St Ives Cl LU3 . . . . .116 B3
St James CE Lower Sch
MK40 . . . . .37 C1
St James Cl
Houghton Regis LU5 . . . . .114 E4
Pulloxhill MK45 . . . . .96 E8
St James Ct MK40 . . . . .38 C2
St James Rd AL5 . . . . .131 B4
St James' Rd LU3 . . . . . . .116 B3
St James's Ct AL5 . . . . . . .131 B3
St John Cl LU3 . . . . .123 B5
St John Rigby RC Lower Sch
MK41 . . . . .38 F2
St John's Ave MK42 . . . . . .49 D3
St John's Homes MK42 . . . .49 D4
St John's Rd Arlesey SG15 .90 A4
Moggerhanger MK44 . . . . .53 C7
St John's Specl Sch MK42 49 F6
St John's St Bedford MK42 50 C7
Biggleswade SG18 . . . . . . .67 A7
Kempston MK42 . . . . .49 D3
St John's Terr MK42 . . . . . .50 C7
St John's Wlk MK42 . . . . . .49 D3
St Johns Cl LU7 . . . . .112 C5
St Johns Ct LU1 . . . . .123 B5
St Johns Ctr MK42 . . . . . . .50 C7
St Joseph's Cl LU3 . . . . . .116 A4
St Joseph's Inf Sch LU3 .116 A4
St Joseph's Jun Sch
LU3 . . . . .116 A4
St Katharines Cl SG5 . . . .100 D3
St Kilda Rd LU4 . . . . .114 F4
St Lawrence Lower Sch
NN10 . . . . .8 A5
St Lawrence Wlk NN10 . . . .8 B5
St Lawrences Ct LU3 . . . . .116 C3
St Leonard's Ave MK42 . . .50 C6
St Leonard's Cl LU7 . . . . .103 B3
St Leonard's Lower Sch
LU7 . . . . .103 A5
St Leonard's St 1 MK42 . .50 C6
St Leonards Ct MK42 . . . . .50 B6
St Loyes St 18 MK40 . . . . .50 B8
St Luke's Cl LU3 . . . . .115 E2
St Margaret of Scotland
Inf Sch LU1 . . . . .123 B5
St Margaret of Scotland
Jun Sch LU1 . . . . .123 B5
St Margarets Ave LU3 . . . .116 B3
St Margarets Cl
Lidlington MK43 . . . . .72 C3
Streatley LU3 . . . . .108 A6
St Margarets Gdns SG17 . .67 C4
St Margarets Sch MK43 . . .25 A1
St Mark's Cl SG5 . . . . .100 D3
St Marks Cl MK45 . . . . .84 F4
St Martin de Porres
RC Inf Sch LU4 . . . . . . .115 A4
St Martin de Porres
RC Jun Sch LU4 . . . . . .115 A4
St Martin's Ave LU2 . . . . .116 F2
St Martins Bsns Ctr MK42 51 B5
St Martins AL5 . . . . .131 C4

St Martins Way MK42 . . . .51 A5
St Mary's SG19 . . . . .44 E5
St Mary's Ave SG5 . . . . . . .90 F6
St Mary's Cl
Felmersham MK43 . . . . .26 C8
Letchworth SG6 . . . . .101 F2
Pirton SG5 . . . . .99 D4
Tebworth LU7 . . . . .105 C2
St Mary's (Clophill)
Lower Sch MK45 . . . . . .75 D1
St Mary's Ct
8 Dunstable LU6 . . . . .121 B8
St Neots PE19 . . . . .22 E4
St Mary's Gate LU6 . . . . .121 B8
St Mary's Glebe LU6 . . . .119 E4
St Mary's Pl SG17 . . . . .88 B5
St Mary's RC Lower Sch
LU1 . . . . .121 F6
St Mary's Rd LU1 . . . . . . .123 F7
St Mary's St Bedford MK42 50 C7
St Neots PE19 . . . . .22 E4
St Mary's (Stotfold)
Lower Sch SG5 . . . . .91 A6
St Mary's Way LU7 . . . . . .110 E8
St Mary's Wlk SG19 . . . . . .43 C3
St Marys Cl Bletsoe MK44 .17 C1
Elstow MK42 . . . . .50 B3
Marston Moretaine MK43 . . .72 D7
St Marys Rd MK43 . . . . . . .60 F7
St Mathews Cl MK42 . . . . .49 D3
St Matthew's Inf Sch
LU2 . . . . .116 E1
St Matthews Cl LU2 . . . . .123 E8
St Mellion Dr MK40 . . . . . .49 B7
St Michael's Cres LU3 . . .116 D3
St Michael's Cts MK40 . . . .38 D2
St Michael's Rd MK40 . . . .38 D2
St Michaels Ave LU5 . . . .114 B4
St Mildreds Ave LU3 . . . .116 C3
St Minver Rd MK40 . . . . . .38 D2
St Monicas Ave LU3 . . . . .116 B3
St Neots Mus PE19 . . . . . . .22 E5
St Neots Rd Bedford MK41 .40 B3
Bolnhurst MK44 . . . . .19 E4
Little Barford PE19 . . . . .33 F7
Sandy SG19 . . . . .54 B8
St Neots PE19 . . . . .22 D4
St Nicholas Ave AL5 . . . .131 A1
St Nicholas CE JMI Sch
Harpenden AL5 . . . . .131 A1
Letchworth SG6 . . . . .91 C1
St Nicholas Cl MK17 . . . . . .94 F5
St Nicholas Ct AL5 . . . . . .130 F3
St Ninian's Ct 7 LU2 . . . . .123 D8
St Olam's Cl LU3 . . . . . . .116 B6
St Olives SG5 . . . . .90 E6
Saint Paul's Gdns LU1 . . .123 E5
St Paul's Rd Bedford MK40 .49 F7
Luton LU1 . . . . .123 E5
St Paul's Sq MK40 . . . . . . .50 B8
St Pauls Cl MK45 . . . . .84 F3
St Peter's Ave SG15 . . . . . .90 A7
St Peter's Cl MK44 . . . . . . .16 C4
St Peter's Rd LU5 . . . . . . .121 C8
St Peter's St MK40 . . . . . . .38 C1
St Peters Cl MK45 . . . . .84 F4
St Peters Ct SG19 . . . . .56 A8
St Peters Rd LU1 . . . . . . .123 B7
St Saviour's Cres LU1 . . .123 D6
St Swithun's Way SG19 . . .54 D7
St Swithuns Lower Sch
SG19 . . . . .54 C6
St Thomas More
RC JMI Sch SG6 . . . . . .101 D4
St Thomas More
RC Upper Sch MK41 . . . .38 C6
St Thomas's Rd LU2 . . . .117 A4
St Vincent Gdns LU4 . . . .115 D3
St Vincent's
RC Lower Sch LU5 . . . .114 C5
St Vincents MK17 . . . . .81 C4
St Winifreds Ave LU3 . . .116 C3
Salcombe Cl MK40 . . . . . . .38 E1
Sale Dr SG7 . . . . .91 F1
Salford Rd
Aspley Guise MK17 . . . . .81 D7
Brogborough MK43 . . . . .82 B8
Salisbury Ave AL5 . . . . . .131 A1
Salisbury Ho 8 MK40 . . . . .38 A1
Salisbury Rd Baldock SG7 . .91 F1
Flitwick MK45 . . . . .84 E4
Harpenden AL5 . . . . .131 D3
Luton LU1 . . . . .123 D6
Salisbury St MK41 . . . . . . .38 B2
Sallowsprings LU6 . . . . . .120 F2
Saltash Cl MK40 . . . . .38 E2
Saltdean Cl LU2 . . . . .117 D4
Salters Way LU6 . . . . .113 F3
Saltfield Cres LU4 . . . . . .115 C4
Sambar Cl PE19 . . . . .22 B5
Sampshill Rd MK45 . . . . . . .95 E5
Samuel Whitbread Upper
Sch & Com Coll SG17 . .77 E2
San Remo Rd MK17 . . . . . .81 F4
Sand La Barton-le-C MK45 . .97 B8
Biggleswade SG18 . . . . .67 A6
Northill SG18 . . . . .53 E1
Sandy SG19 . . . . .54 E7
Sand Rd MK45 . . . . .85 E3
Sandalwood Cl LU3 . . . . .116 B7
Sandell Cl LU2 . . . . .116 F2
Sanderling Cl SG6 . . . . . .101 E8
Sanders Cl MK42 . . . . .49 D6
Sanders Way MK43 . . . . . . .60 F8
Sanderson Cl MK45 . . . . . .95 E6
Sanderson Rd MK45 . . . . . .95 E6
Sandfields Rd PE19 . . . . . .22 F5
Sandford Rise SG19 . . . . . .54 A7
Sandgate Rd LU4 . . . . . . .115 D2
Sandhill Cl MK45 . . . . .73 A1
Sandhills LU7 . . . . .103 B1
Sandhouse Cotts LU7 . . . .103 D8
Sandhurst Pl MK42 . . . . . . .50 B6
Sandhurst Rd MK42 . . . . . .50 B6
Sandland Cl LU6 . . . . .114 A1
Sandon Cl SG19 . . . . .54 C8
Sandpiper Cl SG18 . . . . . . .66 F5
Sandringham Dr LU5 . . . .114 E4
Sandringham Rd MK45 . . .84 D1
Sandy Acres MK45 . . . . . . .74 B1
Sandy Bsns Pk SG19 . . . . .42 C2
Sandy La Chicksands SG17 .76 E5
Husborne Crawley MK17 . . .82 D3
Leighton Buzzard LU7 . . . . .103 A3
Tilbrook PE18 . . . . .6 C6
Woburn Sands MK17 . . . . . .81 B2
Sandy Rd Bedford MK41 . . .39 A1
Everton SG19 . . . . .43 B2
Potton SG19 . . . . .55 E7
Willington MK44 . . . . .52 E8
Sandy Sta SG19 . . . . .54 D6
Sandy Upper Sch
& Comm Coll SG19 . . . . .42 A1
Sandy View SG18 . . . . .67 B8
Sandye La MK44 . . . . .11 D8
Sanfoin Rd LU4 . . . . .115 A4
Santa Pod Raceway NN29 15 C6
Santingfield N LU1 . . . . . .123 B6
Santingfield S LU1 . . . . . .123 B6
Sarum Rd LU3 . . . . .115 F4
Saturn Cl LU7 . . . . .111 D8
Sauncey Ave
Harpenden AL5 . . . . .131 B3
Harpenden AL5 . . . . .131 C2
Sauncey Wood AL5 . . . . . .131 E4
Sauncey Wood La AL5 . . .131 E6
Saunders Gdns MK40 . . . . .49 E7
Saunders Piece MK45 . . . .84 F8
Savannah Cl MK42 . . . . . . .49 F5
Savile's Cl PE19 . . . . .22 D7
Saville Cl MK44 . . . . .41 A5
Sawtry Cl LU3 . . . . .116 A6
Sawyers Cres NN9 . . . . .3 B8
Sax Ho SG6 . . . . .90 E1
Saxon Ave SG5 . . . . .90 F8
Saxon Cl Dunstable LU6 . .120 E8
Flitwick MK45 . . . . .84 F4
Harpenden AL5 . . . . .131 C4
Letchworth SG6 . . . . .90 F1
Roxton MK44 . . . . .31 E1
Saxon Cres MK45 . . . . .97 C4
Saxon Ctr MK42 . . . . .49 E4
Saxon Pl PE19 . . . . .22 F4
Saxon Pool & L Ctr SG18 .67 C5
Saxon Rd LU3 . . . . .116 C2
Saxon Rise NN29 . . . . .7 C8
Saxons Cl LU7 . . . . .111 C7
Saxtead Cl LU2 . . . . .117 D1
Saywell Rd LU2 . . . . .117 B1
Scawsby Cl LU6 . . . . .113 E1
School Cl SG19 . . . . .44 D5
School Hill NN29 . . . . .7 B8
School House Mews
MK45 . . . . .86 C4
School La Carlton MK43 . . .25 A2
Colmworth MK44 . . . . .20 A2
Eaton Bray LU6 . . . . .119 F6
Great Barford MK44 . . . . . . .41 A5
Greenfield MK45 . . . . .85 C2
Husborne Crawley MK43 . . .82 B4
Irchester NN29 . . . . .7 A8
Luton LU4 . . . . .115 D4
Roxton MK44 . . . . .31 F2
Shefford SG17 . . . . .77 B2
Southill SG18 . . . . .65 D1
St Neots PE19 . . . . .22 C2
St Neots, Eynesbury PE19 . . .22 E4
Stewartby MK43 . . . . .61 C1
Wootton MK43 . . . . .60 F7
School Rd NN29 . . . . .7 A8
Scotchbrook Rd MK43 . . . .72 D7
Scotfield Ct LU2 . . . . .117 D3
Scott Ave MK42 . . . . .51 A2
Scott Ct LU5 . . . . .114 C1
Scott Lower Sch MK41 . . .38 C5
Scott Rd LU3 . . . . .115 C7
Seabrook LU4 . . . . .115 B3
Seaford Cl LU2 . . . . .117 C3
Seal Cl LU4 . . . . .115 D3
Seamons Cl LU6 . . . . .121 D6
Sears Cl SG17 . . . . .78 B3
Sears The LU6 . . . . .119 B5
Seaton Dr MK40 . . . . .38 E2
Seaton Rd LU4 . . . . .115 F3
Sebright Rd AL3 . . . . .128 E5
Sebright Sch AL3 . . . . . . .128 C4
Sedbury Cl LU3 . . . . .116 A6
Sedgwick Rd LU4 . . . . . . .115 B7
Seebohm Cl SG5 . . . . .100 C1
Segenhoe Cl MK43 . . . . . .82 F5
Selbourne Rd LU4 . . . . . .116 A2
Selina Cl LU3 . . . . .115 C7
Selsey Dr LU2 . . . . .117 D4
Selsey Way MK41 . . . . . . .38 E2
Sergeants Way MK41 . . . . .39 C2
Setchel PE19 . . . . .22 C6
Severalls The LU2 . . . . . . .117 B3
Severn Cl MK45 . . . . .84 D2
Severn Way MK41 . . . . . . .38 C5
Severn Wlk LU7 . . . . .103 B3
Sewell La LU6 . . . . .113 D3
Sexton Ave MK42 . . . . .50 A4
Seymour Ave LU1 . . . . . . .123 F5
Seymour Rd LU1 . . . . .123 F5
Shackleton Lower Sch
MK42 . . . . .50 C5
Shady Wlk PE19 . . . . .22 F5
Shaftesbury Ave
Bedford MK40 . . . . .50 E8
St Neots PE19 . . . . .22 F5
Shaftesbury Rd LU4 . . . . .116 B1
Shakespeare Dr SG18 . . . .66 C8
Shakespeare Rd
Bedford MK40 . . . . .38 A1
Harpenden AL5 . . . . .131 C1
Luton LU4 . . . . .115 B2
St Neots PE19 . . . . .22 C3
Shaldon Ct MK40 . . . . .38 E2
Shanklin Cl LU3 . . . . .116 A7
Shannon Cl
Lower Stondon SG16 . . . . . . .88 F2
Sandy SG19 . . . . .42 B1
Shannon Ct SG19 . . . . .54 C7
Shannon Pl SG19 . . . . .55 F7
Sharnbrook Ct MK44 . . . . .16 D3
Sharnbrook Rd MK44 . . . . .16 B7
Sharnbrook Upper Sch
MK44 . . . . .16 B3
Sharnside MK44 . . . . .16 D4
Sharose Ct AL3 . . . . .128 E5
Sharp Cl MK45 . . . . .86 B7
Sharpenhoe Clappers
LU3 . . . . .107 F7
Sharpenhoe Rd
Barton-le-C MK45 . . . . .97 B2
Streatley LU3 . . . . .107 F7
Sharples Gn LU3 . . . . . . .116 B8
Sharps Way SG4 . . . . .101 A1
Shay La PE18 . . . . .5 B4
Shearley Cl MK40 . . . . .49 F7
Sheepcote Cres LU7 . . . .103 A5
Sheepfold Rd MK45 . . . . . .84 F3
Sheeplands MK41 . . . . .39 B3
Sheeptick End MK43 . . . . .72 B3
Sheffield Cl SG19 . . . . .56 A7
Shefford Bsns Pk SG17 . . .77 C3
Shefford Ind Pk SG17 . . . .77 C2
Shefford Lower Sch SG17 77 B2
Shefford Rd Clifton SG17 . .77 F2
Clophill MK45 . . . . .76 A2
Meppershall SG17 . . . . .88 C7
Sheldon Ct MK17 . . . . .81 B4
Shelford La MK44 . . . . .20 B3
Shelley Ct 16 AL5 . . . . . . .131 B1
Shelley Pl PE19 . . . . .22 D6
Shelley Rd LU4 . . . . .115 B2
Shelton Ave LU5 . . . . .105 F4
Shelton Cl LU5 . . . . .105 F4
Shelton Ct MK44 . . . . .40 F5
Shelton Lower Sch MK43 .60 C3
Shelton Rd Hargrave NN9 . . .1 A3
Upper Dean PE18 . . . . .5 A5
Shelton Way LU2 . . . . . . .117 A3
Shenley Cl LU7 . . . . .103 B3
Shenley Hill Rd LU7 . . . .103 C3
Shepherd Rd LU4 . . . . . . .114 F4
Shepherds Cl MK45 . . . . . .95 F1
Shepherds Mead
Hitchin SG5 . . . . .100 F2
Leighton Buzzard LU7 . . . . .103 A1
Shepherds Way AL5 . . . .130 D4
Sherborne Ave LU2 . . . . .116 D6
Sherbourne Way MK41 . . .38 F5
Sherd Cl LU3 . . . . .115 F7
Sheridan Rd LU3 . . . . . . .116 C2
Sheriden Cl LU6 . . . . .114 B1
Sheringham Cl LU2 . . . . .116 C7
Sherwood SG6 . . . . .101 F8
Sherwood Rd LU4 . . . . . . .116 A2
Sherwood Terr NN29 . . . . . .7 B8
Sherwood Wlk MK41 . . . . .39 B3
Shillington Lower Sch
SG5 . . . . .87 E1
Shillington Rd
Gravenhurst MK45 . . . . .87 D4
Lower Stondon SG5 . . . . . . .88 C2
Meppershall SG17 . . . . .88 B4
Pirton SG5 . . . . .99 B5
Shingle Cl LU3 . . . . .116 A8
Ship Rd LU7 . . . . .110 E6
Shirdley Rd PE19 . . . . .22 F4
Shire La MK16 . . . . .58 E4
Shires The LU2 . . . . .116 D1
Shirley Rd LU1 . . . . .123 C8
Short Path LU5 . . . . .114 C6
Short St MK40 . . . . .49 F7
Shortcroft Ct MK45 . . . . . .97 B2
Shortmead St SG18 . . . . . .66 F6
Shortstown Lower Sch
MK42 . . . . .50 F2
Shrubbery La MK44 . . . . . .29 C4
Shuttleworth Collection
Mus The SG18 . . . . .65 D6
Shuttleworth Coll
SG18 . . . . .65 D5
Shuttleworth Ct
Bedford MK41 . . . . .39 C3
Biggleswade SG18 . . . . .67 A6
Shuttleworth Rd MK41 . . .39 C2
Sibley Cl LU2 . . . . .117 B3
Sibton Abbey MK41 . . . . . .51 B8
Sidmouth Cl MK40 . . . . . . .38 E2
Sidney Rd Ampthill MK45 . .84 E7
Bedford MK40 . . . . .37 F1
Silbury Ct MK45 . . . . .86 B5
Silecroft Rd LU2 . . . . .124 B8
Silsoe Lower Sch MK45 .86 C4
Silsoe Rd Flitton MK45 . . . .85 E3
Maulden MK45 . . . . .85 E7
Silver Birches The
MK42 . . . . .49 F2
Silver End Rd MK45 . . . . . .63 F1
Silver Jubilee Mid Sch
MK42 . . . . .50 E6
Silver St Bedford MK40 . . . .50 B8
Great Barford MK44 . . . . . . .40 F5
Guilden Morden SG8 . . . . . . .69 F4
Luton LU1 . . . . .123 E7
St Neots PE19 . . . . .22 F4
Stevington MK43 . . . . .36 B7
Silverbirch Ave SG5 . . . . . .90 F8
Silverbirches La MK17 . . . .81 B2
Silverdale St MK42 . . . . . . .49 F4
Silverweed PE19 . . . . .22 C5
Simdims MK43 . . . . .59 A1
Simpkin Cl PE19 . . . . .22 C2
Simpkins Dr MK45 . . . . . . .97 C4
Simpson Cl LU4 . . . . .115 D2
Singer Ct MK42 . . . . .49 D2
Singer Way MK42 . . . . .49 D2
Singlets La AL3 . . . . .129 C2
Sir Herbert Janes Village
The LU4 . . . . .115 D4
Sir John Lawes Sch AL5 131 C3
Sir Malcolm Stewart
Homes MK43 . . . . .73 C8
Sir Peter's Way HP4 . . . .126 E6
Skegsbury La SG4 . . . . . .125 F1
Skelton Cl LU3 . . . . .108 B1
Skerne Pas MK41 . . . . .38 C7
Skimpot Rd LU4 . . . . .115 A1
Skipton Cl SG19 . . . . .54 C8
Skua Cl LU4 . . . . .115 A5
Slade The Clapham MK41 . .37 E6
Clophill MK45 . . . . .75 C1
Wrestlingworth SG19 . . . . . .57 B3
Slapton La LU6 . . . . .118 F6
Slate Hall LU3 . . . . .107 A4
Slate Row MK44 . . . . .16 A8
Slater Cl MK42 . . . . .49 D5
Slickett's La LU6 . . . . . . .119 F3
Slip End Lower Sch LU1 .123 B1
Slip The MK43 . . . . .26 C7
Slype The AL5 . . . . .131 F6
Smiths Lane Mall 5 LU1 .123 E7
Smiths Sq 6 LU1 . . . . . . .123 E7
Snagge Ct MK43 . . . . .60 E1
Snailswell La SG5 . . . . . .100 E5
Snow Hill MK45 . . . . .74 B1
Snowdrop Wlk SG18 . . . . .67 C5
Snowford Cl 1 LU3 . . . . .116 A7
Sollershott E SG6 . . . . . . .101 F4
Sollershott Hall SG6 . . . .101 F4
Sollershott W SG6 . . . . . .101 E4
Solway Rd N LU3 . . . . . . .116 A4
Solway Rd S LU3 . . . . . . .116 A3
Someries Inf Sch LU2 . . .117 C3
Someries Jun Sch LU2 . .117 C3
Someries Rd AL5 . . . . . . .131 C4
Somersby Cl LU1 . . . . . . .123 E5
Somerset Ave LU2 . . . . . .117 A1
Somerton Cl MK41 . . . . . . .39 A5
Sopwith Way MK42 . . . . . .51 A2
Sorrel Cl LU3 . . . . .116 B8
Souberie Ave SG6 . . . . . .101 F5
Soulbury Rd LU7 . . . . . . .110 D7
Souldrop Rd MK44 . . . . . . .16 C5
South Ave MK42 . . . . .50 C1
South Dr MK42 . . . . .51 A2
South Drift Way LU1 . . . .123 B5
South End Jun & Inf Schs
NN10 . . . . .8 B8
South End La LU6 . . . . . .119 B4
South Gr NN10 . . . . .8 B5
South Luton High Sch
LU1 . . . . .123 F5
South Rd Luton LU1 . . . . .123 D6
Sandy SG19 . . . . .54 B7
South St
Leighton Buzzard LU7 . . . . .111 B7
St Neots PE19 . . . . .22 E5
South View
Biggleswade SG18 . . . . .67 A5
Letchworth SG6 . . . . .101 F5
South Wlk SG18 . . . . .67 B7
Southampton Gdns LU3 .107 D1
Southbridge St SG17 . . . . .77 C3
Southcott Lower Sch
LU7 . . . . .110 D7
Southcott Village LU7 . . .110 D6
Southcourt Ave LU7 . . . .110 D6
Southcourt Rd LU7 . . . . .110 D7
Southcroft Ho LU7 . . . . . .110 D7
Southdown Rd AL5 . . . . . .131 B1
Southern Ave SG16 . . . . . .89 C3
Southern Rise LU2 . . . . . .130 F7
Southern Way
Letchworth SG6 . . . . .101 E8
Studham LU6 . . . . .127 C4
Southfield Jun & Inf Schs
LU4 . . . . .114 F4
Southfields
Letchworth SG6 . . . . .90 F1
Roxton MK44 . . . . .31 E1
Shefford SG17 . . . . .77 E2
Southfields Ct SG17 . . . . . .77 E2
Southfields Rd
Dunstable LU6 . . . . .121 D6
Kempston MK42 . . . . .50 A3
Southgate Ct 5 AL5 . . . . .131 A2
Southill Lower Sch SG18 .65 D1
Southill Rd Broom SG18 . . .66 B2
Cardington MK44 . . . . .51 E2
Southland Rise SG18 . . . . .78 F5
Southlands Lower Sch
SG18 . . . . .67 B4
Southlynn Ho 2 LU2 . . . . .123 F8
Southview MK44 . . . . .40 F5
Southview Gdns LU7 . . . .111 B6
Southview Rd AL5 . . . . . .131 D3
Southville Rd MK42 . . . . . .50 B5
Southway MK42 . . . . .50 E5
Southwood Rd LU5 . . . . . .121 E6
Sovereigns Quay MK40 . . .50 B8
Sowerby Ave LU2 . . . . . . .117 C3
Spa Ho PE19 . . . . .22 F5
Sparhawke SG6 . . . . .91 A1
Sparksfield SG16 . . . . .78 D2
Sparrow Cl LU4 . . . . .115 A4
Spayne Cl LU3 . . . . .116 B8
Spear Cl LU3 . . . . .115 E6
Speedwell Cl LU3 . . . . . . .116 A8
Spencer Cl Potton SG19 . . .56 A8
St Neots PE19 . . . . .22 D6
Spencer Ct LU7 . . . . .103 B1
Spencer Ho SG5 . . . . .90 F6
Spencer Rd Luton LU3 . . .116 C2
Sandy SG19 . . . . .54 D6
Spencers The MK44 . . . . . .41 A5
Spenser Ct MK40 . . . . .37 F1
Spenser Rd
Bedford MK40 . . . . .37 F1
Harpenden AL5 . . . . .131 C1
Spensley Rd MK45 . . . . . . .95 E5
Spinney Bglws LU7 . . . . .118 C6
Spinney Cres LU6 . . . . . . .120 F8
Spinney La MK17 . . . . .81 F4
Spinney Rd
Chawston MK44 . . . . .31 E4
Luton LU3 . . . . .115 D7
Spinney The
Bedford MK41 . . . . .39 B3
Harpenden AL5 . . . . .130 E3
Spitfire Rd SG17 . . . . .77 C1
Spittlesea Rd LU2 . . . . . .124 C7
Spoondell LU6 . . . . .121 A6
Spratts La LU6 . . . . .121 F1
Spreckley Cl SG16 . . . . . . .89 B5
Spring Cl Ampthill MK45 . . .84 F7
Biggleswade SG18 . . . . .67 B6
Spring Gdns MK42 . . . . . . .50 A4
Spring Gr Sandy SG19 . . . . .54 B7
Woburn Sands MK17 . . . . . .81 B5
Spring Hill MK44 . . . . .13 A3
Spring La Stagsden MK43 . .48 C6
Yelden MK44 . . . . .4 A3
Spring Pl 5 LU1 . . . . .123 D6
Spring Rd Clifton SG17 . . . .78 A2
Harpenden AL5 . . . . .130 A4
Kempston MK42 . . . . .50 A4
Letchworth SG6 . . . . .101 E4
Letchworth SG6 . . . . .101 E6
Springbrook PE19 . . . . .22 F4
Springfield SG18 . . . . .68 C5
Springfield Ave MK42 . . . .49 E4
Springfield Cres AL5 . . . .131 B5
Springfield Ct LU7 . . . . . .110 E7
Springfield Ctr MK42 . . . . .49 F3
Springfield Dr MK43 . . . . .36 E3
Springfield Lower Sch
MK42 . . . . .49 F3
Springfield Rd
Dunstable LU6 . . . . .120 D5
Leighton Buzzard LU7 . . . . .110 E7
Luton LU3 . . . . .116 C6
Springfield Way MK43 . . . .59 C2
Springshott SG6 . . . . .101 E5
Springside LU7 . . . . .110 E7
Spruce Wlk MK42 . . . . .49 F3
Spurcroft LU3 . . . . .108 C1
Square The
Aspley Guise MK17 . . . . .81 E4
Dunstable LU6 . . . . .121 B8
Wilstead MK45 . . . . .62 E4
Squires Cl SG17 . . . . .77 E2
Squires Ct PE19 . . . . .22 C4
Squires Pl LU5 . . . . .105 F6
Squires Rd
Marston Moretaine MK43 . . .72 D7
Wootton MK43 . . . . .60 F6
Stables The MK45 . . . . .84 F7
Stadium Est The LU4 . . . .115 B1
Stafford Rd MK42 . . . . .50 A6
Stagsden Rd MK43 . . . . . . .36 E2
Staines Sq LU6 . . . . .121 C7
Stainmore Rd MK41 . . . . . .39 C4
Stakers Ct AL5 . . . . .131 B1
Stanbridge Lower Sch
LU7 . . . . .112 D5
Stanbridge Rd
Billington LU7 . . . . .111 F1
Leighton Buzzard LU7 . . . . .111 C6
Tilsworth LU7 . . . . .112 F5
Totternhoe, Lower End LU6 112 E2
Totternhoe, Stanbridgeford
LU7 . . . . .112 E3
Stanbridge Road Terr
LU7 . . . . .111 B6
Stanbridge Way MK45 . . . .74 B8
Stanbrook Way MK44 . . . . .4 A3
Stancliffe Rd MK41 . . . . . .38 E3
Standalone Farm SG6 . . .101 D7
Stanford La SG17 . . . . .78 A3
Stanford Rd Clifton SG17 . .78 A5
Luton LU2 . . . . .117 A1
Shefford SG17 . . . . .77 D3
Southill SG18 . . . . .77 F8
Stanhope Rd MK41 . . . . . . .38 E4
Stanley Cl MK45 . . . . .96 E8
Stanley Livingstone Ct
LU1 . . . . .123 D6
Stanley Rd LU3 . . . . .108 A5
Stanley St Bedford MK41 . . .38 B2
Kempston MK42 . . . . .49 F4
Luton LU1 . . . . .123 D6
Stanmore Cres LU3 . . . . .115 F4
Stannard Way MK44 . . . . . .51 C6

Stanton Rd
Kempston MK42 ....49 D5
Luton LU4 ....115 C1
Stapleford Rd LU2 ....117 C4
Stapleton Rd MK42 ....50 D4
Staploe Rd MK44 ......21 D2
Starey Cl MK44 ....27 B5
Starling Cl SG19 ......42 B1
Starling Way MK41 ....38 C4
Startpoint LU1 ....123 C7
Stately Ct LU3 ....116 D1
Statham Cl LU3 ....108 B1
Station App AL5 ....131 B1
Station Cres MK43 .....72 B3
Station Ct SG19 ....55 F7
Station Par SG6 ....101 F6
Station Pl SG6 ....101 F6
Station Rd Ampthill MK45 ..84 C7
Ampthill MK45 ....84 D7
Arlesey SG15 ....90 A4
Baldock SG7 ....91 F1
Bedford MK42 ....50 A4
Biggleswade SG18 ......67 A5
Blunham MK44 ....41 D2
Cheddington LU7 ....118 A1
Dunstable LU5 ....121 D8
Flitwick MK45 ....84 F2
Gamlingay SG19 ....44 F4
Hargrave NN9 ....1 B7
Harlington MK45 ....95 F1
Harpenden AL5 ....131 C2
Irchester NN29 ....7 C8
Langford SG18 ....78 F6
Leighton Buzzard LU7 ..110 E7
Letchworth SG6 ....101 F6
Lidlington MK43 ....72 B3
Lower Stondon SG16 ...88 F3
Luton, High Town LU1 ..123 E8
Luton, Leagrave LU4 ...115 E5
Marston Moretaine MK43 ..72 D6
Oakley MK43 ....37 A8
Potton SG19 ....55 F7
Ridgmont MK43 ....82 D6
Sandy SG19 ....54 D6
Sharnbrook MK44 ......16 E4
Stanbridge LU7 ....112 D4
Tempsford SG19 ....42 C8
Tilbrook PE18 ....6 C7
Toddington LU5 ....106 A7
Turvey MK43 ....35 B5
Willington MK44 ....52 C8
Woburn Sands MK17 ....81 B5
Station Sq MK45 ....84 E2
Station Way SG6 ......101 E6
Staughton Pl PE19 ....22 C4
Staughton Rd MK44 ....12 D5
Staunton Ho MK17 .....92 F7
Staveley Rd
Dunstable LU6 ....121 B6
Luton LU4 ....115 C1
Stephens Cl LU2 ......117 A3
Stephens Gdns LU2 ...117 A2
Stephenson Cl LU7 ...110 E6
Stephenson Lower Sch
MK42 ....50 E5
Stepping Stones
The LU3 ....115 E5
Steppingley Hospl MK45 ..84 C4
Steppingley Rd MK45 ..84 D3
Steppingley Road Trad Est
MK45 ....84 E3
Steppingstone Pl LU7 ..111 B6
Stevenson Ct PE19 ....22 D6
Stevington Windmill
MK43 ....36 C6
Stewart Cl MK43 ....37 A4
Stewart Clark Ct LU6 ..114 A1
Stewart Ct MK43 ......61 A6
Stewart Rd AL5 ....131 B2
Stewartby Lake Ctry Pk
MK43 ....60 F1
Stewartby Sta MK43 ...61 B1
Stewartby Way MK43 ...61 C1
Stile The LU7 ....103 A5
Stileman Way MK44 ....16 C4
Stirling Cl SG19 ....42 B1
Stirling Rd MK42 ......51 A2
Stivers Way MK45 ......95 F3
Stockbridge Rd SG17 ..78 C3
Stockdale LU5 ....105 F5
Stockgrove Ctry Pk LU7 ..102 F7
Stockgrove Park Ho LU7 102 F8
Stockholm Way LU3 ...115 E8
Stockingstone Rd LU2 ..116 B3
Stocks La SG19 ....44 D5
Stockton End SG19 ....54 D8
Stockwood Craft Mus
& Gdns LU1 ....123 D4
Stockwood Cres LU1 ..123 D6
Stockwood Cl 16 LU1 ..123 D6
Stockwood Pk LU1 .....123 D3
Stoke Albany Mews 3
MK40 ....38 A1
Stoke Rd LU7 ....102 D1
Stokesay Cl MK41 ......39 A4
Stondon Lower Sch SG16 88 E3
Stondon Rd SG17 ......88 C4
Stone Cl MK40 ....49 B6
Stonecroft SG19 ......54 D7
Stonedale Rd MK42 ....50 A4
Stonehill JMI Sch SG6 ..90 E1
Stoneland Ave LU6 .....67 A4
Stoneleigh LU3 ....116 B7
Stoneley SG6 ....90 F1
Stonemason Cl AL5 ...131 A3

Stonesdale LU4 ....115 C4
Stoneways Cl LU4 .....115 C6
Stoneygate Rd LU4 ....115 D3
Stonnells Cl SG6 .....101 F3
Stopsley High Sch LU2 ..116 F4
Stopsley Inf Sch LU2 ..117 A4
Stopsley Jun Sch LU2 ..117 A4
Stopsley Way LU2 .....117 A3
Stormont Rd SG5 .....100 F1
Stotfold Ho SG5 ....90 F6
Stotfold Rd Arlesey SG15 ..90 C7
Hinxworth SG7 ....80 C1
Letchworth SG6 ....90 D1
Letchworth SG6 ......101 C4
Stour Way MK41 ....38 C5
Stow Rd PE18 ....6 F5
Strafford Cl MK45 .....95 F1
Strand The MK45 ......75 C1
Strangers Way LU4 ...115 C4
Stratford Cl LU3 ....105 E6
Stratford Rd MK40 .....38 A2
Stratford Pl LU2 ....22 C3
Stratford Rd Luton LU4 ..116 B1
Sandy SG19 ....54 E5
Stratford Way MK43 ...60 D2
Strathconon Rd MK41 ..39 C4
Strathmore Ave
Hitchin SG5 ....100 F1
Luton LU1 ....123 F5
Strathmore Ct SG5 ...100 F1
Strathmore Inf Sch SG5 ..100 F2
Strathmore Wlk LU1 ...123 F6
Stratton Bsns Pk SG18 ..67 B3
Stratton Ct 7 SG18 ....67 A6
Stratton Gdns LU2 ....116 D4
Stratton Mews LU7 ...111 B7
Stratton Pk SG18 ......67 C4
Stratton Upper Sch
& Com Coll SG18 .....67 C6
Stratton Way
Bedford MK41 ....39 D3
Biggleswade SG18 .....67 B7
Straw Plait SG15 ......89 F4
Strawberry Field LU3 ..115 E7
Strawberry Hill Cotts MK44 ..9 F2
Streatley Rd LU3 ......107 D4
Street Cl MK43 ....25 A3
Streetfield Mid Sch LU1 ..121 F6
Stringfellow Cl MK43 ...58 E2
Stronnell Cl LU2 ......117 B3
Stuart Rd Barton-le-C MK45 97 C4
Kempston MK42 ....49 E4
Stuart St Dunstable LU6 ..114 A1
Luton LU1 ....123 D7
Stubbs Cl LU5 ....114 D5
Studham La Dagnall HP4 ..126 D4
Whipsnade LU6 ....127 A7
Studham Lower Sch LU6 127 B4
Studio Ho MK40 ....50 A8
Studley Rd Luton LU3 ..116 D1
Wootton MK43 ....60 E7
Sturgeon's Rd SG4 ...101 B2
Styles Cl LU2 ....117 C2
Sudbury Rd LU4 ....115 B6
Sudeley Wlk MK41 .....39 B4
Suffield Ho 1 PE19 ....22 F5
Suffolk Cl LU4 ....115 A3
Suffolk Rd LU5 ....121 F6
Sugden Cl LU6 ....121 A8
Sullivan Cl SG17 ....77 D3
Summer St
Leighton Buzzard LU7 ..111 B7
Slip End LU1 ....123 C1
Summer Wlk AL3 ......128 E5
Summerfield Dr MK43 ..60 F6
Summerfield Rd LU1 ...122 F8
Summerleys LU6 ......119 E4
Summers Rd LU2 ......117 C1
Sun La AL5 ....131 A2
Sun St Biggleswade SG18 ..66 F7
Potton SG19 ....56 A7
Sunbeam Rd MK42 ....49 D1
Sunbower Ave LU6 ....113 F3
Suncote Ave LU6 .....113 E3
Suncote Cl LU6 ....113 E3
Sunderland Cl MK44 ...28 F1
Sunderland Hill MK44 ..29 A4
Sunderland Rd SG19 ...54 D8
Sundew Cl Bedford MK42 ..50 F8
St Neots PE19 ....22 B6
Sundon Hills Ctry Pk
LU3 ....107 C6
Sundon La LU5 ....114 C5
Sundon Lower Sch LU3 ..107 B4
Sundon Park Jun Sch
LU3 ....115 C8
Sundon Park Rd LU3 ..115 C7
Sundon Rd Chalton LU4 ..107 A2
Chalton LU4 ....107 B8
Houghton Regis LU5 ..114 D7
Streatley LU3 ....107 F5
Sundown Ave LU6 .....121 D7
Sunningdale LU2 ......116 E2
Sunningdale Wlk MK41 ..38 E5
Sunnyside Special Sch
SG18 ....67 A6
Sunridge Ave LU2 ....116 E2
Sunset Dr LU2 ....116 F3
Surrey St LU1 ....123 E6
Surrey Street Prim Sch
LU1 ....123 F6
Sursham Ct AL3 ......128 E5
Sussex Cl LU4 ....114 F4
Sussex Pl LU2 ....117 D2
Sutherland Pl LU1 ....123 D5
Sutton Ave SG18 ......67 B6
Sutton Cross Roads SG19 ..55 E4
Sutton Gdns LU3 ......115 D6

Sutton Lower CE Sch
SG19 ....56 A3
Sutton Mill Rd SG19 ...55 F6
Sutton Rd Eyeworth SG18 ..68 F8
Potton SG19 ....56 C7
Sutton SG19 ....56 B3
Swaden SG19 ....54 E6
Swaffield Cl MK45 .....73 E1
Swale Path MK41 ......38 C7
Swallow LU4 Flitwick MK45 ..84 D4
Luton LU4 ....115 A4
Swallowfield
Upper Caldecote SG18 ..66 D8
Wyboston MK44 ....31 F6
Swallowfield Lower Sch
MK17 ....81 B5
Swamsholme Garden Ct
SG19 ....54 C7
Swan Cl LU1 ....119 A1
Swan Ct LU6 ....121 B8
Swan La
Guilden Morden SG8 ...69 F4
Sandy SG19 ....54 B7
Swan Mead LU1 ....115 B4
Swanbourne Cl SG18 ...67 B5
Swannells Wood LU6 ..127 C4
Swansholme Gdns SG19 ..54 C6
Swansons LU6 ....119 F3
Swanston Grange LU4 ..115 B2
Swasedale Rd LU3 ....116 A6
Swift Cl Bedford MK41 ..38 B4
Flitwick MK45 ....84 D2
Letchworth SG6 ....101 E8
Sandy SG19 ....42 C2
Swifts Green Cl LU2 ...117 B5
Swifts Green Rd LU2 ...117 B5
Swinburne Ave SG5 ...100 C1
Swindale MK41 ....38 D6
Sworder Cl LU3 ....107 F1
Sybil's Way MK45 ......74 A7
Sycamore Cl
Biggleswade SG18 .....67 A8
Flitwick MK45 ....84 F2
Luton LU3 ....107 C1
Sycamore Rd LU4 .....114 C6
Sycamores The
Baldock SG7 ....91 E1
Kempston MK42 ....49 F3
Silsoe MK45 ....86 B5
St Neots PE19 ....22 F6
Sylam Cl LU3 ....115 E7
Symond Gdns NN10 ....8 A7
Sylvester St LU2 ......103 A5
Symonds Cl MK43 .....36 F1
Syon Path MK45 ......84 D1

T

Tabor Cl MK45 ....95 F2
Taddy Cl SG18 ....66 B8
Tadlow Rd SG19 ....57 C3
Taft Pl SG17 ....76 E2
Talbot Ct LU7 ....111 A8
Talbot Rd Bedford MK40 ..38 E1
Luton LU2 ....116 F2
Talbot Way SG6 ....91 B1
Talisman Ct SG19 ......42 B1
Tall Pines LU7 ....102 F2
Tallents Cres AL5 .....131 D3
Tamar Rd MK41 ....38 D5
Tamar Wlk LU7 ....103 B3
Tameton Cl LU2 ....117 F2
Tamworth Rd MK41 ....39 A5
Tan Yd PE19 ....22 E5
Tancred Rd LU2 ....117 A4
Tandys Cl Pavenham MK43 ..26 C4
Turvey MK43 ....34 C5
Tanfield Gn LU2 ....117 E1
Tanglewood LU4 ......130 F2
Tannery La MK43 ......15 D1
Tanqueray Ave MK45 ...86 C8
Tansur Ct PE19 ....22 F8
Tansy Cl Bedford MK42 ..50 F4
St Neots PE19 ....22 B5
Tarnside Ct LU6 ......121 B6
Taskers Ho LU6 ....119 F4
Taskers Row LU6 ......119 F4
Taunton Cl MK41 ......39 A5
Taunton Rd LU2 ....117 B1
Tavistock Cl MK17 .....81 B6
Tavistock Cres LU1 ...123 E5
Tavistock Ct PE19 .....22 E6
Tavistock Pl MK40 ....38 B1
Tavistock St Bedford MK40 38 B1
Dunstable LU6 ....114 A2
Luton LU1 ....123 E6
Taylor St LU2 ....123 F8
Taylor's Rd SG5 ....80 A1
Taylor's Ride LU7 .....102 F2
Taylors Cl SG17 ....88 B5
Taylors End MK45 ......74 B1
Teal Rd SG18 ....66 F5
Teasel Cl LU5 ....22 C5
Tebbutts Rd PE19 .....22 E5
Tebworth Rd
Tebworth LU7 ....105 A1
Wingfield LU7 ....105 E1
Tedder Ave SG16 ......89 B5
Teesdale LU4 ....115 C5
Telford Way Bedford MK42 51 B5
Luton LU1 ....123 D8
Telmere Ind Est 18 LU1 ..123 E6
Telscombe Way LU2 ...117 C3
Templars Way MK44 ...16 E4
Temple Cl LU2 ....116 E5
Temple Way MK45 .....84 E2

Templefield Lower Sch
MK45 ....84 E3
Templer Way SG17 .....76 F3
Tempsford Rd
Everton SG19 ....42 E5
Sandy SG19 ....42 A3
Sutton SG19 ....43 C3
Tempsford SG19 ......41 F5
Tempsford St MK42 ....49 E4
Tenby Dr LU4 ....115 F3
Tenby Mews LU4 .....115 E3
Tenby Way LU7 ....22 F1
Tennyson Ave
Biggleswade SG18 .....67 A5
Houghton Regis LU5 ..114 D4
Tennyson Ho LU1 .....123 E5
Tennyson Pl PE19 .....22 D6
Tennyson Rd
Bedford MK40 ....50 E8
Flitwick MK45 ....84 D3
Harpenden AL5 ....131 A2
Luton LU1 ....123 E5
Tennyson Road Prim Sch
LU1 ....123 E5
Tenth Ave LU3 ....115 C7
Tenzing Gr LU1 ....123 C6
Terrace The MK17 .....81 E5
Test Cl MK41 ....38 D7
Tetworth Hill SG19 ....44 A8
Teversham Way PE19 ..22 C6
Thames Cl MK45 ......84 D2
Thames Ct LU3 ....116 B3
Thames Ind Est LU6 ..121 B8
Thatch Cl LU4 ....114 F4
Thaxted Cl LU2 ....117 F2
Thelby Cl LU3 ....115 F6
Theobald Bsns Ctr SG4 ..101 A3
Therfield Wlk LU5 ....114 E6
Thetford Cl MK42 .....49 F4
Thetford Gdns LU2 ...116 E6
Theydon Ave MK17 ....81 B4
Thickthorn La MK45 ...62 A3
Thinnings The MK45 ...84 E3
Third Ave LU3 ....115 D7
Thirlestone Rd LU4 ...115 D1
Thirlmere Cl SG18 .....67 B4
Thirlmere Gdns MK45 ..84 E2
Thirlmere Rd MK42 ....49 E3
Thistle Rd LU1 ....123 F7
Thistley La MK41 ......36 E1
Thomas Johnson
Lower Sch MK43 ......72 B3
Thomas St LU2 ....103 A5
Thomas Whitehead Sch
LU5 ....114 B5
Thompsons Cl AL5 ...131 A1
Thompsons Mdw SG8 ..69 F4
Thomson Ave MK42 ....51 A2
Thor Dr MK41 ....39 D3
Thorn Rd LU5 ....113 E6
Thorn View Rd LU5 ...114 B5
Thornage Cl LU2 ......116 D7
Thornbury Dunstable LU5 114 F2
Harpenden AL5 ....131 D1
Thornbury Ct LU5 .....114 C7
Thorncote Rd SG18 ....53 E4
Thornhill Cl LU5 ......114 D7
Thornhill Lower Sch
LU5 ....114 D7
Thornhill Rd LU4 ......115 F2
Thornton St MK42 ....49 F5
Thorntondale 5 LU4 ..115 C5
Thorpe Cl MK40 ....37 B1
Thorpe Way MK43 .....60 F8
Thrales Cl LU3 ....115 E7
Thrapston Rd PE18 .....6 F5
Threave Cl MK41 ......38 F5
Three Closes SG5 .....99 C4
Thresher Cl LU4 ......114 F4
Threshers Cl LU7 .....111 D7
Thricknells Cl LU3 ....115 E7
Thrift Rd LU7 ....103 A5
Thrift St NN29 ....7 A7
Thrift View MK41 ......59 C2
Thrupp End MK43 .....72 B3
Thurleigh Lower Sch
MK44 ....18 C2
Thurleigh Rd
Bolnhurst MK44 ....19 C2
Milton Ernest MK44 ...27 D5
Ravensden MK44 ......28 E2
Thurlestone Rd MK40 ..38 F1
Thurlow Cl LU4 ....114 F4
Thurlow St 12 MK40 ....50 B8
Thurne Way MK41 .....38 D7
Tibbett Cl LU6 ....121 D7
Tiberius Rd LU3 ......115 F6
Tidbury Cl MK41 ....81 A4
Tiddenfoot L Ctr LU7 ..110 E5
Tilbrook Rd PE18 ....6 D6
Tilgate LU2 ....117 D3
Tiller Ct LU7 ....111 D7
Tilsworth Rd LU7 .....112 D5
Timber La MK17 ....92 F7
Timbers Ct AL5 ....130 F2
Times Cl SG5 ....100 D4
Timworth Cl LU2 ......117 D1
Tindall Ave LU7 ....103 B1
Tingey's Cnr SG18 ....54 E1
Tingrith Rd MK17 ......94 D6
Tinker's Cnr MK43 ....48 E1
Tinkers Hill MK42 ......51 A3
Tinsley Cl Clapham MK41 ..37 C7
Luton LU1 ....123 B5
Tintagel Cl LU3 ....116 B4
Tintagel Ct PE19 ......22 F2
Tintagel Wlk MK41 .....39 B5
Tintern Abbey MK41 ...51 A8

Tintern Cl AL5 ....130 C4
Tipcat Cl MK42 ....50 B4
Tippett Ct SG17 ....77 D3
Titan Ct LU4 ....115 F1
Titchfield Dr MK42 .....50 C3
Tithe Barn MK43 ....26 C8
Tithe Barn Rd MK43 ....60 F7
Tithe Farm Cl SG18 ....78 F7
Tithe Farm Lower Sch
LU5 ....114 B6
Tithe Farm Rd LU5 ....114 B6
Tithe Rd MK43 ....48 E3
Tithe The MK43 ....26 C8
Tiverton Rd MK40 .....38 E2
Toddington Manor LU5 ..105 E8
Toddington Rd
Harlington LU5 ....95 C2
Luton LU4 ....115 C6
Tebworth MK17 ....105 C3
Toddington St George
Lower Sch LU5 ....105 F6
Toland Cl LU4 ....115 C1
Tollfield PE18 ....6 F4
Tollgate Cl MK43 ......36 E1
Tomlinson Ave LU4 ...114 F4
Tompions End SG18 ...65 E8
Top End MK41 ....39 F6
Top Row MK44 ....17 C1
Topham Ct PE19 ......22 F7
Tornay Ct LU7 ....118 D6
Torquay Dr LU4 ......115 D4
Torre Abbey MK41 .....51 B8
Torridge Rise MK41 ....38 C5
Torrington Cl SG19 ....55 F8
Totnes Cl MK40 ....38 E1
Totternhoe Knolls
Nature Reserve LU6 ..120 B8
Totternhoe Lower Sch
LU6 ....120 B7
Totternhoe Rd
Dunstable LU6 ....120 E7
Eaton Bray LU6 ....119 D7
Tower Cl LU2 ....117 A1
Tower Rd LU2 ....124 A8
Tower Way LU2 ....124 A8
Town Cl MK45 ....62 E4
Town Farm Cl SG8 .....69 F4
Town Farm Ct SG16 ....78 D1
Town Lot La MK43 .....26 B8
Town Meadow La SG17 ..77 C3
Town Shott MK45 ......75 E1
Town The PE19 ....13 E6
Townfield Rd MK45 ....84 F1
Towns End Rd MK44 ...16 C4
Townsend Cl
Cranfield MK43 ....71 A8
Harpenden AL5 ....130 F1
Townsend Farm Rd LU5 114 B3
Townsend Ind Est LU5 ..114 B4
Townsend La AL5 .....130 F1
Townsend Rd AL5 ....131 A2
Townsend Terr LU5 ...114 A4
Townside LU6 ....119 F3
Townsley Cl LU1 ......123 E6
Townwell La NN29 ......7 B8
Tracey Ct 15 LU1 .....123 E6
Trafalgar Dr MK45 .....84 E4
Trafalgar Rd PE19 .....22 C5
Trailly Cl MK44 ....4 A3
Tree Cathedral LU6 ...120 F1
Trefoil Cl LU4 ....114 F4
Trenchard Ave SG17 ...76 D4
Trenchard La SG17 ....76 E4
Trent Ave MK45 ....84 D2
Trent Rd Bedford MK41 ..38 D5
Luton LU3 ....116 B4
Trescott Cl LU2 ......117 E2
Trevor Dr MK43 ....36 E2
Trevor St MK40 ....38 A1
Trident Dr LU5 ....114 E6
Triggs Way LU2 ......117 E3
Trimley Cl LU4 ....115 B5
Tring Rd Dunstable LU6 ..120 C4
Dunstable LU6 ....120 D7
Trinity Rd Biggleswade SG18 66 F6
Felmersham MK43 .....26 C8
Roxton MK44 ....31 E2
Trinity Rd Bedford MK40 ..49 F7
Luton LU3 ....116 A4
Stotfold SG5 ....90 A4
Tristram Rd SG4 ......101 B2
Triumph Way MK42 ....49 E2
Troon Cl MK41 ....38 E5
Troon Gdns LU2 ......116 F7
Trowbridge Gdns LU2 ..116 E3
Trowley Hill Rd AL3 ...129 B1
Trowley Hts AL3 .....129 B2
Truemans Rd SG5 ....100 D2
Truman Pl SG17 ....76 E2
Truncals LU1 ....123 D5
Trunk Furlong Est MK17 ..81 D6
Truro Gdns Flitwick MK45 ..84 E4
Luton LU3 ....116 C5
Trust Cotts HP4 ......126 A1
Tudor Cl Barton-le-C MK45 ..97 C4
Bedford MK40 ....38 A1
Bromham MK43 ....36 F3
Tudor Ct Dunstable LU6 ..114 A2
Kimbolton PE18 ....6 F5
Leighton Buzzard LU7 ..110 F7
Tudor Dr LU4 ....114 E4
Tudor Rd LU3 ....116 B2
Tudors The MK44 .....20 B2
Tuffnells Way AL5 ....130 D2
Tulip Cl LU5 ....67 C5
Tulip Dr NN10 ....8 B7
Tunstall Wlk MK41 .....39 C3
Turnberry Wlk MK41 ...38 E5

Turner Cl LU5 . . . . .114 D5
Turner Rd PE19 . . . . .22 C6
Turner Way MK41 . . . . . .38 A2
Turners Cl AL5 . . . . .131 C4
Turners Rd N LU2 . . . . . .117 A2
Turners Rd S LU2 . . . . . .117 A2
Turnpike Cl LU6 . . . . . . .121 C6
Turnpike Dr LU3 . . . . . . .108 C1
Turnpike La SG5 . . . . . . .100 E3
Turnpike Rd MK43 . . . . . .82 B3
Turnpike Way MK41 . . . . .39 B3
Turvey Lower Sch MK43 . .34 E6
Turvey Mill MK43 . . . . . . .34 D5
Turvey Rd Astwood MK16 . .46 F5
  Carlton MK43 . . . . .24 E2
Tweedsmuir Rd MK41 . . . .38 F4
Twigden Ct LU3 . . . . .115 E5
Twinwood Rd MK41 . . . . .37 C7
Twyford Dr LU2 . . . . .117 D1
Tyburn La Pulloxhill MK45 . .96 D8
  Westoning MK45 . . . . . . .95 E6
Tylecote Rd MK43 . . . . . .72 C7
Tylers AL5 . . . . .131 D1
Tylers Mead LU2 . . . . . . .116 E5
Tyne Cl MK45 . . . . .84 D2
Tyne Cres MK41 . . . . . . .38 C6
Tyne Rd SG19 . . . . .42 C2
Tythe Barn Cl MK45 . . . . .95 E6
  Sharnbrook MK44 . . . . . .16 E3
Tythe Cl Flitwick MK45 . . .85 A1
Tythe Mews LU6 . . . . . . .119 E3
Tythe Rd LU4 . . . . .115 C6

U

Ullswater Cl
  Biggleswade SG18 . . . . . .67 B4
  Flitwick MK45 . . . . .84 D2
  Kempston MK42 . . . . . . .49 E3
Ullswater Ct MK42 . . . . . .49 E3
Ullswater Dr LU7 . . . . . .110 C7
Ullswater Rd LU6 . . . . . .121 D8
Ulverston Rd LU2 . . . . . .121 A6
Underwood Cl LU3 . . . . .107 F1
Union Chapel Ho 🏠 LU1 .123 E6
Union St MK40 . . . . .38 A1
  Dunstable LU6 . . . . .114 A1
  Luton LU1 . . . . .123 E6
Unwin Cl SG6 . . . . .101 E4
Uplands Bedford MK41 . . .38 F4
  Luton LU3 . . . . .115 D8
Uplands Ct LU1 . . . . .123 E4
Upper Coombe LU7 . . . . .110 E8
Upper George St LU1 . . .123 D7
Upper Shelton Rd MK43 . .60 C3
Upperstone Cl SG5 . . . . .90 F6
Upton Cl LU2 . . . . .116 D6
Upton Ct MK41 . . . . .38 C5
Upton End Rd SG5 . . . . . .87 F2
Upwell Rd LU2 . . . . .117 B2
Urban Way SG18 . . . . .67 A7
Ursula Taylor Lower Sch
  MK41 . . . . .37 E5
Ursula Taylor Wlk MK41 . .37 E5

V

Vadis Cl LU3 . . . . .115 E7
Vale Cl AL5 . . . . .130 D4
Vale Ct MK43 . . . . .59 D2
Valence End LU6 . . . . . . .121 D6
Valentine Gdns PE18 . . . . .6 F5
Valerian Cl PE19 . . . . .22 C6
Valiant Cl MK45 . . . . .95 F1
Valley Cl Studham LU6 . . .127 B4
  Whipsnade HP4 . . . . . . .126 E1
Valley La AL3 . . . . .128 E1
Valley Rd Letchworth SG6 .101 D7
  Studham LU6 . . . . .127 B3
Valley Rise AL4 . . . . .131 F2
Vanbrugh Dr LU5 . . . . . .114 D5
Vandyke Cl MK17 . . . . . . .81 B6
Vandyke Rd LU7 . . . . . . .103 C2
Vandyke Upper Sch
  & Com Coll LU7 . . . . . .103 D6
Vanguard Cl MK42 . . . . . .49 D6
Varna Cl LU3 . . . . .116 A3
Vaughan Rd
  Harpenden AL5 . . . . . . .131 B1
  Stotfold SG5 . . . . .90 E7
Vauxhall Rd LU1, LU2 . . .124 B5
Vauxhall Way LU2 . . . . . .117 C1
Venetia Cl LU2 . . . . .117 A4
Ventnor Gdns LU3 . . . . . .116 A7
Verey Rd LU5 . . . . .114 C2
Verne Dr MK45 . . . . .84 F8
Vernon Pl LU2 . . . . .114 B1
Vernon Rd LU1 . . . . .123 C8
Verulam Gdns LU3 . . . . .115 F6
Vespers Cl LU4 . . . . .115 A2
Vestry Cl LU1 . . . . .123 D7
Viaduct Cotts LU1 . . . . . .130 F8
Vicarage Cl Arlesey SG15 . .90 A8
  Langford SG18 . . . . .78 E6
  Ravensden MK44 . . . . . . .29 B1
  Shillington SG5 . . . . .98 F8
Vicarage Gdns
  Flamstead AL3 . . . . .129 B1
  Leighton Buzzard LU7 . . .110 E6
Vicarage Gn MK44 . . . . . .18 C1
Vicarage Hill MK45 . . . . . .84 E1
Vicarage La MK45 . . . . . . .62 E3
Vicarage Rd
  Houghton Regis LU5 . . . .114 D6
  Leighton Buzzard LU7 . . .110 E6
  Silsoe MK45 . . . . .86 C4

Vicarage St Luton LU1 . . .123 F7
  Woburn Sands MK17 . . . .81 C4
Vicarage Wlk PE19 . . . . . .13 F6
Vicars Cl MK40 . . . . .49 C8
Vicars Wlk MK41 . . . . .39 B2
Viceroy Cl PE19 . . . . .22 A3
Viceroy Ct LU6 . . . . .121 C8
Victoria Cl Langford SG18 . .78 E6
  Wrestlingworth SG19 . . . .57 B4
Victoria Cotts LU5 . . . . . .114 A6
Victoria Ct 🄯 SG18 . . . . . .67 A6
Victoria Dr
  Houghton Conquest MK45 . .74 A8
  Stotfold SG5 . . . . .91 A5
Victoria Pl SG18 . . . . .67 A6
Victoria Rd Bedford MK42 . .50 B6
  🄻 Harpenden AL5 . . . . . .131 B1
  Leighton Buzzard LU7 . . .110 E6
  Shefford SG17 . . . . .77 D2
Victoria St Dunstable LU6 .114 A1
  Luton LU1 . . . . .123 E6
Victoria Terr LU7 . . . . . . .111 D7
Viking Gr MK41 . . . . .49 D6
Viking Ind Est MK41 . . . . .39 D4
Villa Ct 🄳 LU2 . . . . .123 D8
Villa Park (Mobile Home
  Pk) MK43 . . . . .70 F7
Villa Rd LU2 . . . . .123 D8
Village Rd MK43 . . . . .36 F3
Villiers Cl LU4 . . . . .115 B8
Vimy Rd LU7 . . . . .110 F7
Vincent Rd LU4 . . . . .115 D5
Vinegar Hill SG19 . . . . . . .54 A3
Vines The SG5 . . . . .90 E6
Vineyard Way MK41 . . . . .49 E5
Violet Cl Bedford MK42 . . .50 F4
Violets Cl SG18 . . . . .67 C4
Violets Cl MK16 . . . . .58 B6
Virginia Cl LU2 . . . . .116 F3
Viscount Cl LU3 . . . . .116 A5
Viscount Ct 🄻🄻 Luton LU2 .116 D1
  St Neots PE19 . . . . .22 B4
Vulcan St MK42 . . . . .50 C6
Vulcan Way PE19 . . . . . . .22 B1
Vyne Cl MK42 . . . . .49 D5

W

Waddesdon Cl LU2 . . . . . .117 D2
Wadhurst Ave LU3 . . . . . .116 C4
Wagstaffe Cl MK41 . . . . . .38 E6
Walcot Ave LU2 . . . . .117 A5
Walcourt Rd MK42 . . . . . .50 A5
Waldeck Rd LU3 . . . . . . .123 C8
Waldegrave Pk AL5 . . . . .131 D1
Waleys Cl LU4 . . . . .115 E8
Walgrave Rd LU5 . . . . . . .114 F2
Walk House Rd MK43 . . . .59 B1
Walkley Rd LU5 . . . . .114 B4
Wallace Dr LU6 . . . . .119 E6
Wallace Mews LU6 . . . . . .119 E6
Wallace Way SG4 . . . . . . .101 A2
Waller Ave LU4 . . . . .115 F3
Waller Street Mall 🄳
  LU1 . . . . .123 E7
Wallnut Cl MK43 . . . . .26 B3
Walmsley House Sch
  MK40 . . . . .38 D2
Walnut Acre LU5 . . . . . . .105 F6
Walnut Cl
  Biggleswade SG18 . . . . . .66 F8
  Blunham MK44 . . . . .41 D3
  Bromham MK43 . . . . .36 D1
  Luton LU2 . . . . .117 B4
  Stotfold SG5 . . . . .90 F6
Walnut Gr MK43 . . . . .72 B3
Walnut Tree Rd SG5 . . . . .99 D3
Walnut Way SG5 . . . . . . .100 E4
Walnut Wlk MK42 . . . . . . .49 F3
Walnuts The LU7 . . . . . . .103 B2
Walsingham Cl LU2 . . . . .116 D7
Waltham Cl MK41 . . . . . . .38 F5
Waltham Ct LU2 . . . . . . .117 C3
Walton Ct SG17 . . . . .77 E3
Wandon Cl LU2 . . . . .117 C4
Wansbeck Rd MK41 . . . . .38 C5
Wantage Rd MK29 . . . . . . .7 B8
Warden Abbey MK41 . . . .39 B1
Warden Hill SG19 . . . . . . .43 C3
Warden Hill Cl LU2 . . . . .116 C8
Warden Hill Gdns LU2 . . .116 C8
Warden Hill Inf Sch LU3 .116 C7
Warden Hill Jun Sch
  LU3 . . . . .116 C7
Warden Hill Rd LU2 . . . . .116 C8
Warden Rd SG18 . . . . . . .65 D7
Wardhedges Rd MK45 . . . .85 E4
Wardown Cres LU2 . . . . .116 D2
Wardown Ct LU3 . . . . . . .116 D2
Ware Rd PE19 . . . . .22 E6
Waresley Rd SG19 . . . . . .44 D7
Warkworth Rd SG19 . . . . .54 C8
Warminster Cl LU2 . . . . .117 F1
Warren Cl
  Biggleswade SG18 . . . . . .67 A7
  Irchester NN29 . . . . .7 C7
  Letchworth SG6 . . . . . . .101 D7
  Toddington LU5 . . . . . . .105 F7
Warren Dr The LU1 . . . . .124 C1
Warren Rd Ampthill MK45 . .84 F7
  Luton LU1 . . . . .122 F1
Warren The MK41 . . . . . . .37 E5
Warton Gn LU2 . . . . .117 E2
Warwick Ave MK40 . . . . . .38 A1
Warwick Cl MK45 . . . . . . .84 D1
Warwick Ct Luton LU4 . . .123 B8
  St Neots PE19 . . . . .22 C3

Warwick Ho MK40 . . . . . .38 A2
Warwick Rd E LU4 . . . . . .123 B8
Warwick Rd W LU4 . . . . .123 B8
Washbank Rd PE19 . . . . . .22 E4
Washbrook Cl MK45 . . . . .97 C1
Washburn Cl MK41 . . . . . .38 D6
Washingleys MK43 . . . . . .59 C2
Washington Ave SG17 . . . .76 F2
Water End Cople MK44 . . . .52 B4
  Great Gaddesden HP1 . . .132 F2
  Workhouse End MK41 . . .40 A4
  Wrestlingworth SG19 . . . .57 B3
Water End La LU4 . . . . . .106 C2
Water End Rd MK45 . . . . .85 F7
Water La Chelveston NN9 . . .3 B1
  Flitwick MK45 . . . . .85 A2
  Hitchin SG5 . . . . .100 F1
  Kempston MK42 . . . . . . .49 C3
  Leighton Buzzard LU7 . . .110 F7
Waterdell LU7 . . . . .111 C7
Waterloo Cl MK45 . . . . . . .84 E4
Waterloo Dr PE19 . . . . . . .22 F3
Waterloo Rd Bedford MK40 .50 D8
  Leighton Buzzard LU7 . . .110 E6
Watermead Rd LU2 . . . . .115 F6
Waters End SG5 . . . . .90 E6
Waterside LU6 . . . . .119 F4
Waterslade La LU3 . . . . . .116 B6
Watery La AL3 . . . . .129 E3
Watling Ct Dunstable LU6 .114 A2
  Houghton Regis LU5 . . . .114 B4
Watling Lower Sch LU6 .121 C7
Watling Pl LU5 . . . . .114 B4
Watling St LU6 . . . . .113 C4
Watson Rd MK45 . . . . . . .52 C6
Wauld Prim Sch LU3 . . . .115 E1
Waulds Bank Dr LU3 . . . .115 E7
Wavel Cl MK43 . . . . .73 C8
Wavell Cl MK43 . . . . .61 D1
Wavendon House Dr
  MK17 . . . . .81 B8
Wavendon Rd MK17 . . . . .70 C2
Waveney Ave MK41 . . . . .38 D5
Waveney Rd AL5 . . . . . . .131 C3
Waverly Ave SG19 . . . . . . .42 B1
Waverly Pre-Prep Sch
  MK45 . . . . .84 E3
Wayside LU6 . . . . .121 D5
Wear The MK41 . . . . .38 C7
Weatherby LU6 . . . . .120 E8
Weatherby Rd LU4 . . . . . .115 D2
Weathercock Cl MK17 . . . .81 B5
Weathercock La MK17 . . . .81 C4
Weatherfield Specl Sch
  LU6 . . . . .113 E1
Weaver Cl MK41 . . . . .38 D6
Weavers Gn SG19 . . . . . . .42 C2
Weavers La MK43 . . . . . . .26 C4
Webber Cl SG17 . . . . .77 D3
Webbs Cl MK43 . . . . .36 F7
Wedgewood Rd LU4 . . . . .114 F4
Wedgwood Rd MK41 . . . . .38 B3
Weedon Ct LU2 . . . . .117 D2
Welbeck Gdns MK41 . . . . .38 F5
Welbeck Rd 🄳 LU2 . . . . . .123 E8
Welbourne Gdns MK42 . . .49 E5
Welbury Ave LU2 . . . . . . .116 C7
Weldon Cl LU2 . . . . .117 E1
Well Head Rd LU6 . . . . . .120 C6
Well La LU1 . . . . .123 E6
Welland Ct Bedford MK41 . .38 D5
  St Neots PE19 . . . . .22 C4
Wellfield Ave LU3 . . . . . . .115 C8
Wellgate Rd LU4 . . . . . . .115 D2
Wellhouse Cl LU1 . . . . . . .123 A7
Wellingham Ave SG5 . . . .100 D1
Wellington Ct 🄳 LU1 . . . .123 D6
Wellington Dr SG17 . . . . .76 F3
Wellington Ho LU7 . . . . .103 A4
Wellington Rd MK42 . . . . .50 F2
Wellington St
  Bedford MK40 . . . . .38 B1
  Luton LU1 . . . . .123 D7
Wellington Terr LU5 . . . . .121 C8
Wellpond Cl MK44 . . . . . . .16 D3
Wells Cl Harpenden AL5 . .130 E4
  Kempston MK42 . . . . . . .49 E6
Wells Rd MK44 . . . . .10 F2
Wellsfield MK44 . . . . .41 E3
Weltmore Rd LU3 . . . . . .115 F6
Wendover Cl AL5 . . . . . . .131 D1
Wendover Dr MK41 . . . . . .39 A1
Wendover Way LU2 . . . . .116 C8
Wenlock Jun Sch LU2 . . .124 B8
Wenlock Rd MK42 . . . . . .49 C3
Wenlock St LU2 . . . . .123 E8
Wensley Dale LU2 . . . . . .116 E1
Wentworth Ave LU4 . . . . .115 C6
Wentworth Cl LU5 . . . . . .105 F7
Wentworth Ct LU5 . . . . . .105 F7
Wentworth Ct MK45 . . . . .95 F1
Wentworth Dr
  Bedford MK41 . . . . .38 F5
  Leighton Buzzard LU7 . . .111 A8
Wentworth Gdns LU5 . . . .106 A6
Werth Dr MK17 . . . . .81 B2
Wesley Cl SG15 . . . . .90 A4
Wesley Rd Markyate AL3 . .128 E5
  Sandy SG19 . . . . .42 C1
West Arc 🄴 MK40 . . . . . . .50 B8
West Cl SG4 . . . . .101 B1
West Ct MK41 . . . . .39 A2
West Dene HP2 . . . . .132 F8
West Dr SG15 . . . . .90 B4
West End Elstow MK42 . . . .50 B3
  Stevington MK43 . . . . . . .36 A8

West End La SG19 . . . . . . .56 A8
West End Rd
  Kempston MK43 . . . . .48 D5
  Silsoe MK45 . . . . .86 B3
West Gr MK40 . . . . .49 F8
West Hill
  Aspley Guise MK17 . . . . . .81 D4
  Dunstable LU6 . . . . .121 C5
West Hill Rd LU1 . . . . . . .123 E5
West Hill Rd N
West La SG5 . . . . .99 D5
West Lodge Cotts LU2 . . .117 D5
West Par LU1 . . . . .123 D6
West Rd Gamlingay SG19 . .44 C4
  Sandy SG19 . . . . .54 B8
  Wharley End MK43 . . . . . .58 D2
  Woburn Sands MK17 . . . .81 B5
West St Dunstable LU6 . . .121 A4
  Leighton Buzzard LU7 . . .110 F7
  Lilley LU2 . . . . .109 D1
  St Neots PE19 . . . . .22 E5
West View Beeston SG19 . .54 B5
  Langford SG18 . . . . .78 F6
  Letchworth SG6 . . . . . . .101 E5
  Letchworth SG6 . . . . . . .101 E5
West Way Harpenden AL5 .131 C2
  Moggerhanger MK44 . . . .53 C7
West Wlk SG18 . . . . .67 B7
Westbourne Rd
  Bedford MK40 . . . . .49 F7
  Luton LU6 . . . . .116 B1
Westbury Cl LU5 . . . . . . .114 B3
Westbury Ct Ampthill MK45 .84 F8
  Bedford MK41 . . . . .38 C5
Westbury Gdns LU2 . . . . .116 E3
Westbury JMI Sch SG6 . .101 E5
Westbury Pl LU5 . . . . . . .101 E5
Westdale Wlk MK42 . . . . .49 F4
Westdown Gdns LU6 . . . .120 F7
Westerdale LU4 . . . . .115 B5
Western Ave SG16 . . . . . . .89 B3
Western Cl SG6 . . . . .90 E1
Western Rd LU1 . . . . .123 D6
Western St MK40 . . . . . . .50 B8
Western Way
  Dunstable LU5 . . . . .114 E1
  Letchworth SG6 . . . . .90 E1
  Sandy SG19 . . . . .54 B8
Westfield Ave AL5 . . . . . .131 A3
Westfield Gdns SG19 . . . . .54 B8
Westfield Mid Sch MK40 . .49 F8
Westfield Pl AL5 . . . . .131 B4
Westfield Rd Bedford MK40 .49 F8
  Dunstable LU6 . . . . .113 F1
  Harpenden AL5 . . . . . . .131 B4
  Henlow SG16 . . . . .78 C1
  Oakley MK43 . . . . .36 E8
  Wyboston MK44 . . . . .31 F8
Westgate Ct LU5 . . . . . . .121 A8
Westholme SG6 . . . . .101 F8
Westlecote Gdns LU2 . . .115 E5
Westmill La Hitchin SG5 . .100 C2
  Ickleford SG5 . . . . .100 C3
Westmill Lawns SG5 . . . .100 D1
Westmill Rd SG5 . . . . . . .100 C1
Westminster Gdns
  Houghton Regis LU5 . . . .114 D6
  Kempston MK42 . . . . . . .49 E5
Westmorland Ave LU3 . . .115 F5
Weston Ave LU7 . . . . .111 C6
Weston Ct PE19 . . . . .22 C4
Westoning Lower Sch
  MK45 . . . . .95 E6
Westoning Rd
  Greenfield MK45 . . . . . . .85 B1
  Harlington LU5 . . . . .95 E3
Westoria Ct MK45 . . . . . . .95 E5
Westrope Way MK41 . . . . .38 D7
Westside
  Leighton Buzzard LU7 . . .110 F7
  Leighton Buzzard LU7 . . .111 A7
Westway LU2 . . . . .117 C4
Westwood Cl MK42 . . . . . .51 A8
Wetherne Link LU4 . . . . .115 C5
Wexham Cl LU3 . . . . .115 E8
Weybourne Cl AL5 . . . . . .131 D2
Weybourne Dr LU2 . . . . .116 C7
Wharfdale 🄳 LU4 . . . . . . .115 C5
Wharfe The MK41 . . . . . . .38 C6
Wheat Hill SG6 . . . . .101 F8
Wheatfield Cl LU7 . . . . . .111 D7
Wheatfield Ct LU4 . . . . . .114 E4
Wheatfield Rd LU4 . . . . . .114 E4
Wheathouse Cl MK41 . . . .38 F4
Wheatlands Cl MK45 . . . . .85 B4
Wheatsheaf Rd PE19 . . . . .22 C3
Wheel Wright Cl SG5 . . . .87 F1
Whinnett's Way MK45 . . . .85 E1
Whipperley Ct LU1 . . . . . .123 C5
Whipperley Inf Sch LU1 .123 C5
Whipperley Ring LU1 . . . .123 A6
Whipperley Way LU1 . . . .123 C5
Whipsnade Rd LU6 . . . . . .120 F7
Whipsnade Wildlife
  Animal Park LU6 . . . . . .126 E7
Whistler Rd PE19 . . . . . . .22 C5
Whiston Cres SG19 . . . . . .78 B3
Whitbread Ave MK42 . . . . .50 A6
Whitby Rd LU3 . . . . .116 C1
Whitby Way MK42 . . . . . . .50 C3
White Beam Cl MK42 . . . . .49 F2
White Crofts SG6 . . . . . . .90 F6
White Hill Rd MK45 . . . . . .97 C3
White Ho LU7 . . . . .111 A7
White Horse Cl LU7 . . . . .104 E2
White Horse Ct LU7 . . . . .111 A7
White Lodge MK42 . . . . . .49 C5
Whitechurch Cl LU2 . . . . .117 D2

Tur–Win 149

Whitecroft Rd LU2 . . . . . .124 A8
Whitefield Ave LU3 . . . . . .115 C7
Whitefield Inf Sch LU3 . .115 E8
Whitefield Jun Sch LU3 . .115 E8
Whitefriars Jun & Inf Schs
  NN10 . . . . .7 F8
Whitehall MK43 . . . . .72 B2
Whitehall Wlk PE19 . . . . . .22 F4
Whitehaven LU3 . . . . .107 F1
Whitehicks SG6 . . . . .91 A1
Whitehill Ave LU1 . . . . . .123 D5
Whitehorse St SG7 . . . . . .91 A1
Whitehorse Vale LU3 . . . .107 F1
Whitehouse Cl LU5 . . . . . .114 B4
Whitehurst Ave SG5 . . . . .100 F1
Whitethorn Way LU1 . . . .123 A6
Whitewaybottom La SG4 .125 F5
Whitings MK40 . . . . .49 B6
Whitings Cl AL5 . . . . .131 D4
Whitley Gn LU2 . . . . .117 D2
Whitley Rd MK42 . . . . .51 A3
Whittingham Cl LU2 . . . . .117 F1
Whittingstall Ave MK42 . . .50 A4
Whittle Cl SG16 . . . . .89 B4
Whitwell Cl LU3 . . . . .116 B8
Whitworth Ct MK42 . . . . . .49 E4
Whitworth Jones Ave
  SG16 . . . . .89 C5
Whitworth Way MK45 . . . .62 F3
Wick Hill LU6 . . . . .127 F8
Wickets The LU2 . . . . . . .116 E1
Wickmere Cl LU2 . . . . . . .116 C7
Wickstead Ave LU4 . . . . . .115 E4
Widecombe Cl MK40 . . . . .38 E2
Wigmore La LU2 . . . . .117 D2
Wigmore Park Ctr LU2 . . .117 E1
Wigmore Pl LU2 . . . . .117 E1
Wigmore Prim Sch LU2 . .117 E2
Wigram Cl LU4 . . . . .50 A4
Wilbury Cl SG6 . . . . .101 C7
Wilbury Dr LU5 . . . . .114 E3
Wilbury Hills Rd SG6 . . . .101 C7
Wilbury Jun Sch SG6 . . . .101 D6
Wilbury Rd SG6 . . . . .101 E8
Wilbury Way SG4 . . . . . . .101 A3
Wild Cherry Dr LU1 . . . . .123 D5
Wildber Cl PE19 . . . . .22 F4
Wilden CE Lower Sch
  MK44 . . . . .29 F3
Wilden Rd
  Colmworth MK44 . . . . . . .30 A6
  Renhold MK41 . . . . .39 C7
Wildflower Way MK42 . . . .50 F4
Wilhamstead Lower Sch
  MK45 . . . . .62 F4
Wilkinson Cl PE19 . . . . . . .22 B3
Willenhall Cl LU3 . . . . . . .116 A7
William Austin Inf Sch
  LU3 . . . . .116 C4
William Austin Jun Sch
  LU3 . . . . .116 C4
William Dr PE19 . . . . .22 F1
William St Luton LU2 . . . .116 E1
  Markyate AL3 . . . . .128 E5
William Sutton Ct
  Bedford MK40 . . . . .50 A8
  Luton LU2 . . . . .117 B5
Williams Way MK45 . . . . .84 D4
Williamson Cl MK42 . . . . .49 C2
Williamson Rd MK42 . . . . .49 D2
Williamson St 🄻 LU1 . . . .123 E7
Willian Rd SG4 . . . . .101 C1
Willington Lower Sch
  MK44 . . . . .40 C1
Willington Rd MK44 . . . . .52 A6
Williton Rd LU2 . . . . .117 C2
Willmers Cl MK41 . . . . . . .38 E4
Willoughby Cl MK44 . . . . .40 F5
Willoughby Rd LU3 . . . . .131 B4
Willow Bank Wlk LU7 . . . .111 C8
Willow Cl PE19 . . . . .22 F3
Willow Ct LU3 . . . . .115 E5
Willow Rd Bedford MK42 . .50 D5
  Potton SG19 . . . . .56 A7
  Shefford SG17 . . . . .77 D2
Willow Rise SG19 . . . . . . .54 D6
Willow Tree Way SG5 . . . .100 F2
Willow Views 🄻 PE19 . . . .22 E5
Willow Way Ampthill MK45 .84 F7
  Flitwick MK45 . . . . .84 F1
  Harpenden AL5 . . . . . . .131 C4
  Houghton Regis LU5 . . . .114 D6
  Luton LU3 . . . . .115 E5
  Toddington LU5 . . . . . . .105 F5
Willowfield Lower Sch
  LU1 . . . . .122 F1
Willowgate Trad Est
  LU3 . . . . .115 B8
Willows The Flitwick MK45 .84 E3
  Leighton Buzzard LU7 . . .111 B6
  Wootton MK43 . . . . .61 A8
Willsheres Rd SG18 . . . . . .67 A7
Wilman Ct SG18 . . . . .78 E5
Wilsden Ave LU1 . . . . . . .123 C6
Wilshere Cres SG4 . . . . . .101 D1
Wilstead Hill MK45 . . . . . .74 F7
Wilstead Ind Est MK45 . . .62 B6
Wilstead Lower Sch
  Elstow MK42 . . . . .62 C8
  Wilstead MK45 . . . . .63 C5
Wilton Rd SG5 . . . . .100 E1
Wimborne Rd LU1 . . . . . .123 C8
Wimple Rd LU4 . . . . .115 A2
Winch St LU2 . . . . .116 F1

Winchester Gdns LU3 ...107 E1
Winchester Rd
Bedford MK42 ....50 F4
Sandy SG19 ....54 C8
Windermere Cl
Dunstable LU6 ....121 B7
Flitwick MK45 ....84 E2
Windermere Cres LU3 ...115 F5
Windermere Dr SG18 ...67 A4
Windermere Gdns LU7 ..110 C7
Windermere The MK42 ...49 D3
Windmill Cl MK41 ....39 B3
Windmill Ct MK44 ......16 D3
Windmill Hill MK40 .....37 D2
Windmill Path 4 LU7 ...111 A7
Windmill Rd Flitwick MK45 .84 D4
Luton LU1 ....123 F6
Markyate AL3 ....129 B6
Windmill Row 5 PE19 ...22 E5
Windmill Way MK43 ....59 C3
Windrush Ave MK41 ....38 C5
Windrush Cl MK45 ......84 D2
Windsor Ave LU7 ....110 F7
Windsor Cl Flitwick MK45 .84 D1
St Neots PE19 ....22 F2
Windsor Ct 10 LU1 .....123 D6
Windsor Dr LU5 ....114 D4
Windsor Gdns MK40 ....38 D2
Windsor Rd
Barton-le-C MK45 ....97 C4
Bedford MK42 ....50 D4
Windsor St LU1 ....123 D6
Windsor Way
Langford SG18 ....78 F6
Sandy SG19 ....54 C7
Windsor Wlk 7 LU1 ...123 D6
Winfield St LU6 ....114 B1
Wing Rd Ascott LU7 ....110 B4
Leighton Buzzard LU7 ....110 D5
Wingate Ct LU4 ....115 F2
Wingate Dr MK45 ......85 A8
Wingate Rd
Dunstable LU5 ....114 F1
Harlington MK45 ....95 F2
Luton LU4 ....115 F2
Wingfield Cl MK40 ......49 E7
Wingfield Ct MK45 ......84 F8

Wingfield Rd
Bromham MK43 ....36 F4
Maulden MK45 ....74 C1
Tebworth LU7 ....105 C2
Winhills Schs PE19 ......22 F4
Winifred Rd MK40 ......49 F8
Winkfield Cl LU4 ....115 B1
Winsdon Ct 1 LU1 .....123 D6
Winsdon Rd LU1 ....123 D6
Winslow Cl LU3 ....116 C4
Winston Cl LU7 ....103 A1
Winston Cres SG18 .....67 A7
Winton Cl LU2 ....116 D6
Wintringham Rd 7 PE19 ..22 F5
Wiseman Cl LU2 ....116 E7
Wistow Ct PE19 ....22 C6
Wistow Rd LU3 ....116 A6
Witham Cl MK41 ....38 D7
Withy Cl LU4 ....115 B4
Withybrook MK45 ....84 E3
Witter Ave SG5 ....100 E4
Wivelsfield LU6 ....119 E6
Wiveton Cl LU2 ....116 D7
Woburn Abbey MK17 ....93 D6
Woburn Cl MK45 ....84 C1
Woburn Ct Kempston MK42 49 D3
Luton LU4 ....115 D5
Woburn La MK17 ....81 E4
Woburn Lower Sch MK17 .92 F7
Woburn Pl LU7 ....103 A1
Woburn Rd Bedford MK40 .50 A8
Heath and Reach LU7 ....103 B7
Hockliffe LU7 ....104 E3
Kempston MK42 ....49 D2
Kempston MK43 ....61 C8
Marston Moretaine MK43 ..72 C7
Millbrook MK45 ....73 B1
Woburn Sands MK17 .....81 C1
Woburn Road Ind Est
MK42 ....49 D1
Woburn Sands Sta MK17 .81 A5
Woburn St MK45 ....73 D1
Wodecroft Rd LU3 .....116 B6
Wolfsburg Ct 4 LU4 ...115 C5
Wollaston Rd NN29 ......7 A8
Wolseley Bsns Pk MK42 .49 D1
Wolseley Rd MK42 ......49 E1
Wolston Cl LU1 ....123 C7
Wood Cl Biddenham MK40 .37 C1
Kensworth LU6 ....121 E1

Wood End Hill AL5 .....130 D4
Wood End JMI Sch AL5 .130 D3
Wood End La MK43 .....48 F2
Wood End Rd
Cranfield MK43 ....71 B7
Harpenden AL5 ....130 D3
Kempston MK43 ....48 D2
Wood Green Cl LU2 ....117 B5
Wood Green Rd LU2 ...117 C5
Wood La
Aspley Guise MK17 ......81 D4
Cotton End MK45 ....63 D7
Renhold MK41 ....39 E6
Willington MK44 ....52 D7
Wood Rd MK43 ....24 F7
Wood St Dunstable LU6 ...121 C8
Luton LU1 ....123 F6
Woburn Sands MK17 .....81 B4
Wood The LU7 ....111 A8
Woodbridge Cl LU4 ....115 E4
Woodbury Hill LU2 .....116 E2
Woodcock Cl SG19 ......42 B2
Woodcock Rd LU1 ......123 A7
Woodcock Wlk MK45 ....84 D1
Woodcote MK41 ....39 A3
Woodend La MK44 ......31 C2
Woodfield Gate LU5 ....121 E6
Woodfield La MK41 ....40 A6
Woodford Rd LU5 ......114 E1
Woodhurst SG6 ....101 F8
Woodland Ave
Leighton Buzzard LU7 ...102 F2
Luton LU3 ....116 B2
Woodland Cl
Heath and Reach LU7 ...103 A5
Potton SG19 ....56 A8
Woodland Dr MK43 .....36 F4
Woodland Mid Sch MK45 .84 D2
Woodland Rise LU6 ....127 B7
Woodland Way MK17 ....81 B4
Woodlands Bedford MK41 .38 B6
Caddington LU1 ....122 E3
Harpenden AL5 ....130 E3
Tebworth LU7 ....105 C2
Woodlands Ave LU5 ....114 C4
Woodlands Cl MK44 ....52 A5
Woodlands Rd NN29 ......7 A7
Woodlands The SG18 ...66 C3
Woodman Cl LU7 ....111 B7
Woodmer Cl SG5 ....87 E2

Woodmere Bedford MK41 ..38 F3
Luton LU3 ....108 A1
Woodside
Aspley Guise MK17 ......81 D3
Eaton Bray LU6 ....119 E6
Woodside Farm
& Wildfowl Park LU1 .129 A8
Woodside Ind Est LU5 .114 D3
Woodside Mid Sch MK41 .39 B4
Woodside Park Ind Est
LU5 ....114 C3
Woodside Rd LU1 ......123 B3
Woodside Way LU7 .....110 D6
Woodstock Rd MK40 ....49 F7
Woodville Dr MK40 .....49 B6
Woolfield SG19 ....54 D6
Woolgrove Ct SG4 .....101 B1
Woolgrove Rd SG4 .....101 B1
Woolpack Cl LU6 ......121 C7
Wooton Field SG19 ......44 D4
Wootton Cl LU3 ....116 B7
Wootton Lower Sch MK43 60 F7
Wootton Rd MK43 ......49 A1
Wootton Upper Sch MK43 60 E7
Worboys Ct SG8 ....69 F5
Worcester Rd MK42 .....50 F4
Wordsworth Ave PE19 ...22 D5
Wordsworth Cl SG18 ...66 C8
Wordsworth Ct MK40 ...37 F2
Wordsworth Rd
Harpenden AL5 ....131 A3
Luton LU4 ....115 A2
Worthington Rd LU6 ...120 F8
Wrayfields SG5 ....91 B8
Wraysbury Cl LU4 .....115 D3
Wren Cl Flitwick MK45 ...84 D1
Luton LU2 ....117 C6
Wren Wlk LU6 ....119 E4
Wrest Park Gardens
MK45 ....86 E3
Wrestlingworth Lower Sch
SG19 ....57 B3
Wrestlingworth Rd SG19 .56 C6
Wroxham Way
Bedford MK40 ....49 D7
Harpenden AL5 ....131 C3
Wulwards Cl LU1 ......123 B6
Wulwards Ct LU1 ......123 B6
Wyatt Cl SG5 ....100 D4
Wyatt Rd MK42 ....49 D3

Wyboston Ct PE19 ......22 C4
Wyboston L Pk MK44 ...32 C7
Wybridge MK44 ....12 B1
Wybridge Cl MK44 .....12 B2
Wychwood Ave LU2 ....116 C3
Wychwood Rd MK41 .....39 B4
Wycklond Cl SG5 ....90 E6
Wycliffe Cl LU3 ....116 C6
Wycombe Way LU3 ....116 C8
Wye Cl MK41 ....38 D5
Wyken Cl LU3 ....116 A7
Wymington Rd
Podington NN29 ....7 E3
Rushden NN10 ....8 B8
Wynchwood La SG17 ....77 B2
Wynd Arc The SG6 .....101 F6
Wynd The SG6 ....101 F6
Wyndham Rd LU4 ......115 C2
Wyngates LU7 ....110 E5
Wynnefield Wlk SG19 ...54 C8
Wysells Ct SG6 ....101 D7
Wyton Ct SG17 ....76 F2
Wyvern Cl LU4 ....115 E3

Y

Yardley Ct 14 AL5 .....131 B1
Yately Cl LU2 ....116 D7
Yelnow La MK44 ....16 A3
Yeomans Ave AL5 .....130 D3
Yeomans Gate MK44 ....51 D4
Yeovil Ct LU2 ....117 B2
Yeovil Rd LU2 ....117 B2
Yew St LU5 ....114 D7
Yew Tree Cl
Eaton Bray LU6 ....119 F5
Silsoe MK45 ....86 C3
Yew Tree Ct 2 LU7 ....111 A7
Yew Tree Wlk SG17 .....78 B2
York Cl Barton-le-C MK45 .97 D4
Biggleswade SG18 ......67 B5
York Ct LU7 ....110 F7
York Rd SG5 ....100 E1
York St Bedford MK40 ...50 E8
Luton LU2 ....123 F8
Young Ind Est LU7 ....111 D6

IG	NH	NJ	NK
M	NN	NO	NP
IR	NS	NT	NU
	NX	NY	NZ
	SC	SD	SE	TA
	SH	SJ	SK	TF	TG
M	SN	SO	SP	TL	TM
R	SS	ST	SU	TQ	TR
W	SX	SY	SZ	TV

Any feature in this atlas can be given a unique reference to help you find the same feature on other Ordnance Survey maps of the area, or to help someone else locate you if they do not have a Street Atlas.

The grid squares in this atlas match the Ordnance Survey National Grid and are at 500 metre intervals. The small figures at the bottom and sides of every other grid line are the National Grid kilometre values (**00** to **99** km) and are repeated across the country every 100 km (see left).

To give a unique National Grid reference you need to locate where in the country you are. The country is divided into 100 km squares with each square given a unique two-letter reference. Use the administrative map to determine in which 100 km square a particular page of this atlas falls.

The bold letters and numbers between each grid line (**A** to **F**, **1** to **8**) are for use within a specific Street Atlas only, and when used with the page number, are a convenient way of referencing these grid squares.

Example   The railway bridge over DARLEY GREEN RD in grid square B1

Step 1: Identify the two-letter reference, in this example the page is in **SP**

Step 2: Identify the 1 km square in which the railway bridge falls. Use the figures in the southwest corner of this square: Eastings **17**, Northings **74**. This gives a unique reference: **SP 17 74**, accurate to 1 km.

Step 3: To give a more precise reference accurate to 100 m you need to estimate how many tenths along and how many tenths up this 1 km square the feature is (to help with this the 1 km square is divided into four 500 m squares). This makes the bridge about **8** tenths along and about **1** tenth up from the southwest corner.

This gives a unique reference: **SP 178 741**, accurate to 100 m.

Eastings (read from left to right along the bottom) come before Northings (read from bottom to top). If you have trouble remembering say to yourself "Along the hall, THEN up the stairs"!

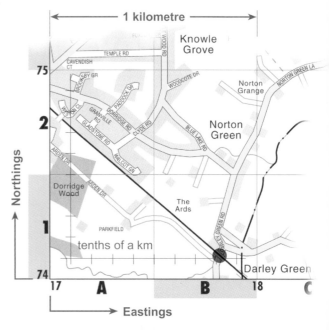

Street Atlases from Philip's

Philip's publish an extensive range of regional and local street atlases which are ideal for motoring, business and leisure use. They are widely used by the emergency services and local authorities throughout Britain.

Key features include:

◆ Superb county-wide mapping at an extra-large scale of 3½ inches to 1 mile, or 2½ inches to 1 mile in pocket editions

◆ Complete urban and rural coverage, detailing every named street in town and country

◆ Each atlas available in three handy formats – hardback, spiral, pocket paperback

'The mapping is very clear... great in scope and value'
★★★★ BEST BUY   AUTO EXPRESS

1 Bedfordshire
2 Berkshire
3 Birmingham and West Midlands
4 Bristol and Bath
5 Buckinghamshire
6 Cardiff, Swansea & The Valleys
7 Cheshire
8 Derbyshire
9 Durham
10 Edinburgh and East Central Scotland
11 North Essex
12 South Essex
13 Glasgow and West Central Scotland
14 North Hampshire
15 South Hampshire
16 Hertfordshire
17 East Kent
18 West Kent
19 Lancashire
20 Leicestershire and Rutland
21 London
22 Greater Manchester
23 Merseyside
24 Northamptonshire
25 Nottinghamshire
26 Oxfordshire
27 Staffordshire
28 Surrey
29 East Sussex
30 West Sussex
31 Tyne and Wear
32 Warwickshire
33 South Yorkshire
34 West Yorkshire

How to order

The Philip's range of street atlases is available from good retailers or directly from the publisher by phoning 01933 443863